# *Conceived in Liberty*

ALSO BY MARK PERRY

*Four Stars: The Inside Story of the Forty-Year Battle
Between the Joint Chiefs of Staff and
America's Civilian Leaders*

*Eclipse: The Last Days of the CIA*

*A Fire in Zion: The Israeli-Palestinian
Search for Peace*

*Mark Perry*

# CONCEIVED
# *in* LIBERTY

---

*Joshua Chamberlain, William Oates,*
*and the American Civil War*

VIKING

VIKING
Published by the Penguin Group
Penguin Putnam Inc., 375 Hudson Street,
New York, New York 10014, U.S.A.
Penguin Books Ltd, 27 Wrights Lane,
London W8 5TZ, England
Penguin Books Australia Ltd, Ringwood,
Victoria, Australia
Penguin Books Canada Ltd, 10 Alcorn Avenue,
Toronto, Ontario, Canada M4V 3B2
Penguin Books (N.Z.) Ltd, 182–190 Wairau Road,
Auckland 10, New Zealand

Penguin Books Ltd, Registered Offices:
Harmondsworth, Middlesex, England

First published in 1997 by Viking Penguin,
a member of Penguin Putnam Inc.

3   5   7   9   10   8   6   4   2

Library of Congress Cataloging-in-Publication Data
Perry, Mark.
Conceived in liberty: Joshua Chamberlain, William Oates, and the American
Civil War / Mark Perry.
p.   cm.
Includes index.
ISBN 0-670-86225-8
1. United States—History—Civil War, 1861–1865—Biography.   2. Chamberlain,
Joshua Lawrence, 1828–1914.   3. Oates, William C. (William Calvin), 1835–1910.
4. Soldiers—United States—Biography.   5. Soldiers—Confederate States of America—
Biography.   6. Gettysburg (Pa.), Battle of, 1863.   I. Title.
E467.P47   1997
973.7'092'2—dc21
[B]        97-24284

This book is printed on acid-free paper.
(∞)

Printed in the United States of America
Set in Bulmer
Designed by Francesca Belanger
Maps by Victoria Russell and Michael J. Keating, Papertiger Studio, Washington, D.C.

*To the graduates of*
*Northwestern Military and Naval Academy,*
*Lake Geneva, Wisconsin*

# Contents

. . . certainly it is more fit that an event of so great importance, and which is attended with such an infinite train of great consequences, should be disposed and ordered by infinite *wisdom,* than it should be left to blind *chance.*

Jonathan Edwards,
"The Justice of God in the Damnation of Sinners"

# The Rocky Hill

THE FIRST THAT WILLIAM OATES knew a battle was raging somewhere off to the east was on the early afternoon of July 1, 1863, when his regiment of Alabama soldiers was on picket duty outside the small Pennsylvania mountain hamlet of New Guilford. The men from Alabama could tell that the distant contest was serious, though the distinctive blast of cannon was muffled by the sultry mountain air. By midafternoon the low booming shook the ground beneath Oates's regiment and rumors of a major battle began to circulate among his soldiers. The low muffled thudding went on and on, as if a distant thunderstorm were fast approaching. Near sunset, brigade commander Evander McIvor Law, a native South Carolinian who called Alabama home, told Oates and his four other regimental commanders to get their men ready to move. Oates ordered his men to cook their rations and prepare to break camp. To the men of the 15th Alabama his instructions were well understood: they would be marching and fighting and have little time for anything else; but his true meaning, they knew, was that somewhere up ahead Robert E. Lee's 75,000-man army was engaged in battle, perhaps was fighting even now for its survival.

The 15th Alabama had been on the move since the morning of June 15, when it stepped off from its encampment at Culpeper Court House in central Virginia and headed north, marching up the eastern fringe of the Blue Ridge Mountains. As part of Law's Brigade of Hood's Division of Longstreet's Corps—one of three such corps in Lee's army—the men of the 15th were all soldiers of the Deep South, veterans of seven battles, dozens of lesser engagements, and hundreds of skirmishes, who took pride in their ability to march quickly and strike fast.

They had moved northward steadily throughout June at a rate of advance taught them when they first arrived in Virginia nineteen months before: a precise 180 steps per minute, at 33 inches per stride, the steady step prescribed in *Rifle and Light Infantry Tactics*, the infantryman's bible. If anything, however, the movement north had been faster than that. The days were long and hot, the stops infrequent, and water scarce. During the first three days of the march the men had suffered from fatigue and thirst. Finally a violent thunderstorm on the night of June 18 had broken the oppressive heat. This was not a respite that the Alabamians coveted, however, since the regiment was forced to shelter from a torrent of hail and sleet. Temperatures plummeted; sleeping on the soaked ground was impossible.

The 15th had reached Snicker's Gap, northwest of Culpeper, on June 19, just in time to hear a distant exchange of rifle fire from Confederate Jeb Stuart's cavalry, which was guarding the Blue Ridge passes against Union horsemen. The Alabama men moved out after a short rest, zigzagging north, then west, then north again, passed over the Shenandoah River, backtracked west, recrossed the Shenandoah, and then headed toward the hamlet of Berryville. The pace quickened. The three divisions of the corps—Hood's, McLaws's, and Pickett's, 24,000 men in all—waded armpit-deep across the ice-cold Potomac into Maryland, marched swiftly north to Hagerstown and then into Pennsylvania. They had marched from Virginia to the Mason-Dixon Line in just under two days. The bands played, the men shivered, and frightened northerners watched in silence.

For William Oates, the movement north went well. While there was some straggling, the 15th Alabama maintained strong discipline. There were four desertions, but most of the men held up well: fifty dropped from exhaustion and heatstroke along the route, but many of these were revived and returned to ranks. In Hagerstown General Hood issued his division several barrels of captured whiskey, but the damage was minor; even the most alcohol-addled soldiers fell back into the long butternut columns, recovering in time to make a smart and proud march into Chambersburg, across the Pennsylvania line. On the thirtieth of June, James Longstreet dispatched Hood's Division to Greencastle. From there, Hood placed Law's Brigade, including the 15th Alabama, on picket duty at New Guilford, well back from the rest of the

Corps. William Oates thought his Alabama regiment never looked better, or more ready for a fight.

❦

The men of Alabama had never seen anything like Pennsylvania. Dorsey Pender, one of the Army of Northern Virginia's rising young officers, described the commonly held view in a letter he wrote his wife on June 28: "This is a most magnificent country to look at; but the most miserable people. I have yet to see a nice-looking lady." If there was hatred in the eyes of "the Dutch," as the Alabamians called southern Pennsylvania's German population, then Oates and his men did not see it. Most of those they met stood by the side of the road gawking at them, as if not quite believing that a southern army had made it so far north. While at Greencastle, Oates was entertained by two young ladies, with whom he spent the afternoon talking about Jefferson Davis, Abraham Lincoln, and the war. Were the northerners filled with resentment toward him? With fear? Malice? His judgment, recorded years later in his memoirs, was that they were "remarkably ignorant of the causes of the war and the real character of the Government."

Oates spent much of his time looking after his regiment, readying them for the battle that would surely come and enforcing Robert E. Lee's General Orders No. 72, which strictly prohibited the destruction of private property. Lee's instructions harshly condemned pillaging and gave instructions for the posting of guards to protect local businesses and citizens. But Lee, for all of that propriety, knew that his army had to live off the land, and so allowed the requisitioning of supplies from local merchants and farmers upon payment of Confederate currency, which was useless in the North. In truth, while the Army of Northern Virginia kept clear of wanton theft, the liberal requisitioning of beef and pork went unchecked. Oates himself was not above looking the other way when it came to feeding his regiment and, while he may have chased soldiers away from one home outside of Greencastle, he later smiled approvingly when he found some of his soldiers catching the milk of cows in their canteens, "which seemed," he said, "to be very expert work of that kind."

On the afternoon of July 1, Oates and his men first heard the sound of battle to the east and waited in expectation of orders to move. Finally, in the early morning darkness of July 2, a rider came down the road into New Guilford and pounded breathlessly into Law's Brigade camp. Within the hour, Oates's 450-man Alabama regiment was on the road to Chambersburg, their march hurried by the knowledge that twenty-five miles away at Gettysburg there was a growing bloody fight, perhaps the bloodiest of the war, that had already taken the lives of some one thousand of their fellow countrymen.

〇━━✦━━〇

The 15th Alabama was not the only regiment on the move that early July morning. Some sixty miles to the east, the 20th Maine, commanded by an unassuming professor by the name of Joshua Chamberlain, was also marching toward Gettysburg. Like the 15th Alabama, the 20th Maine had made the march north from Virginia in nearly record time: when Oates's regiment was guarding Snicker's Gap on the nineteenth, the 20th was just across the way near Manassas. The Maine men heard the same smattering of shots that marked the collision of their cavalry with Jeb Stuart's southern troopers, then ran into some trouble of their own. While east of Ashby's Gap, the regiment was suddenly formed into line of battle and moved west, running up against unidentified Confederate pickets. The firefight was short and the rebels were driven off. "The shot and shell flew pretty lively for a few minutes time," Private William Lamson wrote in a letter home. "None in our company were hurt."

After chasing the rebels west toward the gap, the 20th Maine turned east and then north, mirroring the movements of the 15th Alabama. They made a short and painful pause at the old Bull Run battlefield (where the northern army had been sent into headlong retreat twice in the last two years) before Chamberlain led his men on a forced march north. On June 26, soaked by constant drizzle, the 20th Maine marched just over twenty miles, from Aldie in northern Virginia to Poolesville, in Maryland. The next day the 20th marched another twenty miles, to Frederick, where they stopped to rest. The respite was attended by rumors, which are as common to an army as hardship— that the beloved George McClellan was once again leading the troops, that Lee was far to the north at Harrisburg, and that the regiment would be moving north again tomorrow. The rumors covered the spectrum, from totally false to partially true to absolutely accurate: McClellan was not in command, only one of Lee's corps was nearing Harrisburg, and the 20th Maine would, in fact, be moving again.

Like the Army of Northern Virginia, the northern Army of the Potomac was strung out in a long thin line from northern Virginia to southern Pennsylvania. But for Union commander George Gordon Meade—who had only been appointed to command on the day after the 20th marched into Frederick—the situation was far worse than it was for Lee. Not only was Meade new to his command, he had sole charge of saving the Union. Henry Halleck, Lincoln's general-in-chief, had appointed Meade to command in place of the departed Joseph Hooker in a telegram that was remarkably laconic: "Your army is free to act as you may deem proper under the circumstances as they arise." Lack of instruction was precisely the problem: Meade knew where his army was, but he had little idea where Lee was, despite the fact that his galloping cavalrymen had been hounding the southern force for two weeks. To his credit Meade acted quickly. Looking down at a map of Virginia, Maryland, and Pennsylvania, Meade would only comment was that his troops were "rather scattered." He then fired off a return telegram to Halleck: "I propose to move this army tomorrow in the direction of York."

If Meade knew little, Joshua Chamberlain knew less. But that was not unusual. Regimental officers were told where to go and what to do by their brigade commanders, who were told where to go and what to do by their division commanders, who received their orders down a chain of command from the very top. Over the course of the last twelve months, since his appointment as a lieutenant colonel and then as regimental commander, Chamberlain had learned to live with the system and suppress his natural curiosity. He had succeeded admirably, striving to obey quickly and efficiently, making the 20th as battle-ready as possible. He welcomed the short delay in Frederick for just this reason: it allowed him the chance to reinvigorate his footsore troops. He took care to feed them from the town's plentiful larder, liberally supplementing the standard fare of hardtack and coffee. Where purchase was not possible, they simply took what they needed and told the shocked storekeeper to "charge it to Uncle Sam"—a promise as reassuring as receiving Confederate scrip.

In the months since he joined the regiment, the otherwise soft-spoken Chamberlain, known to his Bowdoin College colleagues back in Maine as a man who, given enough time, could do just about anything, had learned that the first principle of military leadership was to care for his troops. It was not just that Chamberlain commanded men from his home state (which was not always the case in the northern army), it was that hard experience had taught him a regiment travels from meal to meal and that to fight well it must be fed well. Like Oates, Chamberlain looked the other way when his men foraged for food and welcomed the warmth of a fence-post fire, though such warmth was always purchased at the expense of a local farmer. To his mind this was the price that war exacted on noncombatants.

Chamberlain also knew that a regiment's stomach was one thing and its feet another. A stomach could always be filled, but there was little cure for sore feet, except for frequent rest stops. The hard marching had cost the regiment dearly; Chamberlain's second-in-command, Major Charles Gilmore, was one of the casualties, becoming so sick that he was left in Frederick, his place in the regiment taken by Ellis Spear, an earthy schoolteacher from Wiscasset. Others were in far worse shape, broken down from fatigue and the teeth-gnashing and nearly constant shifts in the weather. All of this could be solved by a longer rest in Frederick, but just when that seemed possible, orders came to move north. As the Maine men marched out of Frederick, the skies reopened, soaking them. On July 1 they entered Pennsylvania, and after a twenty-two-mile march, the regiment camped near Union Mills.

❦

Early on the morning of July 2, a horseman galloped into the Alabama brigade's camp, reined in his horse outside the tent of General Law, and passed on the orders given him by General Longstreet, twenty-five miles away. Longstreet instructed Law to bring his Alabama regiments through the mountain defiles, following the road east and into Gettysburg, where the army was waiting. Law, an accomplished and friendly lawyer-turned-military-officer and a graduate of South Carolina's Kings Mountain Military Academy, sensed the desperation hidden in the message. He knew that this march, unlike many others that preceded it, would be conducted with few, and shorter, rest stops. Longstreet expected Law to march without break, or nearly so, after which (as Law now certainly expected) he would be put into line of battle. The brigade would not stop for laggers, but plunge on, hoping that those who fell out would catch up later. The march would be a test of Law's skill, but just now awakening, rousing, and putting over 3,000 men into a line of march took time. Law did his best, but it wasn't until nearly four A.M. that the brigade was on the road east.

At nearly the same moment that Law was ordering his five regiments out of camp at New Guilford, Colonel Strong Vincent, a twenty-six-year-old West Point graduate, was marching his brigade from Union Mills west along the Baltimore Pike toward Gettysburg. Chamberlain's regiment was in the lead, as they had been for most of the past twenty-six miles and twenty-three hours. The march was one of the most difficult that Chamberlain's regiment had yet endured, made worse by the heart-quickening and ghastly sight of bloodied and frightened veterans streaming back along the road toward them from the northwest. Sixteen miles east of Gettysburg the brigade rested, along with the rest of the Fifth Corps, until a bugler called them to order and onto the road once again. Slowly word filtered back through the ranks that the army's First and Eleventh Corps had clashed and been ravaged by Lee's army the previous morning, were driven from position to position, flanked, pursued through the town itself, and only rallied many hours later on a low hill that contained a cemetery—where they now awaited reinforcement. The pace picked up, the word of the defeat filtering back along the line.

Chamberlain was not a superstitious man by nature, but the sight of all the wounded men could not have given him confidence. Nor could he have been cheered by the news that the army's Eleventh Corps had been sent into headlong retreat. The same thing had happened to the Eleventh at Chancellorsville just two months before, when the Army of the Potomac was flanked and soundly beaten by an army just over one-half its strength. The 20th had not been part of that debacle, having been kept in camp north of Chancellorsville at Falmouth for smallpox vaccinations. It was small consolation that the battle was lost without them. Still, this was different. The South could win in Virginia, but winning in Pennsylvania, on northern ground, would be more difficult. Like much of the rest of the army, Chamberlain was confident that this battle would result in a victory.

The same could be said for Oates, who watched the dawn slowly brighten while on the road to Chambersburg. After the early morning excitement and anticipation of coming battle, his Alabama regiment had fallen into their experienced march habits. The road led north and down, winding its way through the forests of the northern Appalachians. They were at Chambersburg for breakfast, moving through the camps recently abandoned by the rest of Hood's Division, which had preceded them on the road east. The brigade did not stop, but swung through the town in an easy march step. Five miles farther on, the Alabamians saw the first signs of the previous day's fight, but they, like the 20th Maine, pressed ahead. By noon they were near Gettysburg, where it became clear that the battle ahead would be vicious, far worse than Fredericksburg, perhaps even worse than that hell, Antietam. Oates remembered the scene: "For two or three miles before we arrived we saw many field hospitals—wounded men and thousands of prisoners, evidencing the bloody engagement of the previous evening." There were bodies lying along the ridgelines, dead.

Law's Brigade arrived at Gettysburg shortly before two P.M., ending what James Longstreet, their corps commander, later described as "the best marching done in either army to reach the field of Gettysburg." Oates and his men marched twenty-eight miles in ten hours, a feat rivaled only by the march of Chamberlain's Maine regiment to the same battlefield. What was even more impressive was that Law brought his brigade to Gettysburg nearly intact. The straggling from New Guilford was virtually nonexistent. As the Alabama troops topped Herr Ridge, just west of Gettysburg, Oates spotted Longstreet and Lee ahead, conferring. The Alabamians filed into a nearby field on the banks of a small creek and rested. The balance of Hood's Division was there, nearly 7,500 men in four brigades. Camped nearby were another 7,500 soldiers of McLaws's Division. These 15,000 men from Longstreet's Corps were the cream of Lee's army, the only division absent being that of George Pickett, who was awaiting orders in Chambersburg.

Lee intended to use Longstreet's men as he had in the summer of 1862, when he sent them into the Second Battle of Manassas: as a knockout blow to an opponent who was still reeling from the previous day's grueling fighting. If Longstreet's men could not do it, then it could not be done. Or, as one of Longstreet's brigadiers, Joseph Kershaw, put it, "There was a kind of intuition, an apparent settled fact [that] after all the other troops had made their long marches, tugged at the flanks of the enemy, threatened his rear, and all the display of strategy and generalship had been exhausted in the dislodgment of the foe, and all these failed, then when the hard, stubborn, decisive blow was to be struck, the troops of the First Corps were called on to strike it." Oates had that same belief: that his men could not be defeated and would only be overcome by superior numbers. They were, as he said, "terribly in earnest." At a little after three in the afternoon, the 15th Alabama was put into a column with the rest of Longstreet's Corps and ordered to move south, behind the low ridge, screened from Union observers on the hills to the east.

Hood's Division took the lead, marched for an hour, and then suddenly, inexplicably, were ordered to stand, silent. Officers galloped back up the line, past the Alabamians, then galloped back down again. Finally, after a confused wait, Oates's men retraced their steps, moved west away from the battlefield, and then headed south once again. The division stopped as more orders were passed down the line. The entire corps then filed across a road and headed straight east, past a farm, and down into a low swale. Two hills that Oates spied in the distance came ever closer. Finally, nearly two hours after they had started, Law's Brigade was prepared for battle, facing north, with Oates's 15th Alabama in the center and two sister regiments, the 44th and 48th Alabama regiments, to his right and left. Back up the line, in a great arc that stretched from east to west and then north, Longstreet's two divisions of 15,000 men faced the two low hills in the distance.

It was three-thirty when the artillery opened.

Joshua Chamberlain heard them open. The cannonade surprised his Maine men, who expected a Confederate attack on their right. But this artillery was firing on the left. Within minutes, Chamberlain was told to form his regiment and prepare for battle. He put them all into the column, even the most footsore and sick—"all but the drummer boys and hospital attendants"—because everyone would be needed. As the Maine men once again waited, William Oates instructed twenty-two of his own soldiers, eleven from each company, to fill the regiment's canteens. They rushed off to a creek one hundred yards in the rear. A few moments later, Oates realized that he had made a mistake: all along the line, the brigade was forming for battle, stripping off their knapsacks and blankets, and checking their ball and powder. General Law was out in front, preparing the line for the assault. The cannon sent rocketing shells into the woods to the north toward the low but looming hills.

At about the same time the 20th Maine was instructed to move to the west and into the battle. To Chamberlain's left, through a low and rocky ground, past a thick stand of trees, and across an open field, the Alabama troops of William Oates waited, and waited, through three minutes of the bombardment—what was called "artillery preparation." The artillery shelling was designed to scatter unrallied and skittish opponents, but the Alabama men had learned from long experience that it more often merely served as a signal that an attack was coming. From the beginning of the cannonade to its pause must have seemed like a lifetime. Chamberlain could not see Oates or his men, but he knew that the southerners were there, forming for battle, as drawn to this field as he was. Oates steadied his troops and steeled himself against the coming combat. Then, just as Chamberlain had been ordered forward, on the far side of the low hill to his front, Oates was given a signal to begin the attack. He looked back at his men, hesitated for just one moment, then stepped off into the field.

Over the course of the next two hours, William Oates and Joshua Chamberlain would create a shared history that would influence the course of American life for the next one hundred years. They were very different men, these two. One was a college professor, born naturally to a life of personal achievement. The other was a small-town self-made lawyer. But different as they were, history or accident—or fate—had brought them to Gettysburg, together, and would now animate their lives for the next five decades. Though they never laid eyes on each other, from the moment they led their regiments forward—into the sweltering, midafternoon maelstrom of July 2, 1863—William Oates and Joshua Chamberlain would be forever inextricably tied, their names and fortunes linked, their lives a monument to the battle before them.

# PART ONE

# 1

## *I Went Out Among Strangers*

IT WAS NOT FATE that brought William Oates's father to Alabama, but land. The elder William Oates came to Montgomery from South Carolina in 1828, then moved forty miles to the southeast, near the city of Troy. There, in Pike County, he set down roots and built a farm on land that was intersected by two trails cut through the wilderness. The journey from South Carolina must have been arduous, but thousands of young settlers like him made the trip in the first three decades of the nineteenth century. Most of southern Alabama was populated by farmers who came west from the soil-poor upland districts of Virginia, North and South Carolina, and Georgia. They followed the old Indian trails that skirted the southern edge of the Appalachians, or hugged the lands just north of the Gulf Coast, stopping by circumstance or plan to put in crops and start a family.

Small farmers were not the only ones moving west. Planters from the tidewater regions of the mid-Atlantic were also on the move, fleeing the bleached-out cotton lands that produced smaller and smaller yields. While most of Alabama's newest settlers planted small plots of corn, tobacco, sugar, fruit, and vegetables, the lowland immigrants came with their slaves, cutting away thousands of acres of woodland and building plantations. These new planters settled mainly in the "black belt" country of central Alabama, where the soil was rich. They engaged in the nineteenth-century equivalent of industrial farming. With few exceptions, these planters did not learn from their failures in the east, however, and gave little thought to rotating and diversifying their crops or resuscitating their fields with potash and phosphates.

By the third decade of the new century, most of the South's

planters and farmers realized that their methods were spawning an agricultural disaster, but they kept on as before, pushed by necessity. Edmund Ruffin, a slaveholder and plantation owner in Virginia, recognized the effects of southern farming methods on his own holdings as early as 1832 and pushed his fellow planters to institute more progressive farming methods. He received little support. When his neighbors asked him why his estate, Marlbourough, was thriving while their own were going to ruin, he pointed to his fields of planted corn and wheat, his thriving herd of livestock, and his small plots of green vegetables as proof that his methods resulted in increased yields. Cotton was a huge cash crop that promised immediate profits, he pointed out, but a farmer should not plant it everywhere year after year. It destroyed soil fertility. But instead of being viewed as agricultural innovations, Ruffin's methods were looked on with suspicion, and he was labeled a cranky eccentric.

By the early 1850s, however, Ruffin would no longer be alone in his views and the South would be faced with a looming agricultural crisis. In 1857, agricultural expert J. Foster Marshall told a South Carolina conference of planters:

> Our present system is to cut down our forest and run it into cotton as long as it will pay for the labor expended. Then cut down more forest, plant in cotton, plough it uphill and downhill, and when it failed to give a support leave it. . . . Then sell the carcass for what you can realize and migrate to the Southwest in quest of another victim. This ruinous system has entailed upon us an exhausted soil, and a dependence upon Kentucky and Tennessee for our mules, horses, and hogs, and upon the Northern States for all our necessaries from the clothing and shoeing of our Negroes down to our wheelbarrows, corn-brooms and axe-handles.

In spite of these and other warnings issued over the years, southern farmers believed that no matter how poor their soil became, anyone who worked hard and planted in cotton could strike it rich; all that was needed was for new lands to be opened in the West that would support the cotton economy, and the slaves that went with it. The belief was pervasive; many of the subsistence farmers of Virginia, the Carolinas, and Georgia who moved west in the 1820s were lured by a vision of easy cotton-bought wealth that would transform them from the South's poor cousins to men and women who lived in the manor. With a little luck and enough cotton, they believed, they could form the new cotton aristocracy of Alabama and Mississippi.

The elder William Oates carried the family name, a capacity for hard work, and an iron disposition into the wilds of southeastern Alabama. It is nearly impossible to trace the Oates line past William's father, Stephenson Oates, except to confirm what is written in the sparse family biography: that the Oateses were of Welsh stock and poor, had been in America since before the Revolution, and that an ancestor had fought in the Revolution as a soldier for Francis Marion, the "Swamp Fox."

When Oates arrived in southeastern Alabama in 1828, he surveyed a virgin country untouched by the plow. Until then, the only excitement southeastern Alabama had seen was the day in 1813 when Andrew Jackson's tattered western militia came sweeping through in pursuit of the Creek Indians. Jackson fought a series of engagements that broke the power of the Indian confederacy, made them wards of the federal government, and opened new settlement lands. The excitement lasted long enough for hundreds of Creeks to be slaughtered at the Battle of Horseshoe Bend, two dozen miles northeast of Montgomery, after which Jackson set out along a new trail that took him to New Orleans and, later, to the White House. But if the Creeks were defeated, they were not subdued. The year William Oates arrived in Montgomery, the state's leading politicians were embroiled in a bitter controversy over Indian removal with the administration of John Quincy Adams, who not only believed that the Indian nations should be as "states within states," but who had decreed that one-third of Alabama should be left in the hands of its natives.

Adams's policy was unpopular in the South; in Alabama, opposition to the plan grew so violent that the state government would likely have considered armed resistance had Adams been reelected to a second term. The election of Andrew Jackson eased the crisis, but the danger did not pass. During Jackson's term Alabama's tribes agreed, in principle, to cede their lands to the state government in exchange for an understanding that they could remain as residents until they chose to move. In turn, the federal government promised the Indians it would protect them. Buried in the treaty was the implicit understanding that the Indians *would* move, but not just yet. Such fine print did not matter, however, to the hordes of settlers who descended on the state in a breathless rush. Over a period of two years, 30,000 settlers moved onto Indian lands in defiance of federal orders, staked claims, and began to farm. Surprisingly, Jackson—who came to office on the strength of his ties to the simple frontiersman—ordered federal troops to remove the settlers, by force if necessary. Alabamians were defiant; local militias were immediately raised and public meetings were held to organize resistance. But just when it seemed that the state was on the verge of outright rebellion, Jackson announced that the settlers could stay where they were.

The conflict bore all the hallmarks of southern frontier society: an aristocratic pride in defiance, a deep-seated loyalty to a state's right to nullify federal law, and a romantic belief in the sovereignty of farmers armed with muskets. That Andrew Jackson might simply have been more willing to break a promise to the Indians than shed the blood of those who elected him did not occur to many Alabamians. They believed, instead, that their opposition to the federal government had been justified by their victory. Furthermore, Jackson's initial orders to remove the settlers convinced many Alabamians that New Englanders (like the hated Adams) were trying to strangle the South, first by closing off the settlement of fertile lands and—when this strategy failed—by agitating for an end to slavery. Alabamians were not far wrong: by the mid-1830s a nascent but dedicated abolitionist movement, led by men and women pledged to eradicate the institution, had already taken root in the North. At first southerners dismissed the movement, but they feared that the promise of freedom held out by the abolitionists might lead to a slave revolt, and an end to their way of life.

There were 85,000 whites and 41,000 slaves in frontier Alabama in 1820, but the ratio of white to slave decreased decade by decade over the next forty years. By 1830, two years after William Oates had settled at what came to be known as Oates's Crossroads, there were 117,000 slaves in the state. The figure doubled during the next twenty years. At first no one doubted that the master-slave relationship could be maintained, but the increase in the number of black families sparked doubts among Alabama planters, who began to enforce stringent new slave codes to ensure the peace. The slave codes made everyone feel secure for a time, but they failed to address the increasingly obvious demographic imbalance. The one thing Alabama's planters most feared—that they would be drowned in a sea of black faces—was also the very thing that made them rich, gave them their status, and infused every part of their culture.

Alabama was being gradually transformed into three distinct districts: a slaveholding region in the central counties, a white anti-slaveholding section in the northern counties, and a poor white region of largely small farmers and few slaves in the southern counties. This division began to poison the state's social order. While most of the residents of Pike County mistrusted the federal government, they also resented the affluence and social influence of the planter class. It was a simple matter of geography; just miles north of Oates's Crossroads, the thick, rich soil of central Alabama supported a class of influential planters and a disgruntled and potentially violent population of slaves. There were four whites for every one slave in Pike County, but twenty miles to the north the numbers were nearly even. The distance a man could travel in one day marked the difference between a life of unceasing toil on poor land and a life of comparative comfort on land as yet unspoiled by cotton's demands. Alabama society was shot through with the language of southern propriety and later accounts describe William Oates as a "planter." The term is a social conceit—he cleared and cut the land, planted, harvested, and sold a crop and, after three years, returned to Montgomery to marry Sarah Sellers, whose family roots were French and Irish. William and Sarah were farmers, not "planters." They started poor and stayed that way, their days taken up with the spine-breaking work of scratching a living from the soil, and trading the paltry surplus they produced at the nearby crossroads. They were typical of the new settlers of the "wiregrass country"; their lives had few amenities and little in the way of enrichments.

Within a year of their marriage, William and Sarah began to build their family, which soon consisted of as many mouths as they could feed. Their oldest child, William, was born on November 30, 1833, and was followed, in quick succession, by seven others—Thomas, John, Amanda, Melissa, Mary, James, and Louisa. There may have been more; infant deaths were left unrecorded. This was a common enough event on the frontier, for while the passing of a child was deeply mourned, it was only a temporary interruption of the monotony of everyday life. William and Sarah struggled to keep up with their growing family, bringing more of their land under cultivation, but the farm produced only enough for their immediate needs. The elder William worked from sunrise to sunset, while Sarah raised the children to meet her standards. She believed in hard work and religious devotion and was a strong-willed woman with a formidable consitution. She ran Oates's Crossroads with patient firmness, never deviating from her own belief that steely ambition would overcome any obstacle. She had a high regard for education, pushing her oldest son to learn under the most adverse circumstances.

There were moments of delight for William and Sarah Oates: healthy births, baptisms, visits to nearby families and friends, and visits to trading towns that lay within easy distance. Over the years, this extended group of families became a tightly knit community, with the Oates children marrying the children of family friends in the nearby towns of Eufaula and Tuskegee. The young William Oates made friends for life on the farms nearby: M. E. Meredith and Jefferson Hussey. Within miles of the Oates home, the Linton and Long families became friends, and relatives of the Sellerses and Oateses—aunts, uncles, cousins—were sprinkled throughout the southeastern part of the state. In the years ahead, the Oates family would become associated with families who were typical of frontier Alabama, large and poor, but dedicated to improvement, and whose descendants are still prominent citizens of the state.

William Oates's best friend, his closest confidant, and his ally in all of his adventures was his brother John. Unlike most brothers close in years, they never seemed to have fought, and came to rely on each other in doing chores and defending each other in schoolyard fights. Their closeness came as a result of their work for their father, a strict and demanding disciplinarian, and grew over the years because of their shared intelligence, adventurousness, ambition, and dream of finding a way of life away from Oates's Crossroads. They felt stifled by working on a farm, cultivated an abhorrence for hard labor, and took whatever opportunity they could to go off to the local school.

Their father, who is described in histories of Pike County as being "an honest, upright, and godfearing man," knew this and did his best to sustain his family, educate his children, and offer them opportunities outside of Oates's Crossroads. Yet he could do little to appease his sons' restiveness—the family was simply too poor to allow much deviation from the day-to-day round of chores that were essential for its survival.

When the settlers of Virginia, the Carolinas, and Georgia came to Alabama, they brought with them their dreams of a better life and their belief in individual initiative. And they brought their religion. When they arrived they found that the frontier, much like their homelands farther east, had been set afire by itinerant ministers who preached a new and potent religious message of self-reliance and salvation. These evangelists rejected the rising popularity of New England deism and reinforced the belief that a family chosen of God could make its way in the wilderness. The "Second Great Awakening," as it is now called, was sparked in 1801 by James McGready, a Presbyterian minister whose initial three-day encampment at Cane Ridge, Kentucky, attracted 25,000 worshipers, a crowd unheard of for that time. McGready's hellfire sermon at Cane Ridge and his continuing ministry, with its heady potion of down-home morality, had an enormous appeal to frontier families. He preached salvation through hard work and churchgoing, and alluded to far-off unnamed devils who plotted to undo the work of God. Such preaching was especially well suited to frontier Alabama, where its message of individual salvation through hardship took deep root.

During the years when William and Sarah Oates were raising their children, religious encampments and revivals were drawing thousands of settlers throughout the South and West. Those who witnessed them would never forget the scenes of crowds of people pressing forward to receive the blessing: "Will I ever see anything more like the day of Judgment on this side of eternity—to see the people running, yes, running from every direction to the stand, weeping, shouting, and shouting for joy. O! glorious day they went home singing shouting," one observer wrote in 1837. The revival movement burned itself out in the early 1850s, but it had an enormous impact on frontier life, combining with its call for a rejection of sin a belief that God alone ruled and gave to each, regardless of his or her station, a chance at personal redemption. The pious would be rewarded no matter what hardships they met along the way.

It was an inspiring message for hardscrabble settlers aspiring to be planters. Yet it resonated even in New England, where devout church-goers were struggling with the Calvinist notion of predestination. In Rochester, New York, Charles Grandison Finney used the language of frontier revivals to preach a gospel of redemption that questioned the precepts of New England Puritanism and emphasized the primacy of human freedom. Sin, Finney said, was not universal, but personal. He initiated what he called "new measures," like six-hour religious services and the "anxious seat," where sinners sat facing the congregation to confess their most intimate sins and to wrestle publicly with the devil for the dominance of their soul.

Finney's enormous popularity was undoubtedly rooted in his flair for drama, but stage props like the anxious seat were also a symbol of the dramatic changes that frontier revivals were having in the more staid congregations of the North and East. While McGready and his col-leagues called themselves "harvesters" who had come to gather God's bounty, Finney adopted the language of the revivalists to urge his congregants not simply to harvest new souls, but to remake the world. Sinners who stood by in the face of evil, McGready and Finney pro-claimed, could not join the harvest but would be condemned, cut like fields of wheat before the scythe, their seeds scattered to the winds, their redemption bought with blood. This above all, the evangelists claimed, was plain for everyone to see: the sinful would be punished, and the devout would be rewarded.

At first Finney was viewed as a quaint country parson by many of the Northeast's traditional ministers and their upper-crust congregants, but the power of his message eventually made itself felt, especially in upstate New York. In New England, free-thinking deists used Finney's message to build a small but vocal core of social reformers, including abolitionists, who used the church to spread their message. This is cer-tainly not what Finney had intended (the "great political, and other worldly excitements that agitate Christendom, are all unfriendly to religion," he wrote pointedly), but his message was fraught with the belief that human action could change the world. Like McGready, Finney believed that revivals contained the seeds of change for established religious institutions, just as, in the Bible, "the word of God is compared to grain, and preaching is compared to sowing seed, and the results to the springing up and growth of the crop."

The message that appealed to a small core of reformers in the North was used to great effect, but to different ends, in the South. In Alabama and throughout the Deep South, McGready's disciples emphasized his message of personal salvation (just as Finney had), telling their audiences that those who believed in God and followed his path could reach salvation. But they did not stop there. McGready's constant reference to work of the godless outsider had great local appeal and helped to bind fragile frontier communities together. The "Second Great Awakening" reinforced the status quo in the South, where families like the Oateses of Alabama lived a day-to-day existence timed to the rhythms of the crops. Like most of their neighbors, they believed that while the lot of the human race might someday be improved, it was unlikely to happen anytime soon. Instead, God gave to each man and woman a role in life, and a station. In the North personal salvation required individuals to work to end society's evils, but in the South personal salvation became rooted in the defense of the God-fearing against the wicked ways of the devil's agents.

⌖

There was a certain pride in the pioneer spirit that McGready and his disciples understood well, and the frontier mentality of hard work and accomplishment was an invariable part of his sermons. That hard work leads to salvation is something the elder William Oates already believed. While the life of the plantations clustered just to the north might seem beyond his reach, it was the elusive but ever-present goal toward which he worked—as did every member of his family, including his increasingly frustrated firstborn son.

Beginning in his early teenage years, William continually asked his father to send him to school, but was always met by the same answer. There was too much work to be done on the farm and there were too many mouths to feed. The son understood necessity as well as his father, but the memory of watching others attend school bothered him then and embittered him for years thereafter. "The facilities for obtaining an education in the country at that time were indeed poor," he wrote later, in a hand shaken by age. "Two or three months in the year to a common school in the country was the only chance we had for a scholastic education. And then one out of ten of the teachers employed should have gone to a good school for years before they would have been properly qualified as teachers."

The result was that Oates's education was spotty at best—the teachers were themselves nearly illiterate, the schoolrooms disorganized, the older boys strong and intimidating. There were some exceptions: a school taught by Gamalael Sellers, a relative, and a teacher by the name of F. J. Braswell. But Oates could not attend the single-room schoolhouse for more than three months in any year because of the requirements of the farm. Worse yet, he had to pay for the education himself with funds he earned taking jobs in the neighborhood. "My father, seeing that I had a desire for education, told me . . . that he was too poor and had so many children he could not afford me or them any better advantages than the schools [near Oates's Crossroads], and that if I saw proper at any time to go out and try my hand at getting on in the world that he would not object . . . [but] I would not leave him but stuck to my plough daily until the crop was made." Oates was intent on getting an education, however, even if that meant working at two jobs— one at home, for which he would not be paid, and as a field hand on nearby farms, to earn the money for his tuition.

"I went out among strangers and hired myself to one Allen Pryor for a time and then to Tom McDonald to work on the farm for ten dollars a month," he later recounted, "a part of which I saved and paid my way through a three months county school." Eventually, even with the paucity of education that he was receiving, Oates became proficient enough that he was able to hire himself out as a local teacher, helping younger children learn to read and write. He even "got up a little school in the neighborhood" that brought in extra money for the family. Oates's budding career as a local teacher was cut short, however, by an argument he had with his father, who unfairly blamed him for an undefined act of disobedience, and undoubtedly for taking time away from his chores, and beat him. The son ran away from home in rebellion, making his way as an itinerant laborer in southern Alabama. While he came home only weeks after leaving, his relationship with his father remained strained. It was then that the temper for which he would be known in his youth first began to show. Returning to the local school, he fought with a schoolyard bully by the name of Bill Crauswell, who beat him badly "but did not whip me." Oates "then tried to get a gun to shoot him, but failed. I had it in me for years afterwards to kill him, but I never got the chance." Just a few months later, Oates was still packing a pistol for Bill Crauswell, and working to pay his way through school, when another violent misadventure sent him fleeing the Crossroads, and changed his life forever.

❦

The episode that Oates remembered with a mix of horror and pride throughout his later life had its beginnings just over one thousand miles north of Oates's Crossroads, in the small town of Hydesville, New York. There, in the tiny hamlet of some forty houses thirty miles east of Rochester, an event occurred that was so strange, it gave new meaning to the phrase "burned-over district," which is what that part of the state was then called. The phrase is used by historians to reflect the feverish religious movements that swept through Hydesville and other towns like it in the region; so many movements, in fact, that the communities were spiritually "burned over"—as if scorched by God's power. Joseph Smith first revealed the Book of Mormon in upstate New York, where he gained his first converts in the search for the New Jerusalem. The region also spawned the ministry of Charles Grandison Finney. But neither the experiences of Smith nor Finney nor the religious epiphanies claimed by other upstate religious movements could compare to what happened in the house of John and Margaret Fox on a cold day in March 1848. On March 31, the Foxes learned that their fifteen-year-old daughter Maggie and her twelve-year-old sister Kate were communicating with the dead.

It started in the evening when, suffering from colds, the two daughters moved their trundle bed into their parents' bedroom. Soon after, the two parents and their daughters heard several distinct but irregular raps, as if someone were knocking on the walls. The family had heard the rappings before, but passed them off as the sounds of the old house creaking and settling in the weather. But this night, the two girls began snapping their fingers in imitation of the sounds. The younger girl, Kate, then asked the sounds to imitate her snapping fingers—one rap for yes and two for no. Whoever (or whatever) was rapping responded. Their mother then conducted an experiment of her own, which was duly noted by later investigators: "I then asked if it was a human being that was making the noise? and if it was to manifest it by two sounds. I heard two sounds as soon as the words were spoken. I then asked, if it was an injured spirit? to give me the sound, and I heard the rapping distinctly. I then asked if it was injured in this house? and it manifested it by the noise. If the person was living that injured it? and got the same answer. I then ascertained by the same method that its remains were buried under the dwelling, and how old it was."

Neighbors were called, confirmed the rappings, and testified that despite hours of intense searching they could not find the source. Then more neighbors came, and more, until the story of the two young Fox girls and how they learned to communicate with the spirit world had spread well beyond Hydesville. Within weeks, crowds began to descend on the Fox home and local committees of investigators were appointed to locate the source of the rappings. No one could. Doors were shut, windows closed, and sentries posted in the cellar and all the rooms, yet no one could determine any trick the girls had used to mislead the community. Finally, a chief investigator was forced to admit that while the young Fox daughters might not be communicating with the dead, they were certainly not involved in a massive charade: "I am willing to testify under oath," this investigator said, "that I did not make the noises or rapping which I and others heard, that I do not know of any person who did or could have made them, that I have spent considerable time since then in order to satisfy myself as to the cause of it, but cannot account for it on any other ground than it is supernatural."

That was good enough testimony for many and sufficient for most. The investigation brought even larger crowds to Hydesville. Eventually, at the urging of their parents, the Fox girls worked out a complicated code to communicate with the spirit world and a regular series of messages passed between the living and the dead. The Fox sisters were now famous—so famous, in fact, that just one year after the Hydesville rappings began, the Foxes decided to move Kate to Rochester to keep her away from the excited crowds. That turned out to be a very good decision because in Rochester (as Kate quickly informed her growing flock of admirers) the first complete message from the world of the dead was transmitted to the world of the living. This message became as well known to spiritualists as Graham Bell's "Watson, come here, I need you" became known to a later generation of scientists. "We are all your dear friends and relatives," the spirit said. The message was soon hailed by Kate's growing group of followers as a communication as important as Morse's telegraph (invented four years before)—or more so, since this new "spiritual telegraph" opened a world that Morse did not even know existed.

On November 29, 1849, the sisters received their first payment for a private séance. The drama during such readings rivaled anything that James McGready had presented at Cane Ridge and made Finney's "anxious seat" pale by comparison: tables moved, beds and mattresses were overturned, blankets fluttered unaided about rooms. The Fox sisters' power, prestige, and popularity was known far and wide, with journalists and society mavens traveling from New York City to participate in their private readings. Even the most outspoken skeptics were convinced: "In justice to the family," one journalist wrote, "we must acquit the girls of any attempt to impose upon the public—in truth they are the most imposed upon by the public—and when we see published statements of their trickery and deception, we do not hesitate to pronounce the authors of them liars."

In early 1850 the Fox family moved to Albany, where they continued their work. Here they were put upon by a gaggle of agents and the equivalent of twentieth-century public relations experts. Soon afterward, the two young girls decided that they should follow the advice of their handlers by taking quarters in the luxurious Barnum Hotel in New York City. Their arrival in New York drew throngs of people, from the curious to the convinced. The great and near-great of the city were also attracted by the new wonder and crowded quickly into the Fox sisters' public demonstrations and private readings: Horace Greeley, the influential editor of the *Tribune*, the poet William Cullen Bryant, and author James Fenimore Cooper all made the pilgrimage to the Barnum to meet the sisters, confer with them, participate in their "rap sessions," and then discharge an endless patter for a nation consumed by the news. Cooper was particularly impressed when a spirit from "the other side" correctly answered his most private questions—especially when it rapped fifty times for the number of years that his beloved sister had been dead.

It did not seem to matter to the public that one year after taking New York by storm, the Fox sisters failed an examination conducted by doctors of a recently organized school of medicine in Buffalo. The doctors concluded that the two girls made the sounds of rappings by deliberately popping their knee joints, cracking and uncracking them, but the report caused little interest. The public simply did not want to believe that the sisters were frauds. For many, the issue was put to rest by the dead themselves, who reassured their loved ones that the Fox sisters had been specially chosen as their communicants. Besides, spiritualism not only soothed the pain of loss for the living, it was good for business. Inevitably, the Fox sisters phenomenon gave birth to myriad other wild claims that all attracted adherents: believers in animal magnetism, clairvoyants, summoners of poltergeists, and speakers of tongues (who communicated with the dead while in a trance). It was as if the public testimonies of the "Second Great Awakening," which featured fearful screams, faints, and terrified shaking, had been transmuted into something far more wondrous—or sinister. In an age still dominated by church leaders who claimed that only the elect could be saved, the popularity of spiritualism proved that anyone could have access to the truth, even two unprepossessing hayseed country girls.

American spiritualism swept through New York and then out across the Midwest. It came to Alabama in the early 1850s, carried there by new settlers from the northern states who, like the earlier frontier peoples, came looking for a better life—or a fast way to make a dollar. On a hot June day in 1851 a spirit medium called Miss Post set up business near Oates's Crossroads and claimed that she could communicate with the dead through rappings that were similar to those heard by the Fox girls. Of course, ever since the first Hydesville Rappings, as they came to be known, the use of innocent children as communicators with the dead was standard fare as parents all over America (some as convinced of their children's special gifts as the Foxes themselves) promoted the mediumship of their children for personal gain. The temptations of proving this fraud were too much for William Oates, however, who visited the young girl for a special spiritualist reading.

At first, everything went well, or as well as the Posts had hoped, but when Oates insisted on firmly holding down the table at which he and the young lady were seated—thereby causing the rappings to stop—the trouble began. The girl was disconcerted, increasingly flustered, protested against his skepticism, and insisted that he put his hands out of sight so that she could continue with her reading. Oates was delighted by this and unintimidated by the looming figure of the young girl's father, who entered the room to watch the session and to keep an eye on his daughter's customer. When Oates repeated his actions, the father could barely contain his anger. He was so enraged, in fact, that he ordered the young man off of his property and followed him down the road, shouting at him and shaking his fist in the air. When Oates continued to hoot about his trick, the man picked up a piece of lumber and chased him, apparently intent on protecting his investment from a youth who would broadcast the fraud throughout the community. The man swung at Oates, believing that it would take little effort to scare him away, but Oates, instead, turned to face him. When the man kept coming, Oates grabbed a nearby shovel and, swinging wildly to protect himself, knocked him down. The damage was worse than Oates had intended: by his own account he "hit him a glancing lick which fractured his skull, [and] knocked him senseless, inflicting a terrible wound." As fortune would have it, a passerby who had heard the argument came upon Oates standing over the man, shovel raised. There could be only one conclusion; within hours a warrant was issued for Oates's arrest.

But it was too late. Oates was gone, headed south, convinced that somewhere behind him the local authorities were telling his father and mother that their oldest son was being charged with murder. He left Alabama with a bag over his shoulder and fifty dollars in his pocket.

∘━━◆━━∘

The next twenty-four to thirty-six months in the life of William Oates—from the early summer of 1851 until about the beginning of 1854—were some of the most important of his entire life and, for later historians, some of the most confusing. Writing about the events that followed his flight from Pike County more than six decades later, Oates not only failed to give clear chronological markers of his journey (it is still uncertain just exactly *when* he left Oates's Crossroads), he made it nearly impossible to tell when he went where, how long he stayed, and when he decided to return home. Oates may well have purposely clouded the record; he certainly had good reason to do so. Over the next months, the young Alabamian wandered the untamed and violent footpaths of frontier America with little concern for his own safety and little reflection on the higher purposes of life—he consorted with criminals, gambled, brawled in public, had numerous run-ins with the law, and tasted the fleeting pleasures of meaningless romance. His journey was certainly exciting, but it was also sybaritic—something that many years later, as a mature and established man of means, he would not want many people to know. That we have a record of his adventure at all is unusual, for he only wrote of his time "a roving in the southwest" at the very end of his life, leaving his sole written account to his son "that he may profit by following my good examples and be happy by avoiding my errors." It is obvious that he did not want his adventures made public.

Oates seems to have left Alabama in late June 1851 and, after a short and uneventful journey through Pike and Henry counties, found himself in the small Florida panhandle town of Milton, a nondescript crossroads village of ruffians and gamblers just across the Alabama–Florida state line. Milton must have been one of the most unattractive places on the Florida frontier, a town of transients and those who served them: bartenders, a few storekeepers, a handful of prostitutes, and rough men looking for work. There was little work to be had, except farther south, along the Gulf Coast itself, where a small fishing trade had grown. Oates had little idea what he would do with himself in Milton, though he believed firmly that fifty dollars (a fortune, really, for a seventeen-year-old southern boy in the early 1850s) was enough money for him to start a business and prosper. Certainly there was nothing else to do, so after making certain the Alabama authorities had not followed him across the state line, and believing he could make up in ambition and good intentions what he lacked in experience, Oates rented a small stand to sell cigars.

It was an odd idea. Oates had little business knowledge and almost no contacts in Milton, and he soon learned that, despite the town's ever-shifting population, there was little need for cigars in the community. Eventually he was forced to supplement his meager income by playing cards, a way of life that was not only exciting (and chancy, considering the lack of gambling laws—or anyone to enforce them), but for which he believed he had an almost inexhaustible talent. But the learning curve for gambling is, if anything, steeper than it is for selling cigars and it was not long before Oates and the money he had earned from his cigar business were separated in "a game or two or a dozen of cards." Within a few short weeks Oates was forced to close his cigar stall and hire himself out as a housepainter, which provided a constant, though unexciting, source of income. By then, just weeks after setting out, Oates received word from his friends in Pike County that while he had not killed the father of the medium, he could not return home, since a warrant for assault had been issued in his name. The local constable was waiting for him.

He had only been gone a few weeks, and yet because Milton offered even fewer prospects than Oates's Crossroads, the young Alabamian decided to once again take to the road. This time he headed farther south to the Gulf Coast itself, where he had heard there were jobs to be had aboard a number of local fishing schooners. But his time as a hired hand on a Gulf schooner was a brutalizing experience, cold and physically exacting. He was mistreated by the schooner captain, who worked him to the point of physical exhaustion and then, when he complained, refused to pay him his wages. Oates later recalled that the only friend he had on his first voyage was "a big long negro" who kept him warm during the cold Gulf nights and fed him during the day. When Oates finally put his feet back on dry soil, he wisely decided to give up the life of a deckhand and once again struck out west, down the single dirt road to Pensacola.

Yellow fever had begun to sweep through the South, claiming hundreds of lives each year in the region's larger cities. It struck Pensacola in early 1852, at about the same time that Oates arrived there. It was only a matter of time before he also became ill. As the disease worsened, he began to vomit blood, turning a deathly yellow as the fever racked his body. One night, when the disease was at its height, the few friends he had made in Pensacola gathered at his bedside to witness his death. In due time they called in a minister to give him a last blessing, then waited for the inevitable. By the next morning, however, Oates had made a miraculous recovery: he was awake, the fever was gone, and after several days he had rallied completely. Others in Pensacola were not so lucky and dozens died before the fever swept on farther west.

After several months of working in Pensacola without any improvement in his prospects, Oates decided that he had had quite enough of Florida, packed up what few belongings he owned, and moved west to Mobile. The yellow fever epidemic had preceded him, however, and Oates was not willing to wrestle with death one more time; so he gave Mobile a wide birth and struck out along the well-traveled wagon-rutted road to New Orleans. It was a memorable journey, peopled with itinerant Americans heading to the new southwestern frontier where jobs could be found along the waterfront in New Orleans, or in the new state of Texas, where the sparsely populated plains were being broken for farms or divided into cattle ranches. Near the Louisiana–Florida border, Oates fell in with some "creamy looking Mulattoes, spanish speaking, quite pretty and attractive in appearance," whom he accompanied for a time before leaving them to find work in New Orleans.

Even in early 1853, New Orleans, the South's first city—a boomtown of wharves, warehouses, ornate homes, slums, bars, gambling dens, and slave markets—was famous across the nation as the gateway to the Gulf and the heartbeat of America's greatest river. Like Abraham Lincoln, who sculled his way from Illinois south to New Orleans on a flatboat (making an unimaginable eight dollars per month doing so), Oates undoubtedly believed that his visit to the Crescent City would be the high point of his young life. It was, but only for a short time. While Oates was impressed by the sheer numbers of people who crowded the New Orleans docks (more people than he had seen in one place, ever) and promenaded along its still young streets, he was disappointed, even scandalized, by New Orleans' seamy underside. He spent some time there (whether days or weeks is uncertain) taking in the sights and doing odd jobs, but then coolly decided what was plain for everyone to see: that despite its legendary sophistication, New Orleans was a "filthy" place. One day he had had enough and moved on north, to Shreveport.

His decision may have been influenced by the yellow fever that seemed to have followed him to New Orleans from Pensacola. The sickness hit the city hard; where it had once felled a handful, and then dozens (in Milton, Pensacola, and Mobile) it now afflicted hundreds, and then thousands. For several weeks the fever swept through the city seemingly unchecked, driving people into their homes in fear and emptying the newly fashioned Latin Quarter, where Oates had heard French spoken for the first time. The first cases of yellow fever appeared in New Orleans in the spring of 1853, and it reached epidemic proportions during the humid midsummer months. Over the next two years, 5,000 people died of the fever in New Orleans. It was only in 1855, after the disease moved north along the river (where it claimed one-sixth of the population of Vicksburg, Mississippi, in two short months) that the city recovered.

Although it isn't clear when Oates arrived in Shreveport, his luck began to change there. He was able to find work as a housepainter and quickly settled into a predictable routine of work and entertainment. It appeared that he had finally found a home; he befriended Shreveport's natives and became known around the town. After a few weeks he even found himself attracted to "a pretty rosy cheeked, black eyed country girl who," he added, "had not been reared to closely observe the rules observed in the more cultured circles of society."

One night near Shreveport, while Oates and the girl were carrying on "a little love affair" in the family wagon, the girl's father burst in and grabbed Oates by the shirt. Oates could see that the girl's father was enraged and about to haul him off to the local constable or, worse, demand that he marry his daughter. Oates would not have any of that, firmly refused the suggestion, and began to grapple with the man. Luckily, Oates was saved by a very timely interruption. In the midst of the angry tussle, the girl's father was himself arrested by the local sheriff, who accused the man of stealing a slave—a very serious criminal act. Oates later recounted this episode in his autobiography, commenting at length on the pitfalls of love and the temptations of romance and warning his son against the temporary pleasures of such liaisons. "It is only the puny, feeble and lifeless chap who is too pious, prudent and pure to be allured by the natural attractions of the world," he wrote, but then added that such attractions can be dangerous.

Oates said later the important lesson he learned was that not all is what it seems and that it is precisely when you are most vulnerable you should think about the future. After the Shreveport incident, Oates resolved never to be shackled to a plow and determined to make the best of his ambitions before being saddled with a family. Clearly Oates hoped to avoid his father's fate: a brood of children and a mounting pile of bills. He followed this vow well into his adult life, ultimately marrying only when it suited his purposes.

<hr/>

While Oates's "little love affair" had brought him a maturity he had not had when he set out on his journey, the events of the next few months proved that he still had not mastered his temper. It flared up once again when a man he worked for in Shreveport failed to pay him what he promised. Oates confronted him angrily and, when the man still refused to pay what he owed, Oates "seized him and threw him back into his chair, grappled his throat with my left hand, held him as a vise, and while choking him, I hit him in the face eight or nine times with my right fist and made the blood spatter." He left the scene in a hurry, feeling better that he had taken his revenge, though the local authorities were once again on his trail.

Oates was now on the run again. He wandered aimlessly off toward Texas and soon found himself in the small town of Marshall. Though he had few prospects and even less money, Marshall seemed much more to his liking than any other place he had been, not only because almost everyone carried a gun, but also because open public gambling and the violence that went with it were common. Oates was attracted to this kind of danger, and knew it. So he promised himself he would stay away from the gambling dens as long as he could (his Milton experience must have still been on his mind), do his best to make a living at his old job as a housepainter, and stay clear of young marriageable girls. It was not that Oates had suddenly decided to follow the path to respectability, but rather that having always been attracted to books and ideas, he began studying at a local school and doing the best he could to stay out of trouble. It was one of the few times since he had left Alabama that there had been any routine in his life.

Marshall was a frontier town, growing and dangerous, and it was almost inevitable that he would get into a fight. This time, though, Oates was more victim than aggressor. The incident took place when Marshall's town drunk, a man by the name of Sweeney, insulted him in a local bar. When Oates hurled an insult back at him, the argument grew heated. Sweeney pulled out a long Bowie knife and waved it threateningly in front of Oates's face. Oates was thoroughly frightened (he later wrote vividly that the knife "glistened like new silver") and ran down the street with Sweeney huffing after him. Again, as so often in the past, the young Alabamian was saved from almost certain death by accident when a group of close friends spied him running through the city with Sweeney close behind. Acting quickly to change the tide of events, one of Oates's friends threw him a large "brick bat" that was lying on the ground nearby. The weapon appeared just when Oates most needed it and, brandishing it, he turned on Sweeney menacingly. Sweeney stopped, hesitated, backed up, then turned and ran the other way, with Oates pursuing him back the way they had come. Sweeney eventually outran an almost certain beating, or worse. Yet he was dissatisfied with the results and within days he accused Oates of not fighting fair, challenging him to a stand-up fight—but this time, he said, Oates could only use his fists.

The two met several days later and Oates was pummeled by the more adept boxer. But Sweeney had underestimated his opponent, who stayed on his feet long enough to corner the larger man. Oates struck back, stunning Sweeney. With the older and larger man set back on his heels by this surprising onslaught, Oates pounced on him, put his thumbs in his eyes, and squeezed as hard as he could. He only let up after attempting to pull Sweeney's eyes from their sockets, then smothering him with his hands until be gasped for breath. Oates finished the fight by kicking Sweeney in the stomach. Oates left Sweeney on the street, doubled over in pain, and went off to celebrate his victory. But he had to leave town the next day, when he was told that there was another arrest warrant (his third) issued in his name.

After several days, or weeks, of wandering off to the southwest, Oates made his way to the Texas town of Waco, which over a period of just half a decade had grown from a small frontier fort guarding the Brazos River into a thriving settlement. It was the roughest town yet visited by Oates and served as a kind of magnet for every kind of outlaw that could be found on the Texas frontier. Despite this, Waco was in the midst of an economic boom and there were jobs to be had; within days,

Oates had hired himself out as a shingle maker, a trade that demanded backbreaking labor in mosquito-infested swamps under a broiling sun. It was the most brutal work he had ever done and it paid little.

The monotony of shingle making, which consisted of stripping bark off of hardwood trees growing in three feet of water, was alleviated to some degree, however, by the fact that Oates now enjoyed the friendship of a distant cousin who had met up with him in Marshall and agreed to travel with him through Texas. The two young men worked in the swamp during the day and stalked the streets of Waco at night, marveling at the lawlessness of the town, but steering clear of trouble. While Waco was a wild frontier town that promised new and more dangerous experiences, Oates had become almost indifferent to the lure of such excitement and he began to think about returning to Alabama. He had been gone from home for at least two years and word of his family had only reached him intermittently, through some family friends in Texas and through distant relatives of his mother's whom he had met along the way. Except for his stay in Shreveport, he had spent hardly more than four months in any one place and he was getting tired of "roving."

In spite of this, Oates decided that he would postpone his return to Pike County at least for a little while in order to get a feel for Waco, on the outside chance that it had something to offer that he had not yet seen. This was not long in coming. One night, with Oates looking on, a notorious outlaw by the name of Bill Long murdered a Texas Ranger in the middle of the town and coolly walked away—certain that he would never be punished. The sheer arrogance of the act impressed Oates even more than the horror of the victim's quick and meaningless death. But it also worried him. As a witness to the murder, he knew he would be questioned by the Rangers and that he would be watched by Long's friends to make certain he remained quiet. He quickly considered his options—facing the Rangers or facing Long's friends, a group of gamblers for whom taking the life of a teenager to protect an outlaw would mean nothing. If Long could kill a Texas Ranger, Oates thought, then he could kill anyone. But before he could flee, Oates got into yet another scrape when he was insulted by a local doctor by the name of A. D. Baldwin. Oates would have responded to the insult in the same way he had responded to Sweeney, but Baldwin, Oates later noted, had "killed three men, was a gambler and half crazy all the time with whisky and morphine."

Even so, Oates admitted, his fight with Baldwin (and, he believed, his resulting death) had been a near thing: when Baldwin threatened him for making derogatory comments about Waco (a habit, it seems, of frontier Texas—we would call it "picking a fight"), Oates ran through the streets of the town telling everyone he would take his revenge, then ran into his room and started to load his gun. We can imagine Oates with pistol in hand, sitting in his room, deciding whether he should again place his life in jeopardy. As easy as it was to imagine he could be as tough as Bill Long, it was just as easy for Oates to imagine himself in the place of the Ranger, facedown in the street, dead. So after reflecting on his situation for a short time, Oates "pocketed the insult" and put away his gun.

He left town for Austin, where he stopped for only a short time before heading west and south to Bastrop. Here he spent six weeks drinking and gambling, winning a large stake in a card game. Being good at cards had its bad side, however, and Oates decided to move on again before anyone would question his honesty. One morning Oates simply walked out of Bastrop, heading south to Port Lavaca, where he found work as a laborer on a plantation owned by a "Yankee" named Allison. For the first time on his journey west, he stayed out of trouble, spending much of his time over the next several months working in and around Port Lavaca (which was much more civilized than either Marshall or Waco) and gambling away his wages at local card games.

Surprisingly, however, especially given his earlier vow not to marry young, Oates fell in love with a Port Lavaca girl and became engaged. But the romance was short-lived; one night, as he was about to announce his arrival at his sweetheart's home, he spied her in the family garden kissing another man. The next day, without saying his farewells, he left Port Lavaca for Henderson, Texas, infinitely wiser about the shape of the world that his father had told him he "should try his hand at." He was now convinced that his earlier belief—that it is only "the puny, feeble and lifeless chap" who is immune to the natural attractions of the world—was the correct one, and that whatever the temptations of romance, he should do his best to avoid them.

Oates was ready to go home. He missed his family and was tiring of his life on the frontier. He was heading back east toward Alabama, perhaps without knowing so, when miraculously he met up in Henderson with his brother John, who had been sent by their mother to bring her oldest child home. John explained that while the Alabama arrest warrant served on him was still in force, he could hide out at the family farm before deciding what he should do. William needed little convincing and, after visiting relatives in East Texas, the two brothers started back.

By now, however, it seemed inevitable that Oates would find trouble no matter where he was. So when the brothers became involved in a wild card game in East Texas, it was only natural that it would end in a fight. This one was vicious. William found himself facing off against a man named McGuire, as tenacious a scrapper as the burly Sweeney. The result, however, was the same. After trading insults, McGuire attacked Oates and got the better of him for a time. But Oates's sheer tenacity eventually tipped the scale and McGuire ended up with gouged eyes, a tactic that Oates found repeatedly useful. With honor served, William and John finally set out for Alabama.

⊙━━✦━━⊙

The brothers traveled quickly through Louisiana and arrived at the family farm at Oates's Crossroads in short order. It was more than two years since William's departure, but not much had changed. William helped his father with the farm for a time, kept himself out of the eye of the law, and looked up old friends—but his relationship with his family, and especially with his father, was no better than it had been when he first went off to Texas. There were still too many mouths to feed and the work was as physically exhausting as it had been when he left. So while he was happy to see his family, he knew that eventually he would have to start out on his own. He had now seen the world, or as much of it as he wanted, and decided that he could do as well in Alabama as anywhere else—maybe even better.

After a stay of only a few weeks, Oates announced to the family that he was moving to Henry County, only a short distance away. The move seemed like a perfect solution to all of his problems: it would allow him the liberty he craved, and at the same time he could keep in close touch with his brother John. Henry County had another inducement as well.

There, a small community had need of a teacher and Oates thought he might fill the post. All he needed to teach a country school was a minimal ability to read and write, which he had. The modest job in a small Henry County settlement offered a chance for him to earn a steady income as he set about the task of gaining a more formal education. So in early 1854, at the age of twenty, William Oates left home again, this time for good, and headed south to Cottonwood, a small settlement carved out of the wilds of southeastern Alabama.

# 2

# *Shadows Luminous in the Sunset Glow*

LIKE ALABAMA, Maine was settled by families needing land. The state's first European inhabitants were hardy people who thought they saw opportunity and riches in its impenetrable pine forests and political freedom in its comparative isolation. As in Alabama, the people of Maine came first from other places (primarily from Massachusetts) and spent years of punishing work to clear the land. But unlike Alabama, Maine was not the object of a land rush: the environment was simply too harsh—with short growing seasons and long, cold winters. There were many cases of settlers coming north, farming for several years, and then returning south in frustration.

For one hundred years, Massachusetts colonists claimed Maine as theirs—as a kind of safety valve for its own growing population. There was no disagreement about this until 1785, when a group of Maine citizens began a separatist movement. But it was not until 1816 that Maine's statehood seemed assured: a convention was held in Brunswick to draft a constitution, and in 1819 the Massachusetts General Court agreed to an act of separation. By coincidence, the federal Union just then needed another state, to balance the entrance of Missouri, which southerners insisted should be set aside for slavery. Maine was founded, then, as an integral part of the Missouri Compromise, in 1820.

Maine entered the Union as the twenty-third state and there were grand hopes that its virgin lands would attract huge numbers of land-starved New Englanders. But there were few takers: Maine had barely 300,000 settlers in 1820, most of them nestled along the Merrimac and Kennebec rivers, and much of the state remained unsurveyed. The economic boom promised by statehood went largely unrealized, and the state's major exports remained lumber and ice for food packing. Still, there was prosperity for those who worked hard and had acclimated themselves to Maine's harsh realities. Among the most successful of Maine's families were those, small in number, who had come to the state a generation before the statehood convention, including the Chamberlains of Orrington. By the time Lawrence Joshua Chamberlain was born in Brewer, in 1828, the Chamberlains had been in Maine for three generations—since 1799—and proudly counted themselves as one of the state's original pioneer families.

❦

Lawrence Joshua Chamberlain was given his name by his father, Joshua Chamberlain, who admired the American naval hero Commodore James Lawrence, the commander of the warship *Chesapeake* during the War of 1812. In the heat of battle with a British frigate, Lawrence incited his men with the words "Don't give up the ship." It is likely that Joshua Chamberlain hated the British as much as Commodore Lawrence, since the Chamberlain family had been separated from their family fortune during that war by the British navy when it sailed up the Penobscot River and burned Ebenezer Chamberlain's warehouse and ruined his shipbuilding business. Despite this legacy (and his father's wishes) Lawrence Joshua Chamberlain—the oldest son of the Chamberlain family—insisted on shifting his name to Joshua Lawrence Chamberlain. He eventually relegated his new middle name to a simple middle initial. His preference meant nothing to his immediate family, however, who called him Lawrence throughout his life. Lawrence, or Joshua (as we now know him), gave no explanation for his decision. Perhaps he admired his father.

Joshua Chamberlain's father was an old-fashioned New England Puritan: he believed in the worth of work, the sanctity of the Sabbath, the value of self-discipline, financial prudence, and hope for the future. He had expansive ambitions for his children, hoping that they would become great Americans. There were five children in all: Lawrence, (born September 8, 1828), followed by Horace, Sarah, John, and Thomas. It was important to Joshua's father that each of the children be given a strong, distinctive name, or one that honored an American. John, Joshua's younger brother, was named for John Calhoun.

The Chamberlains came to America from England in the 1640s and settled in Massachusetts. The male descendants carried the proper British names of William and John, but the family's names took a bibli cal turn in the colonies. The son of the first Massachusetts settler was named Jacob, followed by another William, then Ebenezer, who became the family's first soldier when he fought in the American Revolution. Ebenezer's grandson—Joshua, Jr., named for his father, was born in 1800—moved north to Maine, where the family set down roots as shipbuilders and farmers.

The senior Joshua Chamberlain was a respected member of his community, serving as county commissioner and commander of the local militia. He was attracted to the military life, with its honors, uniforms, and weapons. In 1839, when his son was just a boy, the father had his own flirtation with military greatness. Joshua marched the Brewer militia off to war in a border dispute with Britain in Maine's Aroostook River Valley. Captain Joshua Chamberlain was an officer in the militia's second regiment, a responsibility he took all the more seriously in light of his family's past experience with the British.

Chamberlain's regiment marched and countermarched, but calm eventually prevailed. While the Brewer soldiers stood waiting for orders to fight, British-American relations improved and General Winfield Scott was dispatched to Maine to settle the dispute amicably. The senior Chamberlain, who was probably disappointed that he could not retrieve his grandfather Ebenezer's honor (or win such honors for himself), returned home to his fields. It was undoubtedly with this experience in mind that the senior Chamberlain set about teaching his son how to fight with a broadsword, though even then such weapons were clearly going out of style. The lessons were taken seriously, nevertheless, and the two Chamberlains—the older man and young boy—could be seen endlessly dueling, clearly enjoying the sport, in the fields of the family's one-hundred-acre farm.

Chamberlain's mother, Sarah Dupee Brastow (whom everyone called Sallie), was the granddaughter of Captain Thomas Brastow, Jr., a soldier of the French and Indian Wars and an officer in the American Revolution. She was descended on her mother's side from Jean Dupuis, of a family of French Huguenots who had made their way to New England in the mid-1680s. Sarah inherited warmth, a quick mind, and a prodigious physical capacity for work from her family, and a Huguenot tolerance for those who were different. She was suited to her husband in many ways: both were religious, strong-willed, believed in the worth of a good education, and felt that there was a direct relationship between personal salvation and hard work. But Sarah Chamberlain was gentler and more trusting of the formalities of education than her husband, and she was more committed to the family religion. She was comforted by the conventional beliefs of New England Calvinism, with its daily strictures, dour traditions, and sense of closemouthed propriety. She took care to wear a muslin cap when she did her everyday chores, never missed church, and fervently hoped that her oldest son would become a minister.

She disagreed with her husband's view that the life of the ministry was not as honorable as that of a military officer. But that was their only major disagreement. Both believed that Joshua should excel in whatever he chose to do and were single-minded in their effort to provide him with the best education New England's schools could offer. In this way, the Chamberlains were wholly different from the Oateses of Alabama: while both families struggled to make a living (the Chamberlains were themselves nearly caught several times on the edge of bankruptcy), the Chamberlains were not poor and, despite their occasional financial problems, it was not out of the question that their eldest son could someday graduate from the Military Academy at West Point or become a minister.

In either case, Joshua and Sarah wanted to make certain that their children, and most especially their firstborn son, would continue the family tradition of hard work as the only sure path to heavenly reward. To emphasize this belief, Sarah made certain that religion was an important part of life in the Chamberlain household, and the family diligently attended the local Brewer Congregational Church. The Chamberlains' religious beliefs were simple, and simply stated: church attendance was required; family quarreling was forbidden; profanity was not allowed; punishment was strict, certain, and immediate; modesty and moderation were displayed in all things; public expressions of any kind of emotion, fear or even affection, were viewed as undignified. The young Joshua was diligently taught that the path to salvation was paved by a life of good works.

The eldest son rebelled only slightly against these strictures, tending in his early years to follow the path dictated by his mother, who had a more gentle and studious personality. It was primarily due to her influence that he began to think of himself as a minister. Nevertheless, in his teens Joshua Chamberlain agreed to attend a boy's academy in nearby Ellsworth; Whiting's Military and Classical School combined the strong discipline of regimentation with exposure to French, Latin, and the obligatory Rhetoric. Joshua attended the school as a full-time student at the age of fourteen. He hired himself out to help pay his tuition during the first year, but in the following year he was forced to return home when his father, because of poor investments, could not pay his tuition.

The picture we have of the young Joshua Chamberlain is the one that has been passed down to us by no less than four major biographers. He is treated admiringly as a young man who lived an idyllic life in the fields of eastern Maine. Much is made of his family history and the Chamberlains' stable stock, and what hint of scandal exists is passed off as a part of history that is better forgotten. Unlike the Oates family of southeastern Alabama, the Chamberlains knew their ancestry well and could trace their line to revolutionary soldiers and shipbuilders who were all well-known to their community. The men of the family are painted as dour, erect, God-fearing, and patriotic, while the women are religious, hardworking examples of nineteenth-century womanhood. Much is made of the great family successes: the elder Joshua Chamberlain's two brothers, John Quincy Adams Chamberlain and Elbridge Gerry Chamberlain, moved west, where Elbridge became a congressman from Indiana. Both became valued members of their communities and, while not affluent, made an economic success on the frontier.

Joshua Chamberlain's boyhood is treated similarly. He was born in a modest cottage and grew up in the small tight-knit farming community of Brewer. Joshua Chamberlain is said to have inherited his immense self-confidence and self-discipline from a father who taught him that willpower could prove an adequate defense against any challenge: when told to move a huge stone in a field (it is said), Joshua balked, asking his father how such a thing could be done. "Just do it," his father replied. Admirably, we are told, Joshua complied, "and it was done." The portrait is effective and in keeping with what we know of his later, heroic life: Joshua Chamberlain spent his time learning, working, and worshiping.

There is, however, something not quite believable about this history. It is too idyllic. The portrait we have of Joshua Chamberlain, his parents, and his brothers and sister are stereotypes and, ultimately, uninformative. In the winter, the biographers tell us, the senior Chamberlain would come home to his family, blowing off the Maine snow after a day in the town, then join them around the fire while Sarah read from *Pilgrim's Progress* and he puffed contentedly on his pipe. In the spring there was planting to do, with the boys coming into the fields to help their father with the sowing, then returning home to chop wood to heat the evening meal. But such labor, while intense, was not brutalizing. In the summer the boys sailed the family sloop and searched the woods for remnants of Maine's aboriginal Indians. Stories were swapped about the ancient tribes and their chiefs and the family listened in pride as the eldest son played on a bass viol he had miraculously carved from raw wood. In autumn the harvest came in and the children were schooled locally, attending to their books under the watchful eyes of their loving mother. The family excelled and prospered, the children were bright students, their parents were loving, but properly stern.

There is little doubt that the family was healthy and happy—and there is nothing in the historical record to suggest otherwise. Nevertheless, the ethic of the time dictated that every family's most basic troubles would remain unstated, not simply to friends and neighbors, but even (or especially) to posterity. There were troubles in the Chamberlain family of course and, while they were not dire, they are instructive. With his brothers gone west, it was up to Joshua's father to keep up the family name in New England, but that was a difficult and sometimes even suffocating responsibility. Joshua's father was, in fact, much less successful than either of his two brothers. Hardworking and modest though he was, the senior Chamberlain was not thrifty, as befits a prudent Congregationalist, but took large gambles with the family savings, bringing the Chamberlains to the edge of financial ruin. This family secret was, predictably, no secret in Brewer despite the Puritan admonition against gossip, and it was generally known among the townspeople that the senior Joshua Chamberlain was a careless man who hoped by his investments to reach beyond the narrow confines of rural Maine.

In the early 1840s, Joshua Chamberlain's father made several questionable investments and fanciful loans, including one in a shipbuilding enterprise in Portland that he believed would make him rich, thereby fulfilling his son's wishes for a better education. But while Portland was becoming a shipping boomtown and the center of commercial activity for northern New England, the local economy was susceptible to small but vicious recessions. It was largely the result of one such economic slide that Chamberlain's shipbuilding gamble failed: his loans went unpaid and the ships were only partially built. The family hardship lasted for several years; it was during this period that Joshua was forced to return from Whiting's and the Chamberlain family had to sell all of its holdings except for the hundred-acre family farm. The senior Chamberlain staved off bankruptcy, but his family was thrown back on its most constant resource, which came from hoeing, chopping, plowing, planting, harvesting, and selling the crops from their farm. There was little the senior Chamberlain could do except to begin to rebuild his savings.

The family financial difficulties had a significant impact on Joshua, who was forced to work in a brickyard and in Portland's burgeoning timber industry. He was strong, above average height for his time, and inured to manual labor, but he preferred books to farming and enjoyed his time as a member of the church choir—his one break from the daily round of farm chores. By the time he was seventeen, his single year at Whiting's seemed long past, his education was put on hold, and a wide and prosperous future was thrown into doubt. To make matters worse, there was a far more serious problem that Joshua Chamberlain had to wrestle with, especially if he ever hoped to expand on his modest educational beginnings. As a child, Joshua had developed a distinctive stammer, tripping over words that began with the letters *p, b,* or *t.*

Chamberlain's stammer was more than a worrisome problem: left unsolved, it would have an enormous impact on his life—and on his mother's dream that he become a minister. While the impediment did not bar him from teaching or the ministry, it would certainly cause him problems; it would certainly serve as a major handicap if he decided to become a minister. New England's traditions were oral, and much of public discourse took place from the pulpit, where ministers were not only judged by their ability to interpret Scripture, but where a good Sunday sermon was a symbol of religious devotion. Chamberlain's inability to communicate and his subsequent withdrawal from family and community activities hindered his social growth. The stammer added to the adolescent frustrations brought on by his father's financial difficulties. While the problem undoubtedly focused the young Chamberlain on the written word (and helped to focus his attention on scholarship), the stammer was a constant worry that no one in the family knew how to solve.

As Chamberlain's efforts at communication became increasingly difficult, and sometimes embarrassing, he spoke as little as possible and spent more and more of his free time in isolation. With no books as an outlet (few were allowed—outside of the Bible and occasional family readings from, of course, *Pilgrim's Progress*), Joshua Chamberlain turned to writing. Even as an adolescent, he was an accomplished writer. A compensation for his shyness, he was able to put onto paper emotions and feelings that rarely received public recognition. His written compositions are talismans of nineteenth-century romantic hyperbole, with pretensions to deep romanticism that he copied in style from the one poet, Byron (oddly), that his mother allowed him to read. Memorizing passages from Byron was a prodigious feat that he would repeat throughout his life, but the most immediate effect was that this made his writing drip with sentimentality. It is difficult to shake the conclusion that Chamberlain used this florid style not simply to describe, but also to conceal what was an uncertain childhood and adolescence. In "Early Memoirs," penned when he was an adolescent, Chamberlain wrote:

> Now in the declining day of the sower, guiding the faithful, knowing mare, companion to his youthful toils, traverses breadth by breadth the field—the figures standing out against the shadows luminous in the sunset glow which has touched the mists above the city across the river with wondrous glory,— and thus, all bathed in a golden dream, tenderly pressing that precious earth, for the last time of the dear old times.

Writing allowed Chamberlain to remember his youth for what it was not: a pastoral heaven on earth in which the financial troubles of his father, the comforting but naive musings of his mother, and his inability to speak without stumbling could be forgotten, ignored, or transformed into "shadows luminous in the sunset glow" that were "bathed in a golden dream." The idyllic life of the young Joshua in the Maine woods, a childhood he spoke of in monotonous pastoral tones throughout the rest of his life (he wrote a cousin, at the age of seventeen, that his boyhood was "unbeclouded") was actually one of constant work to make certain that the family stayed fed and that he become educated.

⌒═══✦═══⌒

In 1846, after his stint working in the brickyard, and thoroughly exhausted by working on the family farm, Joshua Chamberlain took a job as a teacher at a school in the rural hamlet of North Milford, just up the Penobscot River from Brewer, breaking the hours of teaching by conducting a singing class at the local church—he even sent home for his bass viol, which he used as accompaniment. The respite from home and family gave him the opportunity to think about what he would do with his future.

It did not take him long to decide, though he knew it would be difficult for him to lead the life he imagined. While his education was sparse by today's standards, it was extensive by those then applied in rural Maine, and Joshua decided to use it to attempt to gain entrance to Bowdoin College in Brunswick. He would thereby defer his decision to enter the ministry, at the same time he applied himself to studies that would prepare him for divinity school. He knew gaining admission to Bowdoin would be a difficult task and would cause financial hardships to his still struggling family. Chamberlain would be required to pass a stringent entrance examination that included a command of ancient Greek. Returning home from keeping school in North Milford, he set aside a part of his family attic for a study and applied himself to an in-depth review of Latin, Greek, mathematics, and rhetoric. He was helped in his study of the classics by a tutor from Whiting's (paid for by the hard-earned funds that he gained from keeping school, and by the diligent application of his father to scrape together every extra penny the family then had), spending nearly ten hours of each day in an isolation broken only by the need to gather firewood—a time that Chamberlain later referred to as "woodsplitting and head-splitting."

Over the course of the next year, Chamberlain worked unrelentingly, being drilled again and again by his old Whiting's master, William Hyde. The teacher was exacting and knew precisely what Chamberlain would be asked by the Bowdoin admissions committee; Hyde was not only a Bowdoin graduate and friendly with the committee, he was an accomplished classics scholar and an apparently gifted teacher. Much of the Greek and Latin was a matter of drill and memorization and Chamberlain was tested for three hours every day on what he had learned, delving first into Homer, Herodotus, and Thucydides, and then into the Latin classics of Cicero and Sallust.

In February 1848, the nineteen-year-old Chamberlain set out with Hyde on a two-day journey to Bowdoin College, passing through Maine's small coastal towns, and arriving at the campus on a cold and snowy morning. Hyde escorted his young student into a small poorly lit room, where a committee of professors waited. They were undoubtedly skeptical that the somber young man from Brewer could pass their exacting test or that he would be able to recite the Greek and Latin texts they required, but Hyde had done his work well.

After nearly a half day of questioning in Latin and Greek—which included, for the stammering Chamberlain, the nerve-racking recitations of key passages from the classics—the committee said they were satisfied that Chamberlain had learned his lessons well, complimented Mr. Hyde on his abilities, but commented that his young student's Greek needed more study. They warned Chamberlain to pay special attention to his texts and not be diverted by the lure of college life, and welcomed him officially to their community. Without a fuss, Chamberlain was given his class schedule, assigned to a room in one of the two small dormitories, and told to report to his first class the next morning, before sunrise. Hyde returned to Brewer, proud of his charge and convinced that he would make his way as an honored scholar or even, as his mother hoped, a minister. Chamberlain was suddenly "a Bowdoin man."

The four buildings of the Bowdoin College campus must have seemed especially intimidating to a farm boy from rural Maine. This was a new world for Joshua Chamberlain, complete with first-year hazings, endless pranks, after-hours forays, and late-night study sessions. For a short time, at least, Chamberlain was uncomfortable in his new surroundings. But the thin country boy, who stood one inch short of six feet, was much less naive than he appeared. He struggled in his first term, scrambling to make up for his lost semester in a curriculum that included algebra, Greek, Latin, and a liberal sprinkling of English composition. But he remained confident that he could do the work, and even excel. In the tradition of the time, language study was done orally—which caused him the most problems—but Chamberlain applied himself to his studies and ignored the rites of passage that accompanied a new man's appearance on campus. While he good-naturedly endured a smoke-out, with upperclassmen filling his room with clouds of tobacco (the room lamp, he later wrote, "looked like a red moon in a foggy night"), he decided to abstain from alcohol and followed his own strict personal regimen of studying and churchgoing.

Even at Bowdoin, which was known for its strict Puritan traditions and twice-daily religious services, Chamberlain was more devout than most of his classmates. He taught Bible class, participated in the church choir, improved his musical skills on the church organ, attended Thursday and Saturday evening prayer meetings, and prepared himself for the quiet life of a clergyman. Sunday mornings found him at the nearby First Parish Church, as diligently intent on finding his way into a life of service as he had been intent, during the previous week, to learn how to navigate the treacherous shoals of Latin cases and verb tenses. There were some lonely moments: because of his self-imposed temperance, a number of Chamberlain's classmates dropped him from their social outings, and there were few letters from his family. Chamberlain shrugged off his discomfort: "They seem to understand my duty pretty well," he wrote of his fellow students. "I have sometimes found myself alone but all came out right."

Chamberlain got along best with his professors, who took a liking to his scholarly tenacity. While few thought Chamberlain brilliant,

everyone admired his endless capacity for work and his bottomless diligence. Mr. Hyde had done an admirable job preparing his young student for the endless hours of memorization and oral testing and
Chamberlain was even better prepared for the rigors of college work
than many of his classmates. He was able to sit for hours, without moving, poring over a text, then recite it from memory in class the next
morning. Even his most distant classmates eventually sought out his
help, but he could offer little except to advise them to do what he did,
which was to commit everything to memory and work long hours. He
did not want to be diverted, so he tried to associate with what one of his
friends described as "the right sort of fellows," that is, those who were
short on cursing, drinking, and pranks, and long on study. He joined a
campus social group, a quasi-fraternity, because he was expected to do
so, choosing the Peucinian Society because of its scholarly members.

Chamberlain knew that he could not always remain so aloof. During the middle of the term he joined in a class romp loosely called
"Class Tree Day," during which the men of the school searched for a
tree to transplant to the college grounds. The tradition was little more
than an excuse to swig down enormous quantities of liquor (or "cider,"
as it was called) and sing the freshly cut tree back through the town of
Brunswick to the campus. During Chamberlain's freshman year, the
boisterous celebration went well beyond Bowdoin traditions. When
the townspeople complained about the rowdiness to school officials
the next morning, Chamberlain was called into the president's office,
told that the drunken behavior was "disgraceful," and was ordered to
give the names of the offenders. He refused. The president, Leonard
Woods—a stiff, prickly, and self-important man—threatened him with
suspension, but Chamberlain was not intimidated and defiantly refused
to name the perpetrators. Woods was enraged, especially since he had
picked out Chamberlain as the most likely student to cooperate with
the school administration. Woods berated Chamberlain, telling him
that his silence came from "a false sense of honor" and declared him
summarily suspended from the college. Chamberlain would not go quietly. Standing before the imposing Woods, the nineteen-year-old summoned up his courage and told Woods that, even with a suspension, he
would not be known as "an informant" and "a betrayer of confidence,
which is much like a traitor."

This might have been enough for the hair-trigger Woods, but Chamberlain, who had already gone too far, added an extra comment: "I know well my father will be proud to see me coming home for this," he told Woods, his stammer apparently under strict control, "more so than I shall be to return here again." Woods harrumphed his disgust, pointed to the door, and Chamberlain returned to his room at 21 Maine Hall to pack his bags. He was met there by his classmates, who crowded around him, fearful of what he might have said to the school president. Chamberlain reassured them that he would never betray a friendship: "I'm going home, boys," he said simply, sadly, "there's no help for it," and he reiterated his view that he had had little choice in the matter. Embarrassed by such an unpredicted show of friendship and loyalty from this stammering farm boy—the newest, greenest member of the class—Chamberlain's classmates grew sheepish and agreed that they would go to Woods to confess to their rowdy crimes. "Boys, let's go down and own up to the cider," one of them decided, and off they marched. Woods, who was viewed as a man who made good on his threats, surprised everyone by relenting and, after the traditional lecture on good manners and the proper behavior of Bowdoin men, satisfied himself that justice was served by passing out a small number of reprimands. Chamberlain was reinstated; but, more important, he was confirmed in the affection of his classmates by gladly taking on the new nickname of "Jack" that they had given him in an ironic play on his serious nature. The incident became one of his proudest memories.

Staid as Bowdoin was, the school had gained its reputation in New England more for its adherence to exacting classical standards than for its traditional religious practices. The school attracted revered scholars, men like the ageless, but doddering, chemistry professor Parker Cleaveland, who began teaching at Bowdoin in 1805. He was joined at the college by the faculty terror, mathematics Professor William Smyth, whose impenetrable lectures threw the students into equally impossible tasks—trying to understand what he was saying, and then applying it to their puzzling texts. Many believed that Smyth should not be a teacher at all, but they ruefully admitted that at least he was an egalitarian, since he disliked all of his students equally.

Cleaveland and Smyth were joined during Chamberlain's time as a student by Thomas Cogswell Upham, Bowdoin's professor of mental and moral philosophy. Upham was viewed as a progressive—a radical, even—because he sprinkled his lectures with quips about that well-known European "revolutionary," Immanuel Kant—whose belief that morality could be derived from reason was considered breathtakingly original by Bowdoin's board of trustees. Thankfully, the administrators recognized Upham's powerful teaching abilities and the fact that his brilliance added to the college's growing prestige. Its most talented professor, Daniel R. Goodwin, however, was neither eccentric nor stooped, but young and cheery. Goodwin was a born teacher, considered by many to be a genius, and a man who would be remembered by Chamberlain many years later as the person who gave him a deep love of languages. He befriended Chamberlain, invited him to family dinners, and saw the boy through his coursework.

Chamberlain recognized that Bowdoin offered him opportunities only dreamed of by his forebears, so he kept to his strict regimen of study, working late into the night to master his Latin and Greek. He applied the same attention to overcoming his stammer, to which he now gave increasing attention. The speech impediment loomed over everything in Chamberlain's life, interfering with his scholarly recitations, his personal life, and his stillborn friendships. Despite the "Class Tree Day" incident, after five months on campus, he was still an outsider at Bowdoin. He finally sought help from Alpheus Packard, Bowdoin's professor of ancient languages. Under Packard's tutelage, Chamberlain taught himself to recognize word hurdles in his speech—and then learned to "sing" his way through them. "The old Spartans used to sing their laws for [an] after-dinner past-time," Chamberlain reflected later. "And Spartan laws were no laughing matter." This was the closest Chamberlain ever came to admitting to his discomfort, or to his feeling that his classmates viewed his strange malady as a personal flaw—or even laughable.

With the help of Packard, and the rigorous application of the same principles that helped him to pass Greek, Chamberlain slowly mastered his problem, but his speech was never effortless. To the end of his life his sentences were filled with strange hesitations and irregular rhythms, a habit of speaking that some put down to his great erudition. He was an expert at pausing at just the right spots, as if reflecting on some larger point, when in fact he was thinking ahead to how he would overcome the next *p, t,* or *b.* Chamberlain allowed, later, that his stammer undoubtedly affected the way he viewed others, and how he was viewed by them, and that his struggle with speaking "may have reached into the whole of [my] life." He had touched on only one small part of the truth, however: Chamberlain's strange hesitations, his seemingly erudite demeanor, and his flowery, singsong delivery served as protection against the prevalent view that those with speech impediments were somehow touched by the devil. While such judgments now appear primitive and uninformed, the devil was still a constant presence in mid-nineteenth-century New England. For Chamberlain any such hesitation in speech might be viewed as evidence that the devil had laid his hand on his tongue—and might therefore be a possible disqualification for a man of God.

⟡

The religious revival led by Charles Finney that spread through most of the Northeast during Chamberlain's freshman year at Bowdoin led to a deep questioning of the region's accepted belief—that all alike were sinners—and its views of eternal punishment. Yet in 1848, a majority of Maine's citizens would have likely agreed with Hawthorne, who was then writing of the evils of long-buried family secrets: "In the depths of every heart, there is a tomb and a dungeon, though the lights, the music, and revelry above may cause us to forget their existence, and the buried ones, or prisoners whom they hide." One of the buried Chamberlain family secrets was that Rebecca Chamberlain, the wife of the family's first American settler, was burned at the stake during the Salem witch trials of 1692. The man who passed judgment on her was John Hathorn, who condemned her to her "tomb and dungeon." John Hathorn was one of reclusive and witchcraft-obsessed Nathaniel Hawthorne's more storied ancestors. The horror of the trials imbued in both the Chamberlain and Hawthorne families a distaste for heresy and quick condemnation. In this they were no different than their neighbors. Having witnessed New England set upon by a pious throng bent on striking the devil from their midst, Maine's Congregationalists—especially those who attended both the First Parish Church and straightlaced Bowdoin College—simply did not join movements, or mobs, and frowned on those who did.

Many in Maine mistrusted abolitionists, who were as rare in the state as warm winter days. The abolitionist William Lloyd Garrison, publisher of the *Liberator*, critic of "gradualists" and "colonizers" and head of the New England Antislavery Society, made a speaking tour in the state in 1849, thundering his radical abolitionist gospel. But few came to hear him. Nor were Maine's churches as consumed with the slavery debate as their neighbors. But during Chamberlain's second year in college, students at Bangor Theological Seminary, which Chamberlain had decided to attend once he graduated from Bowdoin, began to contest the issue. Many of Bangor's young seminarians quickly became radical abolitionists, seeing in the movement a confirmation of their own religious commitment. Many of them also enlisted as messengers along the Underground Railroad, whose northernmost spur now extended into the state. Despite Chamberlain's decision to enter the ministry after completing his studies at Bowdoin, he does not seem to have wrestled much with the question of slavery. If Joshua Chamberlain had any thoughts of his own on the dispute, he did not commit them to writing or speak of them in public. It is most likely that he was influenced by his father in his views: while both practiced at broadswords and celebrated the discipline and glory of military life, they remained cautious about the kinds of wars they would fight. The senior Chamberlain, especially, believed there was too much controversy over slavery—which was none of Maine's business anyway. This, coupled with his innate mistrust of the central government and his admiration of the South, affected his views and influenced his sons.

If anything, Chamberlain's second year at Bowdoin was even more successful than his first. He became one of Professor Daniel Goodwin's library assistants, which was the best and most public evidence of his scholastic abilities, and maintained his friendship with the Packard family, who provided him with a secure second home. Packard's constant tutoring was also still a necessity, occasioned by Chamberlain's continued and still tortured attempts to master his confused tongue. Packard drilled him again and again, making him repeat his *p*'s, *b*'s, and *t*'s until he could recite his texts without stumbling. But other than spending time with Packard, Chamberlain's regimen remained unchanged. He once again gave little time to socializing, but set aside hours for prayer meetings and studying. His Sunday mornings at the

First Parish Church were as important in his mind for his spiritual growth as memorizing his Greek was for his intellectual growth. He participated in every aspect of the church's life.

During his second year at Bowdoin, all of Chamberlain's scholastic work began to show rewards: he started the year ranked near the middle of his class, but was near the top at the end. It was not a feat to be taken lightly—he had climbed the academic ladder despite his stammer, and by surmounting the difficulties of decoding Professor Smyth's barely comprehensible lectures on trigonometry. Chamberlain was a scholastic success, a valued and respected member of his church, and was established as "Jack," a valued if not always collegial member of his class. At the end of the second year, he returned home and was greeted by his proud parents, who were buoyed by his success. The entire Chamberlain family seemed to gain by his success. Though there had been years of hardship and poor investments, Chamberlain's father was now viewed as a prosperous, though hardly affluent, member of the Brewer community, having reassumed the commercial respectability he had had prior to his poor investments. Not only could he continue to send his son to Bowdoin, he was planning the education of his other children, a number of whom decided to follow the example set by their brother Joshua. But just as the life of this eldest son seemed set out on a very successful course, fate intervened: as he was preparing to return to school for his third year, Joshua Chamberlain fell mysteriously ill and was confined to his bed.

When school opened at Bowdoin in late August, Chamberlain was still in Brewer. By mid-September his condition had grown worse. He was running a high fever, had lost all of his strength and quite a bit of weight. The Chamberlain family doctor prescribed bed rest and cold compresses for his fever, but could do little else. One by one, the maladies that afflicted nineteenth-century America were ruled out: there was no yellow fever, no measles or smallpox, no flu or cold, and no pneumonia. The family was left to find its own remedies. But nothing seemed to work, and Chamberlain's condition grew worse every day. During the first days of 1850, when his Bowdoin classmates were preparing for their midyear exams, Joshua Chamberlain lay bedridden and near death in his room in Brewer. At this point, and almost frantic with fear that she would lose her eldest son to an unknown sickness,

Sarah Chamberlain dismissed the family doctor and sent for a local homeopathist, with his bag of home remedies. It is not known exactly what the homeopathist did to help, but his treatment probably followed the common-sense principles of nineteenth-century homeopathist belief: Chamberlain was put on a strict regimen of exercise and rest and his body was filled with nutrients. He was fed at regular intervals, despite his protests, and ordered to exercise, no matter how exhausted he seemed. Slowly he recovered, then faded, and then recovered again, building his strength step by step.

Chamberlain later credited his mother with saving his life. He never knew exactly why he had become ill, but it is likely that the last opinion he had received, from the homeopathist, was the most accurate: months of studying trigonometry, Greek, Latin, French, religion, and composition, followed by prayer meetings and religious services, had so exhausted Chamberlain that he suffered a general physical collapse. By the early spring of 1850 he was doing simple chores on the farm, and by the beginning of the summer he was jousting with broadswords in the yard with his father. At the end of the summer he was fully recovered and was ready to return to Bowdoin. Not surprisingly, he had kept up with his studies during his recovery, applying himself for ever longer periods of time to his Greek and Latin. Nevertheless, he had missed a full year of school and would not be rejoining his classmates for their senior year. He was disappointed, but had little choice. In September he journeyed to Bowdoin, where Professor Goodwin and Packard welcomed his return.

Bowdoin could not be expected to change in the short year that marked Chamberlain's absence. Nevertheless, the school was undergoing something of a slow, though perceptible, transition. While Professors Smyth, Cleaveland, Goodwin, and Packard were still consumed by their normal routines and a new class of freshmen were learning the school's traditions, the national debate over slavery had become more prominent among Bowdoin's students. There was also startling news that Calvin Stowe was coming to Bowdoin from Ohio. His wife, the novelist Harriet Beecher, was already living in Brunswick, waiting for him to join her. The Stowes' odyssey from their home in Cincinnati, however, had actually begun many years before, when abolitionism first came to Alabama.

# *3*

# *Written in Blood*

ABOLITIONISM CAME TO ALABAMA on the heels of the religious
revival, and in much the same way. Just as the "Second Great
Awakening" was symbolized by the ministry of Presbyterian
preacher James McGready, abolitionism in Alabama would forever be
associated with James G. Birney, a callow Kentucky dandy for whom
the eradication of slavery became a lucrative business—though not
nearly as lucrative as he wished.

Lanky, loud, ostentatious, and ambitious, Birney had first come to
Huntsville in northern Alabama from his father's lush Danville, Kentucky, estate in the 1820s with a retinue of forty slaves trailing closely
behind. With a dream of becoming a genteel southern planter (and,
someday, president), the young Birney had a Princeton education, a
bad drinking habit, and an obsession with cards. Within a few years of
his arrival, Birney had gambled away his birthright, sold his slaves and
new estate, and begun a career as one of Huntsville's local lawyers. He
was a failure and was forced to return to Kentucky, where, having rid
himself of his drinking habit as well as his slaves, he began to urge others to do the same. He talked first of the evils of drink and then signed
on as an agent of the American Colonization Society, an organization
that advocated the removal of slaves to Africa. Backed by the colonization society's well-funded program, Birney returned to Alabama in the
early 1830s to preach the gospel of colonization at a series of well-
attended public meetings.

Being a former resident, Birney knew he needed to sculpt his message to appeal to Alabama's most primal fear—that someday its slave
population would rise up and murder its white masters. The problem

was not slavery, Birney told his audiences, but slaves. He knew this because he had spent time in the North, where a burgeoning abolitionist movement was forcing border state slaveholders, like those in Kentucky, to sell their property farther South. That trend, he said, would continue. Eventually the rising tide of surplus slaves would swamp Alabama, he argued, thereby changing forever the increasingly fragile white-to-black demographic equation. Birney, however, had not come to frighten his audiences, but to reassure them: the inevitable eclipse of the white South, lost forever in a sea of black faces, need not happen at all, he said. All that Alabama's slaveholders needed to do was give money to ship the surplus slaves to Africa. When he was criticized for being an abolitionist, Birney vehemently denied the charge—that was simply not true, he said, and he could prove it. He had once owned slaves and understood the necessity of the slave system to southern commerce. He did not want to abolish slavery, but only keep the black population in check, thereby providing demographic stability to the slave system. Abolitionism threatened that stability.

For all of his eloquence and compelling revival-meeting style, Birney was not able to convince Alabamians to give money to help rid slaveholders of their excess slaves, or to send the money to Kentucky to keep slaves from swamping the Deep South. Even Birney had to admit that there was a certain "deadness" in his audiences, no matter how articulate his pleas. He was met with polite silence wherever he went, as well as condescending smiles from planters whose own solution to the problem of an increasing black population was infinitely simpler than shipping money to Kentucky. Certainly they feared a slave insurrection, a number of planters told Birney; they would be foolish not to. But their slaves were not rebels and, for those few who were, there was the certainty of swift and awful punishment. Alabama could deal with its slave problem, the planters argued, by passing strict new slave laws and by making certain that abolitionist propaganda did not make its way south.

After his last public address in New Orleans (where he thought his program would have its greatest appeal), Birney returned to Kentucky, a depressed and embittered man, enraged that Alabama had so cavalierly ignored his warnings and that his audiences were so "deplorably inert." But he refused to admit defeat. After reflecting on his Alabama experience for a few months, Birney started to think that maybe the abolitionists were right: southern planters were incapable of listening to reason and would only respond to the sting of a more radical message. The real problem was not the slave, Birney decided, but slavery. As convinced by this new reasoning as he was by the back-to-Africa scheme, Birney formed the Kentucky State Antislavery Society in 1833, received funds for his society from the New York philanthropist Arthur Tappan, and began to publish an abolitionist newspaper. This time, however, his message was not met with polite silence.

Birney was not only hated by Kentucky's small planter population, he was viewed with suspicion by the state's free-soil farmers, who feared the competition for land from an influx of newly freed black settlers. Colonization was one thing, Birney was told, but abolitionism was quite another. Birney had his defenders, however, among citizens who liked his message. After a local citizen's committee was formed to urge him to leave, another group was formed to urge him to stay. There was talk of forming a lynch mob to deal with the neighborhood abolitionist, but the threat was mostly talk. Birney's allies would not have stood for it. The controversy ended only after Birney learned that the owner of his printing press had decided to sell his holdings, apparently because all the fuss over Birney made him nervous. With the pressures against him mounting and his publisher unwilling to support him further, Birney decided to move north across the Ohio River to Cincinnati. There, in 1835, he began publishing an abolitionist newspaper he called the *Philanthropist*.

Birney commented often on his personal journey from colonizer to abolitionist, telling his audiences his life story in the form of a parable. It was, he said, the tale of a man who put away the bottle, found God, sold his slaves, and so, as he implied, attained personal redemption. His eloquent message of salvation—sprinkled liberally with portraits of harsh overseers, oblivious masters, and torch-lit crowds of hangmen—made him one of the most popular anti-slavery figures in the North and one of its leading and most controversial political figures. He even ran for president as a candidate of the free soil Liberty Party (winning 7,000 votes in 1840 and 62,000 in 1844). Of course, in all of his dramatic recountings, Birney was careful not to mention that he sold his forty slaves to pay his gambling debts, or that he once preyed on southerners' racial fears to raise money for colonization. But if Birney thought that being a resident of a free state made him safe, he quickly learned otherwise.

Abolitionism was almost universally reviled in southern Ohio as a doctrine put forward by radical troublemakers. In July 1837, Birney's newspaper was attacked by an anti-abolitionist mob and wrecked. He refused to surrender. He started up his press once again, despite a public meeting in Cincinnati that censured him and in spite of a warning that the city fathers could not be responsible for policing the community's grievance should a second mob take up where the first left off. On the night of July 21, 1837, a crowd of Cincinnati citizens descended on the offices of the *Philanthropist*, forced open its doors, and threw Birney's press into the Ohio River. The mob, watched closely but without interference by the town fathers, then marched to the hotel where they suspected Birney was staying and, when they could not find him, went on a rampage and burned one dozen homes and several businesses belonging to blacks. Birney was now a martyr to the abolitionist cause.

With his reputation firmly in place, he moved east to Philadelphia with his wife and two sons, there to be touted as one of the most well-known activists of the growing abolitionist movement. Birney knew that the night of mob violence in Cincinnati made him a national hero, and realized that it would have a profound influence on the rest of his life and his family. But he could not have realized the repercussions the Cincinnati riot would have on others—or the transformations that it worked on the life of a young woman who viewed it from afar.

Watching the events of the summer of 1837 from her home in Cincinnati was Harriet Beecher Stowe, the daughter of the nationally known Presbyterian minister, Lyman Beecher, the new wife of the famed biblical scholar and Beecher disciple Calvin Stowe, and an accomplished writer whose stories had appeared to great acclaim in several national magazines. She was horrified by the mob violence against Birney, since her own family had itself been victimized by the contending forces that abolitionism loosed. On the night of the Cincinnati riot, she was torn between her sympathy for Birney—"I can easily see how such proceedings might make converts to abolitionism," she wrote to her husband, then touring schools with her father in the East—and her loyalty to her family. For while Harriet Beecher Stowe had sympathy for Birney's plight, she mistrusted his motives and those of his closest abolitionist ally, Theodore Weld.

As an ardent abolitionist schooled in the feverish religious tradition of Charles Grandison Finney, Weld had mounted a student revolt over the slavery issue in 1834 at Cincinnati's Lane Theological Seminary, which was founded and headed by Lyman Beecher. The trouble had started when Weld called for an eighteen-day "protracted debate" on the slavery issue among the seminary's students. The school's conservative board of governors looked on Weld's call for a debate with disapproval, but they could do little to stop him. The "Lane Debates," as they were called, debated both immediate emancipation and colonization, and gained national attention. When they were over, the students (even the southerners among them) voted overwhelmingly against gradual emancipation and colonization, and in favor of full and complete black emancipation—"immediateism." At that point the Lane board of governors decided that they had had enough. With Lyman Beecher in Connecticut, the Lane board barred abolitionist meetings at the school and told Weld that they would no longer tolerate any public discussion of the slavery issue. The board's announcement had just the opposite of its intended effect, transforming the confrontation over slavery into a debate over free speech (in which Weld was defended— even by anti-abolitionists). The board's censure of Weld brought a howl of protest, also, from much of Lane's student body, who now lined up in support of their fellow student.

Weld reacted quickly to the board's decision, forming an anti-slavery society and urging the students to begin socializing with Cincinnati's free black population. Weld also organized integrated Bible classes, prayer meetings, and an employment agency to help the freed slaves. Even Lyman Beecher, still in Connecticut, was alarmed by this turn of events. Hurrying back to Ohio, Beecher attempted to dampen the board's anger at Weld at the same time that he told the students they were moving too quickly and well beyond what social convention would allow. "If you want to teach colored schools," he told the students, "I can fill your pockets with money; but if you will visit in colored families, and walk with them in the streets, you will be overwhelmed."

Weld ignored Beecher's warning and expanded his abolitionist activities. He was now intent on broadening his anti-slavery appeal by carrying through with his strategy of confrontation with the Lane leadership. He pointedly ignored their order barring all debate on the issue, testing their willingness to confront him. When the board countered by threatening expulsion unless his activities ceased altogether, Weld and his followers withdrew from Lane—an action thereafter referred to as the "Lane Rebellion"—and enrolled at a small college at Oberlin, Ohio, where Charles Grandison Finney headed the theology department. Lane was left with a handful of students, the resentment of Cincinnati's local leaders, and, because financial backers decided the school was too controversial, a mountain of bills.

Harriet Beecher Stowe was not only a keen observer of the Lane Debates, she was convinced that Weld was right to argue for immediate emancipation. But she resented the rebellion and the betrayal of her father's friendship. Lyman Beecher had long viewed Weld as a gifted seminarian and predicted he would have a brilliant future, but Lyman had been placed in an untenable situation, caught firmly between a conservative board and an increasingly radical student body. Harriet's father hated slavery as much as Weld, but believed that the abolitionist movement's call for immediate emancipation would lead to nothing but violence and a division of the races. No one liked slavery, Beecher said, but the abolitionist movement was setting people against each other, with the result that only the black man would suffer.

Harriet was struck not only by what she viewed as Weld's purposeful abandonment of Lane, however, but also by his disloyalty to her father's Calvinist principles in favor of Finney's doctrine of "perfectionism." As Lyman Beecher worked tirelessly to take the harsh edge off of Calvin's doctrine of the elect, Finney undercut his work by preaching "perfectionism" (soon called "Oberlinism")—the doctrine that it was possible, through prayer, devotion, and hard work, for human beings to attain salvation on earth. Weld's treachery, as Harriet would have termed it, was doubly disturbing: it seemed to imply that Calvinism was as outmoded as gradualism—and that the issue of slavery was in human, not divine, hands.

Now, in the stifling summer of 1837, when black homes were burned in the riot following the destruction of Birney's press, Harriet

Beecher Stowe was struck by the explosiveness of the abolitionist message. Cincinnati remained a tinderbox of racial emotions throughout the summer as crowds of abolitionists faced off against their detractors in the city streets. The potential for violence seemed to extend to the Beechers themselves. One evening, after yet another tension-filled day, Harriet walked into her kitchen to find her brother pouring lead into a small mold. "What on earth are you doing, Henry?" she asked. Henry Ward Beecher, who was soon to set out on his own storied public ministry, hardly flinched: "Making bullets to kill men with," he told her.

Harriet began the summer with doubts about the radicalism of the abolitionist movement. But as the summer wore on, she began to question the more moderate views on slavery advocated by her father. While she still doubted that the tactics for immediate emancipation used by Weld and others would actually work, her own abhorrence for slavery grew. Like much of the rest of her family, she now knew firsthand how divisive the disagreement over slavery was becoming. By the end of the summer of 1837, her transformation from gradualist to "immediateist" was complete: she was convinced that slavery was an abomination and must be ended. Still, she was in the minority; despite the growing antislavery sympathy throughout the North, abolitionists were still widely denigrated or dismissed by those who believed (as she once had) that God gave a station to everyone in life: slaves were slaves because God had decreed that they would be, as part of His greater plan.

⌐═══◆═══¬

By the mid-1830s, every major American religious denomination was embroiled in the debate over slavery and abolitionism, and nearly every church was split by the argument. The Presbyterian church was hardest hit, as southerners accused their northern counterparts of sedition and undermining church teachings, the most significant among them being St. Paul's admonition that a slave should obey his master. Lyman Beecher had been drawn into the debate even before the Lane Rebellion, when he was put on trial for heresy by the church hierarchy in 1835. While he was acquitted, the pro-slavery elements in the church could not tolerate his moderate views. The charge of heresy was reasserted with renewed fervor in 1837 and then again in 1838. The church's indictment—that Beecher was deviating from established church doctrine—was brought by southern ministers who could not abide Beecher's refusal to endorse the slave system as part of God's plan, his tolerance of radical abolitionism, and his studied unwillingness to renounce those who joined the Lane Rebellion. Lyman Beecher was, in fact, much less an abolitionist than was generally believed among the church's hierarchy. But while he was not a radical, he simply would not agree to muzzle those who spoke out against slavery or joined anti-slavery societies.

The church's unrelenting questioning of his actions, the heresy trials, and the loss of Weld to Oberlin destroyed Beecher's dream for Lane and plunged the Beecher family into debt. In 1838, Lyman Beecher was dismissed from the Presbyterian church, along with Harriet's husband and Lane faculty member Calvin Stowe, who had followed his father-in-law's moderate line. "John C. Calhoun was at the bottom of it," Lyman Beecher later reflected. "I know of his doing things—writing to ministers, and telling them to do this and do that. The South finally took the Old School side. It was a cruel thing—it was a cursed thing, and 'twas slavery that did it." Watching from the sidelines, Harriet Beecher Stowe was increasingly frustrated by the silence that greeted her father's troubles, and by the seeming inability of northerners of conscience to speak out on the evils of slavery. Even in Cincinnati people feared any open discussion of the issue. "Pray what is there in Cincinnati to satisfy one whose mind is awakened on this subject?" Harriet asked. "No one can have the system of slavery brought before him without an irrepressible desire to *do* something, and what is there to be done?"

By 1841, their financial situation was perilous. Calvin Stowe pleaded with his wife to keep better account books and to write down every expenditure, but she spent what little money they had liberally, telling him her father had always claimed that God would provide whatever they needed. Calvin Stowe had a better idea, urging his wife to use her considerable talent as a writer to bring in extra income. This was more than a practical suggestion. In April 1842, while on a lecture tour, Calvin Stowe wrote to his wife in admiration, telling her not only that her writing could prove lucrative, but that he was convinced she was part of God's plan:

You must be a literary woman. It is so written in the book of fate. Make all your calculations accordingly, get a good stock of health, brush up your mind, drop the E [initial] out of your name, which only encumbers it and stops the flow and euphony, and write yourself only and always, Harriet Beecher Stowe, which [is] a name euphonous, flowing, and full of meaning; and [take] my word for it, your husband will lift up his head in the gate, and your children will rise up and call you blessed.

Harper's publishers brought out *The Mayflower*, a collection of Harriet Beecher Stowe's short stories, in 1843, but the sales were not enough to offset the Stowes' financial problems. "Our straits for money this year are unparalleled even in our annals," she told her husband. Nor did the family's personal problems abate. Just months after the publication of her book of stories, Harriet's brother George Beecher died unexpectedly—"a bolt from the blue," Harriet called it. In early 1845, Harriet suffered a miscarriage, and that summer nearly died during a cholera epidemic. Four years later, just when the Stowes' financial situation was finally beginning to improve, Harriet and Calvin's newborn son Charley was struck down by the same disease that had nearly killed his mother. For Harriet Beecher Stowe, this was the bitterest injustice: of all her children, Charley was the healthiest and the most even-tempered. Harriet was nearly inconsolable and began questioning her faith. To Harriet Beecher Stowe, Charley's death must have seemed the firmest evidence that the harsh verdict of Calvinism, which she had spent years trying to escape, was everywhere present.

Eventually, racked by grief but energized by the hope held out by the Hydesville Rappings, she turned to séances, attempting to find beyond the hand of death the renewed life of her stricken son. Her husband had similar yearnings. For many years Calvin Stowe had communed directly with the dead, testifying that, as a child, "every night after I had gone to bed and the candle was removed, a very pleasant-looking human face would peer at me [from near a place on the wall] and gradually press forward his head, neck, shoulders, and finally his whole body as far as the waist, through the opening, and then, smiling upon me with great good-nature, would withdraw in the same manner in which he had entered."

Harriet followed her husband into this world of visions, though only for a short time. The mediums she visited could not give her the reassurance she desperately needed: that her son had entered heaven, that he lived there with her harsh God, that his soul was saved. She abandoned the Calvinism of her childhood and turned away from its strict discipline, convinced that a doctrine in which only the elect could be transported to heaven, while the innocent burned in hell, simply could not be true. Following the death of Charley, such a belief appeared to Harriet as a merciless and terrifying doctrine that made a mockery of God's world. She had had enough of it, and turned into a Calvinist exile, feeling greater comfort among the growing body of Congregationalists.

Charley's death marked not only a change in Harriet Stowe's views on religion, however. By the end of 1849, she and her husband were intent on abandoning their home in Cincinnati, believing that while they had done everything possible to make the Lane Theological Seminary a success, their sacrifices—financial, spiritual, and personal—were simply too overwhelming. Both began to look east for new opportunities and Calvin Stowe made discreet inquiries about teaching jobs in Connecticut, Massachusetts, and Maine. Finally, in early 1850, Calvin accepted an offer from Bowdoin College, his alma mater.

In the spring of 1850, still recovering from the emotional thunderclap of Charley's death, six months pregnant with her seventh child, and eight months ahead of her husband's expected arrival, Harriet Beecher Stowe arrived in Brunswick, Maine. She rented the same house Calvin had once shared during his Bowdoin years with Henry Wadsworth Longfellow. The move was arduous, but once she was settled in her new surroundings, the slower pace of Brunswick provided her with a temporary rest from the emotional turmoil of the previous years.

Harriet was met in Brunswick by Professor Thomas Upham's wife, who made her feel at home by organizing a welcoming committee of Bowdoin wives. After the expected rounds to meet the staff and administration, Harriet Beecher Stowe plunged into more immediate tasks: renovating the Federal Street house, planning her husband's arrival, and getting back to her own writing. After the long silence caused by the death of her son and the continued financial troubles of her family, she sat down in June 1850 to begin gathering stories for another book. *The Mayflower* had received generally good reviews and her small but dedicated group of readers believed her second anthology was long overdue. Notices to that effect had even appeared in a New York literary journal, the *Pathfinder*. Knowing that she needed solace and a diversion from her recent troubles, a number of friends urged her on. "Your girls are large enough to copy and arrange them for you— and the thing must be done," one wrote.

The trouble was that Harriet Stowe did not know precisely *what* to write. When she attempted to pen a new set of stories, her work was flat and unemotional. She gathered her past writings and corresponded with a number of editors, and kept up a voluminous correspondence with her family, friends, and admirers. She taught a class of young students in her home for several hours each day, read to her children from the heroic novels of Sir Walter Scott for two hours each night, and attempted to write. But she still felt uneasy, even "haunted by the idea that I don't do anything." Nevertheless, she tried, only to be interrupted again in early July by the arrival of another son, whom she named Charles Edward, after the departed Charley. The arrival of Charles Edward was welcomed and she loved her new baby, but her mind was still on Charley. "I shall never love another as I did him," she wrote to a friend, "he was my 'summer child.' "

By now, Harriet Stowe had abandoned Calvinist doctrine, but she was still obsessed by its message, still driven by its cruelty. Like many adults she found that what is learned as a child is not so easily abandoned as an adult, no matter how rational, learned, principled, or experienced a person might become. The past is everywhere present: the first great awakening, a century before, was led by Jonathan Edwards, the founding father of Calvinism in America, who believed that all human beings were "sinners in the hands of an angry God." Humans dangled like spiders, Edwards wrote, over the hot flames of hell and could not know if they would be saved or condemned. Only God could know that. To Harriet Beecher Stowe, the experiences of the Beecher family and her husband Calvin seemed evidence that God's judgment sometimes fell even on those who served him most loyally.

But it was not simply the death of Charley or the troubles of her family that consumed Harriet Beecher Stowe. These were momentous times, filled with violence and danger. On September 18, 1850, Congress admitted California as a free state, organized two new territories, and strengthened the Fugitive Slave Act, allowing federal authorities to enter homes in search of runaway slaves. The Compromise of 1850 was intended to protect the Union and forever postpone its division. It did just the opposite. Passage of the Fugitive Slave Act transformed the vocal but small abolitionist movement into a popular national cause. Northerners were enraged. It was one thing for the government to protect the right of the slaveholder to have slaves and quite another to empower the government to act on their behalf—by searching for fugitive slaves in private homes. And it was the one thing that men like Joshua Chamberlain's father feared most, a government so powerful that it became an arbiter of public morality or, worse, a tool of what was coming to be called the "slavocracy."

The passage of the Fugitive Slave Act was condemned as "odious" and widely and violently disobeyed throughout the North. In Boston, throngs of abolitionists who once proselytized to small crowds now hammered out their message before larger and larger audiences, their cause now made famous, and just, by the infamous act. Across the North, former slaves were tracked down, sent to local courts, and quickly dispatched back south. Harriet Stowe's minister-brother at the Congregational Church of Brooklyn, Henry Ward Beecher, spoke before rallies of hundreds and then thousands. Harriet herself railed against her family's critics in both the press and pulpit who "keep calm and smile and smile when every sentiment of manliness and humanity is kicked and rolled in the dust and lies trampled and bleeding."

But Harriet underestimated the tenor of the times, supposing that the public press, which maintained a delicate neutrality on the act, represented the views of the majority of Americans. Just the opposite was true. The Fugitive Slave Act transformed gradualists into emancipators, and moderates into radicals. By attacking the most fundamental American right, safety from searches and seizures in one's own home, the Fugitive Slave Act provided the abolitionists with their best recruiting tool. Even Bowdoin's moderate Professor Upham, who defended the act and said he would obey it, was transformed when faced with the reality of a fugitive fleeing the South's bonds. One day, after a disagreement with Harriet on the subject, Upham discovered a young escaped slave at his door asking for bread. He gave him bread, as well as an entire sack loaded with clothing and provisions, and sent the man north to Canada.

The passage of the Compromise of 1850, and the rising tide of violence that accompanied it, made clear that the confrontation between the North and the South was now inevitable. By the spring semester of 1851, the possibility of secession was discussed on the Bowdoin campus, in its classrooms, and, at length, at the weekly gatherings at the home of Calvin and Harriet Stowe on Federal Street, where professors, their wives, and a select group of students gathered to talk about national politics for one afternoon every week. Stowe was consumed by the topic of disunion: it was as if the Compromise that had loosed a torrent of emotions in the North had just as effectively sparked in her a new creative stream. She wrote a piece on the Fugitive Slave Act for the *National Era*, a popular anti-slavery New York paper edited by Gamaliel Bailey (who had, twenty years before, taken over the editorship of the *Philanthropist* from James Birney). She followed this with a series of stories that appeared in the *National Era* in the spring of 1851.

Each of Stowe's stories was more vivid than the last, and more controversial. In one, a man who refuses food to a runaway slave is called before God, who orders him out of heaven with the words "Depart from me ye accursed." The story almost certainly resulted from Harriet's argument with Upham, but it also owes much to her new vision of universal justice—that the emancipators are the "elect," while the slaveholders are damned for all eternity. Implicit in her writings is her belief that acting against slavery is a necessary expiation, a physical sacrifice, that could be exemplified in the shedding of blood. Union soldiers would be blessed in marching off to war against slaveholders, she thought, ever as much as Jesus was in sacrificing himself for sinners. She was urged on by her friends, who now began to look at her as one of the nation's leading anti-slavery voices. "Now, Hattie," her sister pleaded, "if I could use a pen as you can, I would write something that would make this whole nation feel what an accursed thing slavery is." That is exactly what she wanted to do, if she could only find the strength, and time.

Young Joshua Chamberlain could hardly have missed the excitement and fevered political debate over slavery that now consumed Bowdoin. Not only was he an interested political observer, he was a regular guest at the Stowe home on Federal Street. The controversy over slavery also rekindled doubts that Chamberlain harbored over his decision to attend the theological seminary in Bangor. His pursuit of a position as a minister seemed more and more like a retreat from his patriotic responsibilities. In addition, he was increasingly attracted to the military life, just as his father had been before him. Unlike his father, however, Joshua now began to look skeptically at the actions of the South and, as he later made clear in his speeches and letters, was convinced that he would have to fight against the South if war came.

Chamberlain wrestled with his decision to become a minister throughout his third year at Bowdoin, but he did not tell his mother about his doubts. Instead, he kept to his rigorous schedule of studies, his prayer circle, and his weekly work with the choir at Brunswick's First Parish Church. While attendance at Sunday services was compulsory for Bowdoin students, Chamberlain's devotion was zealous—he was a constant figure at the weekly concerts given by the church choir in nearby towns and spent hours rehearsing with the choir's organist, Fannie Adams. Chamberlain met Fannie when he first arrived at Bowdoin, but he began to take an interest in her in late 1850, when they met to talk about religion.

Fannie Adams was the adopted daughter of George Adams and his wife Sarah Ann. The Reverend Adams was a celebrated and highly respected member of the Brunswick community, the minister of the First Parish Church, and a member of the Bowdoin Board of Overseers. Fannie's relationship to the Adamses, however, was unusual. When she was a young girl, Fannie's elderly and ailing parents, Ashur and Amelia Adams of Boston, allowed her to move in with her uncle. While she visited her parents regularly, she looked on George and Sarah as her real family; she referred to the Reverend Adams and his wife as her father and mother, and the two brought her up as their own

daughter. Reverend Adams was quick to scold and an exacting disciplinarian, and often criticized Fannie for being too independent, hint-
ing that he thought her habit of purchasing expensive dresses a sign of
her immodesty.

Joshua Chamberlain was attracted to Fannie because he found her
to be intelligent and witty. He was as intrigued by her streak of independence as her adopted father was repelled by it. The church became
their meeting ground. Yet, while Chamberlain would have seemed to
be an ideal suitor for Fannie, the Reverend Adams stubbornly discour-
aged the relationship, making it clear that he disapproved of it. "Your
father has not much faith in our relation—I cannot call it engagement, it
seems something more—he does not expect that much will ever come
of it, or that it will last very long," Chamberlain wrote Fannie at one
point. "I do not need to be told that—I see it plainly enough. I simply
say he has mistaken his man."

Joshua Chamberlain and the Reverend Adams were very different,
and it is this fact that probably accounted for the older man's disapproval. While Adams was devout, he scandalized the community by
inviting a black minister into his pulpit and by approving the use of an
organ during church services—one of the first New England clergymen
to do so. His congregation condemned both decisions, especially the
former, and when the black minister appeared many of them got up and
walked out. That did not bother Adams, who preached abolitionism
from the pulpit throughout the 1840s and 1850s, an unusual occurrence
in Maine, where the line separating politics and religion was rarely
crossed. Chamberlain, on the other hand, was not then, or later, known
for holding controversial positions in defiance of community norms. It
is also likely that Adams disapproved of Chamberlain's background, for
while the Chamberlains were traditional New Englanders, they lacked
the blood background Adams proudly touted.

The relationship was fraught with other dangers. Adams's views on
the liberation of slaves did not extend to women, a contradiction that
eroded his deteriorating relationship with his adopted daughter. As
Fannie grew older she became less tolerant of his continued hectoring
about the importance of modesty and a woman's place. While this view
was in keeping with the opinions of most men of his time, they were
grating and offensive to Fannie. Chamberlain urged her on in her rebel-

lion: when Fannie purchased expensive dresses or failed to remain modest and silent in the presence of others, Chamberlain encouraged her, knowing that Adams would disapprove.

Chamberlain courted Fannie throughout early 1851, speaking with her at church and during the evenings at the Stowes', when Harriet would read to her guests from her latest work, a novel whose inspiration had come on a Sunday in February 1851. In the middle of the service at Brunswick's First Parish Church, just as Harriet Beecher Stowe had finished taking communion and was seated in pew 23, the likeness of a beaten slave and a white overseer appeared to her, hovering over her head. The portrait was so vivid that she rushed home after the service and wrote down what she had seen on brown grocery wrapping paper. And every night thereafter, she applied herself to sketching out the story that seemed to literally pour from her pen. In May she sent out the first installment of her book to the *National Era* in Washington. It was serialized soon after, appearing under the title *Uncle Tom's Cabin*.

# 4

# *A Fair English Education*

ARRIET BEECHER STOWE said that *Uncle Tom's Cabin* was written by God. And so it seemed: she scribbled away, late at night, without plan or outline, the book flowing effortlessly from her pen as if it were written by someone else. When it appeared in book form Harriet Stowe's "tangible vision" sold 10,000 copies in the first week, 300,000 in the first year, 500,000 in five years, and was translated into twenty languages. It remains one of the great events of American publishing. *Uncle Tom's Cabin* had a shattering impact on northern public opinion. And between 1851 and 1853—Joshua Chamberlain's third and fourth years at Bowdoin—Harriet Beecher Stowe went from a writer with a small following to one of the most popular and successful novelists in American history.

*Uncle Tom's Cabin* was ignored in the South—or rather, read just enough to be condemned. The most enraged and vicious critic was William Gilmore Simms, a South Carolina novelist and competitor of Harriet Stowe's whose response seethed with anger. For Simms, the devil was now made manifest in the figure of a modest but talented northern woman: "Mrs. Stowe betrays a malignity so remarkable that the petticoat lifts of itself, and we see the hoof of the beast under the table," he wrote in one review. Simms's more pointed response came in his counternovel *Woodcraft*, which he was writing as *Uncle Tom's Cabin* was being serialized in the *National Era*. *Woodcraft* was a broad defense of slavery, but with a twist: a revolutionary war hero returns to his impoverished South Carolina plantation and teams up with a widow to rescue their slaves from villainous slave stealers, fellow southerners all. The hero is confirmed, the slaves are saved, and the aristocrat-turned-soldier returns again to his planter gentility to ponder whether he should marry the widow. The soldier has put down his weapons and taken up his plow. And the slaves? Why, they don't even want to be free: "I no guine to be free no way yo kin fix it; so, maussa, don't you bodder me wid dis nonsense t'ing bout free papers," Simms has one of them say.

The idyllic prose and ham-handed defense of slavery presented in *Woodcraft* was viewed as nonsensical by Harriet Stowe and other abolitionists, with the result that Simms's book was as ignored in the North as *Uncle Tom's Cabin* was in the South. Yet *Woodcraft* is a valuable piece of history because it is an unintentionally revealing portrait of relations among southern whites. Its portrayal of poor southern whites as ignorant, uncultured, and animalistic comes through its pages in tones so fevered that it is hard to believe Simms did not understand what he was writing. The enemies of pure low-country, aristocratic white southernness, Simms says, are not the abolitionists (as he intended), but the upcountry bumpkins, who want slaves but must resort to thievery to get them. In *Woodcraft*, the lowlife frontier pioneers are routed and aristocracy is saved. The willing slave, also named Tom, like Beecher's protagonist, is reunited with his owner.

Simms's portrait of southern white relations was confirmed by northern writers who traveled in the regions in the decade before the Civil War. Traveling in the South in the 1850s, for example, Frederick Law Olmsted catalogued the horrors of slavery for thousands of northern readers in a series of letters that appeared twice weekly in the *New York Daily Times* and that were later published, to great acclaim, as a book called *The Cotton Kingdom*. Olmsted tried to be even-handed, or at least not to give offense to southerners. But in the end he could barely contain his condemnation of southern life, especially as it affected poor white southern farmers—the evil slave stealers of *Woodcraft*.

> To work industriously and steadily, especially under directions from another man, is, in the Southern tongue, to 'work like a nigger': and, from childhood, the one thing in their condition which has made life valuable to the mass of whites has been that the niggers are yet their inferiors. It is this habit of considering themselves of a privileged class, and of disdaining

something which they think beneath them, that is deemed to be the chief blessing of slavery.

At the heart of slavery was the simple and insidious belief that white society was superior, and that slavery was actually a "civilizing" institution. The poor white southern farmer might be unhappy, but at least he was white. So long as there were planters and plantations, there was something greater to aspire to, a standard that a very few, but some, had reached. For these reasons, slavery, the pursuit of slaves, the romanticization of southern life, and the desire to be a planter were everywhere apparent, defended, promoted—which is why southern white farmers who owned few or no slaves became slavery's most ardent champions, and the first to fall in its defense.

Furthermore, most southerners believed that emancipation was, for practical purposes, beyond reach. Slavery was not simply an economic system, it was a way of life—the only way of life the South had ever known. Slavery supported every aspect of the region's commercial, cultural, and social environment: shopkeepers depended on planters for business, railroads on cotton for cargo, lawyers on slave disputes for clients, preachers on the master-slave relationship for sermons, writers on the institution for plots, customs collectors on cotton export for duties, auctioneers on slave property for profits, and politicians on the fear of insurrection for votes. Slavery was even more entrenched in the South in the 1850s than it had been in the 1830s. There were more slaves in the region than at any previous time, and slave auctioneers were among the region's newly rich. Even more important, the previous decade had seen an explosion in southern commerce, largely due to the trade in cotton.

Although the South's professional and commercial class could not compare to the North's, Atlanta, Richmond, Charleston, Nashville, New Orleans, Savannah, and Montgomery were thriving cities, while in Alabama and elsewhere, former hamlets had grown into thriving towns, most of them supported by the commerce in cotton. Small industrial centers based on the trade in cotton grew up, supporting a rudimentary rail and water system that in turn enhanced the cotton trade. Iron production began, tentatively, in Richmond and in northern Alabama, producing rails and engines. By the late 1840s, steamboats had replaced flatboats, which could carry double or triple the number of cotton bales. There were still few options for poor southern white farmers, but those who left the farm and worked industriously and steadily could make their way in the expanding economy. In this sense, the obstacles faced by small farmers in Alabama were not much different than those faced by their fellow citizens in Maine. In both places, the keys to affluence and stature were ambition—and education.

William Oates was barely an adult when he left his home at the crossroads for Henry County, but his experiences, so different than those of Joshua Chamberlain in Maine, gave Oates a maturity he might not have otherwise had. He had seen enough of life in 1854 to decide that the farm was not for him. Oates's first stop was the town of Cottonwood, a small crossroads hamlet in the far corner of southeastern Alabama, near the Alabama–Florida state line. After getting settled, he worked as a hired hand in the nearby farms and started a one-room school, where he taught classes to local children and strapping adolescents whose parents believed their children needed the kind of education, and discipline, that Oates could offer.

The little extra time he had Oates spent on his own studies, but after nearly a year in Cottonwood, he knew that in order to get the kind of education he needed he would have to go elsewhere. In 1855, Oates decided he had prepared himself adequately to apply as a student at a private school in Lawrenceville, twenty-five miles away. The Lawrenceville Academy was unusual in southeastern Alabama, for while it lacked the rigorous scholarly discipline of Whiting's in Maine (or many other New England private schools, for that matter), it offered a course of study that would make Oates more than passably literate, and might even, given enough time, prepare him for college. The school's principle was William A. Clark, a semiprosperous teacher whose own education far outstripped any gained by his neighbors and whose erudition was not only widely acknowledged but extremely rare for the region. A graduate of the University of Georgia, Clark had a keen eye for meeting the demand for education among the farmers of the rural wiregrass country, which he combined with an abundant businesslike acumen. Clark established his academy, advertised for students, charged modest fees, and hired two teachers, one of whom, R. R. Fudge, was a professor of mathematics, and the other, a "Miss Pilly," a college graduate of literature and music.

Together, the three had launched a popular and competent school that was apparently open to any student of any age who wanted to apply. The three taught at all hours in every subject, shaping their schedules to the needs of an agricultural community, while providing a rigorous teaching routine and regular classes for the more advanced students. No matter what the need, Clark, Fudge, and Pilly dedicated themselves to providing the best education they could for the students they attracted, whether they be from the large plantations to the north, from farms to the south and east, the children of families living in nearby Abbeville and Eufaula, trading towns that contained small professional classes, or older students, like Oates, who needed the rudiments of an education they had missed during adolescence.

Oates had enough education to immediately win enrollment in rhetoric, composition, and mathematics and within a very short time was able to prove that a self-taught son of a hardscrabble farmer could accomplish great things through the sheer application of will. He was a voracious reader and had an eye for detail, a knack with language, and, most important, the ability to master an immense amount of material in a short time.

"There were over fifty girls and sixty-five or seventy boys [in the school]," Oates remembered in the short memoir he wrote in later life. "They were all more or less advanced, and about thirty of the boys were young men grown, or nearly so; the girls were from ten to eighteen years of age." Oates boarded in a nearby home and worked after school hours and then late into the night mastering his lessons. "I remained in the school during the long session of six months, and made most rapid progress. At its close I was employed to teach school at Rocky Creek Camp Ground, seven miles from Gordon, then the village of Woodville." Off Oates went again, to a Woodcraft-like community, but this time he carried with him the knowledge he had gained at Lawrenceville. Like Chamberlain, Oates's life now fell into a regular routine, the first he had known outside of the life he had led on his father's farm. He gained also a sense that he could control his own future—that not every town was like Marshall or Waco, and that, with a little education, he could throw off the life that saddled his family.

Until his attendance at Lawrenceville, Oates's pro-southern opinions repeated the predictable stock phrases of the time, but at the school he learned how to defend his arguments and focus his thinking. Oates saw in Clark the kind of man he had rarely met before in Alabama: well liked, worldly, tough-minded (a quality that Oates placed above all others), and opinionated, but also well respected. Unlike the men of Waco and Marshall (who, when not drunk, could talk tough and shoot straight) or of innumerable small towns like Oates's Crossroads (where men were indistinguishable from plows), Clark's power was derived not from his ability to simply survive or plant corn rows straight and true, but from his ability to master words and arguments.

Oates was encouraged to speak up in class arguments and master the finer points of public speaking. Unsure at first, he soon became competent enough that he not only wrote well-argued compositions, but became Lawrenceville's unofficial composition tutor and its leading debater. Oates's early efforts at public speaking were undoubtedly unsophisticated, but Lawrenceville took the rough edges off the youth. While he never received the kind of comprehensive scholarly background offered to Chamberlain at Bowdoin, Oates was accomplished enough to impress the town fathers of Woodville, where he was earning extra money as a teacher, who invited him to join the local Masonic Lodge. This was a singular honor: Masonry was a necessary step up the ladder of respectability, and a sign that a man was an acknowledged member of the community.

The people of Woodville hoped Oates would settle in their small town permanently, but he decided to return to Lawrenceville as a full-time student to finish his education at the academy. His second stay at Lawrenceville was much more difficult than his first, however, and he needed to put aside his job as a farmhand to concentrate on the course of studies Clark laid out for him. While Oates does not admit it anywhere, it is likely that Clark helped Oates meet his tuition payments, for there was simply no other way he could have stayed alive. Oates's education now consisted of a crash course administered by Clark and Fudge as well as geometry, algebra, English and Latin grammar, chemistry, and astronomy. It was as rigorous a schedule of studies as any taught by any school in the state:

> I now studied in my room and went to the Academy at regular hours to recite with my class. During this session of the school I belonged to the debating society, and became one of the best debaters in the school. I was apt in composition, and at the close of that session of the school I wrote several speeches, some for other boys, as well as for myself. I had gotten through with the mental and practical arithmetic including the University edition, Algebra and six books in geometry. I had fairly mastered the English and Latin grammars, had read Aesop's Fables and the First Book of Caesar. I stood high in philosophy and had a smattering knowledge of chemistry and astronomy. In other words, I had learned the elementary principles of these sciences. . . . I had learned Hedge's Logic and became proficient in it.

What Oates did not mention was that, over the course of his studies, he became an avid student of local and state politics and began to participate in arguments about the larger questions of his time: slavery, abolitionism, and secession. Not surprisingly, he now viewed himself as a traditional southern Democrat—a party man who believed in states' rights, but not secession, and the right to hold slaves, though he was clearly lukewarm on slavery. In other words, Oates's views were a reflection of his upbringing and class and depended more on the tradition of nullification (inbred in Alabama settlers from the days of the removal of the Creek Indians) than rebellion.

Oates graduated from Lawrenceville in record time, cramming the equivalent of a secondary school education into two years of study. He returned to Woodville to teach for a short period of time. His return was graciously accepted, for the farmers not only prized his teaching abilities and immense patience with their children, but turned to him in local disputes. By the time he left once again, Oates was Woodville's unofficial justice of the peace, mediator of disputes, and judge, jury, and prosecutor of local misdemeanor crimes, applying what the community believed was a fair and impartial hand in nearly every matter. It was quite an honor, even in Woodville, for a man in his early twenties to be viewed with such universal respect. Yet he never seemed overly learned and passed off his seemingly effortless mastery of the indecipherable texts of ancient authors. He continued this practice in later life, purposely understating his accomplishment as a student, saying only that he "acquired by energy and hard study a good English education and a fair knowledge of Latin." When pressed, he allowed that he might have done better than he at first admitted, and hinted that he was purposely careless with dates (which has confounded historians ever since), as well as with the facts—there is little doubt that he graduated from Lawrenceville, though he preferred to have it said that his education was self-obtained, and that he had no special paper to show for it.

One point of pride and one pointed regret seeped into all of Oates's later descriptions of himself: his pride at having mastered the six books of geometry, which proved to be very difficult, and his regret that he had "never attended any college" because he "was not able." In truth, while Oates could have gone on to college, his old restlessness was getting the better of him. He enjoyed his time at Lawrenceville and as Woodville's unofficial mediator, but he simply could not stand to stay in one place for very long. In early 1858, at the age of twenty-four, therefore, he packed up his meager belongings once again and struck out for nearby Eufaula. He said that Lawrenceville had "put" it in his head "to become a lawyer."

⊶⟡⊷

Eufaula was not by any means a thriving metropolis, but it was a step beyond Lawrenceville, far beyond Cottonwood, and a far different world than the one he had grown up in at Oates's Crossroads. The town's name was taken from an Indian word, meaning "high bluffs," which ran into the Chattahoochie River. Eufaula served as a trading town for nearby plantations and a commercial outlet for Montgomery, which was eighty-five miles to the west. Bales of cotton lined the street, awaiting shipment aboard the steamboats that took them north for resale or south for processing. It was a town of growing opportunities as well as a Democratic Party stronghold that consistently voted states' rights conservatives into public office.

Eufaula was also the home of the law firm of Pugh, Bullock, and Buford, an institution in southeast Alabama politics. The firm was

headed by thirty-nine-year-old James Lawrence Pugh, a highly respected, well-read, self-made man. Orphaned at age eleven, Pugh had
studied law under John Gill Shorter, who in 1858—when Oates arrived
in Eufaula—was considered one of the most powerful politicians in the
state and one of the leading advocates of southern nationalism. Pugh
had married into a planter family (from which he received considerable
assistance) and started the law firm. But Pugh owed much of his early
success to his former teacher, Shorter, from whom he inherited his partisan political views, as well as his stump-speaking ability. As the firm's
leading lawyer, Pugh was a master hand-shaker and back-slapper and a
man who was known for taking care of his friends—and punishing his
political enemies.

Edward Courtney Bullock was the firm's legal expert as well as a
master of Democratic Party politics. A graduate of Harvard College,
Bullock was undoubtedly one of the most learned men in the state.
Even at the age of thirty-three, his courtroom skills were legendary. But
Bullock's erudition did not detract from his pride in being thoroughly
southern, having been born in Charleston, the cradle of the states'
rights movement. He was elected to the Alabama legislature the year
before Oates's arrival in Eufaula. He spent much of his time, when not
in Montgomery, managing the firm with Pugh, who needed his steady
hand, obsessive organization, and quick wit. Pugh (and his teacher,
Shorter) received most of the political attention of Eufaula's leading
families, but Bullock, many believed, would become one of the state's
most well-known political figures.

While Pugh was the glad-hander and Bullock the mastermind, Jef-
ferson Buford was the firm's fiery philosopher. At the age of forty-four,
Buford had already nearly gotten himself killed fighting abolitionists in
Kansas—saying it was better to fight evil on the plains of the West than
to "plant bayonets on the Potomac." Like Bullock, Buford was a former
South Carolinian and an outspoken defender of southern nationalism.
He had a volatile and abrasive personality, as well as a short temper.
Standoffish, energetic, and cultivated, with an immense stand of friends
and political cronies, Buford could be boorishly domineering. But
Pugh admired him because there was always a hint of wit even in the
midst of his tirades.

Pugh, Bullock, and Buford were not only hardened Democrats and followers of John Gill Shorter, they were allied with combative Eufaula attorney John Cochran (a constant candidate for the state legislature); John Gill Shorter's brother, Eli Shorter (who represented southeastern Alabama in the U.S. Congress); and another of Shorter's law pupils, Henry DeLamar Clayton—who was renowned for his political abilities. This group included two other influential lawyers, Lewis Cato and Alpheus Baker, both of whom came from well-established Alabama families. The entire southeastern part of the state was, in fact, seeded with Democratic lawyers, all of whom worked in concert to organize and run the party and, through it, the state itself—thereby making certain the legislature in Montgomery paid special attention to the needs of the wiregrass country. Together, the two Shorters, Pugh, Bullock, Buford, Cochran, Clayton, Cato, and Baker formed southeastern Alabama's Democratic political machine, dominating the political and commercial life of Pike, Henry, and Dale counties for three decades—from the 1830s until the outbreak of the Civil War. Their success in party politics, and their hold over an important section of the state, gave them formidable influence in the Alabama statehouse and made them known throughout the South as the "Eufaula Regency"—as important in Alabama state politics as the Democratic Party political machine Tammany Hall was in New York.

In the spring of 1858, William Oates arrived in Eufaula with a small suitcase, took a room at the Barnett house, and the next morning appeared at the offices of Pugh, Bullock, and Buford to study law. It is not known whether James Lawrence Pugh was skeptical of Oates's talent, though it is likely that he was; it would not be the first time a young man with the mud of some Alabama town had come to the firm with a desire to be a lawyer and little else. It is also true that while Pugh undoubtedly knew of Oates's successes in Woodville, he was probably unsure of Oates's educational ability. Being a graduate of Lawrenceville did not guarantee admittance to the bar, or any predisposition to memorizing the vast texts he would be required to cite before a team of lawyers and judges called for the purpose. In addition, much of the firm's practice served the affluent owners of the nearby plantations; Pugh undoubtedly would have welcomed someone into the firm with at least some experience of that world, and Oates was clearly not from that background. Nor did he look the part. While he was above average height, he was stubby-legged—almost boyish—and he was still young, and showed it, with an expression of open innocence.

Even so, Pugh and his partners must have noticed that Oates always had a peculiar look in his eye that seemed to show he was ready for anything and, as others had learned, could be a formidable opponent in any kind of dispute, whether physical or mental. It was probably this last quality, as well as the contacts he had at Lawrenceville and among the firm's clients in Woodville, that convinced Pugh to take Oates on as a clerk. He quickly handed him over to Bullock for schooling. Bullock knew the law and was an exacting taskmaster, but he had met his match in Oates, who set out to be as familiar with the law as his teacher. He studied more than twelve and sometimes as many as sixteen hours each day, reporting faithfully to Bullock, who tested him constantly. By the end of four months, in October 1858—an extraordinarily short time given the amount of material he was called on to master—Oates announced that he was ready for his examination.

"Judge Dougherty was holding the Circuit Court of Barbour County at Clayton, when I applied for admission to the bar," Oates later remembered.

> After an oral examination lasting two hours on criminal law by Attorney General M. A. Baldwin, on the law of real estate by Maj. Jeff Buford, on the law of personal property by D. M. Seals, on pleading and evidence by John Cochran, on chancery and chancery pleading by L. L. Cato, on commercial law by Alpheus Baker, and on the statutes and the code by Judge Dougherty, the Judge did not await the verdict of the examining committee, but remarked: "Gentlemen, the young man has undoubtedly stood the best examination I ever witnessed. Give him his license, Mr. Clark. Mr. Sheriff, adjourn court until nine o'clock tomorrow morning."

And with that, William Oates of Oates's Crossroads—by way of Pensacola, New Orleans, Waco, Cottonwood, and Lawrenceville—was admitted to the bar of Alabama.

Oates stayed on for a time with the Eufaula law firm for extra tutoring and some in-court work. But after a few short months, he decided that there were too many lawyers in Eufaula and that he needed to move to a town where he could set up his own law office. He chose Abbeville, just down the road from Eufaula, for his great experiment, saving up a modest amount of money to rent a small space and buy some law books. There, on December 1, 1858, just one day after his twenty-fifth birthday, he went into business for himself.

⟊⟊⟊

The influential men of the South were all great orators and debaters who made their reputations from their ability to engage the most important questions of the day. Clark and Bullock were Oates's first mentors, but the true architects of the South in which he reached maturity were men with a national following, and the most important of them all was the greatest champion of states' rights in American history, South Carolina's John Calhoun. In the 1850s, southern political discourse was dominated by politicians who gained their education in large part by reading Calhoun's speeches: South Carolina's Robert Barnwell Rhett, Mississippi's Jefferson Davis, Georgia's Alexander Stephens, Virginia's Roger Pryor and Edmund Ruffin, and Alabama's own William Lowndes Yancey.

Yancey, especially, came to define the increasingly intransigent voice of southern politics. He was a character right out of William Gilmore Simms. Hot-tempered and heavy-drinking, Yancey was the son of a Georgia widow who had married a minister from Troy, New York, in the heart of the burned-over district's country of mediums and Mormons. Educated at Williams College in Massachusetts, Yancey settled as a lawyer in South Carolina before moving (coincidentally) to Troy, Alabama, a day's walk from Oates's Crossroads. Northern sentiments and Williams College had apparently little influence on his political thinking: once he had seen the South, he decided that he would be its champion. Yancey became the South's chief defender of slavery and, often well lubricated by whiskey, its most eloquent promoter. It was simply not enough for Yancey to defend the "peculiar institution"; he viewed those who compromised on its extension in any manner as dark allies of abolitionism and travelers with the devil. Using the issue of the legalization of the international slave trade, Yancey pushed southerners toward his own radical views.

Simply by suggesting that the international slave trade should be legalized—a commerce that had long since been outlawed—Yancey transformed the debate over slavery in the South. If slavery was legal in Alabama, Yancey argued, then it was legal everywhere. And if slaves could be bought and sold in Alabama, they could be bought and sold anywhere. It made no sense, Yancey argued, for a slave to be open to trade in one place and not in another. For Yancey it was a matter of principle. Either slavery was right or wrong, but if right it was right everywhere and in every form. He added that those who opposed the international slave trade actually had something else in mind: they hated the South, he said, and wanted it subjugated to their own narrow economic interests. The only solution was secession.

Over the next decade, Yancey almost single-handedly made the slave trade issue a litmus test of southern patriotism. At first Yancey was out of step with his colleagues, who were unwilling to take the South out of the Union over slavery. Instead they struck compromises: over Missouri in 1820, then in 1850, and finally over Kansas and Nebraska in 1854. But when it became apparent that northern Democrats would not defend their southern colleagues from the growing northern abolitionist movement, Yancey gained adherents. By the mid-1850s the situation was desperate; Kansas was lost and everywhere, even in the border states of Maryland and Kentucky, anti-slavery sentiment was on the rise.

There were many turning points in the debate, but one of the most important came during the annual Southern Commercial Convention of 1858, held in Montgomery. It was the sixth in a series of annual meetings that had begun as a forum for southern businessmen to discuss the South's future and had become increasingly political.

That Montgomery was hosting this meeting could mean only one thing—the slave trade would once again be at the top of the agenda. And that is exactly where Yancey put it. Soon after convening, one of his allies proposed that the convention pass a resolution calling for the trade's legalization. The debate that ensued between Yancey and Roger Pryor of Virginia was as important in the South as the Lincoln-Douglas debates were that same year in the North. In response to Pryor's initial arguments against the proposition, Yancey said the South could not wait for full political agreement to take itself out of the Union, and those who called for such unity might wait forever. The South must act now;

it already had the unity it needed, "a unity of climate, a unity of soil, a unity of production, and a unity of social relations." Everyone knew Yancey was using "a unity of social relations" as a way to defend slavery as a positive good. After which he then proposed that the convention call for a reopening of the African slave trade. This brought Pryor to his feet in a fist-shaking fury, arguing that what Yancey really wanted was not a defense of slavery, but "the dissolution of the Union." Pryor argued that slavery was not a good enough cause to spark secession: "Give me a case of oppression and tyranny sufficient to justify a dissolution of the Union," he said, "and give me a united South, and then I am willing to go out of the Union." But many delegates disagreed with Pryor; secession in the defense of slavery was justified. "Slavery is right," one delegate argued, "and being right there can be no wrong in the natural means of its formation."

By the end of the convention it was clear that, while Yancey had stood alone ten years before, he had gained thousands of adherents. Henry Hilliard, a delegate from Montgomery (and one of the few victors in an election against a Regency candidate for Congress, John Cochran of Eufaula, back in 1846) was shocked by the strength of the radicalism shown at the convention and wrote that the slave radicals were as bad as "the black Republicans." But even he had to admit that the people of southeastern Alabama would likely vote to secede if an abolitionist Republican was elected president in 1860.

At the end of the Montgomery convention, Yancey and others formed the "League of United Southerners" to push the South's political leaders into a more radical defense of its rights. In July, Yancey journeyed throughout the state, calling on its citizens to join a new crusade to form a league of slaveholding states. "A republic," he said, "is our only safety."

"We shall," Yancey told one friend, "fire the Southern heart—instruct the Southern mind—give courage to each other, and at the proper moment, by one organized concerted action, we can precipitate the Cotton States into a revolution."

# 5

## *To the Harvest Home of Death*

WHILE WILLIAM LOWNDES YANCEY may have been the South's most radical nationalist, he was not its most popular. The honor went to Mississippi Senator Jefferson Davis, who left Washington's humidity in the summer of 1858 for cooler Maine, where he hoped to recover his deteriorating health and calm his shattered nerves. Tall, gangly, overly formal, Davis suffered from crushing headaches and a splenetic disposition, arguing interminably on nearly every topic. A colleague once characterized him as "quarrelsome, petulant, hot-headed, turbulent." He was all of these, and he was his most venomous when it came to defending southern rights. As the debate over slavery escalated, so too did Davis's rhetoric. He was so outspoken and so quick to anger, in fact, that he had found himself close to engaging in "affairs of honor"—dueling—on no less than seven occasions. At times his temper seemed almost uncontrolled, and his friends, colleagues, and even his enemies looked on his outbursts in awe. Davis was pointedly aware of just how angered he could become and often caught himself, in midsentence, screaming invectives. "I have an infirmity of which I am ashamed," he once admitted. "When I am aroused in a matter, I lose control of my feeling and become personal." But the people of Mississippi loved him and southern senators looked on him as their leader.

By 1858, however, Davis was a spectral figure, emotionally isolated. A bout with malaria at Hurricane, his Mississippi plantation, nearly killed him in 1835, and carried off his first wife, Sarah Knox Taylor, the daughter of General and, later, President Zachary Taylor. Then, in 1837, after drinking champagne with a friend, Davis accidentally walked off a bridge and hit his head on a rock, an incident that might have been humorous except for the fact that he suffered a life-threatening concussion. The blow exacerbated the undefined, and unexplained, facial pains he was then suffering and that continued to plague him throughout his life. During the Mexican War, Davis suffered a painful foot wound that left him bloody and unconscious. And just months before his trip north in 1858, Davis spent seven weeks in bed in Washington, suffering from exhaustion and a painful swelling in his left eye. The swelling receded and he resumed his Senate duties, but he was nearly blind. Davis's most recent encounter with death was so painful that he could barely speak, transmitting his wishes to his wife, Varina, on a slate board. But the greatest blow had come four years earlier, when his two-year-old son, whom he believed would someday take his place at Hurricane, died of a ravaging fever.

After three decades of unbroken service to his country, as a military officer, congressman, secretary of war (under Bowdoin graduate Franklin Pierce), and senator, Davis was now contemplating an end to all that: for the election of 1860 would undoubtedly, and for the first time, place a Republican, anti-slavery man in the White House and if that happened, Mississippi, as he had told his state legislature just months before, would rip its star from the nation's flag and defend its rights by arms. Davis was blunt in his assessment of what such a defense would mean. Secession would send thousands of Mississippi's young men to "be gathered to the harvest home of death," he said.

The Mississippi legislature cheered these words, coming to their feet with a roar, and Davis stood, proudly defiant, listening to the cascading applause. It was with such words that Davis hoped to match the radicalism of Yancey, Ruffin, and Rhett. But despite his bravado, Davis privately hoped that Mississippi would not have to send her sons to fight, that somehow, even at the last minute, a compromise might be found that would allow a man like Pierce, a moderate northerner who was sympathetic to the South and willing to defend slavery, to be elected.

Davis feared the worst, though he was comforted during his trip to Maine by the public sentiment against disunion. He was given a warm welcome in Portland and was asked to speak at a number of public meetings. At one point, the surprisingly sympathetic audiences sparked him to remark that Maine would do well to take itself out of the Union and into an alliance with Canada. The comment was made only partly in jest, for those who came to see Davis were undoubtedly fearful of what secession would bring. The high point of Davis's Maine trip was his visit to Bowdoin College, where he was presented with an honorary doctor of law degree by college president Leonard Woods. Davis was overwhelmed by his reception at Bowdoin and struck a moderate tone in his acceptance remarks, drawing a distinction between patriots who defended secession as a Constitutional right and disunionists, who sowed the seeds of sectional hatred. Davis cherished this argument, implying that, while his most recent remarks on the topic had blurred such distinctions, it would be wrong to count him as a "fire-breather." It was in this seemingly cooperative spirit that Davis was welcomed by the Bowdoin community at the school's commencement and at the informal gathering afterward, during which he was introduced to Bowdoin's faculty. The only sour note came when Davis realized that he would be appearing with Maine Senator, and Bowdoin graduate, William Pitt Fessenden.

Davis and Fessenden had much in common, including a volatile temper, but their views of slavery and secession were uncompromisingly different. Fessenden was a notorious spendthrift and outspoken abolitionist, and Davis despised him. Only six months earlier their last meeting—on the floor of the U.S. Senate—had degenerated into a shouting match, with each man screaming insults at the other. Fortunately for Bowdoin graduates, that display was not repeated during the August commencement, as both men honored a polite but distant truce. Still, it was difficult to miss the differences in the two. While speaking in the moderate tone required for the occasion, Davis defended southern rights, while Fessenden, ever the ardent emancipationist, castigated southerners as defenders of an indefensible institution.

Davis left Bowdoin pleased by his reception, though he should have realized that of the North's numerous colleges, Bowdoin was one of the few that would have openly welcomed him. Not only was Davis a close personal friend of Bowdoin graduate and former U.S. President Franklin Pierce, whose defense of a pro-slavery constitution in Kansas cost him the presidency, but Bowdoin President Leonard Woods thought that all the talk of disunion was the prattle of idle men. While the nation was increasingly caught up in the debate over slavery and secession, Woods counseled Bowdoin students to take a position that was more in line with his own thinking: that disunion was a lesser evil than sectional conflict, that there was much to be admired in southern culture, and that scholars had much better things to do than fight wars. In any event, if it really came to that, the fighting should be left to those with less to lose. Woods, a man of aristocratic bearing (and pretensions), made it clear to his students that he had little use for a debate over slavery and no respect at all for abolitionists—and that he expected Bowdoin graduates to act accordingly. That Jefferson Davis owned slaves mattered not one whit to the Bowdoin president, since he admired anyone who he considered to be educated, upright, and successful.

In the late summer of 1858, however, Woods's views raised eyebrows even among the people of straitlaced Brunswick. New Englanders would never show anything but the strictest courtesy to an outsider like Jefferson Davis, but that did not mean they approved of his views. While both Woods and Davis were respected, both men might have noticed that the people of Maine had consistently elected anti-slavery men to public office, politicians like Fessenden as well as the self-made lawyer and congressman Israel Washburn, who was not only an outspoken opponent of slavery, but a radical who opposed any kind of compromise with the South. That position apparently sat quite well with Washburn's fellow citizens, who returned him to Congress for four successive terms. The Washburn family, Israel and his two brothers Elihu Benjamin Washburne (a member of Congress from Galena, Illinois—who added an *e* to the family name) and Cadwallader Washburn (a congressman from Wisconsin), were more representative of Maine than Woods, and much less likely to forge an alliance with Canada than they were to raise troops to subdue the South.

By the time Davis and Fessenden appeared at Bowdoin, Joshua Chamberlain later said, he was firmly convinced not only that the slave question would lead to secession, but that once it did, war was inevitable. Under those circumstances, he realized, it would be difficult for him to stay in Maine. Chamberlain, now twenty-nine and well on his way to becoming a professional scholar, was torn by this prospect and by his desire to continue the life he had built for himself. This was the old debate from his adolescence, when his parents had disagreed about whether he should enter the ministry or West Point. Chamberlain himself had conducted the debate internally for years and soon, he knew, he would be forced to make a decision. For while Chamberlain was heavily influenced by Woods's patrician conceits and his own father's romantic notions of the South, he was not seduced by them. While he might honor Woods for the favors the older man had shown him in the previous six years (since the day of his graduation), and his father for the hardworking ethic he had bequeathed him, one of the by-products of a Bowdoin education was that it turned its students into independent thinkers.

Despite Leonard Woods's assistance, Joshua Chamberlain's road to a professorship at Bowdoin had been far from easy. There were moments, in fact, when Chamberlain had despaired of any scholarly achievement at all. In the autumn of 1852, Chamberlain had enrolled at the Bangor Theological Seminary and become engaged to Fannie Adams, events that should have excited and energized him. Instead, the next three years became among the most difficult in his life. The trouble began with his graduation from Bowdoin, where he was chosen to give the First Class Oration. He spent hours preparing his speech, diligently committing it to memory, then confidently practicing it aloud, gesturing learnedly, just as he would when he delivered it. But when called on to face his fellow classmates, their parents, and the school faculty at the First Parish Church, he nearly collapsed. After a calm start he lost his way and, gazing out over the expectant faces, he panicked. His old stammer reappeared and he ended by wandering back and forth across the stage. At one point he nearly fainted, catching himself, then continued with his pacing. Realizing that his actions were becoming quite a spectacle, Chamberlain hesitated, then stiffly and hurriedly recited the rest of his speech and sat down, his face red with tension and humiliation.

Before this moment, Chamberlain had been justly proud of his accomplishments at Bowdoin. After recovering from his unexplained illness in his second year, he quickly had made his reputation as one of the college's most accomplished students. When he graduated he was viewed as one of its best scholars and was not only close friends with the school's most prominent faculty members, he had even been taken on board as Professor Cleaveland's teaching assistant. But his truest talent was in languages. He knew German well enough now to teach it, could read Italian, was passable in Latin, and won top ranking in Greek and French. His stammer had all but disappeared and he had become so adept at public speaking (despite the hash he had made of his final address) that he won prizes in oratory. His compositions were excellent and during his senior year he attended Calvin Stowe's lectures on Hebrew. As if this were not enough, his personal commitment to his religion was even greater now than when he had first come to the college. He was now head of the church prayer group and the superintendent of the church choir.

But Chamberlain was far from happy. His most pressing concern was Fannie, who was increasingly miserable in her role as George Adams's adopted daughter. The problem began when George Adams's wife Sarah died unexpectedly. Barely six months later, Adams married Helen Root, whom he had met during a religious conference in Chicago. The marriage, so soon after Sarah Adams's death, seemed undignified to Fannie (this, plus the fact that the new Mrs. Adams was only a few months older than Fannie), who made her outrage at her adopted father's rush to the altar known to the new bride. The situation deteriorated very quickly and at one point was so bad that Adams bluntly suggested that Fannie spend her time elsewhere. Watching uncomfortably from a distance, Chamberlain naturally sided with Fannie, telling her that the Reverend Adams had no right to kick her out of her own house. Fannie should defy him and stay, he said. But Fannie would not hear such advice.

It was particularly galling to Fannie that the new Mrs. Adams spent inordinate amounts of time on her clothes and that Adams, who spent much time talking about moderation and modesty and who criticized Fannie for her own "extravagance," would suddenly find this obsession so charming. Fannie exchanged acerbic and gossipy letters about her frilly habits with the Adamses' other adopted daughter, Anna, then living in Massachusetts. Anna egged her on. "Helen gets along nicely— don't she?" she wrote Fannie at one point. "How do people like her have to dress so much more than mother ever did?" Within a few months, Fannie's open feud with Helen led to bitter words among family members beyond the walls of the parsonage. Fannie searched for a solution to the problem. While it was not unheard of for a woman her age to go into the world on her own, she had no independent income and nowhere to go. She was undecided, frustrated, short-tempered with Chamberlain and terribly unhappy. Chamberlain, already mistrusted by Adams, felt helpless. Adams, however, soon solved the problem by making his own views clear. "Helen cannot stand it long as things have gone lately," he told Fannie, and suggested that she take up work away from Brunswick. Fannie made up her own mind quickly after that, resolving to quit the Adams household to serve as a teacher for three years in the South, a then-accepted quasi-missionary assignment for a young northern woman.

Chamberlain at first opposed Fannie's plan, but then decided to follow her wishes, even though it would mean they would be apart for an extended time. From Chamberlain's perspective, taking on a three-year teaching job in Georgia must have seemed an excessive response to a domestic argument, especially from a woman he now believed would be his wife. But he realized he had little choice in the matter, especially when Fannie insisted that was the only solution to her deteriorating relationship at home.

Chamberlain probably sensed that Fannie was having second thoughts about her relationship with him as well. While historians have always had difficulty removing the varnish from the private lives of nineteenth-century Americans—who were not only private in public, but rarely admitted their own desires to themselves, much less putting them down on paper—Fannie had lived within the protective and puritanical custody of the Adams family for so long that she looked on the sexual union of marriage with fear and doubts. She confided these fears to Chamberlain before she left and then again in letters during their three years of separation, asking him whether he though that "it"—it is unclear whether she means childbirth or sexual union—was "painful," and saying that she thought it might be "better" for the two of them to forgo any intimacy.

Chamberlain too had doubts, though for different reasons. When

Fannie left for Milledgeville, Georgia, in December 1852 Chamberlain began to question her commitment to him and confided that he was "overspread with loneliness and gloom" by her absence. He was not questioning her fidelity (such a thing would have been unthinkable at that time, especially for a woman of her upbringing and background), but simply wanted her to reaffirm her promise that when she returned to Brunswick they would be married. This delicate correspondence reflects the fragile courtship dance of religious New England. Marriage and sex, especially, loomed as a great and embarrassing mystery, all the more so because few men and women of the time ever discussed it. Or perhaps Fannie was simply teasing Chamberlain when she admitted to him that she viewed marriage as prostitution and childbearing as a kind of slavery. Her suggestion that their marriage could be without sex stunned him: "Let me beg of you not to pretend you have no passionate feelings," he wrote to her. "I think you are not so foolish as to suppose either you or I are destitute of a fair degree of humanity."

It may be, however, that Joshua Chamberlain and Fannie Adams had actually consummated their relationship before their marriage. In one letter, Joshua reminded Fannie of "the jar in the cellar way. He would have been three weeks old today . . ." a hint, but only a hint, of this possibility. Clearly, Fannie was attracted to her young Bowdoin fiancé physically, though the language of the time strictly forbade any blunt admission of such carnal desires. "You know dear Lawrence," she wrote to him, "that I may breathe to you, even as to my own heart, in all innocence and perfect trustfulness, those things which would ever sink me in the estimation and respect of any third person; for no other being can know what we are to each other."

Fannie had plenty of passionate feelings, but while she was physically attracted to Joshua Chamberlain, she remained unsure about whether she should eventually marry him. Any eligible woman of Fannie's age, temperament, and time would have been quite happy as Joshua Chamberlain's wife. He was not only an accomplished and well-respected scholar, among the top rank of Bowdoin graduates, he was now a stellar student at the Bangor Theological Seminary (to which he was admitted soon after Fannie's departure for Georgia). And he was, by all accounts, a compassionate, patient, loving man who was totally devoted to Fannie and dedicated (as he reassured her often during her time in Georgia) to making her happy. But Fannie was unlike most of the women of her time. George Adams noticed this first, criticizing her not only for her preening, but for her penchant to adopt what he viewed as strange new ideas. In truth, Fannie Adams's thinking was well in advance of her era, although ideas like hers on a woman's role in society were already beginning to surface in Maine and elsewhere throughout the North. The success and fame of Harriet Beecher Stowe had something to do with this, though her example was just one of many.

There is a suggestion in their correspondence that Fannie's desire for freedom, her distaste for George Adams's marriage with Helen Root, her uncertainty about her own future, and her restlessness led to a whispering campaign among the women of Brunswick that reached the ears of Chamberlain's mother in Brewer. Chamberlain himself dismissed the gossip as the result of envy, but he feared his mother might not. He had reason to be worried. Sarah Chamberlain's disapproval of his interest in Fannie would have placed insurmountable obstacles to the couple's plans and may well have ended the relationship. So, while Fannie was away in Milledgeville, Chamberlain spent time convincing his mother that the undefined chatter about Fannie was the work of idle tongues. Part of the campaign included presenting his mother with a letter to Chamberlain from Fannie's cousin that reviewed Fannie's future plans and her love for Chamberlain.

Everything about the incident leads to the conclusion that Chamberlain carefully orchestrated the exchange of letters; that he had Fannie write her cousin her thoughts on him, then instructed the cousin to pass on the correspondence so he could show his mother that all of the mutterings about Fannie (her willfulness, "inconstancy," her love of expensive dresses, and, most of all, her independent ideas) were intended to denigrate a loving and serious woman. Fortunately for Chamberlain, the ploy worked. His mother read the correspondence, was reassured of Fannie's good intentions, and gave her blessing to the proposed marriage. Chamberlain passed the good news on to Fannie: "It gave the lie to all that had ever been whispered to her by certain ladies about you," he wrote, "and she knew that you were good." Chamberlain was transported by the turn of fortune. His mother's blessing meant they could be married: "I know in whom all my highest hopes and dearest joys are centered I know in whom my whole heart can rest—so sweetly and so surely."

Having secured his mother's approval, Chamberlain, now at the Bangor Theological Seminary, realized that Fannie's sojourn in Georgia was just as well. He had little time for an extended courtship and even less time for meeting the responsibilities of beginning a marriage and starting a family. While the old debate about attending West Point was raised once more in his mind, and talked about with his parents, he thought it best in the end to follow his plan to become a teacher or minister. That meant that for the three years Fannie was in Milledgeville he would have to spend almost every minute mastering a new course of studies. Not only was he now required to learn Arabic, Syriac, and Hebrew, but he must continue to solidify his position in the church. To make matters more difficult, he decided against accepting any financial help from the seminary and turned to teaching German to young students during the school year, supervising the Brewer schools, teaching several days in nearby Ellsworth, and playing the First Parish Church organ in Brunswick. For extra money he accompanied his father on surveying expeditions in the lumber regions of northern Maine and Canada.

Fannie's rebellion gives a hint of the second revolution tucked away behind the antebellum controversy surrounding slavery. The movement for women's rights was long in coming, but it had burst onto the public scene in 1848, when Elizabeth Cady Stanton and Lucretia Coffin Mott organized a women's rights convention at Seneca Falls, New York. While Stanton had been pressing for equal rights for women for many years, Mott was considered even more radical. When her husband James barred women from membership in the American Anti-Slavery Society during an organizational meeting in Philadelphia in 1833, Mott took a group of twenty women down the street and formed the Female Anti-Slavery Society. A second women's convention was then organized in 1850 by Lucy Stone, a graduate of Oberlin—the Ohio college that Theodore Weld attended after his exile from the Lane Theological Seminary. Stone vowed that she would make such meetings an annual event.

Perhaps the two most influential women of the time were Sarah Grimké and her sister Angelina Emily (who married Theodore Weld), both of whom had been raised on a South Carolina plantation. The Grimké sisters became the most outspoken female opponents of slavery and conducted a speaking tour of the North when women were not expected to speak publicly on any subject. In the 1830s, Angelina Grimké wrote one of the most stirring and unique abolitionist appeals in American history; stirring because of its lack of rhetoric and unique because its audience was southern women. "I know you do not make the laws, " Grimké wrote in *Appeal to the Christian Women of the Southern States*, "but I also know that you are the wives and mothers, the sisters and daughters of those who do; and if you really suppose you can do nothing to overthrow slavery, you are greatly mistaken." The *Appeal* got the sisters barred from South Carolina, the tract was burned by the postmaster of Charleston, and its publication led to vicious criticisms in the North. "Why are all the old hens abolitionists?" the *New Hampshire Patriot* asked. "Because not being able to obtain husbands they think they may stand some chance for a negro, if they can only make amalgamation fashionable."

Fannie Adams was obviously influenced by the parallels Stowe, Stanton, Mott, and the Grimkés drew between slavery and marriage. While none of these women had suffered the indignities of slavery firsthand (Harriet Beecher Stowe had never even been in the South), they were certainly more capable of empathizing with the slave's plight than Weld, Garrison—or Birney. Stowe, in particular, "shook the foundations of the patriarchy" by defending Mott and others in print and by defending women who took an active role in the abolitionist movement: "If a ruffian attacks her children, she will defend them even at a risk of appearing unladylike & you may be sure that whenever a poisoned dagger is lifted to stab the nobly unfortunate *in the back* some woman's hand will always be found between its point & his heart, tho the act be unladylike, & the touch poison to her." But it was Angelina Grimké who articulated the connections between the plight of her sex and the Negro slave most clearly: "True, we have not felt the slaveholder's lash; true, we have not had our hands manacled, but our hearts have been *crushed.* . . . I want to be identified with the negro, until he gets his rights, we shall never have ours." But the statement that hit home was much more subtle and pointed: "The investigation of the rights of the slave has led me to a better understanding of my own."

Fannie was neither a radical nor an abolitionist crusader. Her letters to Chamberlain from Georgia indicate that her stay in the region had little effect on her political views. While she found the sleepy South boring (she played the organ, visited women in their homes, chatted endlessly with friends, and not much more), its inhabitants listless, and its black servants and its slaves contented—or quiet—she grew to admire the region. In part, she explained, this attraction was due to her fears of becoming no more than an appropriately quiet appendage to a New England minister. By the time she had spent a full year in Milledgeville, however, the crushing boredom of the small town had an impact; she wrote to Chamberlain that Brewer, Bowdoin, and the prospect of becoming the wife of a respected professor or minister looked better than it had on the day she had taken the boat to Savannah. She urged him to come to Georgia to teach, then changed her mind and said that he should not come. While Fannie constantly expressed her love for Chamberlain, she reiterated her fear of sexual intimacy and, most especially, the pain of childbirth.

Chamberlain read this correspondence with mounting confusion. He was disturbed by what he viewed as her childish flights of imagination and at one point told her that it appeared she did not really know what she wanted. Finally, he suggested that they leave both Maine and the South and head to California, where gold ran in the hills and hard work could make a man rich. He could start college in the West, he said, where such institutions were needed. The suggestion was actually made by Chamberlain's father, who was a keen observer of his son's increasing frustrations, pressures, and doubts about Fannie. Fannie was taken with the proposal, though she ignored the part about starting a college: "There is a man here," she wrote from Milledgeville, "from that land of gold wanting five or six to go back with him." Chamberlain, however, quietly dropped the proposal. As for Fannie's fears of marriage, Chamberlain indelicately wrote that her duties as a wife would not be nearly as onerous as she imagined. He did not mean to "preach all the time," he told her and only felt the "tenderest love for her" that rested on the sure ground that "my first and greatest [is] to God."

Eventually, perhaps calmed by his reasonableness, Fannie became more affectionate and reassuring in her correspondence, though still insistent that he choose a path that took note of her desires. She informed him that she did not want to be a minister's wife, but hoped he would turn to scholarship. In return, she promised, she would make sacrifices of her own and reassured him that the lower salary of a professor could meet the needs of both of them. She then urged him to sacrifice his "over-fastidious pride," even if it meant taking a lesser position than one the church offered. Chamberlain was uncertain of this, hoping their marriage could start without the financial sacrifices a teaching job offered—though he too, as he readily admitted, was more inclined to be a teacher than a minister. Chamberlain was probably also skeptical that Fannie would keep her promise to make sacrifices of her own. He had witnessed her conflicts with George Adams over her extravagance and suspected that Fannie's reluctance to become a minister's wife was in part a reluctance to dress like one. Her cousin echoed these sentiments as well:

> Do dress simply as becometh a minister's daughter and one who expects to become the wife of a minister. You ought to be willing to take advice on this subject and yield your feelings on so trifling a subject, and in other points of view a most momentous subject—as dress—to the feelings, the judgment, the wishes of your friends. Beads and Furbelows, and finery are very unbecoming one in your situation and your expectation. Your love for such things is a weak spot in your character and you ought to fight against it.

Everywhere Fannie turned she was beset by such criticism and by the constant complaint that she was "childish." In fact, she was very intelligent, loved art and literature (and kept up with the latest developments in each), was an avid reader, and spoke her mind clearly on important subjects. While she did not have the structured educational training of Chamberlain, she took pride in the fact that she could think and speak for herself, rebelled against the criticism that she was flighty, and was actually more independent, in many respects, than the more well-known independent women of her time. It is hard to shake the belief that Fannie acted with bitterness and resentment—and, at times, childishly—because, like many other nineteenth-century women, she was treated like a child.

After taking his degree from the Bangor Theological Seminary, and soon after Fannie returned to Maine from Georgia, Chamberlain decided to deliver an oration at Bowdoin, in the hopes of winning a master's degree and a teaching job. While he had been offered three ministries in Maine, he had turned them down in turn, convinced now that he was meant to teach. His Bowdoin lecture was far more successful than his First Class Oration three years earlier. The subject, "Law and Liberty," was a distillation of all of his scholarship, and a thinly veiled commentary on the great debate then shaking the country. While Fannie was in Georgia, Chamberlain had solidified his own thinking on slavery and secession, and while he only indirectly referred to those topics in his oration, nearly every subject at the time was infused with the controversy. Chamberlain put the dispute in scholarly terms, writing that liberty without law leads to chaos, and law without liberty to despotism. He hewed the middle course, firm in his own mind that the South could keep its slaves, but that it would forfeit everything if it left the Union.

The oration was a great success and Chamberlain was offered a junior faculty position at Bowdoin, which he readily accepted. But he kept putting off his marriage to Fannie from one month to the next, so that she was nearly beside herself, wondering whether Chamberlain really intended to marry her at all. But Chamberlain had not hesitated because of his doubts about Fannie; instead he was concerned about whether he could meet the responsibilities that marriage brought. Money was the problem. Bowdoin's offer was good, but it was hardly enough to keep him alive, let alone provide for a new wife. It was only when Chamberlain's mother suggested that the young couple could come to the Chamberlain house in Brewer to live for the summer, thereby saving on rent money, that he finally made up his mind. The two were married by the Reverend George Adams, at the First Parish Church, on December 7, 1855.

Joshua Chamberlain was a gifted teacher as well as a patient and understanding man who took extra time with his faltering students. He had much to keep him busy: preparing lectures, reading student compositions, participating in faculty activities, and keeping an eye on his younger brothers Horace and John, who were both students at Bowdoin. Chamberlain's mother worried constantly about John especially, believing him more sensitive (immature is probably a better word) than his older brothers. By the time Jefferson Davis came to speak at Bowdoin, Joshua Chamberlain had been on the faculty for three years, and the Bowdoin board had just given him more responsibilities and a promotion. And yet, by 1858, he had begun to be dissatisfied with the straitlaced educational traditions of the college. He told his colleagues that Bowdoin needed to change, that the college was preparing its students to work and not to think: that they were providing *training* to young men, he argued, instead of educating them. He emphasized the word in a letter on the subject he wrote to Professor Cleaveland, three months after meeting Jefferson Davis. He soon instituted a number of his teaching innovations—which emphasized student participation, greater science offerings, and less reliance on the classics—without gaining permission from either the Bowdoin president or the board of trustees.

But his primary concern was still Fannie, whom he worried over constantly. In the first five years of their marriage she gave birth to three children: Grace Dupee was born eleven months after their marriage, but their second, a boy, died in infancy, despite the nursing assistance provided by Chamberlain's mother. Another son, named Harold Wyllys, was born in 1858. Fannie managed their home, cared for a husband who was just starting a difficult career, and attempted to satisfy all of her own often expensive habits on a modest salary. Chamberlain was ever mindful that Fannie remained restless and naggingly dissatisfied. But he could not keep himself from chastising her over her overspending and became unreasonably jealous when he discovered a stack of letters she had written, before their marriage, to another man. But the storm soon passed and, after his promotion at the college, he moved his family out of the cramped apartment they had rented and into a house. He, Fannie, and their growing family soon fit into a regular routine of work, church, and visiting friends and relatives. For the most part, they were happy.

In the summer of 1859, abolitionist John Brown, the Connecticut son of a Bible-thumping Calvinist who grew up believing he held a special place in Providence's plan (as the punisher of the unrighteous, the sword of God), organized a militia and stormed the federal arsenal at Harpers Ferry, Virginia (now West Virginia). He called for a slave uprising, hoping to attract thousands of slaves to his standard. The raid at Harpers Ferry stunned the nation, but for those in the North who knew him, Brown's place at the head of the insurrection was not a surprise.

As a boy, John Brown had organized snowball fights at his family home near Torrington, Connecticut, dividing the contending sides into "little Federalists" and "little Democrats." He had received his abolitionist baptism in Ohio, when he saw a slaveholder savagely beat his servant with a shovel. At the age of sixteen, Brown decided to become a minister and set about committing the Bible to memory. The year he attended the Litchfield Academy, Lyman Beecher was the Connecticut town's Congregational minister and its most famous resident.

Brown entered adulthood as a man of strong and outspoken convictions. Married to Dianthe Lusk in 1820, he set up business as a tanner and fathered seven children. Dianthe died seven years after they were married, and Brown married sixteen-year-old Mary Ann Day. They had thirteen children in twenty years. Brown kept a harsh household—maintaining a strict Sabbath silence, a regular schedule of Bible readings, and constant prayer. He believed that God punished the wicked and used the blessed as his instruments. The most wicked sinners were slaveholders; those who tolerated slavery were, he believed, also stained by its sin. Freeing slaves was the duty of every true Christian in America.

Slavery consumed Brown. When not tending his work and family, he read everything he could on the growing controversy, then spent two years in a freedman's community in North Elba, New York. He served as a conductor on the Underground Railroad for several years and became known to the radical wing of the abolitionist movement. When his children reached maturity, however, they began to fall away from his strict beliefs, a fact that saddened and angered him, and which he interpreted as a failure of his faith. He read the Bible even more closely, attempting to discern among its stories a message that God was sending especially to him. He thought he found the special message in the Book of Judges, where Gideon is called by God "out of Gilead" and given an army of thousands to save Israel. Gideon triumphed against great odds, even after most of his followers abandoned him.

Brown was entranced by the story and, after passage of the Fugitive Slave Act, became an anti-slavery pamphleteer and the organizer of the United States League of the Gileadites. "Nothing so charms the American people as personal bravery," he wrote to his followers. "The trial for life of one bold and to some extent successful man, for defending his rights in good earnest, would arouse more sympathy throughout the nation than the accumulated wrongs and sufferings of more than three millions of our submissive colored population." In August 1855, Brown followed five of his sons to Osawatomie, Kansas, to fight the slaveholders. When the abolitionist community of Lawrence was burned, Brown vowed revenge. On the night of May 23, 1856, he led six of his followers to the pro-slave settlement of Pottawatomie Creek, dragged the inhabitants from their homes, and butchered five of them with sharpened swords. Afterward Brown defended his murders: "God is my judge," he said, "we were justified under the circumstances."

In the summer of 1859, Brown left Kansas for western Virginia, where he organized an army of twenty-one men to start a slave insurrection. His army raided Harpers Ferry on the night of October 16. Brown's plan had been to use the weapons he obtained from the arsenal to arm the slaves throughout the South, believing they would rally to his colors. But a platoon of Marines under Colonel Robert E. Lee stormed the arsenal building, which he had turned into a fortress, arrested Brown, and killed ten of his men. The trial that followed caused a national sensation. Brown was found guilty and hung in Charles Town on December 2, 1859. He was conducted to his place of execution riding on his own coffin, clothed in a simple white shirt, his eyes blazing in martyred triumph. Several days before, he had written his wife: "Remember, dear wife and children all, that Jesus of Nazareth suffered a most excruciating death on the cross as a felon, under most aggravating circumstances."

Witnessing Brown's hanging were cadets from the Virginia Military Institute, under the command of their instructor, Thomas Jonathan

Jackson, a devout Presbyterian. Jackson marched his cadets through Charles Town to the field of execution, putting them in neat gray lines. The night before Brown's execution, Jackson had slumped to his knees, praying for Brown's soul. Now, as a witness to the scene, he was shocked by the condemned man's calm and struck by his devotion to his cause. "I was much impressed with the thought that before me stood a man in the full vigor of health, who must in a few moments enter eternity," Jackson wrote in a letter to his wife.

Brown said nothing of his crime as he was led to the gallows, but looked up to the hills: "This is a beautiful country. I never had the pleasure of seeing it before."

His execution electrified the North.

Chamberlain, in Brunswick, followed the events in Virginia with a mix of growing alarm, excitement, and restlessness. Things seemed to be happening everywhere but where he was. Men were preparing for war, the nation was boiling with anticipation. His life seemed a dull and monotonous routine in comparison.

And then the war came.

Most Americans knew it would come. The precipitating cause was the election of Abraham Lincoln to the presidency. Lincoln reassured the South that he would leave slavery intact where he found it, though he promised he would work to bar its introduction into the territories. But the seeds of disunion planted by Yancey, Rhett, and Ruffin began to bear fruit.

Secession need not have been inevitable. On the eve of the Civil War, most southerners opposed secession and many of their leaders counseled caution. But after the election a rumor spread through the South that Senator Robert Toombs of Georgia had resigned his post in Washington. The report was not true, but it was enough to begin the South's precipitous march out of the nation. Secession rallies were held throughout the region, in Charleston, Mobile, and in Montgomery. As predicted, South Carolina moved first, calling for a secession convention in Charleston for January 1861, then moving the date up to December 17, and then to December 6, 1860.

Alabama's secession convention was scheduled for February, but the date for its meeting was also moved forward. A special vote to elect delegates to the Alabama convention was held the day before Christmas. The closeness of the Alabama vote showed just how uncertain southerners were that secession was the right course of action: 28,100 Alabamians supported compromise (or "cooperation," as it was then termed), while 35,600 Alabamians voted for disunion. While there was reason then, and now, to believe that a majority of southerners did not favor disunion, it is also true that the dissenters had neither the power nor the popular following to stop it. As in the argument over slavery itself, moderation was viewed as betrayal; the test of southern patriotism was a southerner's willingness to defend secession as a "right."

William Oates was among the moderates. Long after the war ended, Oates defended the act of national dismemberment as a Constitutional right. But at the same time he argued that he had never been in favor of secession to begin with and reminded friends that soon after he began his law practice in Abbeville he had carried a gun to defend himself from a man who thought his views too moderate, too Yankee. The argument between the two was treated as laughable and insignificant by Oates, but the incident reveals much about the tenor of the debate in the days preceding the founding of the Confederacy.

South Carolina seceded on December 20, 1860, Mississippi on January 1, 1861, followed by Florida (which seceded by a margin of nine delegate votes) on January 10 and then by Alabama on January 11. Georgia, Louisiana, and Texas followed in February. On February 4, a group of secession "commissioners" from each of the Deep South states met to negotiate a confederation of southern states. They adopted a provisional constitution on February 7 and elected Jefferson Davis of Mississippi president of the Confederate States of America on February 9.

Oates was not a delegate to the Alabama secession convention, nor one of the secession commissioners, but he had made a name for himself as a lawyer in Abbeville and became deeply involved in Democratic politics by founding and editing a pro-Democratic Abbeville newspaper, the *Abbeville Banner*. By early 1861, like other moderates he now followed the path dictated by the leaders of his state and believed that the differences between North and South could not be reconciled. Still, he argued that secession did not necessarily have to lead to civil war, since it "did not, could not, and never did put the life of the nation in jeopardy." Oates believed there should have been an amicable solution, as there had been before, if only Lincoln would abandon his position of restricting slavery to where it already existed. Jefferson Davis also believed this, of course, and made the claim a part of his February 1861 inaugural address, given from the front portico of the state capital building in Montgomery. In the crowd below him, William Oates listened intently. Davis gave a stirring oration, hoping to unite the South and induce the border states to come to its aid. He was moderate, saying in even tones that the new nation they were founding should be based on the mutual respect of the states and have as its goal a vigorous commerce. He then quickly spoke of the secession crisis, saying that while he opposed war, the South would defend itself, if need be through the shedding of blood. He hoped that such "folly and wickedness" would not happen.

Lincoln also took a moderate tone in his inaugural address, three weeks after Davis's speech in Montgomery, counseling understanding between the states and reassuring the South that he had no "purpose, directly or indirectly, to interfere with the institution of slavery in the states where it exists." But he also issued a warning: "No state upon its own mere motion can lawfully get out of the Union," and he added that as president he would "hold, occupy and possess the property and places belonging to the government and to collect the duties and imposts."

His remarks were greeted without much comment in the South, which had already cast its lot with secession. In many places, Lincoln's promise to defend federal property was virtually ignored. For while southerners had begun to arm and form militias, there were relatively few confrontations. Indeed, after the crisis caused by Lincoln's election, the secession of the southern states, the founding of the Confederacy, and the election of Jefferson Davis as its president, the pace of events seemed to slow, as if everyone was being especially careful to avoid starting a conflagration.

The Virginia agricultural reformer Edmund Ruffin, the now-famous secessionist, was one of the few southerners who warned that there would be dark days ahead, and blood. After campaigning for secession for many years he was proud now that it had come and that he had had a large part in making it possible. But while the secession of the Deep South was gratifying, he was increasingly embittered that his home state of Virginia had, by February 1861, not joined the cavalcade out of the Union. He left his home near Richmond in voluntary exile and traveled south to Charleston, where he was greeted as a hero. He was made an honorary member of Charleston's militia, the Palmetto Guard, then on duty overlooking the federal garrison in Fort Sumter, in Charleston Harbor, which was still in Union hands.

It was there, at four-thirty on the morning of April 12, 1861, that Ruffin was approached by the guard's commander, General P. G. T. Beauregard, and asked to fire the first shot of the war. Roger Pryor, standing nearby, had waved off Beauregard when given the offer ("I could not fire the first gun of the war," he said), so Beauregard turned to Ruffin. Ruffin stepped forward a few paces, looked out over the harbor, and pulled the lanyard of a small cannon in front of him. The shot arced over Charleston Harbor and burst just above the water near the fort. Behind Ruffin, the people of Charleston—who had gathered on their rooftops for the occasion—cheered.

# PART TWO

# 6

# *If Honor It Be*

T WENTY-FOUR HOURS after Edmund Ruffin sent the first shot arcing over Charleston Harbor, Fort Sumter surrendered. That was a Saturday. On the next Tuesday, Lincoln called for 75,000 volunteers to protect the Union. It was a mistake. Lincoln's call was viewed as an aggressive act in the border states. On Wednesday, April 17, both Kentucky and Virginia declared that they would refuse Lincoln's call. Secession rolled north, from Alabama, Georgia, and Mississippi, into Arkansas, Tennessee, North Carolina, and Virginia. There were soon eleven stars in the Confederate flag and a new capital at Richmond. The electrifying events in Charleston Harbor exploded the myth of peaceable cooperation. In all parts of the South, men began to form local companies and militias, and drill—sometimes with broomsticks—for war. In Alabama, James Cantey, a wealthy planter and South Carolina native, raised a company of soldiers that he called the Cantey Rifles. He built a camp near Fort Mitchell, ordered an assortment of uniforms, and trained his men throughout the long hot summer months of 1861. A regiment of eleven companies was eventually formed, led by the state's most prominent men.

One of these was Company G from Henry County, commanded by William Oates, the self-taught lawyer from Abbeville. He called his company the Henry Pioneers and designed a brown floppy hat that would make them recognizable on any battlefield. "My company was raised in the north end of Henry County, about Abbeville, and the eastern part of Dale County," he later wrote, "and was composed mainly of young men and boys from sixteen to thirty years of age, the sons of farmers. There were but thirteen married men in it, and but five who were forty years old, in a membership of one hundred and twenty-one, that being the number (including myself) with which I left Abbeville [for Fort Mitchell] on Saturday the 27th of July."

Oates made certain his Pioneers were fully provisioned, going so far as to collect money for his men from the most prominent citizens of the county. When the company took the steamboat north on the Chattahoochie River to Fort Mitchell, Oates got off at Eufaula, cashed a check for $2,000 given him by Abbeville's citizens, and bought food, clothing, and tents for his men. "We were entitled to commutation for clothing, and this, with the monthly pay of the men, was as much as any soldier need to have had expended for his comfort," Oates said, "but this sum, together with the large contributions of clothing, tents, mess-chests and other camp equipage, enough to have supplied a regiment in the last year of the war, abundantly proved the generous and patriotic spirit of the people left at home."

Cantey welcomed Oates and his men and set them to drilling; the fields around Fort Mitchell filled with the shouts of command given by the regimental captains who spent their free hours deciphering General William Hardee's classic book on tactics and close-order drill. At first the men did not even know their right foot from their left and units were hopelessly mixed, with men from one company bumping into another in confusion—"a ludicrous scene," Oates later wrote—while their elected officers tried to sort them out. This was predictable: southerners who prided themselves on their martial spirit and willingness to fight had very little experience in either, except for Colonel Cantey, who had fought during the Mexican War in South Carolina's Palmetto Guards and won a reputation as a good commander. Cantey showed great patience with his new soldiers, repeatedly going over the fine points of moving from column to line and back again. Oates admitted that he and his men were "so utterly ignorant of military law and army regulations as well as tactics that we were as clay in a potter's hands and ready to submit to any kind of organization."

Cantey's Rifles contained an assortment of both odd and notable characters, men from thirteen to seventy years old, many of them boyhood friends of Oates from the Crossroads, including two boys from the Linton family. George Linton, who was eighteen, was a private in Company I, and was married to Oates's youngest sister. The youngest

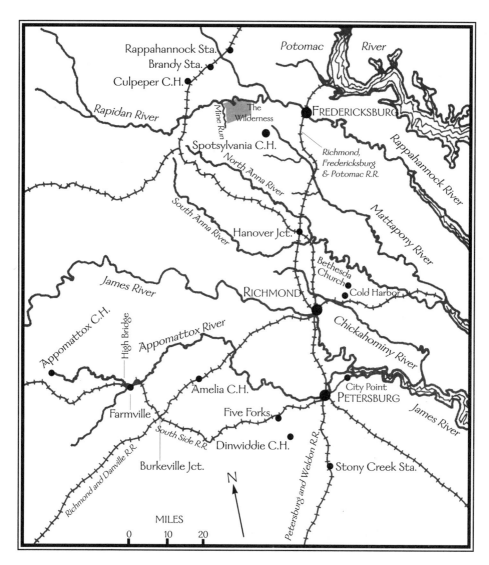

**The Virginia Battlegrounds**

volunteer was thirteen-year-old Pat Brannon, an inveterate gambler who won money from the older soldiers, and who became the regimental drummer boy. The oldest soldier was seventy-year-old Edmond Sheppard, "a northern man and a well-educated physician," who was made the regimental surgeon. But Sheppard was not the regiment's most notable soldier; that honor went to Jefferson F. Beecher, a

sixty-one-year-old enlisted man from Pike County who was widely rumored to be, as Oates testified, "a near relative of the distinguished
Henry Ward Beecher." Beecher did not last long, since, as Oates also
noted, "he was too old for soldiering."

In July, the regiment received word that the newly formed Confederate army had won its first victory in Virginia, routing a Union army
under the command of Irvin McDowell at Manassas Junction. This
First Battle of Manassas (or "Bull Run," as it was referred to in the
North) was greeted by Cantey's Rifles with a mix of joy, arrogance, and
fear: joy that the South had won, arrogance because everyone knew that
the average southern soldier was a better fighter than any Yankee, and
fear that the victory meant the war might end before the Alabamians
training at Fort Mitchell could lend a hand. There was no need to
worry. The southern commanders at Manassas did not follow up their
victory, while the despairing Abraham Lincoln appointed a new commander. In Fort Mitchell, the regiment received uniforms, a mix of
butternut and gray, drilled with wooden stakes, and waited for their orders. The enthusiasm of the Alabama men more than compensated for
the lack of firepower, however, and by early August 1861, when the
southern government ordered them to Richmond, they were ready. On
a hot August day, the regiment left its camp at Fort Mitchell, boarded
rail cars, and headed north.

⚜

That the South was not prepared for war mattered little to its large
cadre of professional soldiers, who believed that the heat of battle was
the best training ground for new soldiers. The unwritten strategy of
the war's early days—that the South would stand its ground, marshal
its resources, and use the experience of its officer corps to advantage—
sprang from these professionals, most of whom were graduates of either
West Point or one of the half dozen southern military academies. While
the North had many fine soldiers, none then were nearly the quality of
Albert Sidney Johnston, who was given command of the South's forces
in Tennessee, or Joe Johnston and Pierre Gustave Toutant Beauregard
(of Fort Sumter fame), who commanded the Confederacy's first army
on the fields of Manassas. Or of Robert E. Lee, who rejected Lincoln's
offer of command of the Union forces to fight with his native state.

The Confederacy was also endowed with a large group of lesser commanders who had years of military service in "the old army." Two of the most prominent were James Longstreet and Thomas Jonathan Jackson. Longstreet, age forty, was large, like a block; serious, imposing, taciturn, and an accomplished student of war. He was one of the few American soldiers who understood that the days of fair fights were being replaced by an age of mechanized killing. A South Carolinian by birth, Longstreet spent his early years on his uncle's farm in Augusta, Georgia, before being appointed to West Point. Longstreet won great distinction in the Mexican War, when he stormed the citadel of Chapultepec with old army buddy George Pickett. In the old army, Longstreet won a reputation as a formidable card player, but in battle he was not a gambler. Nonetheless, he enjoyed battle and could be seen at the head of his troops exhibiting one strange habit: he wore his carpet slippers into battle. The death of three of his children in a single week at the beginning of the war affected him deeply and while he was still a man of ideas, spouting strategy to those who would listen, he was often plunged in moody silence. He could be a nasty, stubborn man, but he was brilliant. During the war Lee came to depend on him and called him "my old war horse." His soldiers often referred to him as a bulldog.

Thomas Jonathan "Stonewall" Jackson had many of the same qualities, with the exception that he would never have uttered an oath, or gambled, or showed anger. Jackson graduated from West Point four years after Longstreet, then fought with him in Mexico. He taught at the Virginia Military Institute and was given responsibility for marching the cadets north to Charles Town to witness the hanging of John Brown. Like the abolitionist martyr, he believed his army was a sword in God's hand and an instrument of His will. Like Brown, he despised human weakness, finding the devil in any sign of exhaustion and pure evil in any wavering from duty. Jackson was also given to odd habits: he sucked on a lemon for strength, traveled with one arm in the air because he said it aided circulation, and believed that pepper weakened him. He was a devout Christian, asked forgiveness from his wife for doing battle on the Sabbath (and rested his troops on Mondays to make up for such perfidy), and prayed often and hard—usually for God's aid in slaughtering the enemy. He was, as William Oates later reflected, "a regular blue-stocking Presbyterian." Jackson won his nickname at

Manassas, when his Virginians stood "like a Stone Wall" against the charging northerners, but his soldiers called him "old blue light" because his eyes shone like beacons in a battle.

When Cantey's Alabamians arrived in Richmond in late August 1861, it was still not certain whether they would join Jackson's or Longstreet's command, but there was little doubt that they would soon see action. Troops were pouring into the Confederate capital from all over the South and Cantey's regiment was soon sent north to Manassas, where they were brigaded with regiments from North Carolina, Georgia, and Mississippi. One day they were marched out to inspect the Bull Run battlefield. What they saw there convinced them that the business of war was far more serious than they had imagined. The regiment, now designated the 15th Alabama, walked the battlefield silently, stepping gingerly over the freshly dug graves. "Some of the mounds where the slain were buried were washed down by the rains until here and there could be discovered a putrefying human hand or foot protruding," Oates wrote. "Such places when approached were offensive."

The regiment was ordered five miles farther north, to Pageland, where they went into camp. Camp life was monotonous, and the close-order drill dictated by higher officers even more so. The men of Alabama wanted excitement, but there was little to be had. It was at Pageland that the first tragedy of war struck the regiment, in the form of the measles, which made its appearance in early September. The sickness reached epidemic proportions in mid-September, when it struck particularly hard among the 21st Georgia regiment before moving into the ranks of the Alabamians. Oates did what he could to allay the spread of the disease, but he was fighting a losing battle. The beautiful Virginia autumn was blighted by the plague: James S. Fears of Henry County was twenty when he died of measles, as was George Sumner; William Mitchell was eighteen, Frederick Hickman, a farm boy, was twenty, Morris Holmes was forty-nine. Later, weakened by the disease, many died of pneumonia, or "camp fever"—an unspecified illness that swept through the southern campgrounds. In this respect, the 15th was typical. Of the nearly 2,000 men who enlisted in its ranks, more than one-quarter died of sickness during the war, many of them in the year that followed its march north.

The thinning of his company's ranks hit Oates hard. He felt responsible for his men, in large part because their fathers and mothers had pleaded with him to pay special attention to "their boy" during the war and asked him to guarantee that their young men would return to their farms unharmed. Oates could not keep these promises and so did not make them, but his status as a successful lawyer in Henry County and the fact that he had single-handedly recruited the company burdened him. By the end of September, Oates was embittered by a new policy that finally segregated the sick from the rest of the regiment, but without making any provision for their care. "I regarded this as a criminally foolish order," he recounted, "and determined to disobey to the extent of sending a good faithful, well man to take care of the sick from my company." He chose twenty-five-year-old Elijah Lingo, who proved to be a selfless soldier. "He had my instructions to stay with those sick boys and give them the best attention possible, which he certainly did. The consequence was that very few of my sick men died, while the number of deaths in other companies was appalling."

December found the 15th Alabama in camp one mile west of the battlefield at Bull Run and reassigned to the division of Virginian Richard Ewell, whose bald pate and confused manner of speaking endeared him to the men from the Deep South. Ewell, called "Old Baldy" by his men, was one of the army's more colorful characters. Somewhat forgetful, he lisped when he was tired or under pressure, and seemed surprised that he had been chosen for command: "Now why do you suppose that Jeff Davis made me a Major General?" he asked his fellow commander, Richard Taylor. Ewell ate "frumentary," a wheat concoction that he claimed aided his digestion, and spoke of himself in the third person, a habit that Taylor found "droll in the extreme." But he was a fighter and Stonewall Jackson liked his style: "The road to glory cannot be followed with much baggage," Ewell told his soldiers—which struck the less wordy Jackson as being about right, if a little windy.

The 15th Alabama was assigned to a brigade with other regiments from the Deep South under the command of Isaac Trimble, a distinguished soldier and West Pointer who at the age of fifty-nine weathered camp life better than most men half his age. Trimble was a fighter and expected his brigade to obey orders without question, but he was not a martinet. Trimble understood the corrosive effects of camp life often left a brigade beaten even before a battle began, so he gave orders that would place his men in a strict military routine of drill, drill, and more drill. In part, Trimble feared that the brigade's power might melt away even before it had proven itself under fire, but he also was doing everything humanly possible to prepare his men for carrying out complex orders in the midst of a firefight.

That the 15th Alabama was part of a brigade that became one of the Confederate army's most effective fighting units was due to Trimble's studious attention to detail, especially when it came to putting them into position to deliver a massed volley of fire. The brigade marched in a column, but fought in a line—as Cantey had once taught them—but now Trimble worked with the entire brigade of four regiments so that it could move and fight as one unit. Trimble understood that being caught in column could have disastrous consequences, so he spent much of his time improving the brigade's time for battle deployment. Trimble also understood the bare arithmetic of battle: since most of his men were equipped with smoothbore percussion cap rifles (which required seventeen precise movements for soldiers to load and fire, which could be boiled down to nine in a pinch), only constant training in the rifle's use would develop the skill necessary to stand without wavering in an open fight. While the rifled musket was a vast improvement over the humble smoothbore flintlock of the Napoleonic Wars, its greater range (of up to 1,000 yards) was offset by its lack of accuracy at great distances.

Trimble knew that most of the coming engagements would be fought against units at one hundred yards' distance or closer. In some cases, in the heat of battle, some units would fire nearly face-to-face. And in a very few cases, when every man knew that the weight of a battle depended on him, not a shot would be fired until the last moment. The effects of such close-range fire were devastating, cutting men down like long sheaves of wheat and laying them in precisely measured rows. It was important to withstand such fire, which was more likely if men fought in compact lines, as much for psychological support as for economy of power. That individual men, or even entire regiments or brigades, would run could not be avoided, but full retreat, disintegration, and surrender could be postponed by the drills that the men of the 15th Alabama, and the other three regiments of the brigade, found excruciatingly routine. Civil War combat was unlike modern war—instead of being brutal and short, it was brutal and long, with the firing of massed volleys going on for hours.

The 15th heard their first shot fired in anger in March 1862, after their brigade broke camp and moved south, taking up a position near the Rappahannock River. The Alabamians were sent east of the river and ordered to destroy a railroad. A Union division appeared out of the afternoon sun and artillery shells began to land nearby. The regiment retreated, crossed a bridge, and fell into line of battle. The bridge was burned while the Union troops threw shells into the ranks and there were "wild looks and low dodging all along the line." But the bluecoats soon tired of the contest and withdrew. With that first test behind them, the 15th returned to camp to resume drilling. At the end of April, the Alabamians were ordered south to Stannardsville and then, on May 1, were directed to join Stonewall Jackson in the Shenandoah Valley—the long, broad, and lush green highway that ran diagonally through Virginia's western reaches. Jackson had already fought two battles in the Shenandoah, at Kernstown and McDowell, and was now about to fight another.

⚬══✦══⚬

Joshua Chamberlain watched from afar. Throughout 1861, the students and faculty at Bowdoin talked of the war and little else, though few at the college believed then (even after the hard winter of 1861 settled onto Virginia's battlegrounds) that the conflict would last much past the summer of the next year. The North had a new commander and hero, George McClellan, who was training an army of thousands in the military camps around Washington. There was a certainty that verged on arrogance among many northerners that "Little Mac"—who posed for the camera with hand in coat, Napoleon-like—would eventually move "on to Richmond" and quickly stamp out the rebellion. Of course, Little Mac would only do that when he was good and ready (which was not just yet, as he constantly told Lincoln), but the outcome was not in doubt. Most northerners expected the war would end with one big decisive battle somewhere near Richmond and everyone would go back to their lives.

Chamberlain thought otherwise. He was convinced the war would last for many years and be far bloodier than many of his colleagues believed. He was influenced by his family's appreciation for the southern spirit and the strength of the region's beliefs, and reinforced by what he took to be incontrovertible facts: that the South would not be forced back into the Union by compromise and that its armies were in deadly earnest. Nor, it seemed to him, did Lincoln think the South could be easily conquered; otherwise why would he call for 75,000 volunteers, or appoint McClellan, or agree to the Anaconda Plan, which called for a siege of southern ports? In truth, 75,000 volunteers were not enough and had barely staved off disaster at Bull Run. More men would be needed, many more. "The slave-holding spirit was not contented with toleration," Chamberlain wrote of his thoughts during this period, "it demanded mastery of the Country. And it got it." Victory would not be won with one battle, but only with the subjugation of the South. The nation would only be reunited by force.

What angered Chamberlain the most, however, was not "the slave-holding spirit" but secession, which he viewed as political heresy, as an erosion of the very law that he spoke of during his Bowdoin master's oration. While slavery was an important issue for Chamberlain, and for every northerner, the Bowdoin professor was not a committed abolitionist. Like others of his generation, Chamberlain's views on the growing national divisions were actually quite moderate up to the time of the passage of the Fugitive Slave Act ("it tried their temper to be summoned from their homes to aid in capturing fugitive slaves," he said), and increasingly radical thereafter. Even so, he was willing to choke down his objections in the name of national unity. But the attack on Fort Sumter changed everything.

"The flag of the nation had been insulted," he later wrote, his anger still inflamed. "The honor and authority of the Union had been defied. The integrity and existence of the People of the United States had been assailed in open and bitter war." Chamberlain did not rush to join the Union forces, but his personal march south began the moment that Edmund Ruffin pulled the lanyard that fired the first gun in Charleston Harbor. It was not simply that Chamberlain believed he must do his duty; he was desperate to go to war. He wanted to fight. By the fall of 1861, he could think of little else.

Fannie Chamberlain knew that her husband wanted to leave and remained silent on the subject, bowing to his wishes. But for Joshua and Sallie Chamberlain, the fact that their son would consider going off to war seemed the height of folly. It was not simply that Joshua was their oldest son, it was that he was a man in the prime of his life at the beginning of what promised to be a long and distinguished career. But they too said little. The war itself had passed the point where the older Chamberlain could influence his son's thinking on the South; even he was enraged by secession. He and Sallie also knew they could do little to stop their son, especially since the war itself seemed to stalk him—in the middle of the summer came news that a Bowdoin student had been wounded and captured at Bull Run; later Joshua was asked to speak at recruiting rallies; and, finally, he was asked to write recommendations for students seeking officer appointments in Maine regiments.

On one hot summer afternoon, Chamberlain found himself standing in a crowd as a unit of young soldiers swung in easy strides through the streets of Brunswick. At their head was Bowdoin graduate Oliver Otis Howard. Chamberlain had witnessed several such parades, but the appearance of Howard in the streets of Brunswick must have had a particularly powerful impact. Chamberlain knew Howard (he graduated in 1850, Chamberlain in 1852) and the two had much in common. Like Chamberlain, Howard was a devout Congregationalist—abstemious, serious, well spoken—and was attracted to the military from an early age. The one key difference, of course, was that Howard had acted on his desire to pursue a military career, leaving for West Point after graduation, while Chamberlain had not. It certainly must have occurred to Chamberlain that, had he made another choice, he and not Howard might have been at the head of that parade, leading Maine's troops into the War for the Union.

That Chamberlain wanted to offer his services to Lincoln's army seems natural for a man who had played at broadswords as a boy and flirted with the life of a professional soldier as a student. But there is another side to the story. In all of Chamberlain's correspondence during the conflict and after, there is a vague sense of unease over his choice of profession. Having been named the college's new professor of modern languages, life for him at Bowdoin was rewarding, but never quite enough. While his life with Fannie and their two children was happy, he seemed almost too comfortable. He had flirted with adventure once before, when he suggested that he and Fannie beat a path to the gold fields of California, but he had firmly put such dreams aside. They were simply not serious, he believed, and not what was expected of him. Now, with the war, he had an excuse to strike out on the adventure he had always craved.

His new resolve was confirmed in December 1861, when his brother Horace died of tuberculosis. Chamberlain was firm in his faith, so the death of his brother did not strike him as meaningless, but seemed to underline his growing conviction that death could appear anywhere and at any time, and not just on a battlefield. "That he should be cut down at the very opening of his career, and when he had so much reason to anticipate a prosperous course, seems almost against the order of nature," he wrote his mother. By the early spring of 1862, he decided that instead of using the two year leave the college had granted him for study in Europe—which was to begin in August—he would offer himself instead for an officer's commission.

Chamberlain was not alone in yearning for adventure. Hundreds of thousands of farm boys North and South were drawn to the killing grounds of Virginia, Tennessee, Georgia, Maryland, and Pennsylvania, not simply by the fight for or against slavery or for or against secession, but by the lure of war itself and the promise it held of showing them something of life they had never seen before. Chamberlain had lived his life according to the well-defined routines of God-fearing New England. But now he went to war for himself. His plan of escape was near completion in March 1862, just as the boys he had seen swinging in even rows through the streets of Brunswick were becoming corpses in Virginia.

❦

The firing was far off at first, then nearby, then far off. The men of the 15th Alabama were ordered to halt on the near side of a low hill and put into a line. They were exhausted, "blown" from the combination of the forced march north through the Shenandoah Valley and the unusual late-May heat. The Alabama men moved forward up a road, crested a low hill, and then halted. Before them lay Front Royal, a small Virginia hamlet. Below them, a Union battery unlimbered, its blue-clad men scrambling for firing position. Moments later a cannonball lofted itself into the air and struck nearby, the shot and shell spraying them with dirt. The Alabama line shuddered, then stood. After a pause, Isaac Trimble ordered the brigade forward and down the hill. On the edge of the town, William Oates saw the men of Confederate General Richard Taylor's 1st Louisiana Brigade push the Yankee picket line back. The federals responded slowly, in confusion. There was a smatter of fire as the gray and blue lines met, followed by the triumphant yell of Confederate soldiers. Beyond the town, cavalry commander Turner Ashby, a full-bearded cavalier with a yen for glory, mopped up what was left of the bluecoats, chasing them into the woods. The remainder fled north.

The Battle of Front Royal was a masterful affair, planned by Stonewall Jackson to fend off a combination of over 60,000 Yankees converging on him from nearly every direction. Knowing that he was outnumbered, Jackson daringly split his command, sending Ewell's Division, including the 15th Alabama as part of Trimble's Brigade, north—down the valley—to hold off troops under the command of Nathaniel Banks, a self-made Republican with a strutting, boastful style. Meanwhile, Jackson moved south and west up the valley—against an army commanded by Union generals Robert Milroy and John Frémont. His plan was simple. As Ewell held off Banks, Jackson would pummel Milroy, sending one arm of the Union pincer back across the mountains into western Virginia. Then Jackson would race north to help Ewell finish with Banks.

The plan was to become a hallmark of Jackson's style: to move without explanation and strike hard and fast. What was intended as a Union pincer movement, with two wings of one army converging to crush the Confederates between them, would, Jackson believed, turn into a rout. The first part of Jackson's strategy went off as planned; a bloody stand-up four-hour fight outside of McDowell sent Milroy's troops scampering west in disarray, after which Jackson gathered his troopers, faced them about, and moved them north. He marched thirty miles in one day, allowed his troops to sleep for a few hours, then marched another thirty miles. On the third day they reached the outskirts of Front Royal, coming up on Ewell's left. The Yankees, were not so much pulverized as forced apart, their separate wings fleeing first west and then north out of the valley. After forcing the federals out of Front Royal, the 15th Alabama moved north toward Winchester in pursuit.

Banks was laconic about the Front Royal defeat, saying that his troops "held their ground manfully, yielding only to the irresistible power of overwhelming numbers." He failed to mention that his troops, while "yielding," did so at an accelerated rate, running back down the Valley Pike with Turner Ashby's plumed cavalrymen nipping at their heals. The forward movement was the only "irresistible" part of the battle and was conducted by southern soldiers who marched smartly north. Many Alabamians wished they hadn't. It was one of the most nightmarish marches of the war: the wind whipped in a gale; rain became sleet, sleet became rain. Ahead, skirmishing southerners chased the rearguard formations of Banks's troops down the Valley Pike, stopping to loot abandoned wagons before surging onward again. But for Henry County's soldiers, the heart-thumping exhilaration of battle that would have warmed them remained only a tantalizing possibility. They were stuck, dead tired, slogging through the mud toward Winchester, while men in line ahead of them fought, lunged, and looted. They did not stop until three hours before sunrise, on the outskirts of Winchester.

The Yankees were there, waiting in the dark, drawn up behind a low wall that stretched across the road. There seemed no way around the formidable defenses. While Richard Ewell tried to find a way to unlock Banks's line, the 15th Alabama stood by unhappily in the pelting rain (a "wholly unnecessary and a cruel punishment," Oates wrote). On that frigid May evening south of Winchester, however, Ewell was no happier than his troops. Over the past two weeks, Stonewall Jackson had ordered Ewell's Division west, then south, then east, and then north in marches that left Ewell short-tempered and deepened his lisp. When it all finally became clear—that the marching and countermarching were intended to confuse the northerners—the balding Virginian still thought Jackson unhinged, though he had a better appreciation for his tactical skills.

Ewell might have thought Jackson eccentric, even crazy, but Oates and his Alabamians were learning to love him. "He inspired his men with blind confidence," Oates said. Marching through the sleet and rain, standing in the cold for hours while he peered strangely into a nearby fire, then fighting and marching without rest should have made the Alabamians, and the 15,000 other soldiers in Jackson's army, resentful and mean-spirited. But wherever Jackson sent them, they won. His temperament suited them; he gave no speeches, few instructions, and remained incredibly calm in the midst of chaos. His lumpy lemon-sucking figure exuded confidence. He never gave an order he did not expect to be followed, and took it for granted that his soldiers would go anywhere he told them. He expected them to win. Jackson gave his army their first victory in the upper valley, when he threw back Milroy, their second at Front Royal (when he joined Ewell), and was now poised to given them their third, at Winchester. Near dawn, the 15th Alabama was finally ordered forward. Jackson had made up his mind—seeing there was no way around Banks, he supposed he would go through him. He told Richard Taylor's men to move against Winchester on the left, while Ewell's Division (with the 15th Alabama) assaulted the town on the right.

Ewell ordered Trimble's Brigade forward—but not the 15th Alabama, which was kept in reserve. As Oates and his men watched closely, resting on their guns, Taylor's men moved smartly forward. They exchanged fire with the federals on the left, while the rest of Ewell's Division converged on the town from the right. Banks was caught in a vise. Again. "Now the firing opened heavily on the Strasburg Pike and southern suburbs of the town," Oates wrote. "A battery in the town was firing vigorously on Trimble's three regiments engaged, and a movement was made by a body of Federals to flank him on the right." The 15th acted quickly, marching to Trimble's aid, maneuvering around a Yankee artillery battery, which had moved to intercept its march. Wet to the waist "with cold dew," Cantey led the 15th Alabama forward, forcing the battery back. By then the battle was nearly over. From his position as a company commander on a ridge east of Winchester, Oates assayed the tableau laid out before him. "Our comrades were now in plain view," he wrote, "driving the Yankees through the streets, and the citizens, whom they had so long oppressed and insulted, shouted to our men from their doors and windows and cheered them on." Banks's men ran through the town and out the other end, north along the bed of the valley railroad.

Spurred on by Trimble, Cantey's men gave chase, attempting to intercept the retreating federal column by running for two miles through thick woods and open fields. It was worth the effort. The 15th emerged from the woods in time "to see the Yankees go out of sight, running pell-mell, the road strewn with guns, cartridge-boxes, hats, cloaks, coats, canteens, and knapsacks." The foraging that had fallen to others was now afforded the 15th, who reprovisioned themselves from the spoils left by the frightened bluecoats. Isaac Trimble could hardly contain his enthusiasm. "The pluck and enthusiasm displayed by my brigade in marching, hungry and partly barefoot, to overtake the retreating foe, and the ready courage and calmness with which they encountered the enemy and met his fire, and the readiness with which my staff officers bore orders cannot be too highly commended," he wrote in his report to Ewell. Banks made no report at all, having decided that it was now impossible to speak of the bravery of retreating troops. Winchester was a debacle.

After a two-day rest the 15th was on the move again, this time north toward Harpers Ferry. So far, at least, Jackson's plan (whatever it was) seemed to be working. His army, with Ewell's Division, had captured over 3,000 prisoners, 9,000 rifles, and two rifled cannon, as well as badly needed medical supplies. Banks fell back, hoping to meet Jackson on friendlier ground. But the fight for Harpers Ferry, just seventy-two hours after the jaunt at Winchester, never happened: "We barely got in sight of the place," Oates remembered. "About 10 o'clock A.M. we were put on a forced march back to Winchester, and reached our old camp at that place about one hour after dark, a distance of thirty miles." The breakneck march led Oates's Alabama men to believe that something was terribly amiss—that, for the first time, Stonewall Jackson had somehow miscalculated. They were right. Jackson was surrounded.

While Jackson was chasing Banks north, Union forces under John Frémont (many of them recovering from the pounding Jackson had given Milroy at McDowell just three weeks ago) were racing north through the valley. Frémont hoped they would be joined by Union General Shields, who marched yet another army through the eastern Shenandoah gaps to Front Royal. Jackson was suddenly faced by three armies (of Frémont, Shields, and Banks) converging on him from the south, east, and north. There were 50,000 bluecoats in all, facing

12,000 exhausted and tattered rebels. Jackson reacted quickly. Ignoring Banks, he ordered his army to march south, past Frémont and Shields, hoping to slip the northern noose before it could close. Midnight on the thirtieth found Oates's Henry County men beyond Winchester, in a camp just off the Valley Pike. At dawn they were up and on the road again, marching south toward Strasburg. "No one could conjecture where we were going," Oates admitted. "But just before we reached the five-mile post [outside of Winchester], about 11 o'clock, two batteries went to the front in double-quick time, unlimbered and opened fire."

The 15th formed into line of battle, moved forward, and, as at Front Royal, topped a hill to find a Union army spread out on the plain below them. It was Frémont with 20,000 soldiers, all bent on redressing the beating Jackson had given Milroy back in early May. The battle seemed set in an almost pristine, tableau fashion. Jackson deployed two artillery batteries, which lobbed shells into the forming blue lines. Frémont responded, straightening—or "dressing"—his lines. The Alabama men prepared for battle, priming their weapons, readying themselves to move forward. But just as they were set to step off, the blue lines inexplicably moved back, south and then west of the town. Frémont was withdrawing, apparently spooked by the gray host before him. Seeing his opening, Jackson formed his men into columns and hurried them south past the closing Union pincers, which slammed shut behind him. It was the closest Jackson ever came to defeat. "Banks, reinforced, would have closed in on his rear and thus would the fame of the immortal Stonewall and his 'foot cavalry' been ingloriously terminated," Oates later reflected.

Jackson slipped past Frémont, taking the Valley Pike south to Harrisonburg in yet another of his hellish marches. All through the rest of that day, June 1, Jackson urged his exhausted men on, though Union cavalry and Frémont's troops continually harassed his column. The heat abated, but then the rain came, in sheets. Hundreds of men fell out along the Pike, exhausted. "We would march a mile or two," Oates remembered, "and form line of battle across the road, facing to the rear, when they would halt and open on us with artillery. We would then move on again. At night some other brigade would take the rear. It rained every day and night. The road was shoe-mouth deep in mud. My feet were blistered all over, on top as well as the bottom. I never was so tired and sleepy." On June 3, Jackson's soldiers burned the bridge behind them at New Market and continued their march south. Jackson studied his maps, searching for a place to rest his army. On Friday, June 6, the 15th Alabama finally halted, near Port Republic, seven days after they had left Harpers Ferry. They slept, finally, in the open on a ridgeline in a grove of maple trees near a small village called Cross Keys.

❦

Ewell's Division was up at dawn, June 7, facing north, waiting for Frémont to attack. They were alone. The previous evening, Jackson had taken the balance of his army farther south to Port Republic, to intercept Shields's troops, who were racing from the east in a vain attempt to link up with Frémont. Jackson was now, once again, right in the middle of two enemy armies—both within easy marching distance. The day was strangely quiet. The Alabama men were tired but confident and noted that the next day was the Sabbath, which made it highly unlikely Jackson would do battle. That meant another day of rest with the Battle of Cross Keys—if Frémont was to choose battle—coming on Monday. But that was not the way it happened. Early on Sunday morning, Frémont sent his troops forward into the sun in long lines, driving in the thin ranks of Confederate pickets that protected the main rebel line. The handful of southern pickets came tumbling back into Cantey's regiment with the Union troops moving forward through a small valley toward them.

The Battle of Cross Keys was a shambling, confused affair that lasted no longer than the jaunt at Front Royal. Frémont sent a part of his army of 10,000 volunteers in ragged lines up a hill at Ewell's brigades, who took the shock of the assault and then, in two distinct volleys, killed more than 300 bluecoats. Frémont pressed the attack and Trimble responded. The fighting was ferocious. At one point, the 15th Alabama became exposed, its men suffering a galling fire from left and right. Cantey ordered their retreat. Trimble agreed, sending the regiment down a fence line and to the right to meet a Union flanking movement. "Away we went for about a mile through wheat fields, crossing two or three rail fences, not firing a shot, and nothing that I could see but a line of skirmishers in hot pursuit, firing up [at] us and doing some execution, until Courtney's battery open on them from a hill in our front," Oates later wrote. "Lieutenant Mills, of Company E from Dale County, was killed, and William Toney, of Company K, from Barbour County, one of the brightest and best boys in the regiment, was mortally wounded."

The 15th ran along a last fence line, was halted, and faced to the north. Out across a field of ripening buckwheat, several hundred yards distance, German immigrants ("Dutchmen," the rebels called them) of Blencker's Division formed and moved forward. The 15th opened, but too soon, sending the Union column to the right, where the fire seemed to have slackened. There, to the right of the 15th, the 21st Georgia, which had held their fire, now let loose with a single volley "which just mowed them down in piles." The bluecoats reeled and fell back. Cantey's men were ordered to the right again and stood in line, taking punishment from a battery of northern artillery. After a short pause, Trimble, riding out along the line, ordered an all-out attack. "Ewell's whole division now advanced," Oates recalled, "and for a few minutes the engagement became general." By nightfall, Frémont had had enough and ordered his men to break off the engagement.

Three miles south at Port Republic, Stonewall Jackson heard the battle raging at Cross Keys but, fearing the appearance of Shields, thought better of ordering his men north to help Ewell. Instead, when he heard Ewell had bested Frémont, he ordered the Virginian to bring his division south. His plan was to pounce on Shields before Frémont could attack again, then turn back north—scoring a double victory. So far, at least, Jackson's plans had always seemed to work. But not this time—when he sent his own Stonewall Brigade forward across the Shenandoah River the next morning, they were met with massed fire from Union troops hidden by a thick woods. Stung by the fire, the southerners nevertheless pressed the attack. They paid a heavy price; within minutes the brigade was met with a fire so intense that it dropped dozens. The brigade was pinned, taking heavy losses. Worse yet, Ewell was nowhere in sight.

Just as Jackson's troops were on the verge of melting away, however, Richard Taylor's Louisianians, the lead element of Ewell's Division, arrived on the battlefield from Cross Keys. Their presence tipped the balance. Taylor ordered three charges in all, two of them against "double-shotted cannister," artillery rounds that sent out hundreds of iron balls into his well-formed ranks. Taylor's men, standing in the wheat, took the fire and returned it, but began to move back. By then more of Ewell's troops had arrived at the scene and Ewell threw two brigades (but not the 15th, which was to bring up the rear) into the fight. They went forward, across a fence line and into the Union lines. Flanked by these two brigades, Shields's attack stalled and his lines began to evaporate, falling out first on the left, before Taylor, and then all along the line. Jackson shouted in exultation: "He who does not see the hand of God in this is blind, sir. Blind!"

It was, indeed, as if God Himself had intervened to even the odds facing Jackson and Ewell. But victory was not certain. Richard Taylor's men raged through the woods at Shields's troops, cutting through the undergrowth only to find themselves suddenly on the bluecoats' flank. A battery was taken and then another, but the Union men fought back, swinging their rifled muskets in hand-to-hand combat. Taylor won the moment, but not the day. His Louisianians were now faced with a mass of blue lines, advancing on them across a wheat field. He was pushed back, his men slowly retreating back over the ground they had just won. Taylor saw the end: "There seemed nothing left but to set our backs to the mountain and die hard." It was then that the rest of Ewell's Division appeared, its lines emerging specterlike from a long stand of woods—stage left. It was not the first time that southern arms were blessed by good timing, but it would not happen often. The southern lines stabilized before darkness, bringing an end to the battle.

Port Republic was a clear victory for the Confederacy, though dearly bought—more than 800 men fell dead or wounded on the battlefield. Trimble's Brigade set the standard for Jackson's army. From Winchester to Port Republic, Trimble suffered 235 casualties of approximately 1,000 men of all arms—more than 23 percent wounded and dead. There were higher percentages in the war, but the numbers here do not reflect the fact that hundreds had fallen out during the march south, so it is likely that the percentage of dead and wounded was much higher. Jackson's aides admitted as much, commenting that the Battle at Port Republic was a desperate affair.

Port Republic brought down the curtain on Jackson's Valley Campaign—arguably the most brilliant ninety days of fighting in American

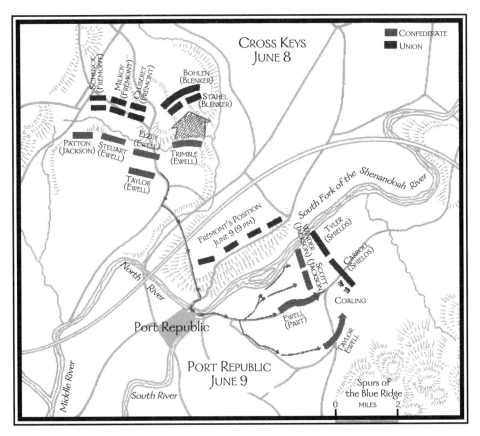

## The Battles of Cross Keys and Port Republic

Jackson's genius was at its best in the upper Shenandoah. While Ewell battled Frémont at Cross Keys, Jackson awaited Shields at Port Republic. On June 9, Jackson brought Ewell south. William Oates saw action in both battles.

warfare. The campaign is studied by military scholars because of its combination of speed and surprise. Looking back on these events years later, William Oates could hardly bring himself to believe that he had been one of its participants. His summary of Jackson's accomplishments remains one of the most elegant:

> In three months, Jackson had marched six hundred miles; fought four pitched battles, seven minor engagements, and daily skirmishes; had defeated four armies; captured seven pieces of artillery, ten thousand stands of arms, four thousand

prisoners, five hundred wagons and teams, three hundred head of beef cattle, and a very great amount of stores, inflicting on his adversaries a known loss of ten thousand men, with a loss upon his own part comparatively small.

Jackson's Valley Campaign had also saved Richmond, siphoning large numbers of Union soldiers from McClellan's army, which was then moving on the Confederate capital, where they now faced a rebel army under Robert E. Lee.

☙———◆———❧

Lee was the commander of the Army of Northern Virginia by accident. After his victory at Bull Run, Joseph E. Johnston—its first commander—moved his troops quickly south to Richmond and then east along a tapered peninsula formed by the York and James rivers to face George McClellan's Army of the Potomac. When McClellan landed his 105,000 men at Fort Monroe in March 1862, Johnston fell back down the peninsula before him—all the way to Richmond, taking up positions along the Chickahominy River, just east of the city. McClellan believed he was outnumbered and complained that he needed Irvin McDowell's 50,000 men at Fredericksburg to launch a successful attack, but Lincoln kept them in place, fearing that Jackson (then bloodying three Union armies in the valley) would head toward Washington. In fact, Johnston faced long odds since McClellan, far from being outnumbered, had a two-to-one advantage in men. Yet fate intervened: first when heavy rains washed out the bridges of the Chickahominy River, isolating two Union corps on its northern bank; and second when Joe Johnston was wounded.

Johnston attacked McClellan's two isolated corps east of Richmond at the crossroads of Seven Pines on May 31, but his attack turned into a southern version of what Banks, Frémont, and Shields were doing that same day in the Shenandoah Valley. Johnston wanted to assault McClellan with three divisions along three different roads heading east out of Richmond, but his orders were verbal, not written, and only one division—led by North Carolina West Pointer D. H. "Harvey" Hill (Stonewall Jackson's brother-in-law)—got into action, pushing the federals back in a series of costly assaults. Riding along the lines late in the day, Johnston was shot and seriously wounded and command of the army devolved to General Gustavus Smith. The next day brought more of the same, as Georgian James Longstreet sent two brigades forward in an ill-fated attempt to pry an entire division out of its line. The battle finally whimpered out along the edge of the Chickahominy. Richmond was saved, but the southern army faced a crisis. His army outnumbered, its commander wounded, Jefferson Davis ordered his chief military aide to take command.

Robert E. Lee was destined to become the most beloved military commander in American history and its greatest strategist. He did more, with less, over a longer period of time than any other commander of American troops anywhere, ever. But none of the southern soldiers than encamped at Seven Pines could have known that in May 1862. Nor did they believe that Lee's assumption of command would lead to anything more than what Johnston had given them over the past several weeks: retreat, confusing assaults, and more retreat. For many of these soldiers, there seemed no alternative but to make one last stand before Richmond, futile though that might be. At first Lee did little to change their opinion. Instead of grand strategy or patriotic orations, the soldiers were handed picks and shovels and told to dig in. This was more than any self-respecting soldier could stand, and Lee was given the name "King of Spades." That fit well with George McClellan's opinion: "Personally brave and energetic to a fault, he yet is wanting in moral firmness when pressed by heavy responsibility, and is likely to be timid and irresolute in action."

Lee did not hear this, but he acted as if he had. In early June he devised a plan to pry McClellan from before Richmond's gates. He told Jefferson Davis he would hold a small force south of the Chickahominy and slip three divisions north across the river and then down, onto McClellan's exposed right flank. This was to be a roundhouse left hook, but it was clearly a gamble; the lines protecting the capital would be stripped to just 25,000 men. To aid in this effort, Lee ordered Jackson (with Oates's Alabama regiment) to march toward Richmond, hoping that the valley army would arrive at the very instant the divisions of Longstreet, D. H. Hill, and red-shirted Virginian Ambrose Powell Hill would begin their descent on McClellan's right. Jackson hurried his men forward, marching them out of the valley on June 18 for an expected convergence with Lee's left wing on June 25. Jackson later moved the day of the attack back by twenty-four hours, to June 26, and that gave his 15,000 exhausted soldiers one week to cover the 100 miles from Port Republic to the Chickahominy. Time enough, Jackson thought.

On June 26, however, Jackson was nowhere to be found. Instead of linking up with Lee's left, he had inexplicably halted his troops at Hundley's Crossroads, six miles from Lee's line of battle, then bivouacked near Hanover Court House. Longstreet and the two Hills waited expectantly for Jackson to open the battle on the left, which would be their signal to move forward. They waited for one, two, and then six hours. Still Jackson did not appear. Powell Hill had been up at dawn, ready for the attack, but by midafternoon he was nearly raging with impatience. At three P.M., unwilling to wait for Jackson any longer, he ordered his men forward across the open ground toward the small hamlet at Mechanicsville. As he sent his men forward, Lee worried—the day before, McClellan had made a lunge from his lines south of the Chickahominy toward Richmond, at Oak Grove, in what would be the first of seven days of constant battle. The Union troops were repelled by the two skeleton divisions Lee had left there, but he feared McClellan would attack again in greater numbers. He needed Jackson.

But Jackson was asleep, exhausted from the month-long Valley Campaign and nearly delirious from the lack of sleep over the last three days as he marched toward Richmond. But if that was not shocking enough, especially given Jackson's appetite for combat, when the thumping of Hill's cannonade five miles to the south woke him, he still did not order his men forward. Jackson's inability, or unwillingness, to move to the sound of Lee's guns still remains one of the war's great mysteries, but Oates probably comes as close as any historian to explaining the unusual lapse, putting it down to the fact that his "resistless" commander was simply "overcome by fatigue."

Lee, waiting for a report that Jackson was at hand, heard A. P. Hill's troops skirmishing with Union pickets, then grew impatient himself when the fighting grew fierce. Fearing the worst, he sent D. H. Hill's Division to reinforce A. P. Hill's hard-pressed troops, who were then throwing themselves at Union entrenchments along Beaver Dam Creek just to the east of Mechanicsville. For the next five hours, the two

Hills fought an unequal battle with a Union corps along Beaver Dam Creek. When darkness brought an end to the fighting, 1,000 southerners were casualties.

The next morning, Lee met the now fully awake Jackson behind southern lines and ordered him to march his division due east, through the Virginia woods and swamps to the small crossroads inn of Cold Harbor. Lee's plans were explained to Jackson. He expected to put all of his troops—the two Hills, Longstreet, and Jackson—into a concerted effort to smash McClellan's two corps north of the Chickahominy. Following that, he would drive the northerners back, destroying them corps by corps, in detail, like a pugilist homing in on a bloodied opponent. Jackson mounted his horse and got his men moving. He was not a moment too soon. While they were on the road, A. P. Hill's Division was cutting forward through thick swamp and woods, driving in Union pickets. Emerging from the morass, they bumped up against the most formidable entrenchments they had ever seen—a triple line of blue-clad soldiers, Union General Fitz-John Porter's entire corps, spread out on a low ridgeline. Hill paid for the knowledge, his soldiers scrambling through a long, low swale below the ridge before being cut down by the bluecoats. Lee assessed the situation, then rode back north to find Jackson. What he found instead was Richard Ewell's lead division of Jackson's army, marching south to Hill's aid.

Ewell sent his troops in, despite a word of caution that the attack had been tried once and failed. The long gray line, stretching more than one-quarter of a mile through woods and swamp, went forward. On the right, A. P. Hill's men, shot through with exhaustion, cheered them on. To the left of Ewell, Jackson hustled Richard Taylor's brigade forward in support. The Louisiana soldiers, who had exhibited so much toughness in the Shenandoah Valley, pushed Porter's thin line of skirmishers back through the small hamlet of Gaines's Mill and onto his main line. Back in Ewell's ranks one of Oates's men, William A. "Gus" McClendon, a simple farmer from Henry County, remembered the day at Gaines's Mill as one of the hardest fought of the war: "The bombshells bursting, their fragments flying in every direction, hitting a fellow occasionally, and the solid shot crashing through the boughs above our heads, and the commands of officers, all added to the excitement and the noise of the occasion."

It was as exciting for Oates, who could be forgiven for believing he had seen the worst war had to offer at Front Royal, Winchester, Cross Keys, and Port Republic. In all of those battles, however, his company had not lost one man. That changed within minutes of Ewell's attack on Fitz-John Porter, when Sam Dickerson of Dale County was shot through the heart and died instantly. Dickerson's death seemed to signal a new crescendo of violence, for as he was falling, McClendon heard a terrible roar on his left as a Union regiment hidden in a bushy swale poured a massive fire into Taylor's Brigade. The fierce Louisiana "Tigers" were nearly all killed in the volley. Oates's men kept moving forward, up a hill, then down the other side and through a woods, and always, in the distance, Fitz-John Porter's three lines of three divisions waited. It was the first real open battle Oates's company had been in and was much worse than anything he had seen in the Shenandoah. "As well as I remember," Gus McClendon wrote later, "it was about 2 P.M. when we opened fire upon the enemy, and there we remained firing as fast as we could for two or three hours."

By sundown, Oates's men were out of ammunition, though McClendon refused to fire his last round; he saved it for an emergency and lay down with the brigade, awaiting orders. Spurred by this lack of firing, Ewell rode forward and was told by William Oates's brother, John, that the command had run out of ammunition. Ewell told the men of the 15th to hold fast while he raced for reinforcements. Minutes later couriers arrived with "buck and ball." They were followed close behind by reinforcements, the 4th Texas regiment. On a signal the two regiments, the 15th and the 4th, moved forward into the smoke. They were joined on the right and left by regiments and brigades from all of Lee's five divisions.

James Longstreet had suggested the assault, though it seemed a dangerous enterprise. Lee's troops were faced by a well-entrenched triple line and the southern army would be charging across open ground. But Longstreet thought they had little choice, and Lee agreed. Spread out in lines along a three-mile arc below an eminence called Turkey Hill, Lee planned for a breakthrough that would send McClellan's entire army reeling off to the south. If he was lucky, Fitz-John Porter's entire corps might be destroyed. If not, the attack still might unhinge McClellan, who was already unnerved by Lee's impetuous assaults. Oates's

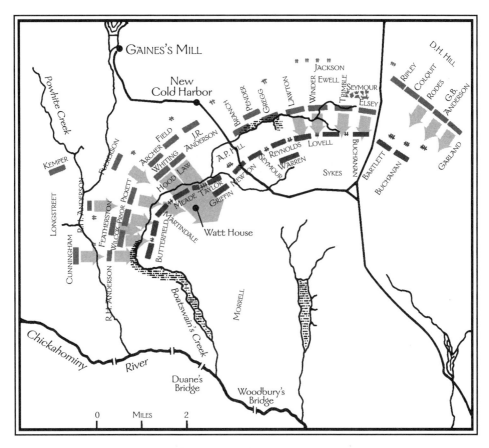

## The Seven Days' Battles

Lee's strategy was to pummel McClellan north of the Chickahominy, trapping most of his army in the tendrils of swamps and woodlands east of Richmond. On June 27, 1862, at Gaines's Mill, Lee accomplished what he had not been able to do during the previous four days: each of his units acted in concert, with Hood and Law leading the way in breaking Fitz John Porter's triple line.

---

men went forward with three regiments of Texans led by John Bell Hood, who would prove to be as tough a fighter as any southern general. There were, in fact, few tacticians who understood the shock of combat as well as Hood, who kept his men moving forward toward the Union lines.

The relentless march apparently had an enormous psychological impact—the first line of Union soldiers scrambled back before the onslaught to a second line. The blue troops opened fire, cutting holes in the rebel charge. But the Texans and Alabamians came on unstaggered. There was a short melee, with men clubbing each other, and then the second blue line dissolved, heading off into the smoke. The gray lines steadied, reformed, and moved forward again, toward the third line of Porter's defense. A volley from the Texans was delivered at close range and the federal line evaporated in the smoke. The massed fire blew a hole a quarter mile wide in the center of the Union line. Longstreet and D. H. Hill's troops widened the breach and entire northern regiments, shaken by the charge, threw down their weapons. Others, running to the rear, attempted to reform and save Porter's Corps from total destruction.

By nightfall, what was left of Fitz-John Porter's three blue divisions were streaming to the rear. Pursuit was impossible. The night enveloped the exultant southern army, which had fought its way to an overwhelming victory in its first engagement under Robert E. Lee. There would be many more ahead, but few would equal the intensity of that attack. It would be remembered fondly, years later, by Confederate veterans as the day they broke Fitz-John Porter's triple line at Gaines's Mill.

Gus McClendon had a special memory. As he moved back to camp from the forward line at dusk, he saw the horrifying and tragic results of war. There was a Confederate soldier shot through the thigh and a Union officer "shot through the bowels," calling for his mother. He helped them, but then went on: "I was so tired and worn out that I left them alone in the dark and returned to camp and went to sleep," he said. When he awakened the next morning he found that many men had not slept at all, but stayed up all night recounting the glory of the charge. He'd had glory enough, he thought: "I claim the honor, if honor it be, of being the first one of Oates's company to fire a gun in this engagement."

# 7

## Kill the Brave Ones

S TONEWALL JACKSON credited the win at Gaines's Mill to the intervention of Hood's Texans. Others disagreed, saying that while Hood had certainly done his part, it was really Charles Winder's Brigade that had done the most damage—or even Lawton's. The disagreement was made in good humor, since the victory seemed to belong to the entire army—the line that assaulted Porter's troops was three miles end to end, from Longstreet on the right through A. P. Hill and Ewell in the middle to D. H. Hill on the left. Alabamian Gus McClendon thought there was glory enough for everyone, and blood too. On this, the third day of what turned into seven days of fighting, 1,483 southern soldiers were killed and over 6,000 wounded. Lee counted it as a victory, but it was not decisive; Porter's troops scampered back to the cover provided by Union gunboats on the Chickahominy. McClellan's army was beaten, but not yet defeated.

McClellan, believing that he faced over 200,000 rebel troops, had clearly had enough. After the battle was over, he called his commanders together to announce that it was time to "save the army," which would retreat or, as he put it, "change its base of operations" to the James River. The race was on; on each of the next three days, from June 29 to July 1, 1862, McClellan pulled the Army of the Potomac back to the safety afforded by his gunboats. Lee desperately struck at his rear guard in a series of clawing, bloody fights: at Savage's Station, White Oak Swamp, and Glendale, battling through the low swampy ground, the chest-high thickets, and impenetrable forests. His army pushed at McClellan, forcing him east and south. Finally the Union commander turned to face his pursuer on the banks of the James River at Malvern Hill.

As fate would have it, the 150-foot artillery-rimmed plateau was held by none other than Fitz-John Porter, who was still smarting from the pounding he had taken at the hands of Hood and Winder just days before. Porter believed the tables might be turned now, if only Lee would order his men across the low swale of ground to his front and up the steep slope. For the Confederate high command, however, such an attack seemed foolhardy, or nearly so, until James Longstreet reported that it might be possible to break Porter's defense by sighting converging artillery fire from opposite points on the line, thus paving the way for a full-scale assault—a "grand" attack. Lee, desperate to get at McClellan, thought Longstreet's idea worth trying, so he gave orders for the bombardment to begin. While the guns were brought forward and put into action, Lee toured the line, searching for an opening in Porter's entrenchments. It was just at this moment, when Lee despaired of finding what he was looking for, that the southern commander received word that there were signs Porter was actually withdrawing.

A twentieth-century aphorism—that anything that is too good to be true probably is—could have been applied at Malvern Hill; but Lee, wanting to destroy McClellan before he could get away, ordered the divisions of Benjamin Huger and John Magruder to exploit the opening. Other Confederate commanders followed, including D. H. Hill, who formed his men and marched them out through a deep woods and onto the open fields below Malvern Hill. What he saw should have convinced him of the futility of any attack; ahead of him Magruder's and Huger's divisions were streaming back, leaving lines of dead on the slopes ahead. Hill advanced anyway, across an open field, and, as Lee himself later described it, "engaged the enemy gallantly." But Hill's assault was also broken, his North Carolinians cut down by the blue-clad men above. Hill was sickened by the results. "It was not war," he said of the attack, "but murder." The next day, McClellan retreated to Harrison's Landing on the James River.

⟡══✦══⟡

The butchery of the Seven Days' Battles before Richmond horrified the North and ended forever any hopes for a quick triumph over the Confederacy. The days when crowds would line the streets of northern cities to shout "on to Richmond" were gone, washed away in the torrential rain that masked McClellan's final retreat, and in the endless list of the dead that appeared in town squares north and south. Sixty thousand men were listed as dead, wounded, or missing during George McClellan's Peninsular Campaign; close to 9,000 of these were killed. There was no getting used to such lists. The most shocking news had actually come two months before, on April 6, when a 45,000-man Confederate army stormed out of the thick southwest Tennessee woods and nearly swamped an army led by Union General Ulysses S. Grant. Shiloh was the first truly bloody battle of the war, accounting for one-half the number who fell before Richmond in just one-third of the time—a scant thirty-seven hours.

By the time of Shiloh, Grant was a household name. After being given command of an army, he set about the task of conquering western Tennessee, which he did with surprising speed, capturing two key Confederate forts—Donelson and Henry—before bivouacking his men at Shiloh. When the commander of Fort Donelson asked Grant for terms, the small cigar-puffing West Point graduate gave a phlegmatic reply, which made "Unconditional Surrender" Grant an immediate hero in the North. That Grant was now a famous general was a shock to his fellow officers in the regular army, who remembered him as a hard-luck soldier who had reacted poorly to the long, boring days of peacetime outpost duty. It had even been reported that Grant resigned his commission after complaints about his drinking.

As McClellan took his army back up the peninsula and Grant moved slowly south, a great fleet of blockaders was put in place to strangle southern shipping, and inroads were made in Confederate strongholds in Missouri, Kentucky, and central Tennessee. The great resources of the Union were being slowly organized, its men put in uniform, its people steeled for the bloody times ahead. This was Grant's strategy all along—that victory lay in "the arithmetic," that if the North traded one of its men for one of the South's the South must lose. Perhaps not immediately, but eventually, and inevitably. War was fighting and killing, Grant thought, and it was best to get on with it.

There were only a few men who had any faith in Grant. One was Confederate General James Longstreet, now fighting with Lee in

Virginia, who had been present when Grant married his cousin Julia Dent at Jefferson Barracks in Missouri. Longstreet liked Grant, served with him during the Mexican War, and thought he was a good soldier. The other was Elihu Washburne, who sized up the squat, quiet, dark-eyed son of a tanner and thought he saw a general. At the outset of the war, Washburne, a Maine native who moved west to become a congressman from Grant's hometown of Galena, was given the opportunity of nominating a man for a brigadier general's star. Washburne sent Grant's name to Lincoln and became Grant's political sponsor.

Recognizing military talent seemed to run as deeply in the Washburn family as politics. At the time of the Seven Days' Battles, Elihu's brother Cadwallader, a former Wisconsin congressman, was leading a cavalry regiment in Missouri, while his other brother, Israel, was serving as the governor of Maine. Like Elihu, Israel was always on the lookout for local military talent that would enhance his own political fortunes. Fortunately, the war with the South gave every politician a golden opportunity to do so, especially since the officer ranks of the regular army were too small to meet the need for talented battlefield commanders. The result was that there was keen competition among state governors not only to fill volunteer quotas, but to produce successful commanders. So when Israel Washburn received a letter from Joshua Chamberlain asking for a commission in the volunteer forces, the Maine governor immediately proposed that the talented Bowdoin professor be awarded command of a Maine regiment.

Chamberlain's letter to Washburn was the result of months of plotting. After nearly one year of watching men march off to war, Chamberlain wrangled a two-year leave of absence from Bowdoin under the pretense that he was intent to study and travel in Europe. In fact, he had no intention of doing so, being persuaded that his "irresistible impulse" to join the fight must be satisfied. He was desperate to get to the war, had told his wife and family of his desire, and had even talked about it personally with fellow Bowdoin graduate Oliver Otis Howard, who had returned to Brunswick to recuperate from the loss of his right arm, the result of a wound he suffered at Seven Pines. Recognizing that the Army of the Potomac needed men like Chamberlain, Howard urged him to ask for a commission as an officer of Maine volunteers. Howard thought Chamberlain's request for a commission would be readily accepted, since Maine was required to find five regimental commanders in July and eight in August to fill Lincoln's call for 300,000 volunteers.

There was more to it than that, of course. With the reputation of Maine riding on every appointment, Governor Washburn wanted to find the right men for the job, who were both educated and had experience in leading others. For Washburn, Chamberlain's request, which explained that "I have always been interested in military matters and what I do not know in that line I am willing to learn," was a godsend. Chamberlain's letter was seconded by a powerful recommendation from Adjutant General John L. Hodsdon, who said that Chamberlain was "a gentleman of the very highest moral, intellectual, and literary worth," and by John D. Lincoln, a Brunswick physician, who issued a prescient recommendation: "[Chamberlain] is as capable of commanding a Regt. as any man outside of a West Point graduate."

There were detractors among Chamberlain's colleagues at Bowdoin, however, who did not want to see him leave the college. In part, some of the faculty and administration felt betrayed by Chamberlain, especially because he had kept his request to Washburn so secret. The first intimation that he was at all interested in going to war came in a report in the pages of the local newspaper, which hinted at his pending appointment. The report was followed by a spate of rumors that he would be named to head one of Maine's newly formed regiments, an appointment that would make him a colonel in the Union army. Chamberlain told Washburn that he was not qualified for such a rank, but such modesty did not matter to his Bowdoin colleagues, who showed a touch of envy that Chamberlain was going off to war while they remained at home.

The anti-Chamberlain movement was led by mathematics professor William "Chalkboard" Smyth, who feared that Chamberlain's loss might upset the precarious balance between liberals and conservatives at Bowdoin. His protest, however, went well outside the bounds of acceptable criticism. Smyth enlisted a number of Maine politicians in his campaign to keep Chamberlain at Bowdoin and hinted that not only was Chamberlain needed at Bowdoin, he was too much of an intellectual to make a good soldier. Such politicking had little influence on Washburn and even less on Chamberlain. When Washburn offered Chamberlain a lieutenant colonelcy in the newly formed 20th Maine on

August 8, Chamberlain accepted. By mid-August he was in uniform and facing a group of new recruits at Camp Mason in Portland.

The 20th Maine was a typical regiment of typical men; its ranks were filled with farm boys, fishermen, and lumbermen, with a small quota of drunks, thieves, and heroes. Like many other of the thousands of regiments organized during the war, the 20th's first exposure to war was the killing routine of drill and training and the acclimation of each soldier to camp life. For many of the regiment's soldiers, it was their first time away from home. Few wrote for posterity intending to provide a historical record, but rather they wrote to reassure fathers, brothers, sisters, wives, or sweethearts. Still, their descriptions of camp life are fascinating and often at sharp variance with the snapshots of glory and gore that make up our vision of the conflict. "I am writing in our tent with a rough board across my knees sitting on a blanket on the ground," a young recruit by the name of William Lamson wrote his sister from Camp Bangor on August 4. "We arrived here . . . a little before 8 this morning. We stopped at Kenduskeag from 12 till 5. . . . Seven of our men are down town three are down to the saloon (there are two on the camp ground) getting pictures. A Garland man, Bill something is curled up in our tent sleeping off a drunk."

Eventually Lamson and his company left Bangor for Camp Mason, where they met Joshua Chamberlain, the regiment's newest, and first, lieutenant colonel and the unit's second-highest-ranking officer. It must have been a daunting experience for Chamberlain, who had never commanded more than a classroom. Worse still, Chamberlain was alone, since the unit's commander, Adelbert Ames, was not due to arrive for several days. This meant Chamberlain was charged with teaching his recruits the fundamentals of a life that he had never led. Fortunately for Chamberlain, Major Charles Gilmore, an ambitious veteran of the 7th Maine, helped to take the new recruits in hand. Gilmore had been in the field since 1861 and served during the Peninsular Campaign. More important, Gilmore learned about army life and combat from Winfield Scott Hancock, one of the Army of the Potomac's finest commanders. Gilmore arrived in Portland having spent hours in the running fight at Savage's Station and therefore knew it would take more than simple drill to prepare the 900 new recruits of the 20th Maine for war. Gilmore took command of the regiment until Ames arrived.

Ames was a striking man, given to poses in profile—but he lived up to his rugged looks and serious demeanor by commanding respect from nearly everyone he met. A native of Rockland, Maine, he had led a life of youthful adventure by signing on as a sailor and then a mate on a clipper ship, before returning home and gaining a place in the West Point class of 1861. He excelled at war. At the Battle of Bull Run, Ames commanded an artillery section and, though wounded, refused to leave the field. He was borne off finally, weakened by loss of blood, but his bravery won him a commission as a major in the regular army. At Malvern Hill, his battery shredded the ranks of the onrushing Confederates. He was promoted to lieutenant colonel and on August 20 was appointed the first colonel of the 20th Maine.

Chamberlain's admiration for Ames grew from the moment he met him. Ames was as impressed with Chamberlain, believing he just might have the spark of leadership that was sorely lacking in the Army of the Potomac. Along with Chamberlain and Gilmore, Ames could count on support from Ellis Spear, a Wiscasset schoolteacher and company commander who seemed one of the more capable new soldiers, and from Captain Henry Merriam of Company H. Back in the ranks were good men, Ames thought, including Chamberlain's brother Tom, who enlisted as a simple soldier. In general, Ames liked what he saw of the rough-hewn men of the 20th—they were green, but willing. Ames quickly imposed a strict regimen at Camp Mason, including a constant round of inspections, drill, instructions in camp hygiene, more drill, and exact attention to the manual of arms.

On August 29, 1862, complete with new uniforms (Chamberlain's was tailor-made) of dark blue coats and dark blue pants (an oddity, as most trousers in the Union army were light blue), the regiment was given its first orders. They were to report to Portland on September 1, where they would be transported by ship to Washington. Ames assumed they would then be added to the Washington defenses or shipped out either to the Army of the Potomac or the newly formed Army of Virginia.

Chamberlain spent the next several days preparing the regiment for its journey, but took time during his last day in Maine, on August 31, to visit with Fannie and the Reverend Adams. Later that afternoon he marched with the 979 officers and men of the 20th Maine through Portland to the railroad station. He carried a note from his father, who gave him his blessing, telling him to "take care of Tom" and to "come home with honor."

❧

As Joshua Chamberlain was making his way from Bowdoin to war, William Oates and the 15th Alabama were making their way from Richmond north, in pursuit of the army of Union General John Pope. Pope was a pretentious little man who so angered Robert E. Lee with his puffery that the southerner took to calling him "that miscreant." The trouble with Pope had started almost as soon as McClellan was tucked safely away at Harrison's Landing back on July 2. Lee decided to leave McClellan there, safe under the daunting fire of the Union gunboats on the James River, and gingerly drew off a portion of the bloodied Confederate army to the northwest to face Pope's 50,000-man Army of Virginia. He sent Stonewall Jackson north, leaving Longstreet on the peninsula, eyeing the kenneled McClellan. When it was clear that McClellan's men were boarding boats for Washington, however, Lee quickly pulled Longstreet back west to help Jackson.

John Pope brought groans of despair to everyone, North and South, when Lincoln first brought him east from Illinois. Lincoln hoped that while McClellan kept the pressure on Richmond from the east, Pope would march on the Confederate capital from the north. Pope, who had first met Lincoln in Springfield before the war, assured the president that that was exactly what he had in mind. Within a few short days, he had mustered the dregs of the Washington garrison and combined them with units smarting from Jackson's offensive in the valley (Frémont, Banks, and McDowell), and marched them out of the capital and down the Orange and Alexandria Railroad. But Pope thought that his first order of business was to issue an address to his soldiers. "I have come to you from the West," he told them, "where we have always seen the backs of our enemies." He then implored them to end their constant talk of holding lines and "taking strong positions" and finished by saying that success "and glory" are "in the advance" while "disaster and shame lurk in the rear."

These remarks brought hoots from the men in blue, many of whom had slogged daily through the Shenandoah Valley in pursuit of Stonewall Jackson. John Pope, they thought, had probably seen the backs of plenty of rebels—he had proven so, in defeating them in a battle for Island Number Ten in the Mississippi—but none of these rebels "from the West" had been commanded by Jackson, Longstreet, or Lee. Fitz-John Porter, a man of few words and many opinions, put much less thought into John Pope than that; he read the address, heard Pope's boast, and promptly labeled him "an ass." That Pope took to signing his dispatches "Headquarters in the Saddle" brought louder hoots, especially from men who were now confident enough to even make fun of the beloved McClellan (the sight of even one lone dog running in fear could bring down cheers of derision that the animal was "changing its base"), let alone a strutting, self-important soldier like John Pope.

Before Lee sprinted north in pursuit of Pope, he reorganized his army, creating two "commands" under Longstreet and Jackson, his most trusted lieutenants. This was not a difficult decision, though Jackson's inability to arrive on time for the Seven Days' Battles had cast some doubts on his abilities. Some of Lee's rank and file critiqued Jackson's performance by saying that he had actually gotten his name at Bull Run from a complaint that, while others fought, Jackson stayed put "like a damned stone wall." Lee, however, never doubted him.

Lee's reorganization reflected Jackson's and Longstreet's personalities. Jackson was adept at playing hide and seek, as his Valley Campaign proved (his new command included seven brigades of hard-marching veterans); Longstreet's head-down intensity made him the army's hook to Jackson's jab. The idea, or so Lee believed, was a combination of speed and surprise. While Jackson set up the opponent, Longstreet would hang back, bringing his twenty-eight powerful brigades into the balance at precisely the right moment. This is what Lee had in mind for Pope, to whom he now gave his full attention. When Pope brought his army south to Culpeper, Lee ordered Jackson to intercept him. To add power to his punch, on July 27 Lee ordered A. P. Hill to join Jackson at Gordonsville. "I want Pope suppressed," Lee told Jackson.

Jackson took his army, including the 15th Alabama, to Gordonsville and then, on August 7, north on the road to Culpeper. The men were in fine spirits, enjoying the warmth of the Virginia summer—a far cry from their shoe-sucking slog through the swamps east of Richmond—but all was not right in Jackson's army. There were changes in the ranks, results of the Seven Days' Battles, including a spate of new commanders and recruits. While most of the soldiers were outfitted with new uniforms and weapons, many of them gleaned from piles of discards left from McClellan's army, the changes in command had left some dissatisfaction. For soldiers only recently acclimated to the ways of war, the loss of friends to wounds and death and the replacement of unfit commanders marked a difficult transition. This was true of the 15th Alabama.

The most important change came at the top of the regiment, when James Cantey reported sick after Gaines's Mill. Alexander Lowther was appointed to replace him, a move that did not appeal to William Oates, who took a strong disliking to the major. Lowther had a number of qualities in common with Pope: he was overweening and given to broad statements of bravery. Oates went so far as to claim that Lowther was given command of the 15th illegally, having been appointed as the regiment's major by Cantey back in Alabama, when the more proper, and traditional, course would have been to have him elected. Oates thought Cantey's actions poisoned the men against Lowther from then on. "[Lowther] was the Colonel's warm personal friend, they had served in Mexico together, and it was natural for the latter to try to secure his promotion," Oates later argued, "but he should have done it by fair means."

Oates also believed he had earned the right to command because he had proved himself a better soldier, both during the fight under Jackson in the valley and again at Gaines's Mill, where he had been in the thick of the fight against Fitz-John Porter. Nor was there much doubt that Oates had gained the respect of his men. After the war he would describe himself as a commander who "gave his men as good care and attention as any captain" and "always contended strenuously and doggedly for their rights," and there is no evidence of any disagreement with his description. Even so, we have only Oates's word about Lowther and Lowther's war record. In this, at least, throughout the months ahead, Oates's judgment of Lowther seemed justified—when there was a fight, Lowther found some excuse to be elsewhere. Oates despised him.

The 15th Alabama was not the only regiment in Lee's army grappling with the changes that resulted from the Seven Days' Battles. From Gaines's Mill until the end of the war, in fact, the Army of Northern Virginia battled just as often with itself as it did with the Yankees. Petty jealousies, stark ambitions, stubbornness, and the competition for honors all conspired to make even the high command a constant skirmish line of contending personalities. Lee did his best to balance these ambitions and soothe frayed nerves, but even he lost his patience on occasion. Such interplays might well fill a stout volume of reminiscences on the always pending duels, arrests, sulks, accusations, criticisms, verbal blasts, and demands for explanations, retractions, and apologies that plagued the army. So it was that Lee sent A. P. Hill to Jackson in central Virginia with these cautionary words: "A. P. Hill you will, I think, find a good officer, with whom you can consult, and by advising with your division commanders as to your movements, much trouble will be saved you in arranging details."

Transferring Hill was Lee's way of separating contentious personalities—in this case keeping the temperamental Hill away from Longstreet, who was furious when Hill was given credit by the Richmond papers for single-handedly winning the most important engagement of the Seven Days' Battles. James Longstreet publicly objected, issuing a criticism of Hill that appeared in the pages of the *Richmond Whig*. Hill was stung by the rebuke and asked Lee for a transfer. The matter would have ended there, but Hill refused to receive any further orders from Longstreet, whereupon Longstreet had him arrested. Hill then challenged Longstreet to a duel. Exasperated, Lee sent Hill north to Jackson—which is where he was on August 9, eight miles below Culpeper, when John Pope attacked him.

⊙━━◆━━⊙

On August 9, in a textbook deployment, Pope sent his cavalry forward as a screen south of Culpeper, then sent troops under Nathanial Banks (who had met Jackson already, at Winchester) headlong into Jackson's army along a small creek at the base of Cedar Mountain. Banks deployed his men in broad but powerful battle lines, then sent them forward through a thick woods at the base of the mountain, where they ran end-on into a division commanded by Charles S. Winder, a

Marylander and veteran of Jackson's Valley Campaign. Winder's troops crumpled like blown paper. Only Ewell held, though just barely, on the right. Jackson himself, seeing his left wing go, rode into the woods to rally his troops. Banks's men kept coming, booming and hooting through the forest, where Jackson was reforming his lines. Oates saw all of this from his vantage point on a small outcropping on Cedar Mountain, just yards in advance of his regiment, which had been placed in reserve.

"While the artillery duel was progressing our lines advanced and so did the enemy, and I witnessed the shock from the mountain top," Oates wrote after the war. "It was a grand sight." What was not so grand was the pursuit of a suddenly tenacious foe. Oates's men were ordered forward along a small stream and halted. "While there a shell exploded within a few feet of my face, but I received no injury except that a few grains of the powder struck in my face. A solid shot struck a man in Company F (I am unable to give his name) and only some few fragments of him were ever found. He had a pair of pants rolled up, which he carried under his arm, and they were carried away and could not be found." That night, Jackson began to maneuver around Pope, moving to Gordonsville, then striking out north. From that moment, on the night of the ninth and for two weeks following, Pope had little idea where Jackson had gone. It was only on August 20 that the man who had "never seen the rebels except their backs," fell back in confusion toward Manassas, thereby exhibiting, as Oates said, "that interesting part of his own anatomy."

Oates's regiment marched north with Ewell's Division, passing the limp bodies of two men "hanged to the limb of a tree." They were Confederate soldiers who had deserted to the Union and then were recaptured by the rebel cavalry and ordered hanged by Jackson. On the twentieth, Oates was wounded by the fragment of an artillery shell in a small skirmish near the Rapidan and for a time the "blood ran down my arm pretty freely, but as the injury was slight I did not retire from the field." The rain came down in sheets that night, soaking Oates, his men, and Ewell's Division. It was one of the few times, amid the carnage, that the Alabamian turned reflective, a fact he put down to the watery torrent his men suffered through.

"I have no recollection of any considerable battle having been fought, but that it was almost immediately followed by copious rains," he later wrote. "The superstitious have said that it was the intervention of Providence to wash from the earth the human gore, etc., but I don't think that the blood of man is held in such high esteem by the Great Creator of all things as to cause Him to interfere with the uniform and perfect operation of His laws for any such purpose. I prefer to attribute the rain to natural and philosophical causes, and am quite certain that the loud noise—the heavy shocks of the atmosphere produced by the artillery firing—causes the rain. If not too expensive, when the farmers' crops are suffering from the drought, it might be well to fire big guns in the neighborhood to bring the rain. I had rather risk it than a prayer meeting."

God was ever-present to the men of both sides of the conflict throughout the war—and to Oates, Chamberlain, and Lincoln. Each of the three turned to God during the war; Chamberlain prayed for deliverance and Oates for the intervention of Providence. Abraham Lincoln prayed for peace. During his campaign for Congress in Illinois more than a decade earlier, Lincoln was forced by his opponent to reaffirm his faith in God, but he did so reluctantly. He did not deny the existence of a Divine Being, he said smoothly, knowing full well that that was the same as saying that he believed in one. The explanation was enough, however, to satisfy constituents who believed that a man's religion was his own business—so long as he had one. Lincoln was not a churchgoer, the true litmus test of religion for that time, but he was deeply religious and, as the war ground on and the lists of the dead grew longer, he often reflected on the place of Divine Will in the contest.

Lincoln felt helpless. Try as he might, he seemed powerless to affect events—to spur McClellan to move, to inspire the North with a single-minded purpose, to end the constant sniping among the leaders in his own army, to bring dry roads and good intelligence to John Pope, and hope to a nation shattered by death. Nothing worked. The more he reflected on the war, the more convinced he became that the fate of the nation was not in his hands at all, but rather, that he was only an instrument of some great purpose. He wrote these thoughts down in the wake of the Seven Days' Battles, his writing hand forming the disciplined arcs of nineteenth-century penmanship, the letters distinctive and personal:

> In great contests each party claims to act in accordance with the will of God. Both may be, and one must be, wrong. God cannot be for and against the same thing at the same time. In the present civil war it is quite possible that God's purpose is something different from the purpose of either party; and yet the human instrumentalities, working just as they do, are of the best adaptation to effect his purpose. I am almost ready to say that this is probably true; that God wills this contest, and wills that it shall not end yet. By his mere great power on the minds of the now contestants, he could have either saved or destroyed the Union without a human contest. Yet the contest began. And, having begun, He could give the final victory to either side any day, yet the contest proceeds.

The issue was slavery—and sin. Lincoln was toying with an idea that was terrible in its breadth, horrifying even to suggest; that southerners and northerners alike (to Lincoln, it was always one nation, not two) were dying because they had tolerated slavery for too long. Such sin could not so easily be washed away by either thunderstorm or shed blood. A toll was being exacted in human lives for a reason, with the final terrible tally known only to God. So it seemed to Lincoln, though not to him alone. It had seemed that way also to Harriet Beecher Stowe, who believed that the coming of war might be God's punishment for the toleration of slavery. She thought the contest would be long and bloody and cautioned her readers that such expiation was only just. She reasoned out the contest in print, making perfectly logical arguments, but when the war came she thundered in a voice that would have made Calvin proud: "The innocent for the guilty!"

Stowe and Lincoln may well have been influenced in their thinking by John Brown, who had been transformed from criminal to martyr in three short years. His prophecy was well known: "I, John Brown am now quite certain that the crimes of this guilty land will never be purged away, but with blood," he wrote during his time in jail. By 1862 Brown was the icon of the abolitionist movement and was fast becoming the unseen spirit of the northern army. In the first year of the war the 12th Massachusetts Regiment, commanded by Fletcher Webster, the son of the statesman Daniel Webster, put new words to an old Protestant hymn that transfigured Brown from icon to blood sacrifice. "John Brown's Body" became the marching song of the Army of the Potomac, confirming to the volunteers and draftees that they were soldiers "in the army of the Lord."

One night in February 1862, an abolitionist and suffragette by the name of Julia Ward Howe heard the song sung by the 12th Massachusetts in their encampment at Washington and returned to her room at the Willard Hotel entranced by its power. She awoke in the middle of the night with the words to the song still running through her head, but as she lay reflecting on Brown, a new poem with the same cadence as "John Brown's Body" began to take form. She got out of bed and began to write out the new words; she folded up the sheets of her poem and sent it off to the *Atlantic* the following day. The magazine published it as "The Battle Hymn of the Republic." The song made the rounds of the Union camps and by the summer of 1862 could be heard distinctly by Lincoln as he sat, waiting for news of the war, in the telegraph office just across from the White House.

> In the beauty of the lilies Christ was born across the sea,
> With a glory in his bosom that transfigures you and me;
> As he died to make men holy, let us die to make men free,
> While God is marching on.

As the 12th Massachusetts marched out of Washington to face Lee, Lincoln wrestled with the idea of translating the battle hymn into reality, of transforming the War *for* the Union into a war *against* slavery. He had rejected the idea again and again; on August 23 (as Oates was marching north against Pope and Joshua Chamberlain was organizing the 20th Maine at Camp Mason) Lincoln wrote to Horace Greeley on the subject:

> My paramount object in this struggle is to save the Union, and is not either to save or destroy slavery. If I could save the Union without freeing any slave, I would do it; and if I could save it by freeing all the slaves, I would do it; and if I could save it by

freeing some and leaving others alone, I would also do that. What I do about slavery and the colored race, I do because I believe it helps to save the Union, and what I forbear, I forbear because I do not believe it would help to save the Union.

At the time Lincoln was writing these words to Greeley, however, he had already finished writing others that were much different. Each day as he waited for news of the war in the telegraph office, Lincoln bent intently over a small desk, writing carefully on a single sheet of paper. The telegrapher, Thomas T. Eckert, watched him: "He would look out the window a little while and put his pen to paper, but he did not write much at once. He would study between times and when he made up his mind he would put down a line or two." At the end of the day, Lincoln folded the paper neatly into his pocket and returned to the White House. The next day he took the paper out again to work on. He did this for many days until he was certain the document was just the way he wanted it. He thought he might present the document after a great Union victory—perhaps one that would be given to him by John Pope.

⚬▬◆▬⚬

That was a forlorn hope. After Cedar Mountain, Jackson moved north along the banks of the Rappahannock, followed by Longstreet; 55,000 southern soldiers in all, who faced over 70,000 Union troops. Pope put the Rappahannock between his army and Lee, which is just what the southern general intended. He sent cavalry commander Jeb Stuart around Pope's far right to Catlett's Station, deep in Pope's rear. Stuart returned with Pope's field jacket and the Union commander's dispatch book—which gave as clear an accounting of the Union army as Lee could ever hope for. On August 24, Lee decided that, while he could not hope to defeat Pope in open battle, he could cause him enormous trouble; so he did what every military textbook advised that a commander should never do: he divided his army, sending Jackson on a long hike to the north to cut Pope's supply line. Jackson set out on August 25, heading straight north in a series of killing marches. Jackson's troops traveled light; knapsacks, extra bedrolls, and even extra rations were left behind. He set his sights on the Union stores at Manassas Junction. After the war, Oates wrote an account of this march North:

> On the morning of the 25th we crossed on a very inferior little bridge, the stream at this point being small and narrow. . . . We passed through the village of Orleans and bivouacked near Salem that night after a long and very fatiguing march. Early the next morning Jackson, with his usual vigor and celerity of movement, had us agoing. We passed through [the] Bull Run Mountains at Thoroughfare Gap. . . . We then marched via the village of Gainesville and reached the Alexandria Railroad at Bristow Station after sunset. . . . We were now completely in Pope's rear and between his army and Washington. We had marched nearly sixty miles in two days, and subsisted mainly on green corn and half ripe apples hastily gathered from the fields and orchards we passed on the march.

Isaac Trimble's brigade, with the 15th Alabama, readily captured Manassas Junction, advancing in line of battle against a group of Union rear-echelon troops that fired once, then again, then ran. The small fight was worthwhile, since the railroad junction contained unimaginable delights that the gray-clad soldiers could have only dreamed of. Jackson's army outfitted itself anew, with pants and shirts and, most important, shoes. But greater delights were in store when the 15th marched out of the junction the next morning. "There was a pile of bacon as large as a small house," Oates remembered in his memoirs, "cut into pieces of convenient size, with hundreds of boxes of hard bread opened and sitting near, and as each regiment marched by on leaving the Junction it was halted for two or three minutes and every man was allowed to help himself to all he could carry." What was left was burned, the smell of frying bacon reaching into the air for miles.

The 15th Alabama marched out of Manassas Junction to Groveton, five miles up the road, then past Groveton to a tree-trimmed ridge rising behind the embankment of an unfinished railroad. There, 22,000 of Jackson's soldiers were already encamped. The 15th fell in, taking its place in a one-mile-long line of battle that ran parallel to the Warrenton Turnpike. Jackson positioned his troops purposely to set an ambush for John Pope, who he hoped would soon bring his army loping up the road in pursuit of the elusive graybacks. If everything worked as planned, Jackson's 23,000 veterans would welcome Pope with an ambush that would shatter his corps and send him scattering back to Washington. Jackson must have loved the fact that, from his vantage point overlooking the turnpike, he could see the top of Henry House Hill two miles away, where he had once stood "like a stone wall."

Jackson remained as patient as he could throughout the long day of August 28, but as the day waned he wondered whether he had overestimated Pope's incompetence. The day moved on, with a variety of reports coming in that Union troops were nearby, but just as they seemed ready to come Jackson's way, they veered off toward Centreville or stopped short of Jackson's position. Jackson, mounted behind the lines, strained to see up the Warrenton Turnpike, keeping one eye on the sun, now halfway down the afternoon sky. Finally, near sunset, a long blue column appeared in the distance, their heads covered with distinctive black hats, and marched up the Warrenton Pike right in front of Jackson's position. Stonewall was ecstatic and, with the sun setting over his right shoulder, ordered his men forward down the hill.

As seemed fitting for this field, the first attack was made by Jackson's old command, the Stonewall Brigade, which opened on the bluecoat column at a distance of several hundred yards. That should have been enough to send the Yankees reeling, but their commander, West Pointer John Gibbon, faced his troops about and returned the fire. This opening exchange seemed to prove the veteran canard that green troops (which is what Gibbon's men were) fought better than veterans, because they did not know any better. Gibbon's four regiments from Wisconsin and Indiana (later to become known as the "Iron Brigade") refused to be budged. Jackson ordered the rest of Ewell's Division to weigh in against the black-hatters, and Ewell ordered his men forward. Only Trimble's Brigade, with the 15th Alabama (now commanded by Isaac Feagin after Alexander Lowther reported sick), was left in reserve. Ewell's men swept down the hill, raised their muskets, took aim—and were met with a timed volley of deadly flame. Men went down all along the line.

Ewell steadied his men, then ordered the right of his line forward in a wheel, designed to flank the federals, lapping around the edge of the buildings of Brawner's farm. "I stood at the end of the woods," Oates later wrote, "and saw more than ten thousand men between sunset and dark march up facing each other in the open field and engage in deadly conflict. Within one minute all was enveloped in smoke and a sheet of fire seemed to go out from each side to the other along the whole length of the lines, with the Confederate right steadily swinging forward and turning on the center as its pivot." At the end of ninety minutes the contest was not yet decided, though Jackson clearly had the advantage in numbers—if only Ewell could bring all of his men to bear. The men of Gibbon's command still stood, unmoved, pouring "volley after volley" into the rebel ranks. With darkness fast approaching, Trimble was ordered forward onto the left of Ewell's line. The battle was now "a long and continuous roll" of musketry.

The 15th Alabama moved forward, down the slope and into a copse of woods, where they met the muscle-hardened farm boys of the 2nd Wisconsin. "We advanced to within hailing distance of each other, then halted and laid down, and, my God, what a slaughter," one of the Wisconsin men wrote in a letter home. "No one appeared to know the object of the fight, and there we stood one hour, the men falling all around; we got no orders to fall back, and Wisconsin men would rather die than fall back without orders." The Alabamians moved through the woods and piled into the ramrod-straight lines of a Wisconsin regiment, but in the twilight the fighting was confused. At one point a report ran through the 15th Alabama that they were firing on friends. A shout to "cease fire" was heard and the musketry died away, but was then followed by another timed volley from the federals. Oates was frustrated by the orders, convinced that the men they were facing were the enemy: "Fire on, men," he shouted to his company, "they are Yankees." But then, only a moment later, the order to "cease fire" was heard again. The confusion cost the Alabama regiment dearly.

"The carnage in our ranks was appalling," Oates later wrote. "Some of the men on the left of the regiment believed so surely that our friends were in front that they refused to fire when I ordered them." Oates's company had suffered severely, reporting at least five dead and thirteen wounded. By the time Oates and his company had sorted out the disaster, darkness had crept into the woods and his men had to grope their way forward. They found a dark blue mass lying neatly in a gully not twenty steps from their own position—all of them dead. Among the rebels, Isaac Trimble, the hard-bitten West Pointer, was down, having taken a bullet in the thigh, and so too was Dick Ewell, his leg smashed. Each army drew off. Lanterns flickered on both sides of the battle line as the wounded were brought to makeshift hospitals in the rear. The 15th Alabama slept in the open, in line of battle, and awoke at dawn for what everyone believed would be a second day of battle. Oates wrote of that day:

> On the morning of the 29th of August, the carnage of the field (which we held) was the most sickening of any I ever beheld. Our dead and wounded were terribly lacerated by the explosion of the balls that struck them. Some of our men, just after sunrise, started a little fire in the edge of the woods in which we had fought, and I had a tin cup on the fire endeavoring to make some coffee, when a Yankee battery, seeing the smoke, threw a conical shell of large field size, which struck the ground about fifty yards off, ricocheted and fell in our little fire, with the fuse burning as it whirled around and around, knocking the fire in every direction. . . . [T]he men [near the fire] sprang to their feet and ran away, and the shell exploded and wounded two of them. I was not hurt, but I confess I was very much frightened.

His breakfast ruined, Oates mounted his horse and rode behind the lines to a small farm, where he enjoyed a breakfast served by "good, hospitable Virginia women." On his way, he passed men of Longstreet's Corps, who had spent the previous day marching to Jackson's relief. Oates had not known they were even there.

But then, neither did Pope.

❦

The previous evening, when the Union general had heard the roar of battle from his headquarters tent eight miles to the east, he had dispatched riders into the night with orders for his army to unite at the small hamlet of Groveton. He was excited by the coming battle, believing that he had Jackson trapped. He now moved to drown the legendary Stonewall in a sea of blue before Lee, with Longstreet's hard-hitters, could come to his aid. Pope spurred his horse forward and prayed that his orders, which had gone out to all points of the compass, would result in the convergence of his 50,000 troops well before dawn and in plenty of time for the double flanking blow he hoped to deliver against Jackson. By early the morning of the twenty-ninth, he had nearly accomplished that feat, bringing three corps under Franz Sigel, Jesse Reno, and Samuel Heintzelman into a line that stretched for three miles, from Bull Run Creek on the right to one mile beyond the Warrenton Turnpike on the left. Ahead, in the woods and along the railroad cut, Jackson's men waited.

But Pope did not attack on the morning of the twenty-ninth. Knowing full well that Jackson always had some surprise in store, he instead sent a messenger pounding back up the turnpike to find Fitz-John Porter's Fifth Corps, which would extend his line farther to the left. This was only a precaution, of course, since Pope confidently believed that Longstreet's 30,000 men were nowhere near. But just to be sure, he placed Fitz-John Porter's Corps well to the south of his main battle line—ready to be called on if needed.

Finally, with all of the troops he wanted on hand, and even the unexpected taken care of, Pope ordered Franz Sigel to start his attack against Jackson. Sigel's First Corps, a polyglot of veterans, volunteers, and immigrants—led by men named Schurz, Krzyzanowski, and Shimmelfennig—wheeled out into the bright eastern sun and marched purposely forward, across the Warrenton Pike and right into the teeth of Jackson's formidable defense. No one believed that the fight against Jackson would be easy, certainly not the voluble and principled Carl Schurz, a Prussian-born Republican Party organizer whose claim to command was that he could deliver the German vote to Abraham Lincoln. His lack of experience belied his ability; Schurz was a bulldog commander. On the morning of August 29, he met his match in the person of A. P. Hill, whose division pounded away at Schurz's compact line of attackers with a fearsomeness that made Ewell's scrape with Gibbon the night before seem mild. In a series of counterpunches that marked the battle for the next two hours, regiments from New York and South Carolina traded volleys at closing distances, then grappled through a woods at the base of the railroad cut until both units were fought to exhaustion.

The battle now moved north, with Pennsylvanian John Reynolds's

Division hitting the center of the Confederate line head-on. Finally, on the right, Pope watched Heintzelman's Corps bloody Jackson's northern wing. By midafternoon, after a solid six hours of fighting, some of it hand-to-hand, Jackson rode off to the right to find Longstreet, whose own corps was now deployed out of sight, waiting expectantly for the order to move forward. Under Longstreet's command were 30,000 veterans deployed in an arc facing Fitz-John Porter's Corps, deployed on Pope's far left flank. Jackson found Longstreet, with Lee, in the rear of his corps, and reported that his troops were sweating and bleeding away the last of their strength along the railroad cut. Lee turned to Longstreet: "Hadn't we better move our line forward?" he asked. He wanted Longstreet to swing his troops forward against Fitz-John Porter and crush Pope's army in a vise.

Coming from Lee this was more than a suggestion, but still something less than an outright order. Longstreet, however, wanted to wait, and cited a report that more Union troops were on the way. "I think not," he said. "We had better wait until we hear more from Stuart about the force he has reported moving against us from Manassas." This was almost too much from Jackson, who now believed his own 23,000 men, or what was left of them, were fighting for their lives. He must have looked long and hard at Longstreet before spurring his horse back to his own line, but he did not object. If Longstreet wanted him to take the brunt of the battle, he would do so. Oates was later reticent about this, reporting only that successive waves of attackers were breaking against the Confederate shoals. A sense of Jackson's intensity is evident in an anecdote that was told again and again after the battle: when a brave federal officer on a white horse was cut down while leading a charge, Isaac Feagin berated his troops for killing such a courageous man instead of capturing him. But Jackson told him, "No Captain, the men are right; kill the brave ones, they lead on the others."

In the midst of this fight, Lee asked Longstreet again whether he thought it best to attack and then, minutes later, he asked again. Three times in all, and each time Longstreet answered no—not yet. Somewhere ahead, Longstreet knew, were Porter's troops, and he wanted to fall on them when they least expected it. If Jackson bore the brunt of the fighting now, Longstreet reasoned, perhaps Porter could be drawn off, leaving the fields in his own front bare. Then, and only then, would he advance, cutting a clear swath all the way into Pope's rear, and perhaps all the way to Washington.

Finally, with darkness coming on, Pope's attack against Jackson ended.

The morning of August 30 found John Pope in good spirits. Not only had he pressed Jackson to exhaustion the day before, it now appeared that the thin gray line of skirmishers left in the railroad cut were what was left of Jackson's command—which, Pope thought, must be retreating. As for Longstreet, Pope was still convinced that the Georgian was back west somewhere, struggling to join the battle. In fact, Longstreet and Jackson were now firmly hinged, their lines coming together just south of the turnpike. Longstreet himself had ridden along his lines, placing his artillery hub to hub facing north and east, so that it could enfilade Pope's attacking forces when they opened the battle. Fitz-John Porter's Corps, just opposite him, Longstreet thought, would be swept out of the way quickly enough. In fact, that is just what Fitz-John Porter feared, for while Pope was convinced that Longstreet was nowhere nearby, Porter knew that his troops were massing in his front and getting ready to attack. Porter told Pope that in a series of breathless messages, but the Union commander ignored him and made his own preparations to continue his attack on Jackson.

Longstreet, Jackson, and Lee had to wait until two P.M. for Pope to order his men to battle. As on the previous day, the federals came on in three two-line waves, as if on a parade ground and without the usual artillery preparation that preceded a battle. Jackson was only slightly caught off guard, ordering his resting troops back into the railroad cut to face the cresting wave of blue. On the federals came, pushing against A. P. Hill's Division of Jackson's command until, like the day before, the Confederate line was near its breaking point. Finally Jackson sent a message to Lee that Longstreet should attack. Lee sent the request on to the Georgian. Longstreet, who had kept his own guns silent, was finally ready and now silently nodded his assent. The lines of artillery barked out in unison, the guns jumping a foot into the air. "Old Pete" then ordered his men forward, across the fields, and into the flank of John Pope's army.

Oates saw Longstreet's advance from his embattled lines, saw the blue soldiers turn to meet this threat to their left and rear, and then moved his own men forward in a general advance. "The scene at this point was indescribably grand," he later wrote. "The Yankees would fall back a short distance, about-face and deliver their fire. The Confederates pressed steadily forward." One Union soldier remembered that the thousands of butternut troops Longstreet had held straining at the leash now "came on like demons emerging from the earth." It was all that Fitz-John Porter could do to keep his command from disintegrating, but he did his best—having warned the scoffing Pope repeatedly over the last day that Longstreet was there right in front of him. But it was not a full rout; here and there along the federal line, units kept fighting, protecting the general retreat to Washington.

As Pope's army was beating a retreat, east, Lee composed a message to Jefferson Davis, announcing the victory at what came to be called Second Bull Run: "We mourn the loss of our gallant dead in every conflict, yet our gratitude to Almighty God for his mercies rises higher and higher each day. To Him and to the valor of our troops a nation's gratitude is due."

# 8

# *All That I Am Called To*

L EE'S VICTORY at Manassas had not been the only great victory for the South in the summer of 1862. On July 24, Confederate General Braxton Bragg—a quarrelsome, migraine-plagued Louisiana planter and West Point graduate—had taken the Army of Mississippi out of its entrenchments around Tupelo and moved it east by rail to Tennessee. In fact the route had been longer: south to Mobile, then by steamboat across the bay and north to Chattanooga, since there was no direct west–east rail line. Bragg's change of base was one of the logistical masterpieces of the war, not unlike McClellan's move to Harrison's Landing during the Seven Days' Battles. There were, however, two major differences—Bragg's army had moved by rail, while McClellan's had moved by foot, and the Confederates intended to end their move by going forward, while McClellan only went back. Bragg gathered his army outside of Chattanooga, issued a patriotic proclamation to his troops, and made for the Kentucky–Tennessee border. By the early fall, he believed, the Confederacy could redraw its northern boundary on the shores of the Ohio River.

Farther west, down the Mississippi River, Vicksburg stood, though assailed continually by the Union navy. The federal intent was to place a stranglehold on the Confederacy's bastion on the Mississippi, thereby cutting the new southern nation in two. Earl Van Dorn, the elegantly handsome and zealous Confederate who was given command of Vicksburg, greeted this new waterborne offensive with a mixture of aplomb and defiance: "Let it be borne in mind by all that the army here is defending the place against occupation," he told Vicksburg's nerveracked citizens. "This will be done at all hazards, even though this beautiful and devoted city should be laid in ruins and ashes." The people of Vicksburg expected the worst, but Van Dorn's victory proved as effortless as his promise.

The Union blockade was broken by the miraculous intervention of the Confederate ironclad *Arkansas*, little more than a square iron box placed tentatively on a single slab, which miraculously outran a fleet of Union boats on the river, slipped past the intimidated Union river navy, and finally scattered the federal fleet. A crowd of Vicksburg citizens stood on the city bluffs to cheer the *Arkansas*'s arrival, though the sides of the ironclad were dented from cannon fire and her gun deck was slick with spilled blood. The victory was celebrated across the South as yet another example of southern ingenuity and courage.

The greatest victory, however, came in Virginia. When the first soldiers of John Pope's routed army started trickling into Washington the day after the debacle at Manassas, Abraham Lincoln realized he had yet another disaster on his hands. Pope, near Centreville, either did not realize he was defeated (in which case he was delusional) or could not bring himself to admit it (in which case he was unfit for command): "I thought it best to draw back to this place at dark," he wired the War Department. "The movement has been made in perfect order and without loss. The troops are in good heart." Translation: the army was not only retreating, it was demoralized.

Two days later, as John Pope was riding at the head of a column on the way into Washington, George McClellan was triumphantly riding out in his role as the newly reassigned army commander. In that instant, with McClellan riding to his new command, John Pope's Army of Virginia went out of existence and the Army of the Potomac was reborn. The decision to reappoint McClellan was made by Lincoln. "We must use what tools we have," he said. Secretary of War Edwin Stanton was flabbergasted, as was much of the rest of Lincoln's cabinet. Stanton hated McClellan and blamed him for inviting the disaster at Bull Run, telling anyone who would listen that McClellan had done everything he could to keep his own troops from helping Pope—hoping thereby to promote his own worth. The claim was not without merit. As Pope raced north in search of Jackson, McClellan put his feelings in a letter to his wife: "I take it for granted that my orders will be as disagreeable as it is possible to make them—unless Pope is beaten, in which case they will want me to save Washington again." He made it sound as if Pope's defeat was exactly what he wanted.

The crisis in command that pervaded the northern armies in 1862 was as bad as any of the infighting that so often plagued Robert E. Lee. The close coterie of officers around McClellan were not only steadfast loyalists and admirers, they fully endorsed his outspoken views of Lincoln, a man whom he viewed with contempt. McClellan, a staunch Democrat, disagreed with Lincoln's conduct of the war, which he believed should be prosecuted on narrow grounds, opinions he had made known in a paper he gave the president during Lincoln's visit to the peninsula in July. "Neither confiscation of property, political executions of persons, territorial organization of States, or forcible abolition of slavery should be contemplated for a moment," he wrote. Freeing the slaves, he said, would mean the death of the Union army. Lincoln had read the paper without comment and put it in his pocket.

Now, in the wake of Pope's defeat, McClellan was again in command. Lincoln had little choice: with Robert E. Lee's legions within marching distance of the capital, McClellan could be expected to give him a fight. At least "Little Mac" knew how to organize an army and give it confidence, which is just what it needed after John Pope mishandled it. Within one week of the Bull Run debacle, McClellan (who was "working like a beaver," as Lincoln himself admitted) had reorganized the army, refitted its battered units, returned the skulkers to their camps, and welcomed regiments of new recruits that poured into Washington from the north. One of these regiments was the 20th Maine, which arrived at Alexandria on September 7, made camp in Washington, then was dispatched back across the Potomac bridges into northern Virginia. On September 12, the 20th was told to strike its tents and head north. Robert E. Lee, they were told, was on his way into Maryland.

The sight of the Army of the Potomac marching north in pursuit of Lee, a streak of blue amid the late summer green, must have been both an impressive and strange sight for the people of Maryland. Never had the farmers and shopkeepers along the old National Road seen so many men, or so much disorganization. But there was no stranger sight than

that presented by the 20th Maine, one of the army's newest regiments—
and one of the army's worst marchers. When the 20th had straggled
into its Virginia encampment out of step and exhausted from its march
from Washington, Colonel Ames was enraged. The march into Maryland was little better. While Ames instructed Chamberlain and his other
officers on the necessity of unit discipline, the regiment was literally
coming apart, dribbling footsore soldiers from its encampment outside
of Frederick all the way back down the road to Virginia.

Chamberlain tried to keep the men in formation on the route north,
but it was a hopeless task. He spent the better part of the first two days
riding up and down the column, attempting to keep the Maine men
together, but only accomplished this task after sunset, when the last
stragglers appeared at the regimental campfires. Ames might have predicted that would happen; the regiment was not only new to the army,
it had undergone only the most rudimentary training. The 20th was
not alone, however. Lincoln's call for 300,000 volunteers had filled the
ranks of the Army of the Potomac with well-meaning but untested
troops; there were over thirty-five new regiments in the army, nearly
one-third of the total. The brigade to which the 20th Maine was assigned contained five other regiments: three from New York, one from
Michigan, and one from Pennsylvania. They were now a part of the
First Division of Fitz-John Porter's Fifth Corps of 15,000 soldiers, the
largest corps in the Union army.

If the breakneck pace bothered Chamberlain, he did not seem to
show it. While other men had lost weight in the weeks that followed the
regiment's organization in Maine, Chamberlain actually filled out.
Army life agreed with him, a fact that apparently surprised his brother
Tom, who wrote home admiringly of how his brother thrived in the
midst of such hardship. For his part, Joshua wrote Fannie often, attempting to calm her fears; but he could not keep his own excitement
out of his letters. He seemed unworried about the dangers that faced
him, and actually seemed to look forward to his first taste of combat. He
felt at home, comfortable, and while he had been in the army for only
three weeks, he and the other men of the 20th had quickly picked up its
young traditions.

Like Lee's army, the Army of the Potomac contained its own group
of oddballs, martinets, and fighters. One of these was Daniel Butter-

field, who gave Chamberlain's Brigade its distinctive field call, later known as "Taps." By the time the 20th marched out of Washington, Butterfield had moved on to higher command, but the brigade remembered him fondly, despite his bad temper. Ambitious and talented, Butterfield seemed just average in an army of colorful characters that included sixty-five-year-old Edwin Sumner (his men called him "Bull Head" for his ability to carry out senseless orders), "Fighting" Joe Hooker (whose name came from an errant newspaper headline: "Fighting—Joe Hooker"), "steel cold" John Gibbon (A. P. Hill's West Point classmate), Israel Richardson (called "Greasy Dick" for his ability to dodge danger), Joseph Mansfield (who owed a prewar promotion to Jefferson Davis), and Ambrose Burnside (the poker-addicted son of a slaveholder whose mutton chops we call sideburns).

The Army of the Potomac was an army of men, not leaders. Despite the embarrassment of the Seven Days' Battles and Bull Run, the northerners could fight, a fact that became clear to Chamberlain in Frederick, Maryland, on the morning of September 14, after his regiment finally made camp. As the Maine men were awaiting orders, they heard the distant thumping of battle, which brought them to a solemn silence. Just miles to the west, McClellan was sending lines of men in blue up the slope of South Mountain, straight into D. H. "Harvey" Hill's dug-in graycoats.

The attack had come as a result of a windfall in the form of a dispatch Lee sent his commanders on September 9. Addressed to D. H. Hill and entitled "Special Order 191," the message fell into McClellan's hands on September 13 after being found, along with three cigars, in a field outside of Frederick. The "Lost Order" detailed Lee's location, the movement of his commands, and his plan of operation. "Now I know what to do!" McClellan exclaimed after he had read it. He ordered his army to turn west and force the gaps of the looming ridgeline of South Mountain that separated the Army of the Potomac from the Army of Northern Virginia. If he could act quickly he would catch Lee with his units strung out north and south. "Here is a paper," McClellan told his staff, "with which if I cannot whip Bobbie Lee, I will be willing to go home. Tomorrow we will pitch into his centre and if you people will only do two good, hard days' marching I will put Lee in a position he will find hard to get out of."

As always, however, McClellan's words moved faster than his orders. His army did not, in fact, move on the thirteenth, but on the fourteenth, when he sent his units up South Mountain to contest control of Turner's and Crampton's gaps. Rebel General D. H. Hill's men fought desperately to hold the gaps against the swarming bluecoats, giving Lee time to gather his scattered army in the valley to the west. Northwest of Hill's position, Longstreet's command received Lee's order to come rapidly south to Sharpsburg, where they would be put in line along the south end of Antietam Creek. At the same time, Lee ordered Stonewall Jackson to bring his troops north from Harpers Ferry. By the afternoon of the fifteenth, Lee had 15,000 men of his army ("half famished and looking like tramps," a Maryland woman commented) in line facing east. Just across Antietam Creek, McClellan rode forward to study the rebel defenses. He would attack tomorrow, on the sixteenth, McClellan said, since it was too late today.

Predictably (for this, as Lee knew, was McClellan) the sixteenth came and went and still the Army of the Potomac did not attack. Instead, McClellan spent the day "examining the ground," "finding fords," "clearing approaches," "bringing up reinforcements," and "restocking ammunition." McClellan did everything except the one thing that Lincoln wanted him to do—which was to attack. A strange kind of paralysis gripped McClellan and he seemed as baffled by Lee now, here at Antietam Creek, as he had been back in Virginia. What faced him across the creek to the west seemed too good to be true—so he reached out, tentatively, to feel for the trick: no commander, he believed, would risk his entire army in one simple throw of the dice, or place it so vulnerably on a series of rolling hills unless he meant to be attacked. And that, McClellan further reasoned, was good enough reason not to do so. At least not yet. By the time the sun was just setting on September 16, Joe Hooker's Corps was across the Antietam facing Lee's left, Mansfield's Corps filled in the line in the Union center, while Ambrose Burnside's men were in line to the south, looking down on a stone bridge over Antietam Creek. The 20th Maine was with Fitz-John Porter's Fifth Corps, in reserve.

Across the way in the darkness, the men of the 15th Alabama slept on their rifles in a small field just south of Mansfield's Corps, who were in the looming woods just two hundred yards away. The 15th was ready for the battle, their morale never better. There was only one problem. For the first time since they had come north, the 15th did not have the services of William Oates, who had become sick on the march. "I was not in the battle of Sharpsburg," Oates wrote after the conflict. "I was at the house of an old Dutchman, between Harper's Ferry and Shepardstown, on a surgeon's certificate of disability, but within hearing distance of the musketry—a safe, but a more uneasy and annoying position than in the thickest of the fight." Oates and Chamberlain were frustrated onlookers, though both must have later realized that the intensity of the battle (now, at nightfall on the sixteenth, just hours away) might well have marked their last day of service. For as the confident armies faced each other above Sharpsburg, neither could have known what was in store for them in the twenty-four hours just ahead, or guessed at how much blood would be shed.

&#8450;━◆━&#8450;

"Fighting Joe" Hooker's bluecoats came out of the misty dawn, their lines moving straight south toward a small Dunker Church that bordered the Hagerstown Pike, which ran straight south through Sharpsburg toward the Potomac River. McClellan's intent, since there were no orders given, was to turn Lee's left and push the rebels back into the Potomac. Facing Hooker were just 7,700 men of Jackson's command, who were deployed west and east of the turnpike, with the 15th Alabama just south of the farmhouse of Samuel Mumma. By the time the first ranks of federals began to take fire, with one man falling and then another and another, the sun had emerged from the mist and begun to burn the low fog from Sharpsburg's fields. The cornfield of Sharpsburg farmer David Miller was the first battleground of the day, as John Gibbon's men from the 2nd and 6th Wisconsin ("them damn black hat fellars") moved forward down the pike. The opening volley, aimed at them by rebels from the Stonewall Brigade, set the tone of the day—the men in blue fell in rows, but steadied and then came on, swishing through the high corn.

The 15th Alabama was in the thick of this fight. The regiment suffered the first withering fire from Hooker's men and held, but were

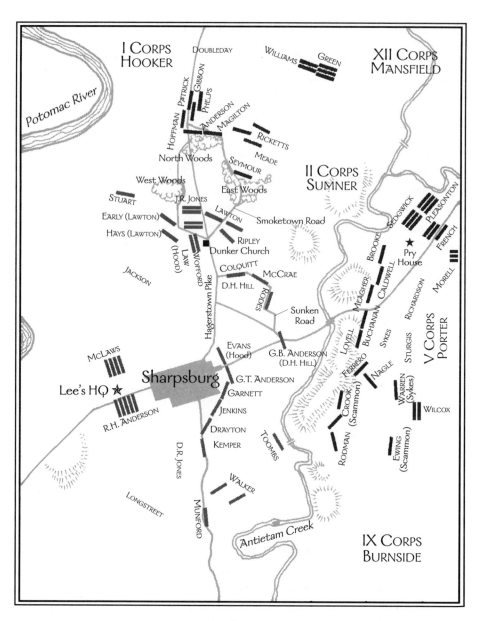

## *Antietam*

By the morning of September 17, 1862, the Army of Northern Virginia was in place behind Antietam Creek, with the Potomac at its back. But McClellan's attacks were disjointed, starting in the north along the Hagerstown Pike, then in the center against the sunken road, and then across the lower Antietam, against elements of Burnside's Corps. At dusk, A. P. Hill, coming up from Harpers Ferry, southeast of Sharpsburg, reinforced Lee.

pushed back, their ranks now thinned by short-range canister. Pressed back from position to position, the firing was so intense that the Alabamians ran low on ammunition. Those who were still standing after thirty minutes clambered among the dead and wounded, searching for powder and ball. Finally, not one hour after the attack opened, and seeing that the brigade on his left had been routed, Isaac Feagin, their commander, ordered his men back to replenish their stocks. As they streamed back toward Sharpsburg, Confederate division commander D. H. Hill angrily watched them go and threatened to court-martial Feagin for leaving the field without orders.

At the end of one hour of the most intense fighting of the war, "Fighting Joe" Hooker's men had gained the cornfield and woods north of the Dunker Church, smashing two of Jackson's divisions. There were hundreds of gray-clad corpses in the woods and fields as well as a surge of fleeing rebels funneling back into Sharpsburg. Back down the turnpike, John Bell Hood, who stood second to none in the Confederate army when it came to courage, rousted his two brigades from their morning meal, put them in line, and moved out to meet the attack. They poured back past the Dunker Church and into the woods and cornfield beyond, supported by Jubal Early's command on the left and D. H. Hill's men on the right. If anything, the fight was more intense than the one that had preceded it and Hooker's men yielded, leaving the field and moving back north. Hood's counterattack succeeded, but retaking the cornfield cost him dearly: "Tell General Jackson unless I get reinforcements I must be forced back," he told one messenger, "but I am going on while I can."

The battle now shifted east and south. As Hooker took his men back across the Miller cornfield, he called on Joseph Mansfield to give him support. Mansfield went into battle believing that Hooker was driving the rebels south, and was shocked to learn that just the opposite was true. Nonetheless, he sent his men forward in compact lines, driving Hood's men back out of the cornfield; but at a key moment Mansfield became confused, believing his troops were firing into the back of a federal line. He ordered them to cease firing and was met with a fusillade of musketry from his front. "Those are rebels, General," a soldier yelled, whereupon Mansfield's horse was shot, bringing the general down in a tumble. Walking back to a fence, Mansfield boosted himself halfway over, at which point he took a minié ball square in the stomach. He died a short time later. Alpheus Williams took command of the corps and drove it forward, then sent back for reinforcements.

This time it was "Bull" Sumner who came on, but at an angle, driving south and west out of the woods, heading straight for the Dunker Church. Unfortunately, Sumner did not trust his volunteers enough to believe they could advance in a single line, so he put them in column. Which is how they died. Sumner's first division was knocked about like ninepins by rebel artillerists, with entire lines falling as straight and pretty as if they were on a parade ground. The other two of his divisions retreated to a nearby woods, where they became hopelessly entangled. "My God, we must get out of this," Sumner yelled; he and his men retreated, trailing corpses as they went. By midmorning, Hooker was down (shot in the foot), Mansfield dead, and Sumner was back in the East Woods searching for his lost divisions.

When he finally found them, he sent them through the fields and due south against the rebels, who had formed a line in the trough of a sunken road. The road, which ran from the Hagerstown Pike to the east before bending sharply to the south, was rutted by years of use by farm wagons, forming a natural trench. On September 17, it became a burying ground, as waves of bluecoats emerged from the woods along Antietam Creek, ran up over the ridgeline in front of the road, and, starkly outlined against the eastern sky, were killed in long rows. The two lines of rebels in the road worked methodically, with one line loading and one line firing, to bring down the Yankees. Sumner's two divisions suffered massive casualties and lost a division commander, when "Greasy Dick" Richardson failed to do what he had done before— dodge—and was felled by a rebel shell. He died four weeks later.

The rebels might have defended the sunken road all day if it had not been for a mistake in command, which occurred when one of the Confederate units was ordered to "refuse" (or bend back) its left company to meet a coming attack. The gray regiment heard the command but misinterpreted it, believing that they had been ordered to withdraw. The butternut-clad defenders in one part of the sunken road turned their backs on their attackers and clambered quickly up the reverse side of the trench, making their way across a cornfield to the distant Piper farm buildings. A Yankee regiment quickly saw the hole formed in the Confederate defense and crashed into the road, where they turned their fire on the remaining rebels arrayed in neat lines to their left and right. The gray line was "flanked" and, unit by unit, the rebels scrambled up the road's far bank. For many, it was a race for life—to stay in the sunken road and be slaughtered, or try their luck, with backs turned, sprinting to the Hagerstown Road. Only a few made it.

Back over the low ridgeline in the rear of the road, James Longstreet worked frantically to mend Lee's shattered center. He ordered up batteries of artillery, placing them hub to hub along the Hagerstown Pike. Behind him, D. H. Hill rallied the remnants of his division, forming them in a long line that helped to stave off the charging Yankees. The center, finally, held and the two Union divisions drew off to the east.

The battle then shifted south, where Ambrose Burnside's Ninth Corps had been attempting to storm the Rohrbach Bridge over Antietam Creek throughout the day. As "Bull" Sumner's fight for the sunken road reached a crescendo, at about four P.M., Burnside ordered his corps to take the bridge by storm—ordering two regiments to run straight down the steep hill on the east side of the creek, then across the 125-foot stone span and up the opposite hill, which was filled with Georgia sharpshooters. At first it appeared the apparently reckless tactic would fail—the Georgians across Antietam Creek brought down several of the lead soldiers in both regiments—but the sheer desperation of the move took the rebels by surprise. By the time the two regiments reached the opposite bank, the rebels on the creekside had begun to pull out of their entrenchments and head for the rear. The day might have been won right then had Burnside pressed the attack, but he did not. Instead, the two lead regiments were sent to rearm and new units were brought forward. The pause gave Lee time to regroup his last line of defense on the rolling hills just to the east of Sharpsburg.

There is a moment in every battle, it seems, when the scales, having been tipped first one way and then another, pause on a hair's breadth as if anticipating the final weight. So it seemed at Antietam, with ninety minutes left to daylight, when Ambrose Burnside's entire Ninth Corps might have been thrown at the thin gray lines behind Antietam Creek; or where, had George McClellan wished, he might have thrown one more division, even one more brigade against D. H. Hill's thin line in the Confederate center. But that is not what happened. Instead, with the scales resting silent, General Ambrose Powell Hill brought 16,000 Confederate soldiers up the Harpers Ferry Road and into the line against Burnside. The saying so often repeated afterward—"and then A. P. Hill came up"—became synonymous with the battle and the Union's tragic, nearly criminal lost opportunity. At sunset, both armies, exhausted by the fight, stood down and counted their casualties.

Antietam became known as "artillery hell" to soldiers on both sides. More than in any other battle, the weapon dominated the field of battle. It played a prominent role for the Army of Northern Virginia and was used with greater effectiveness in the war's early days by the rebels than the bluecoats. A number of Confederate officers were masters of the weapon, including James Longstreet; Colonel E. P. Alexander, who became the army's chief artillerist; and John Pelham, the inventor of "the artillery charge." The rebel army had its own elite artillery units, including the famed Washington Artillery, which seemed ever-present in every battle. Only a handful of high-ranking officers gained similar fame in the Union army, though the Army of the Potomac probably contained America's real artillery genius, Henry Jackson Hunt, who believed that by using cannon in masses he could effectively break up compact assault units—though, after Antietam, lowly privates knew that firsthand.

Artillery officers prayed for the "clean shot," fire that could be brought to bear on charging soldiers at 300 yards or less. Counter-battery fire, which was used to silence other artillery at longer ranges, was far less effective. Both armies used the same tactics: solid shot (like a bowling ball) against columns, explosive shells against enemy cannon, case shot (a hollow shell filled with seventy-five balls, detonated above an attacking line), and canister (a large can filled with iron balls that ruptured when it left the muzzle and blew bloody holes in attacking lines). Both armies used the twelve-pound Napoleon as their weapon of choice, but it was used most effectively by the rebels, to whom it was "the close- and medium-range crusher which achieved the big results." As it did at Antietam. After Antietam, soldiers on both sides took special care to kill artillerists *and* their horses, to keep the animals from dragging the pieces away after a successful assault. The battles ahead would feature the screams of dying horses and, after the battle, great piles of the animals were left on the battlefields.

The carnage of Antietam, the sight of entire lines of blue and gray falling as if in unison, was a numbing experience. "You fought and stood well," a northern colonel told one wounded rebel in the cornfield. "Yes," the Mississippi private responded, "and here we lie." The bloodiest day in American history cost the nation 3,700 dead, 17,000 wounded, and 2,500 missing. It is likely that the final tally was much worse—more than 4,000 dead from twelve hours of fighting. In the wake of the battle, it was clear that the South had suffered a great deal more than the North, with a total of nearly one-quarter to one-third of those southerners who fought at Antietam never returning to the ranks. William Oates, who lay ill in a farmhouse across the Potomac during the battle, was never more ebullient than before the fight, and never more bitter than after:

> The echoes of the artillery in the parting salutes fired by the opposing parties on the banks of the Potomac sounded the death-knell of the infant Confederacy, but the Confederates would not admit it. They refused to see it. The struggle for life, for an independent existence, went on and whole hecatombs of patriots were sacrificed on numerous fields, but the sick man was sick unto death and would not recover.

On the afternoon of September 19, as Lee's army made its way back to Virginia, it came head to head with McClellan yet again. The army crossed at Boteler's Ford, protected by forty-five pieces of artillery commanded by William Pendleton and two brigades of rebel troops that included the 15th Alabama. McClellan sent a detachment of cavalry, as well as elements of the Fifth Corps—including the 20th Maine—to contest the crossing. The rear-echelon units of Lee's army made it across the river without incident, but both sides took shots at each other from opposite banks. The following morning, McClellan continued the pursuit, ordering nineteen regiments and six batteries across the Potomac, where they quickly bumped into several Confederate regiments. The resulting firefight pushed the rebels back toward Shepardstown. Pendleton, a Virginia minister, was commanding the Confederate artillery on the Virginia side of the river. When he saw the federals coming in force, he panicked, reporting to Lee that all of the Confederate cannon had been captured.

Lee calmed the shaken parson and called up A. P. Hill, instructing him to push the pursuing bluecoats into the river. Hill did it by the book. He formed up his men, sent his scouts to the front, felt for the federal flanks, pushed out his pickets, and sent his men forward in a long line toward Boteler's Ford, picking up the remnants of the two rearguard southern brigades, one of which included the 15th Alabama, as he went. Within hours he had cracked the Union line and sent it back in disarray across the Potomac.

The skirmish at Boteler's Ford is no more than a footnote to Civil War history, but it was the first time the 20th Maine and 15th Alabama were directly engaged, and the first time Joshua Chamberlain had been under fire. Chamberlain acted coolly, sitting his horse in the middle of the river, calmly shepherding his men back to the Maryland side as Confederate minié balls splattered in the water near him, as if he had done this many times before. "Come on my men," he told them, "hurry up, hurry up." The men of the 20th waded back across the Potomac River past him, carrying along the three Maine men who were wounded in the skirmish with the 15th. Tom Chamberlain commented on the incident in a letter home, saying that the family would be proud of his older brother's baptism by fire. The regiment spent two days in the muck and mud of the Maryland side, trading potshots with their adversaries, then marched into Sharpsburg and camped near the battlefield.

⚜

Antietam had been a living nightmare. It had been the 20th's first real trial, similar in scope to that faced by the 15th Alabama months before at Winchester. Afterward, dozens of Maine men fell out of the ranks sick, as influenza, pneumonia, and the most dreaded of all diseases, measles, took their toll on the weak. The weather turned cold for a time, but Chamberlain thrived in the harsh conditions, writing to Fannie that nothing could now induce him to return to college life. In his spare time, he continued his crash course on military tactics, writing to his family that he actually enjoyed such dense material, and was applying the lessons that he learned to the ranks of Maine's farmers. When the trees changed with the season, the onetime professor seemed to hardly remember his time at Bowdoin, treating it as a distant memory. He wrote lyrically of this time to Fannie:

> I wish you could be beside me on some gentle palfrey plunging into some rich shaded valley, craggy defile, or along some lovely stream. Or perhaps, as a day or two ago, mount to the summit of one of these blue hills, whence you can see forty miles into Virginia—see the long lines of rebel fires miles away and villages and streams and bright patches of cultivated fields and on our own side the great battle field of Antietam—the hills trodden bare and the fields all veined with the tracks of artillery trains, or movements of army corps. I have enjoyed these rides much. Often I am 12 or 15 hours in the saddle.

Several weeks later he expanded on these thoughts, giving the possibility of his own death only a passing mention:

> I feel it is a sacrifice for me to be here in one sense of the word; but I do not wish myself back [at Bowdoin] by any means. The "glory" Prof. Smyth so honestly pictured for me I do not much dread. If I do return "shattered" and "good-for-nothing," I shall think there are those who will hold me in some degree of favor better than that which he predicted. Most likely I shall be hit somehow at sometime, but all "my times are in His hand," and I can not die without His appointing. I try to keep ever in view all the possibilities that surround me and to be ready for all that I am called to.

Adelbert Ames, the commander of the 20th Maine, was much less reflective. While Ames loved the military every bit as much as Chamberlain, he spoke only of drill and discipline, believing them the best preparation for a new regiment. The war had taken a grim turn, Ames believed, and that called for a new kind of soldier—different than the idealistic volunteers of Bull Run or Gaines's Mill. It was no longer possible to make up in martial ardor for what a unit lacked in discipline. So Ames drilled and drilled and drilled, driving the Maine men to near rebellion. Tom Chamberlain wrote that he wished Ames would either be imprisoned or promoted—anything to end the constant training. "Col. A. drills us sergeants every day to see who is fit to promote," he wrote. "I tell you he is about as savage a man as you ever saw." Joshua (Lawrence) Chamberlain was there, as the regiment's second-in-command. "I wish you could hear Lawrence give off a command & see him ride along the battalion on his white horse," Tom wrote.

Slowly, the sickness abated and the mood of the regiment improved. Lincoln came to visit McClellan and the army crowded forward to see him. Then, on September 22, Lincoln issued the Emancipation Proclamation, which stated that on January 1, 1863, all slaves in the rebellious states "would thenceforth and forever" be free. Lincoln had wanted to time the proclamation so that it followed a victory. Antietam was close enough. The army did not revolt, as McClellan had predicted, or even comment much on Lincoln's move.

At the end of September, the Army of the Potomac moved south to their encampment at Falmouth in Virginia. The northern army was now filled with veterans, with a set of distinctive traditions every bit as important as those of Lee's Army of Northern Virginia. At Falmouth the Union army was refitted, rearmed, and introduced to its new commander, Ambrose Burnside. McClellan was gone, as was Fitz-John Porter, who now spent his days defending himself against charges that he had disobeyed Pope's orders at Bull Run. The southern army had changed also, promoting new brigade and regimental commanders (like William Oates, who took over for the injured Isaac Feagin), though its core of leaders—Lee, Longstreet, and Jackson—remained intact. By December, Burnside and Lee had placed their men (128,000 boys in blue against 78,000 boys in gray) in long lines along the Rappahannock, with the northerners looking down on Fredericksburg from one shore, the graycoats waiting above the town on the other. Almost everyone believed the fighting was done for the year, and the armies settled into their winter camps.

There are moments in history in which time seems frozen. The winter of 1862–1863 was one such moment. On all fronts, east, west, and south—from Fredericksburg in Virginia to Murfreesboro in Tennessee to Vicksburg on the Mississippi and then west, through the great unsettled frontier that once beckoned William Oates, all the way to Galveston on the Gulf Coast—hundreds of thousands of men paused, as if to assess how far they had come.

In the camps of the Army of Northern Virginia, southern commanders struggled to refill their thinned ranks. For them, the war had suddenly taken on a new and darker cast; very few now believed it would end with a single season of campaigning. For southerners, Antietam showed that the road to independence would be far more arduous than any had believed in the bright aftermath of Bull Run. For northerners too the war had changed. Lincoln's proclamation had given the Army of the Potomac, and the North, new life. Its soldiers were no longer attempting simply to suppress a rebellion, they were now leading a crusade.

Fannie wrote Joshua that she missed him terribly and worried that he was lonely. But miss him as she might, Chamberlain often stood alone, empty-handed, after mail call. He wondered why she did not write. In fact, like thousands of others left at home, Fannie worried that if she wrote too often, her husband would become even more lonely than he already was. She did not want to give him any cause for concern about her welfare. Her fears were well placed. She wrote him about the snowy Maine Thanksgiving of 1862, with its "bright red apples, nuts and candy," to which he responded with a cry of woe that he could not be present, and she fell silent again, not writing for many weeks.

But it was not just worry for her husband that kept Fannie Chamberlain from writing. Like many millions of other Americans, Fannie found that the great adventure of civil war not only provided new worries, but untold opportunities. While her husband urged her to stay at home with the children and "occupy [her] mind with pleasant things," Fannie had other ideas. In the midst of the conflict, she spent weeks at a time away from Maine, visiting friends in Boston, Portland, and New York, leaving her children in the care of relatives. She rarely told her husband where she was or what she was doing, leading Chamberlain biographers to explain her absences as reflecting a severe bout of "depression." But it is far more likely that Fannie, like thousands of other women of her time, were now just beginning to wrestle with their new-found freedom, bought by the absence of men.

The tone of the time, and what Fannie must have been feeling, was reflected in one of Harriet Beecher Stowe's more poignant works, *The Pearl of Orr's Island*, set along the rocky coast of Maine. While the book was written in the months immediately preceding the firing on Fort Sumter, its subject foreshadowed one of the most important social transformations wrought by the sectional conflict. The story's protagonist, a young girl named Mara Lincoln, is much like Fannie: she is adventurous, intelligent, but hobbled by the restrictions placed on her gender, a fact that only slowly dawns on her. She is increasingly frustrated that no one notices *her* intelligence, *her* courage, and *her* needs. On the edge of womanhood, she watches in steely resentment as her childhood friend Moses sets off on his fishing expedition—leaving her at home. The story was serialized in the *Independent*, gaining a wide readership. When the war began, however, Stowe abruptly discontinued it. She finally ended the story after an interlude, just as abruptly, in November 1861, with the death of Mara, and apologized to her readers that it was impossible to continue her tale "with Washington beleaguered" and "the whole country shaken."

What Stowe clearly meant, however, was that she was uncomfortable relating the tale of a young woman reaching for her emancipation when the nation was embarking on a revolution to free the slaves. But Stowe had made her point: *The Pearl of Orr's Island* presaged the transformation of abolitionism into a larger movement for women's rights that was to last for more than a century. While the Civil War loosed the great industrial resources of the North, saw its young men off to fight their brothers, and yoked the Union to a single great purpose, it also placed the full responsibility for family and home on the nation's women. Such responsibilities worried most soldiers, who sent detailed letters to their wives and sweethearts on just how to manage affairs that were once their sole concern. Like many of his compatriots, Joshua Chamberlain urged his wife to keep things as they were when he left ("Invite the Juniors over & spend the evening with some of the young ladies, as we used to, & keep up your character for hospitality"). One of his biggest fears was that Fannie might set out alone, much as Mara Lincoln did for a time, on an oceanbound raft, in one of Stowe's more vivid passages from *The Pearl*. He cautioned her against such independence, but then thought better of it, knowing that, in the worst of cases, he might not return at all. As the war went on, his instructions grew less and less specific until, at the height of the killing, he penned a symbolic surrender. "You had better go on without me where you wish," he wrote.

By November 1862, Fannie, and millions of women like her, needed no urging; she was as dedicated to discovering as much about life as her husband—despite his protests. Like Mara Lincoln, who is forced to suffer the indignity of Moses's "continual disparaging tone" of her homebound life, Fannie ignored her husband's offended tone when he learned of such wanderings ("New York! I am sorry you are there . . . I wish you were at home") and began to build a life apart from his.

For the men of the North, the fact that the war had become a great crusade helped to explain its horrors. It seemed that way for Lincoln also, who began to tell those around him that the nation was now paying in human lives the full cost of the unjust punishments meted out by the overseer's lash. The war was God's retribution, the shedding of innocent blood the nation's penance, and the only way that the sin of slavery could be fully expiated. The crusade against slavery did not lessen the tragedy of the thousands dead in the Shenandoah, at Gaines's Mill, at Second Bull Run or Antietam, but it at least gave a reason for such deaths. For many northern soldiers, it helped to explain the struggle.

The lessons of the war were not confined to those men who actually fought it. The war freed thousands of women from the sameness of everyday life. Many rural women, in particular, had to depend on their own abilities to feed their families: to actually put in and harvest a crop, in addition to their other, more traditional duties of educating and raising their children. While women did not leave their homes to serve as workers in war factories—as they did during the wars of the twentieth century—the Civil War inaugurated the process leading to women's suffrage, which became a reality six decades later.

Southern soldiers also found a larger purpose in the war, believing that their fight for independence had been ordained by Providence, and that a just God would reward their sacrifice. The "Cause"—as they began to call it—was no less holy: freedom from tyranny, and the right to lead one's life as one chose. The thousands of dead they left on the battlefields of Virginia and Tennessee were a simple reflection of divine will, the sacrifice necessary to win their rights. This notion, that all the bloodletting was part of a greater plan, was reinforced by the small army of itinerant preachers that descended on the Army of Northern Virginia after Antietam. Armed with religious tracts and small Bibles, this legion of preachers ministered first to a handful, then to dozens, and then to thousands of soldiers who gathered to hear their sermons.

The Great Revival of the Army of Northern Virginia began in the camps of the 12th and 44th Georgia regiments of Trimble's Brigade in the Shenandoah Valley one month after Antietam. Trimble's Brigade (including the 15th Alabama) had long been targeted by ministers, missionaries, and "colporters" (sellers of religious tracts) because it contained a number of devout chaplains. The revival then spread through the rest of Jackson's command, which had been decimated by the fight at Sharpsburg. The religious camp meetings grew in power and size and were carried with the army into Fredericksburg, where they grew in intensity throughout the late fall and early winter. Several members of the 15th Alabama were baptized in the Shenandoah Valley, others in Fredericksburg.

By December 1862, daily prayer meetings and sermons were mobbed. Dr. Joseph Stiles, a chaplain in Trimble's Brigade, wrote of the revival with great excitement:

> In General Trimble's, and the immediately neighboring brigades, there is in progress, at this hour, one of the most glorious revivals I ever witnessed. The audiences and the interest have grown to glorious dimensions. It would rejoice you over-deeply to glance for once instant on our night-meeting in the wildwoods, under the full moon, aided by the light of our side-stands. You would behold a mass of men seated on the earth all around you . . . fringed in all its circumference by a line of standing officers and soldiers—two or three deep—all exhibiting the most solemn and respectful earnestness that a Christian assembly ever displayed.

The most popular tract, entitled "Come to Jesus," was passed hand to hand. One of the most requested readings from scripture began,

"Though He slay me, yet will I trust in Him." The religious services were open, nondenominational, and designed to involve each of the soldiers regardless of rank. There were well-known evangelists in the army like Stiles, but anyone could preach or tell of his own conversion. There were rules, of course, but they remained unstated. A primer for battlefield ministers noted that a devout soldier "does not discuss the 'Relation of Science to Religion,' or the slavery question, or the causes which led to the war, or the war itself. He does not indulge in abusive epithets of the invaders of our soil, or seek to fire his hearers with hatred or vindictiveness towards the enemy. He has no use for any theology that is newer than the New Testament, and he indulges in no fierce polemics against Christians of other denominations. He is looking in the eyes of heroes of many a battle, and knows that the 'long roll' may beat ere he closes."

In one of the most enduring descriptions of the Great Revival, Chaplain J. W. Jones wrote of thousands of soldiers lining the banks of the Rapidan River, just west of Fredericksburg, to witness a mass baptism, as entire companies of men entered the water to "receive Jesus." Impressive as that was, the stirring sight was not unusual. Revival meetings, followed by personal testimonials, brought out thousands of soldiers. The best sermonizers also attracted Lee and Jackson, as well as division and brigade commanders. While the message varied, most ministers emphasized the evils of profanity, drinking, and gambling (but not, apparently, killing). Prints were circulated of a mother or sister or "sweetheart" at home, waiting for her young son, brother, or future husband to reappear, wrapped in glory, unstained and untarnished by the evils of the world.

In late December, the Great Revival spread from Jackson's Corps into Longstreet's. The religious fervor spread through Longstreet's command, taking hold finally in William Barksdale's Brigade, which was billeted in the abandoned homes of Fredericksburg. The rounds of conversions and sermons had barely begun when the Mississippi soldiers, known for their tenacity and marksmanship, were ordered to take their preassigned places in rifle pits facing the Rappahannock River—which separated Robert E. Lee's Army of Northern Virginia from Ambrose Burnside's Army of the Potomac. In the cold early morning darkness of December 11, the Mississippians heard the distinct rustle of

Burnside's men marching across the way, then the splash of pontoons on the mostly frozen river. In the gray light of dawn, Barksdale passed the word to open fire.

⚔

Burnside's plan was simple enough; having feinted up the river and then back down, the Army of the Potomac would steal a march on Lee and cross directly at Fredericksburg before the Army of Northern Virginia could react. But there was the usual critically important mistake: it took an extra week for the pontoons that Burnside had ordered from Washington to arrive, by which time Lee's army was firmly entrenched on Marye's Heights above the city. Burnside was trapped now by his own plan and, thinking that Lee would least expect him to gamble on a straight-ahead attack, decided that that was his best option. The pontoons went across the Rappahannock, therefore, during the early morning hours of the eleventh, though not without cost.

Nine separate attempts were made to lay the pontoons across the Rappahannock, and each time Barksdale's men methodically killed or wounded the lead engineers attempting to lay them. Finally, in a pique of frustration, Burnside ordered the Union artillery to open fire on the town. "It is impossible fitly to describe the effects of this iron hail hurled against the small band of defenders and into the devoted city," Confederate division commander Lafayette McLaws later wrote. "The roar of the cannon, the bursting shells, the falling of walls and chimneys, and the flying bricks and other material dislodged from the houses by the iron balls and shells, added to the fire of the infantry from both sides and the smoke from the guns and from the burning houses, made a scene of indescribable confusion, enough to appall the stoutest hearts."

Lee himself was enraged by the bombardment. "Those people delight to destroy the weak and those who can make no defense," he said. "It just suits them!" Unfortunately for Burnside, however, the artillery fire seemed to be having little effect and it was not until after four in the afternoon that the federals rowed several regiments across the river and landed them on the town's shores. There was a sharp fight in Fredericksburg's streets, after which Barksdale withdrew back under the safety of Marye's Heights. The sun set early, but Burnside was satisfied;

while it was now clear that Lee had not been surprised by this straight-on push, his six pontoon bridges were finally finished and, if all went well tomorrow, he would cross his army into Fredericksburg and begin, on December 13, to push south. For his part, Lee could hardly believe his good fortune. When it was obvious that Burnside meant to come up the hill against his defenses, he sent a message to Stonewall Jackson to hurry his command, just twenty miles down the river, to Fredericksburg, filling in the southern line on the right.

By the morning of December 13, Lee's defenses were nearly impregnable. Longstreet's command of five divisions was stacked in double lines behind a stone wall above the town. The road behind the wall was rutted, allowing the rebel soldiers a chest-high downhill shot at the sloping snow-covered ground over which, if Burnside chose, he would send his blue-clad divisions. Longstreet had nearly 20,000 men to cover his five miles of line along the heights, while to his right Jackson (on land that rolled off the heights and was much lower—but as impregnable) with just as many men covered not quite half the ground. That Burnside would attack, given the depth of such a defense, seemed too good to be true, or too horrible. But Longstreet took no chances, posting successive lines in the rear of the stone wall and sending messages to his commanders dictating positions for a withdrawal. Thomas Cobb, a brilliant Georgia lawyer who commanded the center brigade of Longstreet's defense, looked over his position and gave his own judgment: "Well! if they wait for me to fall back, they will wait a long time," he said.

Cobb's command had been shot to pieces by Burnside at Antietam, but that only deepened the Georgian's dark intensity. Cobb was a firebrand secessionist who had been one of the first southerners to advocate the formation of a Confederacy, saying the South could "make better terms out of the Union than in it"—a proposition that had been sorely tested in the twenty months since Fort Sumter. It was about to be tested again at Fredericksburg, where, it seemed to Cobb, Burnside would make his first attack against his position. But as the fog started to lift off the ground on the morning of December 13, Cobb (who had just finished a breakfast of hard crackers and coffee made from parched corn) came out of the Maryes' house behind his brigade's position at the stone wall and noticed that down the line to his right,

Stonewall Jackson's Corps was drawn up against thousands of Yankees, who were deployed in parade-ground lines in front of Jackson's position.

The Yankees spied by Cobb were the 18,000 men of W. F. Smith's Corps, which was comprised of three divisions, escorted and protected by forty-four separate cannon. As the Union troops formed, Confederate Major John Pelham rolled out his own two-gun battery to give them battle. It was a strange sight, a duel between an undermanned and outgunned battery and a massive wall of flame; for the southern soldiers on Marye's Heights it seemed to symbolize the war itself and to serve as proof of what a rebel Confederacy could do against a larger and more well armed opponent. Pelham was forced to withdraw eventually, but he had proved his point. As Pelham retreated, Smith's Corps came on through the snow to within 800 yards of Jackson's line—then, in what seemed a single crash, were sent back across the field. "No troops on earth, nor any number of them, attacking by the front could have driven Jackson from that position," William Oates said.

Oates's regiment of Trimble's Brigade, now commanded (after Trimble's wound at Bull Run and his successor Alexander Lawton's death at Antietam) by North Carolina's Robert Hoke, saw Smith's Corps break up and retreat, but then form again, this time with Pennsylvania troops under the command of George Meade at the front. When Meade's men came across the field, Oates was ordered to take his regiment into the line. Oates marched his men across the rear of A. P. Hill's division and out to the open edge of a snow-covered cornfield. As his men were ordered forward, the crash of volley fire coming from his front, Oates saw South Carolina General Maxcy Gregg pitch backward off his horse, mortally wounded. Oates's men fired into the cornfield, then charged across it, dislodging a blue line and capturing dozens of Union soldiers trapped in the cut of an unfinished railroad.

The Yankees responded, pushing Oates's men back. Hoke was wounded and, with one of his feet caught in a stirrup, dragged by his horse across the open ground. He was saved by the quick action of some of Oates's men and, while clearly stunned, was remounted. The Alabamians were being raked by grapeshot, thrown into their ranks by the Union artillery. Hoke, seeing his men in trouble, ordered a withdrawal into the railroad cut and then farther back into a ditch at the edge of a woods. Before them, Meade's men came on in closely packed ranks. Oates's troops would have fired at them in a classic stand-up fight, except that a battery of six Alabama Napoleons was firing from behind them over the ditch. "There we were, right under the muzzles of the guns," Oates remembered, "and the Federal replying with thirty-seven pieces, which made the position of the 15th as perilous and disagreeable as well could be." Oates testified that a sergeant of one company was killed by the concussion of an exploding artillery shell: "He was not touched at all."

The battle was touch-and-go for Jackson, especially as he did not have the cover at the lower end of Marye's Heights that Longstreet enjoyed on the Confederate left. As Jackson was pushing and being pushed by 18,000 charging bluecoats in successive lines, and galloping here and there to shore up his battered brigades, Longstreet was observing the battle in front of his own command with something approaching boredom. As Jackson was fighting Smith's Corps on the Confederate right, Longstreet was slaughtering Sumner's Corps on the Confederate left. The numbers, however, were the same—like Smith, Sumner brought three divisions with him in three blue lines that stretched all the way back to the town to their rear. Sumner ordered his men forward just before noon. They marched resolutely forward until barred by a long swale in their front, into which they gladly leaped. They were just 400 yards in front of Longstreet's stone wall. After a short pause, they emerged and headed straight for Cobb's position—in the center of Longstreet's line.

Sumner's men made six distinct charges, each of them running in successive lines closer and closer to Longstreet's position, as if the men in blue were an incoming tide, flowing forward and then back, and then closer and back again, until after the third run-up it seemed they would overpower Longstreet's soldiers. Cobb's men, at the center of Longstreet's line, were the most heavily pressed, but they held on to their position. Lee watched the charges without comment, then turned to Longstreet: "They are massing very heavily and will break your line," he said. Longstreet shook his head, said he doubted that would happen, and told Lee to worry about Jackson. Sumner's men came on for a

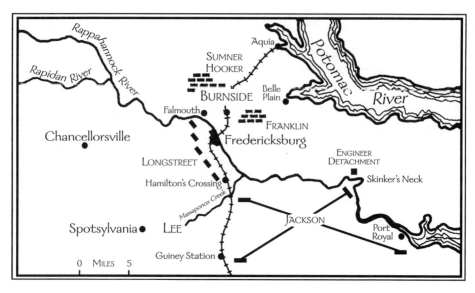

## Fredericksburg

The newest Union commander, Ambrose Burnside, attempted to unlock the puzzle of Lee's position along the Rappahannock but was stymied. Finally, he attacked through the town and against Longstreet's position on Marye's Heights. Even on the Union left, against Jackson, Union troops were met by overwhelming resistance.

---

fourth, fifth, and sixth time, and each time they retreated they left a trail of dead that stretched from within fifty yards of the stone wall all the way back down the hill toward the town.

Cobb's men took their own casualties, but they were not nearly as heavy as those suffered by Sumner. Throughout the afternoon, Longstreet's Corps slugged away at Sumner, if that is what it can be called; it was more like factory work, with the men standing four deep at the walls—each taking a turn at firing before moving back in line to load. In some places one line loaded while another fired, then passed back the rifle to receive another and fire again. In others, two lines did the work—with one firing, then stepping back and letting the second line fire, so that the fight was constant and unrelenting. The work was methodical and deadly. At about the time Sumner was ordering his men to attack for a fifth time, Thomas Cobb, who could be seen pacing up and down his line, and in some places appearing in open sight, was shot by a sharpshooter at the edge of Fredericksburg, the ball breaking his thigh muscle and spilling the blood of his leg out onto the ground. He was taken back to the Maryes' house, where he had breakfasted just six hours earlier, and there he slowly bled to death.

Back across the Rappahannock, Ambrose Burnside watched the futile charges with mounting horror, but still believed he could somehow pry Lee from the heights above the town. He sent orders for Daniel Butterfield's Fifth Corps to cross into Fredericksburg and take its place below the heights. By sundown, Butterfield had his men in a long line below Longstreet's position, with Andrew Humphreys's Division on the far right. Soon a report came to Butterfield from Humphreys that the rebels seemed to be withdrawing in his front. Within moments, Butterfield gave the orders, and Humphreys's division went forward. Butterfield's other two divisions marched out of Fredericksburg to support the latest charge—it was the thirteenth or fourteenth such attempt of the day, no one could be exactly sure—but it too broke in blood in front of Longstreet's position.

The men of the 20th Maine saw Humphreys's vain attack as they moved through the fields in front of Marye's Heights, as part of Charles Griffin's first division. The men kept in their lines, despite having to step over the dead and dying of the Ninth Corps, at least one-third of whom now lay on the fields. Years later, Chamberlain would remember the day as bitterly cold, while others vividly recounted that those who lay around them shouted their warning: "No one lives who goes there." As Humphreys's Division was going in on the right, Griffin's and Sykes's were going in on the left, in one last futile charge against the Army of Northern Virginia. It was nearly dark now, and Chamberlain and Ames could see the flashes of rebel muzzles as the 20th Maine went out across the field. "God help us now," Ames said softly, so that Chamberlain could hear him. The 20th made it into a swale below the rebel position and fired three volleys before making the final advance, but it was stalled almost before it began, with men from the regiment falling to the right and left, until the line gave and slowly yielded.

"We reached the final crest, before that all-commanding, countermanding stone wall," Chamberlain later wrote. "Here we exchanged fierce volleys at every disadvantage, until the muzzle-flame deepened the sunset red, and all was dark." The rebels were unmoved, and Chamberlain ordered his men to lay down where they were and return fire as best they could. When darkness came, they were still there, below the wall, the forward line of the Army of the Potomac, building breastworks with the bodies of dead men, now frozen in grotesque shapes.

⟨══════◆══════⟩

For Joshua Chamberlain, the dark night of December 13, 1862, was the most trying of the war. His men had fought a close-in battle with Longstreet's ranks over ground strewn with the dead and dying, but it was a fight without reason. Chamberlain was disgusted—eighteen of the brigade's men died in front of Marye's Heights, but without ever having the opportunity of fully testing Longstreet's strength. The regiment lay on the field after dark, amid the dead and cold, and made itself as comfortable as it could. Chamberlain pulled the coat of a dead man up over his head and listened closely to the rustlings around him. In the dark, rebel patrols came down the slope, searching among the dead for shoes and coats. "My ears were filled with the cries and groans of the wounded, and the ghastly faces of the dead almost made a wall around me," he wrote several days later.

The 20th was on the field the next day, trading fire with the rebels, while Burnside attempted to find a way out of the battle. He thought about sending another division against the wall—in one final all-out charge—but Edwin Sumner, who had come back across the field, then through the town, and finally across the river, stormed at him that it could not be done. The 20th moved back into the town of Fredericksburg and then, on the night of December 16, covered the withdrawal of the army.

"We had to pick our way over a field strewn with incongruous ruin," Chamberlain wrote, "men torn and broken and cut to pieces in every describable way, cannon dismounted, gun carriages smashed or overturned, ammunition chests flung wildly about, horses dead and half-dead still held in harness, accouterments of every sort scattered by the whirlwinds. It was not good for the nerves, that ghastly march, in the lowering night." Chamberlain thought the battle a waste of lives, a point he made clear during a chance meeting with Joe Hooker, one of Burnside's corps commanders. He told the general that his men had been put in "piecemeal," as if "on a toasting fork." That the regiment had done well was little solace to either Ames or Chamberlain, since the bobbling of the high command meant that there would be another battle, and perhaps another and another into the far future. The Union army lost 12,000 dead, wounded, and missing at Fredericksburg.

In Washington, Lincoln read the wires and was immediately depressed. He had tried three separate commanders—McClellan, Pope, McClellan again, and Burnside—and none of them had found any success against Lee. There had been worse times in the war, but the cold winter of late 1862 seemed particularly harsh. Nor were there many opportunities to break through the gloom, despite his best efforts. He had tried his best to conduct the business at the White House as if the times were normal, but they were not. The war peeked in at every corner. He was obsessed with it. It was the topic of every conversation, the sword hanging over every meeting. Lincoln tried mightily to rechannel these discussions, to make the White House a counterpoint to the blood that was spilled every day elsewhere in the nation, but he rarely succeeded.

Lincoln's December meeting with Harriet Beecher Stowe at the White House symbolized his efforts. Lincoln had great respect for *Uncle Tom's Cabin* and understood its power, so he attempted to make his famous guest as comfortable as possible. The visit passed without incident. But Stowe was bored by Lincoln's endless stories and his midwestern manners and could only shake her head at Lincoln's calm demeanor. "It was a very droll time that we had at the White House I assure you," she wrote in a letter to her sister. Calvin Stowe only said that he had had "a really funny interview" with Lincoln. Neither Harriet nor Calvin would expand on exactly what Lincoln said, but the story soon went around that Harriet Stowe was quite startled when she first met Lincoln. He stretched out his hand and smiled at her: "So this is the little lady who started this big war," he said.

Harriet Beecher Stowe never mentioned the incident, or Lincoln's words, but the greeting has passed into history. Stowe herself would have angrily rejected the claim, especially now that so many young men had left for war, including her son Fred, who was working diligently to be put in a frontline unit. Stowe was horrified at the thought, and frightened when Fred was transferred to the 73rd Ohio of the Army of the

Potomac. "I know not what day the news may come to my house which has come to so many noble families of one more empty saddle and broken sword," she said.

On January 1, 1863, she attended a rally of abolitionists in Boston, called to celebrate Lincoln's Emancipation Proclamation. Her attendance seemed fitting, for the entire nation now acknowledged that *Uncle Tom's Cabin* had helped awaken the North to the evils of slavery. Harriet Beecher Stowe certainly had not "started this big war," but her pen had given it purpose. When it was learned that she was present, the crowd began to chant her name in cadence, over and over: "Harriet Beecher Stowe, Harriet Beecher Stowe," until she rose and acknowledged their cheers.

# 9

# *Men Standing Bright as Golden Grain*

T HE 15TH ALABAMA spent New Year's Day south of Fredericksburg at Hamilton's Crossing, then marched three miles down the Rappahannock to Port Royal, where it made its camp as warm as possible against the winter cold. Several weeks later, in keeping with a new law passed by the Confederate Congress that put state regiments together, Trimble's Brigade was broken up. The 15th and four other Alabama regiments were assigned to Evander Law's Brigade, which was part of Hood's Division in Longstreet's Corps. Oates's new commander, Evander McIvor Law, was a transplanted South Carolina Military Academy graduate who established one of Alabama's first military high schools. He was known as a tough fighter; he had spearheaded John Bell Hood's drive on Fitz-John Porter's triple line at Gaines's Mill and led his former brigade forward into Miller's cornfield on September 17—where it had been butchered.

Most of the 15th was sorry to leave Jackson's command, where they had become part of "Old Jack's" legend. Isaac Feagin's eighteen-year-old younger brother, Noah ("a gallant boy," Oates called him), wrote a letter to his family that reflected the regiment's views:

> The soldiers under him think they are better, tougher, braver than any other soldiers, can stand more hardships, march faster and farther, go barefooted oftener on move and wade the deepest stream than any other soldier, can out flank, out fight, whip oftener, get whipped less, retreat faster and farther, capture more and get captured less, tear up more railroad and ride on it less, burn more commissaries and quarter master's stores . . . than any other soldiers.

Once settled in Law's Brigade and encamped at Hamilton's Crossing, the soldiers had their routine broken up by a thick mid-January snowfall. Feagin wrote of the snow:

> It now lies on the ground 10 and 12 inches deep. Quite an amusing time we had yesterday, snowballing. The Texas brigade came over and whipped the 47th and 48th Alabama Regt., ran them out of their camps, our regiment turned out and went to their relief but when we came up they turned traitors and pitched on us, whipped us and captured our flag and took us prisoners. We likewise turned traitors, joined the band which then composed of Alabamians and Texans, about three thousand in number, marched up and attacked the South Carolina brigade, which was commanded by a Colonel. We routed them, captured their Colonel, took him off his horse, took his saddle off, wallowed him in the snow and turned him loose and rode to his Quarters bareback. The fight is to be renewed on tomorrow.

Oates now commanded the 15th, as the vast majority of its men thought that he should; Alexander Lowther was still on sick leave and Isaac Feagin, while recovered from his wound at Shepardstown, was under a cloud—having charges of leaving his post at Antietam levied against him by D. H. Hill. Everyone knew the claim was unsupported and a number of officers had tried to explain to Hill that Feagin was only attempting to find ammunition for his Alabama men when he had spied him near a haystack south of the Dunker Church. The general would not let the matter drop, however. "D. H. Hill was a very eccentric man," Oates later wrote. In fact, this was an understatement: Hill was a bullheaded commander known for his quick turns of phrase and acerbic manner. While on independent command in North Carolina he responded to an enemy commander's request for term of surrender by saying that while his men would be well treated, he would be "castrated."

Feagin's trial was a minor affair and its results foreordained—especially as his old friend William Oates was appointed the judge advocate in the case. Feagin was quickly acquitted and released; when offered the command of the regiment, he turned it down, saying he now preferred to serve under Oates. The sequence of events would have been enough to raise suspicion among even the most trusting onlooker, but this was the Army of Northern Virginia, where charges, countercharges, "affairs of honor," and even the arrest of high-ranking officers was a nearly everyday occurrence. Oates defended himself against any rumored impropriety by saying simply that not only was Feagin "honorably acquitted by the unanimous vote of the members of the court" but that Oates himself had "made a statement in his favor."

Oates had earned his command. While he was not a striking figure, Oates's men admired his stamina, his great show of chivalry, his earthy humor, and his uncomfortably blunt honesty. Given his background and age (twenty-nine in 1863) he was already viewed as a man of achievement—the farm boy–lawyer turned colonel. He had even changed his appearance, from the dandified look of the mustached rogue to a man who sported a fashionable if somewhat straggly beard. Oates was a large though not imposing man. He had a certain charisma and confidence that his men would go where he led—and they did. In all of his writings, Oates rarely speaks of who he was, focusing more on what he did. He was too often partisan and self-assured; to suggest that there were two sides to a story would have struck him as odd: the cause was obviously just, the principles unassailable, General Lee always right, and William Oates never wrong. Years of experience would soften this view, but in 1863 Oates was what he had been when he first went "a wandering" in the Southwest—a man with enormous talents, deep ambitions, and an insatiable desire for adventure.

Law's Brigade moved south in March, beyond Richmond, as part of Longstreet's effort to gather supplies for Lee's army. April found the 15th east of Richmond, as part of a two-division siege of a federal force at Suffolk. There was skirmishing, but no outright battles. On April 30, Longstreet was ordered north, but he delayed his departure until his foraging parties could be brought in. The corps marched rapidly east, then boarded trains for Richmond, marching through the streets of the capital on their way to join Lee. They arrived at Whitehall, south of Fredericksburg, on the night of May 5. It was too late—the Army of the Potomac's new commander, Joseph Hooker, had crossed the Rappahannock in force and plunged ahead into a region of trees and tangled shrubs called the Wilderness. There, near the crossroads of

Chancellorsville, he was defeated. That was the good news. The bad news was that Stonewall Jackson was severely wounded.

Jackson died on May 10, nine days after he had marched his command through the tangled woods west of Fredericksburg before sending them crashing back east in long battle lines and forward onto the flank of Union General Oliver O. Howard's unsuspecting Eleventh Corps—which Hooker had sent out to guard the federal right flank. In the dusk of a late spring day, in the midst of a victory unparalleled in southern arms, Jackson was shot by his own men—who mistook him for a Union officer—in the gathering darkness. "You must hold your ground General Pender; you must hold your ground, sir!" Jackson said to one of his brigade commanders, Dorsey Pender, as he was borne to the rear. Pender's men followed this order, sweeping past their wounded commander, pushing Hooker's army into a constricted U—with their backs to the Rappahannock River. Thoroughly befuddled by Jackson's assault and stunned by a cannon shot that knocked him down, Hooker collapsed. The evening Jackson was wounded, Hooker took to his bed, mumbled some incoherent orders, and then gave command of his army to a subordinate.

All of this passed Chamberlain by. In February he had taken a leave from the regiment to visit Maine's new governor, Abner Coburn, then spent several days visiting with his family. He talked with Coburn about the need to fill officer vacancies in the regiment and was pleased when his brother Tom was promoted to regimental lieutenant. Chamberlain returned to the 20th less than two weeks after leaving, rejuvenated by his visit to Maine. There was more drilling at the hands of the able Ames, and a Grand Review when Abraham Lincoln visited, but otherwise the weeks had passed without incident. He visited Fannie in Washington and Baltimore for four days in early April, then had returned to find his regiment sick and in quarantine, the result of a spoiled batch of smallpox vaccine. The army's gang of physicians told Hooker that the regiment could not move for two weeks and posted signs at its encampment to keep others out.

Chamberlain was beside himself, describing the encampment as a "pest house" and complaining that the 20th would again be sidelined in the coming fight, just as it had been at Antietam. As the guns were booming around Chancellorsville, Chamberlain rode out of the regimental encampment to plead his unit's case, that they be given any duty at all, even if it was only to "give the enemy the small pox." His sarcasm brought smiles to the headquarters staff and comments that at least here was one man who was anxious to fight. But it was not until the morning of May 3, after the embarrassing collapse of Howard's Corps, led by Chamberlain's school chum, that the 20th was dispatched to guard the fords over the Rappahannock and the telegraph lines that led back to army headquarters. Chamberlain was up at all hours in the saddle, making sure the job was done.

Upon returning to the regiment's camp, Chamberlain wrote to his six-year-old daughter: "My dear little Daisy," he said. "I began a letter to you before the battle [at Chancellorsville] but in the hurry of our moving it was lost. It was night, too, so that we could not see much. I am sorry I lost the letter, for it was almost done. There has been a big battle, and we had a great many men killed and wounded. We shall try it again soon, and see if we cannot make those Rebels behave better, and stop their wicked works in trying to spoil our Country, and making us all so unhappy." Chamberlain was upset by the defeat at Chancellorsville, and with the army's leaders; he had enormous faith in the army and in its soldiers, but he was convinced that they were poorly led.

Lincoln agreed. While Hooker continued to command the army after Chancellorsville, the president continued his search for a leader who would win. The difference now, in May 1863, was that Lincoln had a large number of officers to choose from. With Lee ready to move, Lincoln confined his search to the highest-ranking officers of the Army of the Potomac. The most prominent of these officers was Winfield Scott Hancock, the Second Corps commander. Hancock stood outside the army's tradition: he not only looked like a leader, he acted like one. He was imposing, fearless, plain-spoken, and could fight like the devil. Hancock was joined in the army's upper echelons by forty-two-year-old Pennsylvanian John Reynolds, the hard-charging commander of the First Corps. Reynolds was offered command of the army by Lincoln after Chancellorsville, but he turned it down, fearing he would not be given a free hand. Like Hancock, Reynolds was a superb tactician and a brilliant fighter, but unlike him, he was brazenly impious. The third likely choice to head the army was George Gordon Meade, the commander of the Fifth Corps. Caustic, ill-tempered, self-pitying, and blunt to the point of rudeness, Meade was easily embittered by small slights and imagined plots ("a poor devil like myself, with little merit and no friends," he wrote his wife, "has to stand aside and see others go ahead"). But in the midst of the hardest fights, Meade could not be cowed, bringing to combat a calm that he never found in his everyday relations with his colleagues.

By 1863, there was also a second echelon of talented and dedicated officers who had proven their skills in battle. The 20th Maine's commander, Adelbert Ames, was among this elite. In May, George Meade recommended his promotion to brigadier general and Ames was given a new command in Oliver Howard's shaken Eleventh Corps. After Ames's departure, Chamberlain was named colonel of the 20th Maine. While the promotion was not a surprise, Chamberlain was a virtual unknown; there was also no assurance that the Maine professor could stand up under sustained fighting. The war was certainly not devoid of men who, once promoted, collapsed under fire, and there was a certain tentativeness to Chamberlain's promotion—despite his courage at Fredericksburg, he had not yet really proven himself. That could not be said for the 20th's new brigade commander, Strong Vincent, a Harvard graduate who had distinguished himself as the commander of the legendary 83rd Pennsylvania, which had fought in every battle the Army of the Potomac had engaged in, suffering enormous casualties at Gaines's Mill. The twenty-six-year-old lawyer was cited by McClellan as one of the army's rising young officers, primarily because his regiment was one of the Fifth Corp's most disciplined. But Vincent had other qualities, including a fascination for battle and a heart-stopping yearning for personal glory, a fact that he had proved when he took his regiment all the way to the stone wall at Marye's Heights.

It is easy to imagine how, after the shameful collapse of leadership at Chancellorsville, the Army of the Potomac might have viewed the next engagement with the rebel army with apprehension. But the promotion of Hancock, Reynolds, Meade, Ames, Chamberlain, and Vincent—and dozens of others like them—actually gave the army a certain confidence. The feeling was almost universal that while Lee might win in Virginia and might even outfox someone like Fighting Joe Hooker, it was very unlikely that the rebels could win a slugging match on northern soil. Chancellorsville was a bitter defeat, but it was not decisive. The Army of the Potomac remained a formidable fighting force.

Ironically, on the eve of the summer campaign of 1863, it was not the Army of the Potomac that was facing a crisis in leadership, but the Army of Northern Virginia. The victories at Fredericksburg and Chancellorsville imbued the South with the belief in the inevitability of Confederate victory. The war would be won, it was said, through the intervention of cotton-starved Great Britain, or because of northern disgust with the conflict's mounting casualties, or because of the Confederacy's peerless military leadership. While the common talk that "one reb" could whip "any ten yanks" had long passed, the southern people retained their enormous belief in the commitment of the individual southern soldier. At the very least, to win, all the South need do was survive.

Robert E. Lee knew better. The South was alone, tainted by slavery, its resources limited, its soldiers shoeless and often hungry. This was the real paradox for Robert E. Lee: time was both one of the South's greatest allies and its truest enemy. As long as the war continued there was hope, though each day of killing thinned his army's ranks. At some point, and soon, the South would run out of men, while the North seemed to have an infinite reservoir of ready recruits; already its ranks were being filled by a flood of immigrants, some of whom could not even speak English. The war could not be extended, Lee believed, it must be won. James Longstreet agreed. While returning his command from their foraging campaign, Longstreet stopped in Richmond to talk with Confederate Secretary of War James Seddon. Seddon asked Longstreet's view on the future movements of Lee's army and suggested that a part of it might be able to provide relief to Vicksburg, the South's embattled bastion on the Mississippi. Longstreet listened closely to Seddon's suggestion and agreed that Vicksburg's loss could be fatal, but he did not think that detaching a division, or even two, from the Army of Northern Virginia to Mississippi was the answer. Instead, he said, a part of Lee's army could be sent by rail to reinforce Braxton Bragg, who was then fighting Union forces in eastern Tennessee.

Longstreet took his eastern Tennessee proposal to Lee, who considered it over a period of two days, but finally said he did not want to send a part of the army so far beyond his reach. Instead, he argued, the Army of Northern Virginia should be strengthened and sent north to threaten Washington, in a second invasion of Maryland and Pennsylvania. The invasion would relieve Virginia farmers of the constant threat of battle, allow his army to forage in untouched areas, threaten Washington, and perhaps even defeat the Army of the Potomac "on ground of our own choosing." Lee developed his plans and imagined how his army might win a stunning battle north of the Potomac, engaging the Union forces as they raced north and turned to meet him as he emerged from the eastern ridges of the Appalachians. The federal force would be "strung out" along the roads of Maryland, each corps separated from another, and he could pounce on one, destroy it, then on the next—pushing them aside one by one. Longstreet was against the plan, fearing that Lee's audacity, which had served the cause so well in Virginia, might lead to different results north of the Potomac. Longstreet's only criticism of Lee was that in defensive warfare "he was perfect" but that "when the hunt was up, his combativeness was overruling."

It was a season of long chances. Everywhere the Confederate leadership looked, the forces of the rebellion were in retreat—in Tennessee, along the Mississippi, and in Louisiana and Texas. To make matters worse, the northern naval blockade was strangling southern commerce and making the import of badly need war matériel nearly impossible. The South was thrown back on its own resources, which were increasingly scarce. In this, the beginning of the third full year of the war, Jefferson Davis knew that Kentucky was gone, along with almost all of Tennessee, Louisiana, Missouri, and huge chunks of Virginia. The length of the Mississippi, except for the lone outpost at Vicksburg, was in northern hands. Northern armies were poised at key points along an arc that stretched from Fredericksburg to New Orleans. Facing them were men in tattered gray, organized in regiments that were already bled white.

Lee's proposal for a northern invasion was endorsed by Davis and Seddon, and Lee began preparations for the move into Maryland and

Pennsylvania at the end of May. His first priority was to reorganize and refit the army after Jackson's death. He did so by creating three corps of three divisions each. He kept James Longstreet in charge of a newly enlarged First Corps, but appointed Richard Ewell head of a newly organized Second Corps and named A. P. Hill as commander of a new Third Corps. The army's cavalry, of 14,000 mounted men, was led by the flamboyant and tactically creative (his critics said "reckless") Virginian J. E. B. ("Jeb") Stuart. But the army's veteran command was Longstreet's, where John Bell ("Sam") Hood, Lafayette McLaws, and George Pickett served as division commanders.

Hood was one of the most talented and trusted officers in the southern army and Longstreet's ablest division commander. Evander Law and William Oates, whose brigade and regiment, respectively, were a part of this division, admired Hood and believed him one of the army's great tacticians: "He was singularly devoted to duty; was always present, and exposed himself recklessly in time of battle," Oates wrote. "He was prompt in the obedience of orders and generally too ready to fight, needing to be curbed in his impetuosity. He was a man of many noble traits of character." McLaws, on the other hand, was a stickler for discipline (his soldiers called him "Make Laws") and a man who prized dependability—his own greatest asset. McLaws was one of the few genuinely modest men in the army chain of command, with the result that his great talents often passed without comment. George Pickett was entirely different; he affected a dandified air and talked endlessly of "Dearest Sallie" (his schoolgirl love back in Richmond), and he ached to get into battle.

Richard Ewell's division commanders were clearly as tough as Longstreet's, though more controversial; an added attraction was that many of them had served under Jackson. But the most enduring personality in the corps was not its commander, but Jubal Early—"Old Jube" to his troops. Early was probably the most unpopular man in the army (a "disturber," a "marplot," Longstreet called him). Vain, profane, and quick-tongued, the former Virginia prosecutor had fought well at Fredericksburg, some said brilliantly. But at times Early seemed surprisingly incompetent, as when he took his command forward into a woods near Malvern Hill and lost thirty-three men dead, all without firing a shot. Still, Early was the bright shining star of a corps whose other leaders lacked the aggressiveness that colored Early's personal relations. Robert Rodes was brave, but overly deferential, while Edward Johnson, who carried a club to punctuate his commands, was so gruff that he was virtually unapproachable.

A. P. Hill's three division commanders were as diverse as they were unknown. Virginian Henry Heth was young, impulsive, and eager to please, South Carolinian Richard Anderson was level-headed and steady, while William Pender, a native North Carolinian, was haunted by his wife's outspoken opposition to Lee's northern invasion. The heart of Hill's corps was the famous "Light Division" that Hill himself once commanded, but that was no guarantee that the corps would fight well. Heth, Anderson, and Pender were talented, but none of them had been fully tested in higher command—a fact that underscored Longstreet's importance as Lee's hardest hitting general.

The appointment of Hill and Ewell to command two new army corps disturbed Longstreet (who believed there was "too much Virginia" in the army) and a number of other officers. Longstreet later volunteered that D. H. Hill or Lafayette McLaws should have been given one of the two new commands, but Lee said he trusted Ewell and A. P. Hill because they were fighters; it was an argument that Longstreet could not deny. Longstreet agreed that Ewell was a talented corps commander and admitted that A. P. Hill, despite his constant feuding, was capable of "prodigies."

On June 10, the Army of Northern Virginia, 78,000 strong, slipped out of its camps south of the Rappahannock and moved west and then north, corps by corps, using the Blue Ridge as its cover. Oates's 450 Alabamians stepped off from their camp at Culpeper, swung slightly westward, and into an easy march step headed for the Shenandoah. The morale of the army, Oates said, was "never better." The army moved north slowly, through Virginia's early summer green, enjoying the warm weather and sultry nights. The war seemed far behind, the horrors of Fredericksburg and Chancellorsville forgotten, and only victory ahead. Many soldiers were convinced they were on their way to fight the last battle of the Confederacy, the one that would decide the war.

Within days it seemed that Lee had outfoxed Hooker, moving past his right flank and racing north, shielded by Stuart's cavalry. The march was disciplined but brutal, as the weather turned inconsolably hot. On June 15, hundreds of Hood's Division fell out of the ranks, overcome by the heat. A number died by the roadside. It was only when the air turned cooler and the late afternoon thunderstorms came that the men were afforded any relief, though it was only temporary. As they continued marching, the summer wheat shone yellow at the roadsides and the cherries were in season, which the soldiers ate by the handful. By June 25, Ewell's Corps was in southern Pennsylvania, with Early's Division near York. Rodes's men swung easily into Carlisle on June 27, through the town square, as the Pennsylvanians gawked at them in wonder. They had never seen such a filthy crew, loud and taunting in groups, but unfailingly polite when alone. The Keystoners learned a new American language, every woman became "ma'am" or "miss," and every male "sir," and they were amused to know that none of Pennsylvania's offspring were "children," but "young-uns." Rough-hewn, skinny, with tattered trousers, patched shirts, flop hats, and blankets, it was the strangest army history had ever seen. These were the soldiers of the slavocracy, but to the townspeople of Carlisle, Pennsylvania, they looked like boys.

On the dark night of June 28, a spy by the name of Harrison, hired by Longstreet at the suggestion of the War Department, walked into the flickering firelight of the First Corps encampment with startling news. Not only was the northern army across the Potomac (which meant that Lee had not given it the slip, after all), but it had a new commander: George Meade. Harrison added that the bulk of the federal army was still back in Maryland, but that it had sent out a cavalry screen into southern Pennsylvania. Longstreet immediately sent Harrison to Lee's tent with the news. The Confederate commander was stunned by the report but, in the absence of Jeb Stuart—who had not been heard from in two weeks—he was forced to believe it. He decided to pull his army together. Within the hour he sent messengers galloping off to all points of the compass, ordering a concentration of the army at Cashtown, at the foot of a gap in the last eastern ridge of the Appalachian Mountains. Lee issued strict instructions that the army was to be concentrated before giving battle. He did not want to bring on an engagement with the Army of the Potomac until all of his troops were up.

Henry Heth's Division of Hill's Corps was already at Cashtown. On the night of June 29, its outpost bivouac fires were spotted by a roving squad of northern cavalrymen; a small skirmish ensued, but it was quickly broken off. The cavalrymen were troopers from John Buford's command, who withdrew toward Emmitsburg, just across the Pennsylvania border in Maryland. Heth learned of the skirmish on the same night, but dismissed the idea that the northern army was so close. The Yankees were back in Virginia, he told his aides at Middleburg. A small squad of cavalry was of no concern, he said, especially in light of a report that his men could find shoes at Gettysburg, which was just eight miles down the road. On the morning of June 30, therefore, he rode back into Cashtown to meet with A. P. Hill. "The only force at Gettysburg is cavalry, probably a detachment of observation," Hill agreed. Heth told Hill of the shoes at Gettysburg and asked if he had any objection if he sent his division into the town to get them.

"None at all," Hill replied.

Early on the morning of July 1, Henry Heth threw out a line of skirmishers, deployed the brigades of Marylander James Archer and Mississippian Joseph Davis on either side of the Cashtown Pike, then ordered his men forward toward Gettysburg. The two lines moved into a thin early summer drizzle, crossed a low ridge, and walked through an orchard, then out into the field beyond. There was a single shot from their front and then a handful of others, all of them from blue-clad cavalrymen from William Gamble's Brigade of John Buford's Cavalry Division. Buford stood behind the cavalry line, watching the action, though he would often turn to peer to the southeast, squinting his eyes in the early morning sun, hoping to catch sight of John Reynolds's First Corps coming up the road from Maryland. Buford had sent a messenger to Reynolds at dawn, in the hopes that Reynolds's men would arrive in time to secure the low hills just to the east of the town.

Now, with a full division of rebels deployed in the fields to his west, and marching in long columns for as far as the eye could see back up the road to Cashtown, Buford did not think Reynolds would make it. As Buford watched, Archer and Davis increased their pressure against Gamble, drove in Gamble's pickets, and came forward into a low creek bed. The rebels stopped, exchanged a desultory volley with Gamble's

Brigade, paused to reform and reload, then came on again. To the right, on either side of the Pike, John Calef's Union battery of six guns opened on the neat thin gray lines, sending shot and shell out over the rolling hills. The rebels stopped, then deployed their own artillery, re-dressed their line, and paused to await instructions. Calef threw shells out to the west, his cannon retorts shaking the ground. This was not a full-fledged battle yet, but Buford knew it would be; inevitably the rebels would come at him in strength, down the road, over Herr Ridge, into a low valley, then up and over McPherson's Ridge, then down an-other valley, and finally up and over Seminary Ridge into Gettysburg, and then onto the commanding hills beyond. They would win, again, unless he found more men to stop them.

To get a better perspective on the fight, Buford climbed a ladder to the cupola of the Lutheran Seminary on the ridge to his rear. The semi-nary looked out over the land west of Gettysburg and by eight-thirty the firing had reached a crescendo, with the rebels pressing ahead. Buford was worried and gazed once again to the south. There, two miles away and coming hard up the road toward Gettysburg, he saw the flags of the First Corps. Relieved, he climbed back down the ladder, hoping to usher the Union troops across the fields to reinforce his position. Much to Buford's surprise, Reynolds was there at the bottom of the ladder, waiting and smiling slightly—amused by the cavalryman's worried look.

"What is the matter, John?" Reynolds asked calmly.

"Hell's to pay," Buford replied. After Buford explained that his own division could be easily overwhelmed by the massing rebels, Reynolds galloped off to hurry his men forward. It was a near thing—his troops came onto McPherson's Ridge just as Archer and Davis pressed their attack.

Mere chance saved the Union from an early defeat on that hot July 1. The troops that Reynolds sent into battle were from the first brigade of the first division of the First Corps of the Army of the Po-tomac—the same "black hat fellars," known as the Iron Brigade, that had proved so tough to dislodge at Second Bull Run. The division band played "The Campbells Are Coming" as the Iron Brigade de-ployed, then in a sheet of flame threw Archer and Davis back. The fight grew worse as the morning went on, with neither side willing to give way. More Union troops moved in to support the Iron Brigade from the east, but were trumped by Heth, who added strength to his own lines, moving them north and south on either side of the Cashtown Pike. At ten-fifteen, as Reynolds turned in his saddle to direct more men into line, a minié ball fired by Private E. T. Boland of Brewton, Alabama, struck him in the brain. His death was instantaneous. Command of the shaken but still tenacious First Corps now passed to Abner Doubleday (who had years before—as legend has it—invented baseball at Cooperstown, New York).

By ten-thirty the battle was fully joined. Among Heth's troops, Archer's Brigade was flanked on the right and Archer himself captured, while Davis's Brigade was caught in the bottom of a railroad cut north of the Cashtown Road and cut to pieces. Shaken by the terrible casualties of his brigades, Heth brought new men to the front and sent them once again against the blue lines. The armies paused for the redeployment, but everyone on both sides knew the near silence would be followed by another round of intense fire. The two armies had met and recoiled, met again and recoiled, and were now coming on once again. On the Union side, two new divisions from the First Corps extended the federal lines north and south, racing to overlap the rebel forces coming at them from Cashtown. Finally, the battle settled into a stand-up slugfest as the Union lines held. To John Buford, it appeared that the day had been saved by Reynolds's timely arrival. Every time the rebels came forward, the First Corps responded by pouring new units into the line.

But what Buford had not counted on was the intervention of sheer, stark, and unbelievable luck. Just when it seemed Heth's Division had been stopped cold west of Gettysburg, a shell screamed into the Yankee lines from the north, landing in the midst of the 143rd Pennsylvania regiment—on the Union line's far right. At first the 143rd's commander believed he was taking fire from his division's own batteries somewhere in his rear, but it soon dawned on him that the fire was coming from a low hill behind him. He bent back his line to meet the threat—Robert Rodes's division of Ewell's Corps, at just the precise moment that Henry Heth needed him, was coming down toward Gettysburg from the north. Rodes struck with the fury of a cyclone and for the next four hours the fighting north and west of Gettysburg was nothing less than ghastly, with blue and gray coming at each other from odd angles in unplanned, chaotic, and desperate fighting.

The Civil War changed at Gettysburg. In nearly every previous battle, the two armies had moved toward each other in a kind of delicate dance of move and countermove that was carefully plotted with a sure knowledge of the strengths and weaknesses of the contending sides. But the first day at Gettysburg was not as much a battle as a collision, as the two armies groped forward blindly in an attempt to lock on to each other. In later military parlance, this first day would be labeled a "meeting engagement"—which is what happens when two armies crash unexpectedly together, then pour in reinforcements to stave off collapse, a kind of all-out fight to the death that veteran soldiers fear. So it was that just as Rodes brought his division onto the flank of Doubleday's First Corps, Oliver O. Howard's Eleventh Corps arrived in Gettysburg from the south to extend the Union line to the right. Howard's troops, in turn, were met by a further extension of the rebel line, now bent at right angles—running from south to north and then, without break, from west to east—by troops of Jubal Early. As Rodes arrived to save Heth (on the Confederate side), and Howard to save Doubleday (on the Union side), so Early's rebel division arrived to save Rodes.

The fate of Alfred Iverson's Brigade of Rodes's Division symbolized the carnage of this collision. As Rodes came forward perpendicular to the federal line, he sent Iverson ahead with his brigade of Tar Heels to crush the Union flank. This must have seemed easy pickings for the woozy Iverson (tipsy, it was said, from too much whiskey), who did not even bother to send skirmishers ahead to feel the enemy's strength. The result was that none of his men saw a second Union line hidden behind a low stone wall until it was too late. The North Carolinians were fifty yards from the wall when three regiments of Pennsylvania and New York troops rose up suddenly and fired a single volley into the rebel ranks. Nearly 100 men were killed where they stood in a line so perfectly straight that Rodes, riding across the field later, thought he had come upon a sleeping unit. Of the 1,400 officers and men in Iverson's Brigade, only 400 survived unhurt. Soldiers of both sides always said that blood ran in rivulets during the worst battles, and at Gettysburg it lay in congealing pools on the fields.

By three o'clock on the afternoon of July 1, the battle west and north of Gettysburg was not yet decided, but it was moving quickly toward a resolution. When Oliver O. Howard's Eleventh Corps weighed in against rebel troops north of the town, he was forced to bend back his right, so that the entire Union line now appeared as a broad inverted U, a little over three miles from end to end. Howard hoped to make up for the terrible punishment his corps had taken at Chancellorsville by winning at Gettysburg, but the odds were terribly against him, with rebel troops arriving in long lines from Carlisle and Heidlersburg. His far right was the most vulnerable, as Jubal Early had placed Isaac Avery's powerful, hard-hitting brigade there. Avery's men moved forward against Howard's already spooked "Dutchmen" with a whoop.

From where he stood, in front of his brigade, Avery could look out across the battlefield. On his right the rest of Early's men were going forward; on their right, Rodes's new brigades were forming and moving for a final assault north of the town, while all the way to the west (almost exactly opposite him) Avery could see Pender's Division (in relief of Heth) moving forward for a final match against the Union position on Seminary Ridge. The vivid tableau would remind a modern, more jaded reader of the final scene from a cheap romantic novel, but for the men of Early's Division, the portrait was inspiring. There seemed nothing now, with the Union line bent and cracking, that could save the First and the Eleventh Corps from destruction. Sensing this, and with everything moving as if according to a well-established schedule, the entire Confederate line went forward and the blue lines wavered, cracked, gave, and then, in places, disintegrated entirely. Only the remnants of the Iron Brigade held, on Seminary Ridge, where John Reynolds had placed them hours before.

One of Early's brigade commanders, John Gordon of Georgia, was exuberant, seeing in his mind's eye the victory for which the South had prayed. Independence was there for the taking, just yards away. As he went forward through his own lines, riding his midnight-black stallion, with sword raised in triumph, he was asked by another officer where his fallen were laid. "I haven't got any, sir," he answered. "The Almighty has covered my men with His shield and buckler."

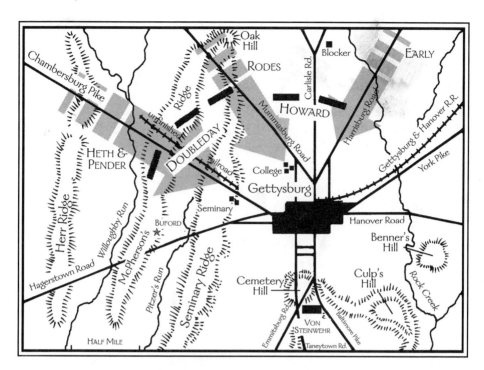

## *Gettysburg* (July 1, 1863)

Henry Heth was after shoes at Gettysburg, but found Union cavalry (under Buford) before being stopped by Union forces arrayed along McPherson's Ridge. The timely arrival of Rodes, and then Early, routed two entire Union corps, which took up defensive positions along Cemetery Hill and Culp's Hill. It was a decisive southern victory, but the Union forces held the high ground.

---

On Seminary Ridge the blue-clad regiments of the Iron Brigade were nearing exhaustion, having fought an unceasing battle against two divisions of A. P. Hill's veterans. They had piled fence posts as barricades against the successive rebel attacks, but it was only a matter of time before their defenses were overwhelmed. As a final line of rebel troops from Pender's Brigade came forward with flags unfurled, walking over the fallen bodies of Heth's command, the Union line steeled itself for the shock. Pender's men stopped, stood and let loose a volley, then came on again. The Union men held, fighting for what seemed like hours (but was only minutes) in a desperate attempt to hold their position, but were finally overwhelmed. Gray-clad soldiers pierced their line, first on the left and then in the center. The Union ranks slowly cracked then, moving back off the ridge and across the fields toward the cemetery on the hills east of Gettysburg.

The bluecoats who had fought north of Gettysburg crowded into the town, searching for roads that would funnel them south to safety. Many of them were rounded up by triumphant rebels, while others hid in storerooms and cellars. The townspeople begged them to stay, with women grabbing at their coats. But they kept going. Watching all of this unfold were Robert E. Lee and James Longstreet, who sat on their mounts on the ridge just west of the McPherson farm, with the Lutheran Seminary visible just to their front. Lee had heard the battle while in Cashtown and rode with his First Corps commander toward Gettysburg. As he watched, Lee ruminated on his plans, then sent messengers north and east to bring up the rest of his army. They would follow up their battle here today and then—if Meade's men were still across the way in the morning—they would attack, with Longstreet, on the right. Now, with the federal troops moving back in disarray toward Cemetery Hill in the distance, Lee must have thought the battle could not have been better handled if he had planned it. The catch was, of course, that he had not.

❧

When Oates and Chamberlain came to Gettysburg on the afternoon of July 2, 1863—one down the Cashtown Road from the west, the other up the Baltimore Pike from the east—neither man could have guessed that the hours just ahead would forever place them in American history. In many respects, and despite their backgrounds and experience, the two were remarkably similar. Born in poverty, William Oates raised himself to a position of eminence through sheer determination, then won the trust of the regiment he commanded by acts of personal kindness and bravery. While born in relative affluence, Joshua Chamberlain had done the same, overcoming personal insecurity and disability to carve a career as a man of learning and influence and then showing compassion and courage in the midst of war.

They were citizen-soldiers. Neither man was fired by the thirst for personal glory, though each believed deeply in his cause. Neither welcomed the conflict. Oates opposed secession; Chamberlain did not believe the nation should fight over slavery. Neither was a fatalist, or sought death, or expected it, but both knew that it might come. Both men were accompanied to Gettysburg by their brothers: Oates by John Oates, Chamberlain by Thomas and John Chamberlain—younger men who looked on them as their best friend.

If there was a difference between the two at this moment, it was this—that Chamberlain was a romantic while Oates was a realist. Chamberlain believed that the idea of the Union would be vindicated by force of arms because right and good always triumphed. Most of the Union leadership believed this—that the United States served a greater purpose, that the events of its history were a symbol for all humanity. To Oates, the right and good had as little effect in the streets of Gettysburg as it did in the gunfights of Waco, Texas. Victory by either side was not ordained or inevitable, but rested on the abilities of simple men in deadly combat. It is not too much to suppose that the history of the nineteenth century could be summarized in the debate over these two views: whether God acted through history, with humans as His agent, or whether events were made by luck, or fate, or accident.

July 2 began early for both men, three A.M. for Oates and the 15th Alabama, camped on a ridgeline south of Greenwood; it was almost exactly the same time that Chamberlain rousted his men after just three hours of sleep on the outskirts of Gettysburg. For Chamberlain, the march to the battlefield lasted only three hours, if that, since his regiment had stopped short of the town at midnight. But the passage of the 20th to Gettysburg was exhausting, since they had marched from Hanover in six hours on the night before. For Oates, the sunrise hours of July 2 were taken up with a march through Chambersburg and then into Gettysburg from the west—a distance of twenty-eight miles in just eleven hours.

Oates found the fields around Gettysburg littered with wounded and dead, the hospitals overcrowded and groups of sullen Union prisoners heading for the rear. At just before two P.M., the 15th Alabama—and the rest of Law's Brigade—filed down the highway from Chambersburg and into the fields just west of McPherson's woods. Law reported to John Bell Hood that his brigade was present and ready for action. The men of Oates's regiment were exhausted and flopped down to sleep where they halted. Oates himself, however, rode on down the Cashtown Pike to find out what lay in store in the hours ahead. "When we arrived," he remembered, "Generals Lee and Longstreet were together on an eminence in our front—on Seminary Ridge—and appeared to be inspecting with field glasses the position of the Federals."

Lee and Longstreet had just finished the latest round in a tense debate that had consumed most of the morning. At issue was how, and whether, to get at Meade's position across the open fields. The Army of Northern Virginia was strung out in a long line, running from east of Gettysburg, almost opposite of where Lee and Longstreet stood, back to the west, and then south, down Seminary Ridge in front of them. The Union's position was in the shape of a fishhook, which ran from Culp's Hill on the far right all the way to a low creek bed just south of Cemetery Ridge. Off in the distance, on the Union's far left, were two hills—Little Round Top and, farther south, Big Round Top.

The position was a puzzle because Lee did not know where the far left of the Union line rested. To determine that (and because Stuart's cavalry had not yet rejoined his army) Lee sent two of his staff officers—engineers—forward to inspect the federal position at eight in the morning. The Confederate commander suspected the Union left was unprotected, but he had to make sure. Longstreet opposed testing the proposition, arguing that the army should move to the right, past the end of the federal position (wherever that was) and "interpose itself" between Gettysburg and Washington. Lee disagreed. "The enemy is there, and we must strike him," he said. Longstreet moved away from the commanding general to speak with Hood: "The general is a little nervous this morning," he said, "he wishes me to attack; I do not wish to do so without Pickett. I never like to go into battle with one boot off." The engineers returned from their reconnaissance and reported to Lee that the left flank of the federal army was, in fact, unprotected (or "hanging in the air," as soldiers described it), with its far left units deployed in the low swampy creekland south of Cemetery Ridge. The two hills farther south were unoccupied.

Lee swept the field with his glasses, tracing the line of Union troops in the distance from left to right, until his eyes rested briefly on the two hills to the south. Longstreet came up then, looked down at a map of Gettysburg spread on a table before Lee, and turned to Lafayette

McLaws. He pointed to the map, indicating the position where he wanted him to place his division.

Lee flared: "No, General," he said, "I want it placed just opposite."

It was the closest the Confederate high command had come to a complete break, but Longstreet moved away, realizing that the argument was lost. Lee gave the command. Longstreet's Corps would move by the right, under cover of the woods and creeks in the rear of Seminary Ridge, and take its positions south of Gettysburg, where it would attack up the Emmitsburg Road, taking the Union position end-on. One of the two engineers Lee had sent on the morning reconnaissance, and who would therefore presumably know the ground, would guide Longstreet's Corps.

Then began one of the most confusing and controversial flank marches in the army's history. Longstreet put his men into column and moved them out, with McLaws's Division leading Hood's. Their goal was to reach the southern part of the battlefield without being detected—much as Jackson had marched a month earlier, before turning on the federal force at Chancellorsville. The two divisions moved from the Cashtown Road down the west side of Herr Ridge, their movement shielded by the woods, toward the Emmitsburg Road. Their plan was to move south and then attack almost directly north along a farm lane to Willoughby Run, then over the creek bed and into the woods on the southern end of Cemetery Ridge; the Union line would be crumpled. If everything went as planned, Longstreet could put his two divisions in position to attack in a line from west to east without being seen.

The column passed across a road to Fairfield, then followed the woods on Herr Ridge as planned, but when it emerged onto the farm lane that would take it east, the staff officer guiding the column realized Longstreet's troops would be plainly visible from Little Round Top. If they walked across the road and field beyond, they would be seen by Union gunners. Their attack would no longer be a surprise. The staff officer halted the column and called Longstreet forward. Longstreet was disgusted. He reconnoitered the ground to his front with Lafayette McLaws and then returned to the column guide and peremptorily ordered him to make the column retrace its steps to its starting point and then begin again. For Longstreet, it seemed, time was not a factor—it was more important that the southern army not be observed.

The column literally about-faced and moved back north, this time with Hood's Division taking the lead. When they reached the point from which they had begun their march south, they moved back west and then about-faced; this time they moved along Willoughby Run, their movements shielded by McPherson's Ridge. They passed the point where, an hour earlier, they could be observed by federal troops (that point was now on their right) and filed across the Emmitsburg Road. E. P. Alexander moved the corps artillery into place on the edge of the woods facing north and ordered his men to their guns. Off in the distance, facing them among the rocks and trees below Little Round Top, were two Union divisions of General Daniel Sickles's Third Corps. John Bell Hood was shocked—there was not supposed to be anyone there at all.

No precise calculations can be made of the full length of Longstreet's march and countermarch, but it undoubtedly took at least three and one-half hours and covered thirteen miles. The delays Longstreet encountered have been given as one of the reasons for Lee's failure at Gettysburg. If Longstreet had arrived hours or even minutes sooner on Meade's southern flank, it is said, the attack he launched would have succeeded. In truth, while Lee's engineers might have arrived at the summit of Little Round Top to find it uncovered, it is quite likely they had arrived there just after one Union unit had left, but just before another arrived. That Little Round Top controlled the southern end of the battlefield was as clear to Meade and Hancock as it was to Lee and Longstreet.

The fault actually lay with Jeb Stuart, who had not yet joined the army at Gettysburg and whose troopers were responsible for scouting the ground, determining the best approaches for an infantry assault, and determining the position of the enemy. Because of Stuart's absence, Lee felt like a blind man, groping his way forward in a strange country. For the previous two weeks he had continually asked anyone within earshot whether they had seen his cavalry. "Can you tell me where Stuart is?" he asked. "Where on earth is my cavalry?" No one knew. Stuart, in fact, was off on another one of his celebrated rides, intending to circle the federal army. But the ride had turned into a night-

ABOVE: Joshua Lawrence Chamberlain's
father, Joshua Chamberlain.
*(Pejepscot Historical Society)*

ABOVE: Joshua's sister,
Sarah Brastow Chamberlain.
*(Pejepscot Historical Society)*

RIGHT: Joshua Chamberlain's
Bowdoin College class picture.
*(Pejepscot Historical Society)*

ABOVE: Bowdoin College, Maine.
*(Bowdoin College)*

LEFT: Edmund Ruffin. *(Library of Congress)*

ABOVE: Frances Caroline Adams
Chamberlain—"Fannie."
*(Pejepscot Historical Society)*

LEFT: Harriet Beecher Stowe.
*(The Schlesinger Library)*

LEFT: William C. Oates at the beginning of the war.
*(Author's collection)*

BELOW LEFT: Confederate President Jefferson Davis.
*(Author's collection)*

BELOW: Abraham Lincoln.
*(Library of Congress)*

LEFT: Robert E. Lee.
*(Library of Congress)*

BELOW: George Brinton
McClellan. *(Library of Congress)*

BELOW LEFT: A. P. Hill.
*(Library of Congress)*

LEFT: John Gordon.
*(Library of Congress)*

BELOW: Evander McIvor Law.
*(Library of Congress)*

ABOVE: Thomas Jonathan "Stonewall" Jackson. *(Library of Congress)*

LEFT: Adelbert Ames of the 20th Maine.
*(National Archives)*

ABOVE: The Confederate dead along the Hagerstown Pike
at Antietam. *(Library of Congress)*

BELOW: Burnside's bridge at Antietam. *(Library of Congress)*

ABOVE: After the battle: the Sunken Road at Antietam. *(Library of Congress)*

BELOW: Ambrose Burnside.
*(Library of Congress)*

ABOVE: Union pontoniers attempting to cross to Fredericksburg in 1862.
*(Library of Congress)*

ABOVE: Joseph Hooker.
*(Library of Congress)*

LEFT: George Pickett.
*(Library of Congress)*

BELOW: Confederate breastworks near Devil's Den at Gettysburg.
*(Library of Congress)*

Little Round Top viewed from the west, looking toward the Union positions; Big Round Top is at the right. *(National Archives)*

BELOW: John Bell Hood, Oates's division commander. *(Author's collection)*

ABOVE: Strong Vincent, the hero of Little Round Top. *(U.S. Military History Institute)*

RIGHT: George Gordon Meade.
*(Library of Congress)*

BELOW: The charge of
Longstreet's corps at
Chickamauga. *(Library of Congress)*

ABOVE: The soldiers' fight at Chickamauga.
*(Library of Congress)*

LEFT: "The Rock of Chickamauga," George Thomas.
*(Library of Congress)*

ABOVE: William Oates leads the 15th Alabama into battle at Spotsylvania Court House (from a sketch made at the time). *(Author's collection)*

LEFT: Ulysses S. Grant.
*(Library of Congress)*

LEFT: Gouverneur K. Warren.
*(Library of Congress)*

BELOW: Joshua Chamberlain.
*(Author's collection)*

BELOW: The McClean House
at Appomattox. *(Library of Congress)*

ABOVE: Fannie Chamberlain.
*(Pejepscot Historical Society)*

ABOVE: Joshua Chamberlain during
the Civil War. *(Pejepscot Historical Society)*

RIGHT: Thomas Davee Chamberlain
in 1865. *(U.S. Military History Institute)*

ABOVE: James Longstreet. *(Library of Congress)*

ABOVE: Jubal Early. *(Library of Congress)*

LEFT: Populist candidate and Oates's nemesis, Reuben F. Kolb.
*(Alabama Archives)*

LEFT: William C. Oates in 1898, at the time of the Spanish–American War. *(Author's collection)*

BELOW: Joshua Chamberlain in the 1870s. *(Pejepscot Historical Society)*

BELOW: The reunion of the 15th Alabama in Montgomery in 1902. *(Author's collection)*

mare; at every point where the southern cavalry commander turned west to find Lee's army, he bumped instead into blue troopers. Finally, Lee had sent riders out looking for him, with orders for him to join Lee's command at Gettysburg.

Although Stuart's lapse was arguably fatal, the southern army was in fact undone by Meade. The new Union commander might have been insecure about his new position ("I know they call me a damned old snapping turtle," he admitted), but he responded quickly to Lee's invasion, telling his aides that his object was to "compel" Lee to "meet me in battle at some point." When he heard about the first day's debacle at Gettysburg and Reynolds's death, he sent the army's best engineer, Andrew Humphreys, forward to inspect the land around Gettysburg—to make certain the army's position could be defended—then dispatched Winfield Scott Hancock to take command of the troops at the battle-field. When Meade himself arrived outside of Gettysburg, in the pitch-black early hours of July 2, he pointedly asked his corps commanders whether they believed this was "good ground." When they agreed that indeed it was, he turned on them. "I am glad to hear you say so, gentlemen," he snapped, "for it is too late to leave it." Meade had no intention of leaving, but thought only of how he would fight. For the first time in its history, the northern army was being led by a commander who meant what he said, a fact well known to Robert E. Lee. "General Meade will commit no blunder on my front," he predicted, "and if I make one he will make haste to take advantage of it."

Meade knew the ground, and as he looked south in the darkness from his headquarters behind the center of Cemetery Ridge, he could see that Little Round Top dominated the field. But he was not convinced the attack would take place there, thinking instead that Lee would attack on the right. So when, the next morning—the sultry day of July 2—Daniel Sickles, the army's combative Third Corps commander and former Democratic congressman, sent a messenger to ask Meade where on the left he should be posted, the new army commander paid him scant attention; he told the messenger to tell Sickles to occupy the ground held by the Twelfth Corps on the night before (which included Little Round Top). This only confused Sickles, who did not think the Twelfth had occupied any position at all, so he rode in person to Meade to ask whether it was in his discretion to post his command as he saw fit. "Certainly," Meade answered, "within the limits of the general instructions I have given you; any ground within those limits you choose to occupy I leave to you." That was all Sickles needed. With drums rolling and flags snapping in the summer heat, Sickles marched two of his divisions out past Cemetery Ridge and occupied a line that stretched along the Emmitsburg Road, facing west, then bent back at a peach orchard, facing south.

Which is where Hood found him on the late afternoon of July 2. With the woods and fields in front of Longstreet's position bristling with cannon and blue-clad troops, Hood aligned his division facing north, with Law's Brigade holding the far right, while McLaws's Division filed in a line next to him, turning to face the east. In the fields, less than one mile from where Hood formed for battle, the Union division of David Birney—the son of Alabama planter-turned-abolitionist James Birney—faced the rebel line, ready for battle. As the cannon opened along his front, Hood sent a messenger galloping to Longstreet requesting that the attack be halted and his division moved to the right, to flank the federal position. When Longstreet received the message he was exasperated. He had made the same suggestion to Lee earlier in the day and been turned down. Longstreet sent back the messenger with explicit instructions. Enough time had already been wasted, he said. The attack would go forward as planned.

Hood was not satisfied. His scouts told him the ground ahead was strewn with boulders, making it nearly impossible to mount his artillery. His brigades could be mauled without such support. Hood sent a second messenger to Longstreet. Longstreet's answer came promptly back: "General Lee's orders are to attack up the Emmitsburg Road," he said. But Hood was still not satisfied. Just as he was about to order his men forward, Longstreet rode up. This time Hood pleaded his case in person, pointing out that if he was allowed to send just one brigade around to the right, the battle might be won. Longstreet's response was peremptory: "We must obey the orders of General Lee." According to a staff courier, Lee himself then appeared and made the final decision, explaining that he could not "take the risk of losing a brigade. We must do the best we can."

Oates stood in front of his regiment and looked out over the field, assessing the ground ahead. A rebel battery less than one-quarter mile to his left was sending shells into the woods beyond—its deep *toomp,* *toomp, toomp* shaking the ground. It was as if someone were blowing holes in the air, sucking out the oxygen. The men from Alabama had had this feeling before, just prior to an assault, their stomachs feeling achy and vacant, their legs shivering with the coming storm. Many prayed. Hood now had his orders and, after saluting Lee, he rode down along the line of his division, talking with his aides for one last time. He then turned and ordered his battle ranks forward—all 6,000 of them, with their muskets at shoulder arms.

The men of the 15th Alabama moved out in the center of Law's Brigade, walking through the field to their front. On their left, men of Arkansas and Texas were going in, walking in lockstep, their muskets at the ready. The artillery bombardment stopped and the men serving the guns lifted their hats as they watched Longstreet's troops go in on the right, heading straight for the large hill and the smaller one just to its north.

☙━━◆━━❧

The noise of the attack was terrible. Almost immediately after stepping forward, the front rank moving down into a shallow swale, Oates heard shots coming from the base of Big Round Top. But there were no casualties yet. Slowly, drawn by the fire, the regiment inclined slightly to its right, toward the hill. With this, two regiments on Oates's right—the 44th and 48th Alabama regiments—slowed, paused, and then passed behind the 15th and became mixed with Oates's men, slowing his march and tangling his disciplined lines. A sergeant in Oates's regiment was annoyed by the mix-up, raising his voice above the noise of battle: "Colonel Oates, make Colonel Bulger take his damned concern out of our regiment!" Oates extricated his command and moved forward.

Oates made his attack with just under 400 men—but there should have been more. Just before the attack opened, the Alabama colonel had sent twenty-two men (one from each company) to the rear to find water, and they had not returned. Others reported sick, including Oates's brother John. Oates had found him behind the lines just before the attack and urged him not to go forward with the regiment. But his brother protested. "If I were to remain here," he had said, "people would say that I did it through cowardice; no sir, I am an officer and will never disgrace the uniform I wear; I shall go through, unless I am killed, which I think is quite likely." Oates was frustrated that his regiment was not up to strength. His tangle with the 48th Alabama could only make the situation worse, as some men might be caught up in the confusion and walk off with the other regiment. In addition, Oates now learned that his assignment, to move straight forward and attack, had changed.

"General Law rode up to me as we were advancing, and informed me that I was then on the extreme right of our line and for me to hug the base of Great Round Top and go up the valley between the two mountains," Oates wrote, "until I found the left of the Union line, to turn it and do all the damage I could." Law rode off, and soon after, the regiment took its first casualties, with first one man and then another going down. One of these was Isaac Feagin, who slumped to the ground, his kneecap shattered. Another was John Nelson, a twenty-three-year-old "shirker" who would go into every battle filled with courage and then, when he heard fire, run away. Sergeant Pat O'Connor was assigned to hold him to his task at Gettysburg, grabbing his shirt collar and leading him across the field. Nelson tried to break for the rear, but O'Connor held him and moved him forward in pace with the regiment. All the way across the fields to the base of Big Round Top Nelson tugged at his captor, trying to get away, until a ball hit him square and killed him instantly. O'Connor let him slowly down and walked on, saying, "Now I guess you will not run away."

Oates moved his men to the right to face the fire, which was coming from the green-jacketed troops of the 2nd U.S. Sharpshooters—the best marksmen in the federal army. Oates sent skirmishers out ahead, then ordered his men up the western face of Big Round Top. "We could see our foe only as they dodged back from one boulder to another, hence our fire was scattered," Oates wrote. His regiment went up the hill hand over hand in the face of the fire, which was now to their right. Oates kept the regiment moving up, straight ahead. "Some of my men fainted from heat, exhaustion, and thirst," he wrote, but he kept going, straight to the top, where he halted, his men collapsing with exhaustion around him. Oates looked out from the mountain, west and north—to the town. "I saw Gettysburg through the foliage of the trees." Below him, among the rocks, the men of Arkansas and Texas were fighting for their lives, their long lines rent by the galling cannon fire from the Union artillery to their front.

Lieutenant Leigh R. Terrill, a brigade staff officer, came up the mountain on horseback. General Hood was down, severely wounded, he said, and Law was now leading the division. Oates should not halt; his orders were to move north down the slope and then up Little Round Top, finding and turning the Union left, 1,000 yards in the distance. "I then called his attention to my position," Oates reported. "A precipice on the east and north, right at my feet; a very steep, stony, and wooded mountain-side on the west. The only approach to it by our enemy, a long wooded slope on the northwest. . . . Within half an hour I could convert it into a Gibraltar." Terrill responded, much as Longstreet had to Hood, that Oates's orders were to move forward and to "drive everything before me as far as possible." Oates obeyed the order, though he believed he held the key to a Confederate victory—he could imagine what a battery of well-handled cannon would do on Big Round Top, sending arcing shells onto the blue-clad men below, who would flee back, up their own line, then down the Baltimore Pike. Oates put this thought out of his mind, allowed his men to rest a few more moments, then ordered them up and into line and led them down the slope toward the Union position.

On the saddle between the two hills, Oates spotted the ammunition trains of the Union army to his right and dispatched a company to capture them. Below him, savage fighting was taking place among the boulders of Devil's Den, while still farther west, Hood's last brigades were fighting their way across a wheat field. Beyond Hood's left, Longstreet was standing with William Barksdale in the front of McLaws's Division, waiting for Hood to bear the brunt of the attack. Barksdale eyed the federal cannon posted in a peach orchard just beyond the road and begged Longstreet to let him go in. "Not yet," Longstreet responded. He was purposely holding Barksdale back in order to develop the attack, which was *en echelon,* moving at intervals from right to left, with first one and then another brigade going forward. Longstreet hoped the federals would shift troops from Barksdale's front to meet Hood's attack. Somewhere there would be a soft spot, and the rebels would punch through the gap, exploiting the sudden chance.

At five P.M., Longstreet finally ordered Barksdale forward and into the teeth of the federal cannon. Barksdale, his gray hair flowing, walked in front of his men, his sword high, as Longstreet walked beside him. Off to the right, the battle for Little Round Top was just beginning. There were now just over 350 men in Oates's regiment—more than fifty fewer than what he had started out with just thirty minutes before. Halfway up the slope, Oates waved his sword and shouted: "Forward, men, to the ledge!" The 15th Alabama moved forward, then were met by a deadly fire from the blue-clad soldiers just above them.

William R. Holloway leaped onto the ledge, with Oates just to his left. A thirty-eight-year-old veteran soldier, he was momentarily blinded by the battle smoke, which wreathed the hillside. He looked at Oates, confused. "Colonel," he yelled, "I can't see them." Oates pointed forward, but then told him to kneel, to look under the smoke on the hillside. "He took deliberate aim and fired," Oates later wrote. "As he took his gun down from his shoulder a bullet passed through his head. I caught him in my arms, laid him down, took up his gun and fired a few rounds myself, and then went to another part of the line. Poor Holloway was a good man."

The ball that killed Holloway was fired by a man of the 20th Maine. Chamberlain's regiment was now deployed in a solid blue line across the southern face of the mountain. But that they were there at all was an accident. George Meade did not plan to have the far end of the Union line defended by a volunteer regiment commanded by a Bowdoin professor. If given the choice, he would much rather have deployed a veteran unit, like the Iron Brigade, cut up though it was. But chance, or destiny, dictated that Meade could not have picked a better group of soldiers to defend his flank. Chamberlain and his men were spoiling for a fight and believed that the fate of the nation rested in their hands. That had not been the case just one hour before, of course, when the 20th Maine was resting in a field near the Hanover Road, behind Cemetery Ridge. The war had still seemed far away to the Maine men, and many of them did not believe they would get into the battle, such glory having eluded them so often before. But just after the guns of Hood's artillery opened on Birney (a cacophony so startling that it brought them to their feet) the men of the 20th Maine had been ordered to the left, with the rest of Vincent's Brigade.

The brigade then went through Plum Run and out into a field beyond, getting a glimpse of the orchard on the high ground to the right where "the havoc was terrible." Chamberlain's men passed the wheat field, "where heroic men standing bright as golden grain were ravaged by Death's wild reapers from the woods. Here we halted to be shown our places. We had a momentary glimpse of the Third Corps left in front of Round Top, and the fearful struggle at Devil's Den, and Hood's out-flanking troops swarmed beyond. Our halt was brief, but our senses alert." The 20th moved farther to the left, then ascended the slope of Little Round Top.

The decision to move up Little Round Top was the result of orders given by the army's chief engineer, General Gouverneur Kemble Warren, who ascended the hill to find it ungarrisoned. Understanding the importance of the position, Warren ordered a cannon to drop a shell into the woods to the south. When the shell exploded, Warren saw the gleam of southern bayonets shimmering in the sun; the rebel army was less than one mile away. He sent a messenger back behind the Union lines to Fifth Corps commander George Sykes, asking that he bring a brigade to Little Round Top immediately. Strong Vincent intercepted Warren's message and headed his regiments up the low hill. Apparently fearing that his first message to Sykes might not get through, Warren ordered the 140th New York up Little Round Top and also dispatched an artillery battery under the command of Charles Hazlett.

The 20th Maine was just starting to go into position when the 15th Alabama started its descent from Big Round Top. As shots started coming at them, Chamberlain placed his men in a compact line, curling a part of them back around the hill, then turned to his two brothers. "Boys," he said, looking over the position, "I don't like this. Another shot might make it hard for mother. Tom, go to the rear of the regiment, and see that it is well closed-up! John, pass up ahead and look out for a place for our wounded." Strong Vincent came up to give Chamberlain his orders. "I place you here," he said firmly. "This is the left of the Union line. You understand. You are to hold this ground at all

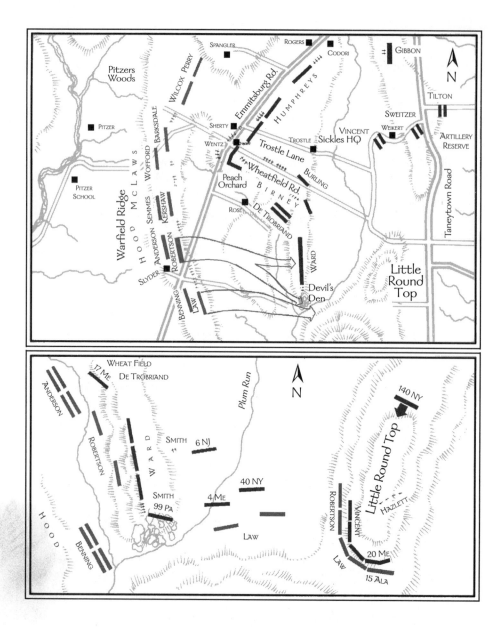

## Gettysburg (July 2, 1863)

After a roundabout march behind Seminary Ridge, Longstreet's Corps emerged along the Emmitsburg Road (*top*). Law's Brigade of Hood's Division stepped off on the right, attempting to crush Sickles's position on Little Round Top and Devil's Den. McLaws followed, attacking Union troops in the wheat field and peach orchard. On the far right, the 15th Alabama attacked the 20th Maine (*below*) in an attempt to turn the Union left.

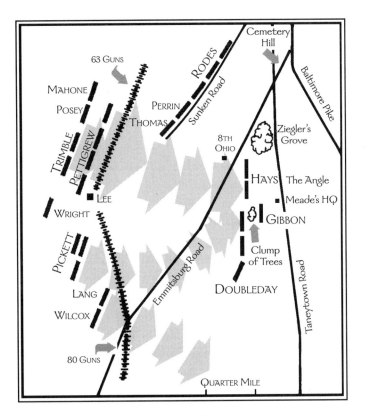

*Gettysburg* (July 3, 1863)

Emerging from the woods on Seminary Ridge, the divisions of Pickett, Petti-grew, and Trimble attacked the center of the Union line on Cemetery Ridge. The assault had been preceded by an enormous bombardment. Confederate soldiers of Armistead's Brigade made it inside the angle, but no farther.

---

costs." The Confederate lines were surging from the right toward the base of Little Round Top like the incoming tide.

After the 20th Maine's first volley killed a handful of Oates's men, he steadied his regiment and faced them forward, moving them up the hill. The gray line stopped and fired, then fired again. Oates could see the Yankee line waver and crack, but it did not disintegrate. The 20th returned the fire, reloaded, then fired again, bringing down half a score of rebels. Oates brought his men on in a rush. Chamberlain responded by moving his men slowly toward the top of the hill, shortening his line. Oates took the ledge that Chamberlain had just held. "It was our time now to deal death and destruction to a gallant foe, and the account was speedily settled," he recalled years later. "I led this charge and sprang upon the ledge of rock, using my pistol within the musket length, when the rush of my men drove the Maine men from the ledge." Oates's regiment was taking catastrophic casualties, but no worse than at the angle of Chamberlain's line where it bent back toward the hill, where whole companies seemed to be swept away by the federal fire.

At one point, a few of the Maine men leaped down, grasping Oates's regimental colors, which were planted on a large boulder. Oates remembered the scene for the rest of his life: "A Maine man reached to grasp the staff of the colors when Ensign Archibald stepped back and Sergeant Pat O'Connor stove his bayonet through the head of the Yankee, who fell dead. I witnessed that incident, which impressed me beyond the point of being forgotten." Oates went back down the hill, realigned his men, and moved them to the right, attempting to flank Chamberlain. The fire now from above was wiping away entire squads of rebels. Oates's brother John fell, pierced by three balls, and lay in the open, bleeding, until Lieutenant Isaac Parks pulled him behind a rock. (After the battle he was found by Union soldiers and taken to a field hospital. He died twenty-three days later. "We were not only brothers, near the same age, but had been reared together, and no brothers loved each other better," William Oates wrote.) Oates could not go to his brother's aid—there were already too many dead men around him. One of them was twenty-four-year-old James Ellison. When Oates gave the command to charge, Ellison cupped his hand to his ear as if he hadn't heard. Oates repeated the command. "I was looking at him when a ball passed through his head, killing him instantly," Oates later wrote. Ellison was wearing his new captain's uniform, presented to him by Oates before the battle.

The battle swung wildly, with first one side and then the other firing massed volleys; then the firing became general as men loaded, fired, reloaded, and fired again. Twice it seemed the 15th Alabama had gained a foothold inside Chamberlain's line, only to be beaten back. Chamberlain later wrote:

Squads of the enemy broke through our line in several places, and the fight was literally hand to hand. The edge of the fight rolled backward and forward like a wave. The dead and wounded were now in our front and then in our rear. Forced from our position, we desperately recovered it, and pushed the enemy down to the foot of the slope. The intervals of the struggle were seized to remove our wounded . . . to gather ammunition from the cartridge-boxes of the disabled friend or foe on the field, and even to secure better muskets. . . . Rude shelters were thrown up of the loose rocks that covered the ground.

After one hour, with the situation more precarious by the moment, Oates moved his men once more to the right, attempting to lap Chamberlain's flank. Chamberlain, standing on a rock above, saw the movement, directed his own regiment to the left, and was openly surprised when the maneuver (called refusing the line) was done without confusion. "My officers and men understood my wishes so well that this movement was executed under fire," Chamberlain wrote in his official report, "the right wing keeping up fire, without giving the enemy any occasion to seize or even to suspect their advantage." Miraculously, the movement of the 20th Maine was mimicked by each Union regiment down the line in turn. "But we were not a moment too soon; the enemy's flanking column having gained their desired direction, burst upon my left, where they evidently had expected an unguarded flank, with great demonstration."

Oates moved his men back down the hill, then put them in line for one last charge. On the hill above them, Joshua Chamberlain was told by his officers that the men were running out of ammunition. The blood of the slain was pooled on the rocks below and around Chamberlain. Oates ordered his men forward. Chamberlain later described the moment: "The enemy seemed to have gathered all their energies for their final assault. We had gotten our thin line into as good a shape as possible, when a strong force emerged from the scrub wood in the valley, as well as I could judge, in two lines in echelon by the right, and, opening a heavy fire, the first line came on as if they meant to sweep everything before them. We opened on them as well as we could with our scanty ammunition snatched from the field."

The few Alabamians who got into Chamberlain's line were either clubbed down or shot while attempting to escape. There was one last pause, while Chamberlain, exhausted, tried to think of what to do. A messenger ran up with news. All of the regiments on the 20th's right were hard-pressed and Strong Vincent was dead. To Chamberlain, it looked like the end. The 20th Maine was out of ammunition; even the cartridges of the dead were gone. But Chamberlain's regiment was the last defense of the last army of the Republic, and his orders were to hold. "It was imperative to strike before we were struck by this over-whelming force in a hand-to-hand fight, which we could not probably have withstood or survived," he wrote. "At that crisis, I ordered the bayonet."

Down the hill, Oates was also nearing the end. His troops exhausted and collapsing from thirst, he sent a messenger to the left to bring help from the 4th Alabama. The messenger returned shortly with news—there was no one there. Oates was alone. Suddenly, above him, he heard the men of Chamberlain's regiment coming down the hill, yelling, their bayonets drawn. "The effect was surprising," Chamberlain said of this bayonet charge, "many of the enemy's first line threw down their arms and surrendered. An officer fired his pistol at my head with one hand, while he handed me his sword with the other. Holding fast by our right, and swinging forward our left, we made an extended 'right wheel,' before which the enemy's second line broke and fell back, fighting from tree to tree, many being captured, until we had swept the valley and cleared the front of nearly our entire brigade."

William Oates would never admit that his men broke before this charge, insisting to his death that he ordered their retreat. But however they went, ordered or not, the 15th Alabama—one of the great fighting regiments of Hood's Division—was scattered by the charge and ran back into the valley between the round tops, then up and over Big Round Top itself, their lines thinned by death. "I found the undertaking to capture Little Round Top too great for my regiment unsupported," Oates later wrote. "I waited until the next charge of the 20th Maine was repulsed, as it would give my men a better chance to get out unhurt, and then ordered the retreat." Then, as an afterthought, he admitted: "When the order was given we ran like a herd of wild cattle." Oates ran too, back down the hill, his men on his left and right, with the minié balls thumping dully past them. Beside him ran thirty-two-year-old John Keels, whose windpipe had been scraped by a ball; he puffed his way down the hill, blowing spouts of blood from his throat.

The rebel attack was over, but not just on Little Round Top. All along the line, Longstreet's men were reaching the end of their strength. Hood was down, wounded, Barksdale was dead, and Oates, reaching the summit of Big Round Top, collapsed in exhaustion. "There never were harder fighters than the 20th Maine men and their gallant Colonel," Oates wrote of the battle. "His skill and persistency and the great bravery of his men saved Little Round Top and the Army of the Potomac from defeat." This was a hard admission, for Oates always believed that if he had just had one more company, or even the twenty-two men who had gone for water, or half a regiment, or perhaps the men he had sent in vain pursuit of the federal trains, he might have won his fight with Chamberlain and given victory to the Army of Northern Virginia. None of that happened. "Great events," he concluded, "sometimes turn on comparatively small affairs."

# 10

# *God Had Nothing to Do with It*

**W**RITING MORE THAN A CENTURY LATER, Shelby Foote was the first to notice the odd symmetry of the struggle for Little Round Top. In *The Civil War: A Narrative*, he noted that the homes of the men of Alabama and Maine lay on a direct line that crossed Gettysburg; that Little Round Top, so unobtrusive as to be past noticing, was and is almost exactly halfway by "crowflight" between Presque Isle in Maine and Talladega in Alabama. A finer calibration, in fact, shows that the line between Brunswick and Oates's Crossroads might well traverse the forward slope of the small hill. More important, Little Round Top, where 800 men from Alabama and Maine fought to decide the fate of the Union, was soon viewed as a microcosm of the war—and one of its most enduring symbols. Gettysburg is now viewed as the single most important battle of America's most important and bloodiest war—and the fight for Little Round Top is almost universally viewed as the single most important struggle of the battle.

The Battle of Little Round Top contains other curiosities. On July 2, Oates not only commanded the 15th Alabama, he was also given command of the 4th Alabama, a demiregiment that had lost its commander. The extra men might have given him an edge in the coming fight, except that Oates's additions were matched nearly exactly by Chamberlain's: on the eve of *his* battle, the Maine colonel was assigned the task of watching over the remnant of the rebellious 2nd Maine, whose remaining men refused to serve when most of the regiment was sent home. Chamberlain was gentle with his prisoners, telling the men of the 2nd that they could fight or not, it was up to them, but that they were needed and he would use them if he could. Most of them volunteered for duty when they heard Hood's guns sounding on the left; some others took arms on the hill itself when they saw Oates's rebels forming below.

It is generally held that the two sides were evenly matched in numbers and in force, but detractors have been heard through more than fourteen decades of national history. The official regimental roster seems to support Chamberlain's claim to being outnumbered, reporting that he entered the battle with under 400 muskets, but Oates made the same contention: "The absence of Company A from the assault on Little Round Top, the capture of the water detail, and the number overcome by heat who had fallen out on scaling the rugged mountain, reduced my regiment to less than four hundred officers and men who made that assault." Each man vied to be outnumbered, to claim that the men of Maine, or Alabama, overcame the odds. Even if equal in numbers, southerners say, Oates's men had the tougher job of assaulting a line while scrambling up a dark, tree-choked hill, making his near-success all the more remarkable. Northerners are usually content to let such protests pass, but when pressed will answer that men facing downhill tend to overshoot their target, implying that Oates's near-success resulted not from diligence or strategy, but simple physics.

The war went on. In Gettysburg's aftermath it was clear to the soldiers of both sides that something had changed. The North gained strength from its victory, the South a new sense of gloom. The ranks of Lee's army were never so strong, so dedicated to victory as in southern Pennsylvania. But after the first day, nothing seemed to go right. William Oates listed the battle's "ifs": Stuart's absence, Ewell's hesitations, Longstreet's countermarch, another brigade at the end of the second day cracking the Union line in the twilight—one more squad, company, or regiment on the right, with the 15th Alabama, on July 2. Oates could nearly see the victory within his grasp, if only one more company had climbed with him that late afternoon. The South would have won, surely, at Gettysburg, if fate, or timing, or even sheer accident had somehow intervened, as they so often had before: at Bull Run, Gaines's Mill, Second Bull Run, Fredericksburg, and Chancellorsville.

For Chamberlain, God's will worked through the Union at Gettysburg, confirming the nobility of the cause, its essential rightness. The dead of the 20th Maine lined the hillside, he remembered, with their faces covered. They were "laid as on the altar," a sacrifice for the nation. Even their burial was modest, their gravestones "rudely carved under tear-dimmed eyes." There was no question that their cause was just, their sacrifice honorable, for the dead were "lifted high above self, pure in heart as they that shall see God" and then reborn: "Oh, the glory that beamed through those nights and days. Nobody will ever know it here! —I am sorry most of all for that. The proud young valor that rose above the mortal, and then at last was mortal after all." Chamberlain even supposed that at Judgment Day, the Gettysburg hills— "which drank in such high heart's blood"—would give up the Union dead and "flame again with transfigured light."

Oates bitterly rejected the notion of Union-dead-as-Risen-Christ. "I do not worship a God who takes sides in battle and gives the victory to the heaviest battalions, greatest numbers and best equipped with arms and implements of war without regard to whether the cause be just or unjust," he wrote, and added, "I am an unwavering believer in God as the Creator of all things. I believe that He created immutable and unchangeable laws for their government and endowed men with the power of acting for themselves and with responsibility for their acts. When we went to war it was a matter of business, of difference among men about their temporal affairs. God had nothing to do with it. He never diverted a bullet from one man, or caused it to hit another, nor directed who should fall or who should escape, nor how the battle should terminate."

Did God intervene? It must have seemed so on July 3, the day after the attack on Little Round Top, when Robert E. Lee sent the divisions of Pickett, Pettigrew, and Trimble—all of them under the command of James Longstreet—against the Union's positions on Cemetery Ridge. The plan seemed perfectly conceived. Lee noted to his commanders that they had attacked on the left and on the right and that Meade would now be weak somewhere; probably in the middle, he thought. Lee had seen such attacks succeed before, during the war with Mexico, when American troops attacked Santa Anna's impregnable position at Chapultepec. The fortress had been the key to Mexico City, as Cemetery Ridge was the key to the Union position. Pickett and Longstreet had scaled the heights at Chapultepec and carried the day against overwhelming odds. Lee must have believed that it could be done again and that Providence would shine on his army.

The center of the attack, which came to be known as Pickett's Charge, was led by Lewis Armistead, who brought his brigade across the field and then up Cemetery Ridge into the very center of the Union line. He is remembered in history as a gentle man, a friend of Union commander Winfield Scott Hancock. Near the end of his attack, as his men were about to make their final assault against the Union position, Armistead placed his hat on a sword point to guide his men forward. In fact, near the end of their long march from Seminary Ridge, Armistead's troops actually stopped short of the Union line to align their ranks—an unprecedented act of courage that astounded the Union line's defenders—before moving forward. The rebels pulled their hats down against the rain of shells, then charged up and over the ridge. Union artilleryman Alonzo Cushing's battery of cannon awaited them with double canister. Armistead placed his hand on one of these cannon, urging his men on. As they swept past him he was mortally wounded by Union infantry fire. The fighting inside the lines, at the point of the rebel army's greatest penetration—the "High Water Mark"—near a copse of trees that could be seen from Seminary Ridge, lasted for many minutes, with men engaged in hand-to-hand combat. Finally, a federal countercharge by more than three Pennsylvania regiments shattered Armistead's command and sent it back across the field.

The charge was an awe-inspiring sight, but that did not keep the Union line from chanting "Fredericksburg, Fredericksburg" as the rebels came at them. Just as Armistead's Brigade was being broken by massed Union fire, Isaac Trimble's line crashed headlong into the Union position along the stone wall to Armistead's left. Trimble's men came across the wall in full tide, but like Armistead, Trimble fell wounded. He watched helplessly as his men ebbed westward, back toward Seminary Ridge. Trimble, the 15th Alabama's first brigade commander, was severely wounded and lost a leg. He remained a prisoner for the rest of the war, but his judgment of the assault remains the most accurate: "No single line of infantry without artillery can carry a line, protected by rifle pits, knapsacks and other cover, and a numerous

artillery, if the assaulted party bravely avails itself of all its advantages."
But that was later. On the field his judgment was pithy: "If the troops I
had the honor to command today couldn't take that position, all hell
can't take it," he said.

Armistead's charge inside the Union lines has become one of the
best-known incidents of the war, and the accounts of his death one of
his generation's most storied legends. In 1861, when Armistead came
east from outpost duty to join the Confederacy, he gave Hancock's wife
a packet to be opened only in case of his death. The package contained
his family Bible, with the inscription "Lewis A. Armistead. Trust in
God and fear nothing." This story, his close friendship with Hancock,
and his prewar pledge that he would never lift his hand against his prewar companion ("or may God strike me dead") was repeated in both
armies after Gettysburg. The stories were embroidered after the battle
by a report that, while laying wounded inside the Union lines, Armistead offered his regrets to his old friend: "Say to General Hancock for
me, that I have done him, and you all, a serious injury, which I shall always regret." The words were tailor-made for those who believed that
God was present, tipping the scales to the just and striking down the
iniquitous.

Armistead's death was a blow to Pickett's Division, which was destroyed by the attack. While Pickett reported 232 killed in his command, only 800 of his 4,500 soldiers returned to his camp after the
catastrophe. The same casualty figures are reflected in the commands
of James Johnston Pettigrew and Isaac Trimble, who had been given
command of Pender's Division on July 3. The men of Pickett, Pettigrew, and Trimble were literally swept away by the cataclysm: "In front
of the Second Corps, the dead lay in great heaps," one Union officer
noted. "Out on the field where Longstreet's Corps had passed, thousands of wounded were lying." Lee immediately grasped the crisis that
faced his army and, with Longstreet (who opposed the assault to the
point of insubordination, then watched it from a fence post, in his slippers), set out to mend the shattered units. It was an impossible task; the
troops fled blindly back west, all the way to the Fairfield Road, far in
the rear of Lee's line. It was a sight that no one in the army had ever before witnessed. "Don't stop my men," Pickett told a guard sent to stop
the retreat. "Tell them to come to the camp we occupied last night."

Pickett's Charge remains one of the most studied events in American history, though at the time it seemed less important than the assault of July 2. In all of the photographs taken of the field by Alexander Gardner and others in the battle's wake, none was taken of the field over which Pickett charged—blessedly, perhaps. But it is hard to believe that, even without Pickett's Charge, the Confederacy could have survived Gettysburg. Lee's army lost thirty percent of its strength during the three-day battle—2,600 dead, 13,000 wounded, and over 5,200 captured or missing. The records for the Army of the Potomac showed 3,100 dead, 14,000 wounded, and 5,300 missing. But the numbers do not tell the entire story. A large portion of Lee's missing were dead. Pickett's Division never really recovered. The losses for the 15th Alabama at Little Round Top were staggering and symbolic of the rebel losses—Oates lost nearly one of every three soldiers he took into battle, 138 dead, wounded, and missing, forty-two percent of the total. It is probable that he underestimated the number of those killed, as Chamberlain reported removing no less than 50 rebel bodies from in front of his position. Of course, the 20th Maine suffered also, counting almost exactly the same number (136) of dead, wounded, and missing.

On July 4, while Lee attempted to maintain his battered lines, Vicksburg surrendered. The next day, Lee moved slowly south with his army, then turned it at the Potomac to face Meade. But the northern commander did not attack. Safely back in Virginia, Lee sent Pickett's Division farther south to rest and refill its ranks, after pleading with its commander to take steps to ensure the integrity of his command. In truth, the Army of Northern Virginia was beginning to disintegrate. Not waiting for the order to retreat, over 5,000 Confederate soldiers left the army's lines at Gettysburg on July 4 and headed south. The high rate of desertions continued after the army returned to its camps along the Rappahannock. In one instance, nearly 60 men of one North Carolina brigade deserted en masse. Lee wrote the Confederate secretary of war recommending that guards be placed at the bridges over the rivers leading to the Carolinas to return the men to the front.

On July 26, the army's inspector general issued a special plea, asking those who had left the army to return to their posts: "To remain at home in this, the hour of our country's need, is unworthy the manhood of a Southern soldier. While you proudly boast that you belong to the Army of Northern Virginia, let it not be said that you deserted your comrades in a contest in which everything you hold dear is at stake." Lee was uncertain about what action to take to stop the desertions, alternating between wanting to "make an example" of those who deserted (by ordering them shot) or issuing a general amnesty to induce those who had left to return. The southern soldier believed he was poorly used at Gettysburg and he showed it. Lee was morose, feeling that he had lost the confidence of his men. He wrote to Davis without recrimination, offering his resignation. "I have seen and heard of expressions of discontent in the public journals at the result of the expedition. I do not know how far this feeling extends in the army. My brother officers have been too kind to report it, and so far the troops have been too generous to exhibit it." In this, at least, Lee was paying tribute to the thousands who deserted, whom he must have thought particularly ungenerous—but they represented only a portion of his army. The rest, the thousands who stayed, were not yet to the point where they would abandon the cause. For them, Lee was still the greatest captain, their only hope of victory. Perhaps one of the most eloquent descriptions of the Confederate general came from William Jordan, a soldier of Oates's 15th Alabama:

> I have seen General Lee under various circumstances and conditions, in the heat of battle, on the march on his horse Traveler, quietly in camps, in pursuit of the enemy, or in retreat. I remember the morning we left Hagerstown to cross the Potomac River back into Virginia at Falling Waters [on the retreat from Gettysburg]. General Lee was there on his horse, on the west bank of the river, having some artillery placed in position in the event it was necessary to protect his rear guard and stragglers; he seemed to be intent, and eager for the last man to get over, without molestation. He showed considerable earnestness with his eagle eyes looking eastward on the Maryland side. A great, grand and extraordinary man was General Lee. It is the opinion of the writer that his caliber was superior to any man that has been tested in America, he had no equal as a commander, North or South.

Davis rejected Lee's offer to resign, knowing that he was the only one who could rebuild the army. "To ask me to substitute you by someone in my judgment more fit to command," Davis wrote, "or who would possess more of the confidence of the army or of the reflecting men in the country, is to demand of me an impossibility." Lee let the matter drop and by early August had begun the process of training new recruits and reorganizing his decimated regiments. At one point, Lee even dispatched his cavalry to harvest grain and mill it, for bread was scarce. According to Jordan, if it had not been for the Virginia black-berries, then coming into season, the 15th Alabama might have starved; this was an exaggeration, to be sure, but the issue of short rations was much on the minds of Lee, Longstreet, Ewell, and Hill.

Meade's army was nearby and, while it had lost heavily at Gettys-burg, was quickly refilling its ranks with new recruits. Lee could not hope to do the same. Everywhere the South was in retreat, and diligent measures needed to be taken to retrieve its fading hopes. The Army of Northern Virginia was fortunate in that Meade had remained on the northern bank of the Rappahannock. This gave Lee time to partially re-coup his losses at Gettysburg as well as to attend a meeting with Davis and Seddon in Richmond to plot the South's next move. Lee suggested another offensive against the Army of the Potomac, but Longstreet thought that a bad idea, particularly in light of the shaky condition of some of its men. Instead, he revived his proposal that he put forward prior to Gettysburg, that a portion of the army reinforce the Confeder-ate forces fighting in southern Tennessee.

This time both Davis and Seddon agreed. The orders were issued on September 7. But instead of moving with three of his divisions, Longstreet would only be moving with two—since Pickett's decimated ranks were still recovering near Richmond. On September 8, his corps broke camp and marched to Richmond, where it boarded rail cars for the journey south, then moved by rail back to the northeast, where it would hook up with the Army of the Tennessee, under rebel General Braxton Bragg. The day that the long line of boxcars, flatcars, coal cars, mail cars, and anything else that the rebel government could scrape to-gether moved south was one of the most poignant in the Confederacy's short history. There was no assurance that Longstreet's men could accomplish in Tennessee what they had failed to accomplish in Pennsylvania, or even that many of them would be coming back.

The cars moved over creaking rails, stopping often, then gathered speed for a time before slowing again, each car swaying through the late summer days. There was widespread knowledge of the move and all along the route women, old men, the infirm, and children gathered, often in near silence, to watch the army pass. The men traveled through the night in North Carolina, their sleeping figures set starkly against the new dawn. The bands were silent in the smaller towns, where people came to watch the soldiers—miles upon miles of them, asleep, going to battle. The specter of rail cars moving in silence, with men laid out sleeping, was particularly emotional for one southern woman: "When a knot of boyish, laughing young creatures passed, a queer thrill of sympathy shook me," she wrote. "Ah, I know how your homefolks feel. Poor children!" Oates remembered the journey in more hopeful terms: "At many places, in anticipation of our coming, the patriotic people, especially the good ladies, prepared abundant and excellent lunches for us. At such points the trains were stopped and the men allowed to partake the feast, which they greatly enjoyed." William Jordan remembered that he rode "the entire way to Atlanta on top of a box-car," adding that "the cars were jammed and packed inside and out."

Not being able to go west due to the Union capture of eastern Tennessee, the trains moved south through the Carolinas to Savannah, then switched to a smaller-gauge train and moved northwest through Georgia. "In Atlanta we were delayed about one day on account of the crowded conditions of the railroads and insufficiency of rolling stock," Oates wrote. On September 16, the 15th Alabama arrived at Ringgold Station, nearly 1,000 miles from its camp on the Rappahannock, and at midnight stacked their arms in a field. The next day they marched west toward the Tennessee line. Longstreet's first units—also men of Hood's Division—had come that way the day before and engaged the enemy in a sharp skirmish before passing on. There were bodies in the fields beside the dusty road. The 15th Alabama marched all day on September 17 and September 18 before camping only a few miles from the Tennessee border. Up ahead, in the woods, Braxton Bragg's Confederate army was camped, in line of battle, along Chickamauga Creek.

Braxton Bragg may well have been the most hated general in the Confederacy, a fact that was already plain to just about everyone except his good friend Jefferson Davis. A martinet, a stickler for regulations, and a man with barely a kind word for anyone, the former Louisiana planter and West Point graduate left a trail of resentment wherever he went, especially among the simple soldiers of his command. Unlike Lee, Bragg rarely debated the need for harsh discipline, but worked his firing squads overtime; he was unconcerned by the criticisms of his subordinates and went about his way, upbraiding his soldiers for slovenliness and his army's commanders for their lack of aggressiveness. Nothing ever seemed to be his fault. The resulting infighting in his army made the relations between his Virginia counterparts seem positively collegial.

But morale was high. The Army of the Tennessee had won victories under Bragg and marched nearly to the Ohio River the year before. Even after their most recent retreat from Chattanooga, during which barely a shot had been fired in anger, most of the soldiers were convinced that they would eventually turn and defeat the Yankees, as they had done before. Much of this success—or perhaps, more accurately, the lack of total failure—was due to the fact that the Army of the Tennessee contained within its ranks some of the most talented and dedicated corps and division commanders in the Confederacy. Among these was William Hardee (the author of *Rifle and Light Infantry Tactics*, the bible of small unit tactics), Leonidas Polk (an Episcopal Bishop), D. H. Hill (who had made his way to Bragg's army from North Carolina), John Breckinridge (the former vice president), and—the most talented of the bunch—Patrick Cleburne (a native of Ireland who had had most of his teeth removed by a minié ball at Shiloh).

Longstreet not only knew most of these men, he looked forward to locking horns with Bragg's northern opponent—the Army of the Cumberland—and its commander, William S. Rosecrans, who had been his roommate at West Point. The two had been close, in part because "Old Rosy" was a brilliant student and helped Longstreet with his homework. As the commander of the Army of the Cumberland, Rosecrans was in the habit of calling his commanders to his tent for late-night strategy sessions that most often turned into long discussions on the nature of religion, one of his favorite topics. It was said that Rosecrans received his nickname from his habit of liberally lubricating his lectures with drink, but Washington wags had taken to calling him "Presently," the answer he most often gave to Abraham Lincoln when asked when he was going to move his army.

When five brigades of Hood's Division marched into southeastern Tennessee and camped in a thick woods on the night of September 18, one day before Longstreet's men arrived, they were unsure of just where they were. They were told that somewhere up ahead was Chickamauga Creek and that just beyond the creek was Rosecrans's army, with its back to the looming mass of Missionary Ridge. Just the week before, Rosecrans had used the ridge as a shield for his troops, who popped in and out of its gaps hide-and-seek style, attempting to find Bragg without being bloodied. Bragg's strategy was to pounce on Rosecrans when he emerged from these gaps, but the southern commander's movements were sluggish and his instructions broadly (he felt purposely) misinterpreted. The result was that Rosecrans's entire army was now camped east of the ridge along the Rossville and Lafayette roads, which led back north to Chattanooga. The rebels faced them in a line four miles long.

William Oates brought his regiment through the woods and into a field in the dark, where they made camp. Like almost every other southern commander, he had only the vaguest idea of just how many troops were across the way, exactly where they might be, or what was expected of him. He had little time to think on this, however, since much of his regiment's camp equipment and their rations were somewhere down the road to the east. There were only two days' battle rations in the 15th Alabama's haversacks, and most of that had already been eaten, so Oates spent the night trying to make his men as comfortable as possible in the unusual late-September chill. That his soldiers were hungry, however, was not unusual; being on short rations was a tradition in the Army of Northern Virginia, which liked to travel light.

"A soldier in active service will eat every time he can get it," Oates explained, "for he never knows when he is going to be put on short rations, and he is generally in anticipation and eats accordingly. I knew a soldier in the regiment named Smith who always ate all his rations at the first halt on the march. It mattered not whether his rations were for one, two, or three days, he ate them all at once just the same, not because he was hungry; but, as he said, his rations were easier to carry that way than in his haversack." The 15th bedded down hungry and cold to await a bright and uneventful dawn.

"The next morning, Saturday, the 19th of September, began in earnest the battle of Chickamauga," Oates later reflected. "We crossed the creek of that name in the woods about 10 o'clock A.M. and went into line without breakfast." As the 15th was going into line, Hood came riding along trailed by his staff, and called out to the 15th: "Remember, boys, we are to whip them." Farther north, beyond the Texas Brigade on his right, Oates heard the opening guns of the battle, with the dull cannonading and the popping of muskets sounding tinny in the distance. The regiment halted then and waited, listening to the sounds of battle to their right and ahead of them. The sounds came down the line to the south and stopped—just before the battle reached them—then receded back north. To some, it seemed, they would never get into the fight.

The 15th, on the left-center of Bragg's extended line, was finally ordered forward in the late afternoon, crossing the Lafayette Road and scattering a group of Union pickets, who retreated to the west. Oates marched his men out smartly, taking desultory fire as he went, but then realized that he was unsupported on the left. He quickly reversed his movement, heading back to the east in confusion. He still had no idea where he was or what exactly he was expected to do. He put his men back into line, looked off to his left and right, and ordered them forward again. It was like this all along Bragg's line as units went disjointedly into action, scrimmaged fitfully with an enemy they could barely see, then recoiled back east. Much like a row of dominoes that fall north to south, Bragg's army moved forward from right to left, fought, fell back, reformed, then moved forward again.

Moving forward again, Oates looked to his right and saw the comforting sight of his Alabama soldiers responding to his lead. But then, farther to his right, he caught sight of a federal regiment marching smartly by into his rear. Oates reversed his regiment, which now scrambled back to the rear. "I ordered the brigade to fall back to the road and as soon as the movement fairly began I saw that a panic had seized the command. I gave the order to halt at the road and for the officers to draw their pistols and shoot any man who crossed it against orders." Oates was chagrined by his latest action, confused by the flowing nature of the battle, and frustrated by his lack of orders. He was not alone. All up and down the Confederate line the fighting was snarled by woods and fields and fought with little rationale. This was due partly to the battleground and partly to the nature of the two armies. Hood's men were learning that the westerners were inclined to slug it out with a lot less bravado than Lee and his enemy commanders back east. These men held much less store in grandiose plans, close-order drill, or grand reviews. The troops here did not "engage" the enemy, it seemed, but "pitched headlong" into his lines. But while the rebel battle lines were less disciplined and the uniforms a motley assortment of homespun and threadbare yellow (the last issue of Confederate gray had come the year before), the fighting was just as vicious—or more so.

September 19 set the tone for the Battle of Chickamauga, which was much more of a soldier's fight than any of the war. Even brigade commanders had little control over their forces, which went forward into woods and fields and were promptly swallowed up in the waving green and brown. The fact that troops were engaged at all could only be determined by the sounds coming from the woods and along the roads, which reminded William Jordan of the sound of burning sugar cane, which crackled, popped, and then exploded in a cataclysmic thunder. Nightfall on September 19 found the 15th Alabama on the west side of Chickamauga Creek, under long-range artillery fire. "Several were killed and wounded," Jordan said. This was another switch from fighting in the east, where by common consent the setting sun most often proclaimed the end of the killing. Not here—where the killing occurred at all hours of day and night.

James Longstreet, who had been busy during the confused battle of the nineteenth bringing the rest of his corps forward, arrived on the field of Chickamauga just after midnight—very early on the morning of September 20—then found Bragg's headquarters and was told that he was in charge of all the forces on the army's left wing. The plan of battle, Bragg told Longstreet, was for Leonidas Polk (another one of "Old Pete's" West Point chums, in charge of all the rebel troops on the Confederate right) to attack Rosecrans's left and roll it up, cutting it off from the Rossville Gap and pummeling it into a corner, where Longstreet's veterans (attacking on the left) could chew it up. That was as much of a plan as Bragg had—Polk's jab from the right, followed by Longstreet's roundhouse left. He eyed Longstreet, grimaced and frowned, and then retired to his tent, leaving Longstreet to grope through the darkness toward his own lines, which were somewhere in the thick woods off to the left. Longstreet carried a crude map of the battleground, but that was all he had by way of information. It was a fit introduction to the way things were done in the west, where the army commander seemed irritated to be awakened from a sound sleep by the new commander of more than one-half his army.

The morning of September 20 dawned bright and cloudless. Longstreet moved down the line of his command, shifting troops and listening, with cocked ear, for the far-off sound of cannon that would signal Polk's attack on Rosecrans. But Longstreet heard nothing. The delay allowed him time to set his own forces in line, scout out the enemy positions, bring up the corps wagons, which had been lost in the woods east of the Lafayette Road, and feed his troops, which now included divisions assigned to him from Bragg's army. He sent for his chief of artillery, but could not find him, then decided that it didn't really matter since (as he later testified) the battlefield was not really a "field" at all "but a heavy woodland, not adapted to the practice of artillery."

Longstreet learned later that the battle's opening, set for just after dawn, was unaccountably delayed by his former classmate, Polk, who whiled away the morning hours sipping coffee and reading a newspaper on a farmhouse porch. The fault, however, was not Polk's at all; he had never received any orders, and so assumed that he had nothing to do. Finally, however, Polk was energized by a courier from Bragg, who told him that his attack was overdue and that the army commander, blue with anger, was looking for him. Polk rode to the front, found Confederate General D. H. Hill, and told him to move his division forward against the lines of Union General George Thomas, whose corps was dug in across the way. Hill, who despised Bragg, laconically said that he would, but first he must gather his men, who were just now having breakfast. Bragg rode up then, glaring at Hill and demanding that he move his men to the attack. Hill turned away in disdain and lurched off, saying he would let his men finish their breakfast. It was nine-thirty before the attack began, with Hill's division heading straight west into Thomas's waiting lines.

As at Gettysburg, the battle was supposed to flow from right to left—from Polk to Longstreet—in the hopes that somewhere along the line the rebels would find a weak spot in the Union defenses. Bragg's intention was to force Rosecrans to reinforce his left by putting all of his pressure there. Polk's Corps, therefore, bore the brunt of the fighting of the battle's early hours, plunging his troops headlong into Thomas's lines. Just as Bragg had hoped, Thomas called to Rosecrans for reinforcements, which were brought from the south end of the field. By eleven A.M., Longstreet could see the federals in his front slowly sidling north and sent a courier to Bragg that "my column of attack could probably break the enemy's line if he [Bragg] cared to have it go in." The Confederate commander had already made that decision, and by the time Longstreet was hoping to receive orders, the men of his right division unaccountably moved out in a long line and crossed the Lafayette Road.

Facing Longstreet's command were the corps of Union Generals Alexander McCook and Thomas Crittenden, whose men had spent the previous night felling trees along their defensive position, their rear secured along the Dry Valley Road, which ran straight north along the base of Missionary Ridge to Rossville Gap. At midmorning, just after Polk launched his attack, Crittenden's troops, with the exception of one division under the command of Thomas Woods, were ordered by Rosecrans to march north, to their left, to reinforce George Thomas's hard-pressed command—which was now bearing the brunt of the Confederate attack. Rosecrans's order left McCook, with just one division, holding a thinning line of blue defenders. McCook was worried that his lines were too thin and that the attack now being launched to the north would spread to his own command. He had, he thought, too few troops to defend his position. He was right. At a little after eleven in the morning, McCook saw a line of rebels three ranks deep burst from the woods in his front and begin an assault on his line. As the rebel troops, regiments from Tennessee, moved forward, McCook gave the order to fire.

The federal volleys ripped into the rebel attack, becoming so intense that the first rank of Confederates went to ground, all one mile of them falling and then returning the fire.

Such massed volleys should have been enough to hold off any attack, but Longstreet's second line now emerged from the woods—men of Lee's eastern army—and walked coolly over the crouching figures of their Tennessee comrades, put their heads down into McCook's withering volleys, and with not so much as even a slight hesitation exploded into the center of Rosecrans's army. It was a glorious sight, fit to compare with anything that had happened under Lee, and later taken as confirmation that men from Longstreet's Corps were cooler under fire than their western counterparts. Rosecrans was shocked by the attack. The rebels lapped up and over his center like a gray flood, vaulting over the makeshift breastworks, capturing guns and men. What was left of McCook's Corps fled toward the west. The entire Union position was now endangered, with Longstreet's men moving ever deeper into the Union rear. How had it happened?

There seemed little reason for the rout, except that here, for one of the few times in the war, a battle plan actually worked, though not exactly in the manner intended by the southern commander. While Bragg wanted to bend Rosecrans's right flank back, his *en echelon* attack forced Rosecrans to strip his center to reinforce his left, thereby creating a soft spot in the federal defenses. Rosecrans had been unperturbed at the thought of thinning his center, believing that all his army needed to do was sidle along to the north, toward Thomas, constricting its lines as it went. The last of these shifts had involved Thomas Woods's Division, the last of Rosecrans's forces on the southern end of the battlefield. Woods had hesitated to follow Rosecrans's plan, fearing that in doing so he would leave a gaping hole in the federal line. But Rosecrans, who had ridden up to see that his order was obeyed, was adamant. "Move your division at once," he had told Woods angrily, "as I have instructed, or the consequences will not be pleasant for yourself."

Woods obeyed the order, moving his men out of their position and left to "close up" with the next unit in the federal line. He made certain that his division met up with the units of the division of his left. But just as he was making certain of this, another courier rode up from Rosecrans with a new order. Woods was to pass behind the unit on his left and fall in one further position up the line. This second order was the result of a terrible miscalculation: Rosecrans thought there was a gap in the Union defenses, and he was moving Woods farther north to close it. In fact, there was no such gap at all—until Woods moved. The gap that was then created, however, was not really a gap at all—it was a chasm; and it was this chasm that Longstreet's men attacked.

As the attack developed, Longstreet, riding behind his lines, could hardly believe what he saw. There, immediately in his front, was something he had never before seen on a battlefield—a hole so big that he could, if he wished, push thirty thousand troops through it. He ordered his men forward, then spurred them on. The two Union units left on that part of the field (one of them north of the chasm, the other south) scrambled desperately to meet his attack. They repulsed his first line, but not his second. The southern ranks hardly hesitated, mounting first one line of breastworks, then another, then another until the last resistance was swept away. The rebel troops poured through the hole in the Union front and then double-quicked forward to within sight of the Dry Valley Road, which was now filled with fleeing troops. The 15th Alabama was one of the regiments moving at the forward edge of the rebel tide. "When we crossed the road it raised a tremendous dust and soon after I could see only a few scattering men of the Union army running away," Oates wrote. Everywhere Longstreet's men were triumphant.

◦▬▬◆▬▬◦

"The scene now presented was unspeakably grand," Confederate Division commander Bushrod Johnson, whose division was in the forefront of Longstreet's attack, testified. "The resolute and impetuous charge, the rush of our heavy columns sweeping out from the shadow of the gloom of the forest into the open fields flooded with sunlight, the glitter of arms, the onward dash of artillery and mounted men, the retreat of the foe, the shout of hosts of our army, the dust, the smoke, the noise of firearms—of whistling balls and grape-shot and of bursting shell—made up a battle scene of unsurpassed grandeur." Deep in the rear, Union artillerymen attempted to hold their ground, even as the gray lines swept past them. In desperation, they actually flung artillery shells at them by hand, hoisting them above their heads and pitching them forward, then swung their artillery rammers at those who tried to claim their guns.

As on the previous day, the rough ground scattered the attackers. While the center of Longstreet's lines kept moving forward, the far outer edges of his battle line (on the far left and on the far right) ran into the exposed edges of the Union chasm. "I discovered that I did not connect with any one on the right or left and halted. I had no idea where the other regiments of the brigade were," Oates later wrote. He moved the 15th back from its exposed position. "Looking around I saw away to my left and front a fight going on; the Federals in solid phalanx along the pine ridge at the edge of a field, with two pieces of artillery in their midst, were beating the Confederates back down the slope through the open field. I did not know what troops they were, except that they were Confederates and were being beaten, and without orders I resolved to go to their assistance."

It was only clear later that Oates's right flank was unprotected because he had gotten far out in front of the army and because the Texas Brigade that had manned his right flank was unaccountably repulsed by a lone New Jersey unit, left over from the Yankee flight north. The Texans fled back across the fields and into the woods, where they were met by a scowling John Bell Hood. After shaming them, Hood turned them about and sent them back into battle. Watching them reform, the luckless Hood was shot from his horse, the minié ball shattering his right leg. Oates did not know any of this—he only knew that he was alone. Being unsupported on either his left or right, he ordered his men to about-face and march back toward the rear to search for the Texas Brigade. They marched to the rear for a few minutes until Oates changed his mind yet again, this time believing that he should not be heading to the rear after all, but to the front—to the sound of battle. He turned his regiment around and headed it off to the left, thereby passing out of that part of the field under the command of Hood and entering the battle lines of General Zachariah Deas. One of Deas's regiments, the 19th Alabama, was under intense fire, trading volleys with a Union regiment under the command of Ohio General William H. Lytle.

Lytle's Brigade was all alone on that part of the field, having been left south of the chasm caused by Woods's march to the right. With little choice but to fight his way out of the converging gray lines to his front, Lytle about-faced his brigade and charged the lines of the 19th Alabama. It was at this point that the 15th appeared, seemingly out of nowhere, to lend a hand. As Oates ordered his men forward in support of the Alabamians, a shell arced out of the trees, exploded nearby, and cut a piece out of Oates's coat. He was knocked to the ground. As his regiment went past, Oates cried to them, "Don't fire, 15th, until you are ordered!" Or so he later said. But other reports, including angry testimony from Colonel Samuel McSpadden, the commander of the 19th, said that Oates's command fired into his right rear. Oates was angered by the report, protested it, but it is quite clear that McSpadden would not have made the statement unless he felt he was right. "I never saw him until that moment," Oates later said. "Colonel McSpadden was an honorable man," Oates later wrote, "[but] he made an egregious mistake in his official report of the battle of Chickamauga."

Nonetheless, Oates's sudden appearance on the right rear of the 19th Alabama undoubtedly helped save that regiment from the uneven charge then being launched straight up at its shaking ranks by William Lytle, who marched his men gamely forward into the disciplined fire of the Alabamians. His men came on shouting, knowing their fate but desperate to save the far right of Rosecrans's army from total destruction. They nearly did so, cutting down dozens of Alabamians. But the weight of sheer numbers took its toll and Lytle was shot and fell while leading his troops, who then abandoned the field. Oates found Lytle on the ground, suffering from his wounds and near death. "The dying General lay in the hot sun. I took him by the arms and dragged him two or three steps into the shade and left him and started in pursuit of my regiment," Oates remembered.

Lytle is one of those numerous Americans, famous in their own time, whose names have been eclipsed by the passage of time. His great-grandfather fought in the French and Indian Wars, his grandfather fought with Daniel Boone, and his father (a peaceable, learned, and gentle man) fought in the halls of Congress, where he represented Harriet Beecher Stowe's Ohio district. Lytle inherited a bit of each of his forebears, including the ability to lead men in battle. His real fame, however, came as a popular poet, whose lines were recited in parlors north and south. His "Anthony and Cleopatra" was by far his most-widely acclaimed, with its opening line—"I am dying, Egypt, dying"—

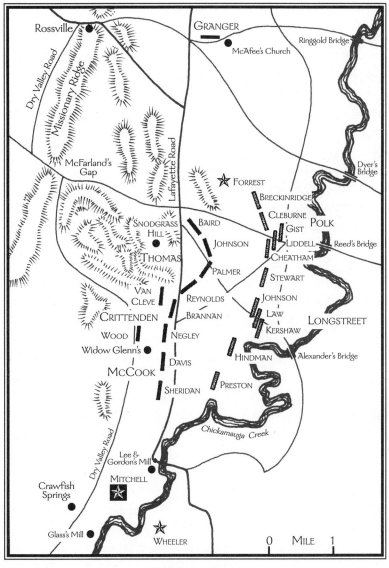

## Chickamauga

Union commander William Rosecrans's army popped in and out of the passes southwest of Chickamauga, but were met just east of the Lafayette Road by Braxton Bragg's reinforced army. After vicious fighting on September 19, Longstreet's command—with Law, Johnson, and Kershaw in the lead—plunged through a hole in the Union line to push Rosecrans north, with Union soldiers retreating along the Dry Valley Road. General George Thomas saved the army from certain catastrophe by making a last-ditch stand on Snodgrass Hill.

one of the great romantic lines of the time. A generation of Americans swooned over the poem. The charge of his brigade and his death soon became one of the most widely reported stories of the war.

Oates now staggered across an open field in the rear of his charging regiment, who were again heading toward the open rear of the Union army. He could see that his regiment had already overrun a Union artillery battery—the first guns the 15th Alabama had ever captured. "After we passed the artillery," William Jordan recounted, "we charged up the hill through a field where there were a few trees standing; it looked as if an old settlement had been there. We made a halt; the enemy commenced firing briskly, killing and wounding several. Great many would seek protection behind the few trees as best they could, but it was so exposed that the men actually went on charging without orders, and continued until an enemy was not to be seen. I am reliably informed, if we had pressed a quarter of a mile further, we would have gotten into the enemy's wagon train."

Oates, lagging behind and still limping from the near-miss of the federal cannon shot, found his men on the hillside. He allowed them little rest, ordering them back into line, and then took them, for a second time, back into the field to the east. The Union dead were laying in the sun on the field. Oates attempted to link back up with his division, but no one seemed to know where it was. "As we moved through the old field I discovered a boy, then about fifteen years old," Oates later recounted, "who belonged to Company G, lagging in the rear and crying. I spoke to him and told him not to cry; that he had not yet been hurt and he might live through the battle, and not to be so unmanly as to become frightened and go to crying. He replied, 'Afraid, hell! That ain't it; I am so damned tired I can't keep up with my company.' " The boy was A. Bryant Skipper, a young Alabama soldier who had run away from home to be with the army.

Skipper was not the only soldier lagging on the field. Longstreet's rifle-shot penetration of the Union center had rolled up Rosecrans's right wing, which was now in full flight. Thousands of blue-clad infantrymen, veterans of every western fight from Shiloh to Murfreesboro, were headed north toward Chattanooga, discarding their muskets as they went. So far, at least, the Battle of Chickamauga was less a set piece of nineteenth-century warfare than, as one Union officer testified, "a mad, irregular battle, very much resembling guerrilla warfare on a vast scale, in which one army was bushwhacking the other." The only thing that stood between the Army of the Cumberland and disaster was the bled-down corps of George Thomas, which made its stand against the full might of Bragg's army on the forward slope of Snodgrass Hill.

Thomas, another of Longstreet's West Point friends, was the only ranking Union officer left on the field by midafternoon of September 20. A man with an unflappable personality, phlegmatic utterances, and blocklike demeanor, Thomas was exactly the kind of commander the Union army needed just now. With nearly three-quarters of the Union's western force headed north back to the safety of Chattanooga, Thomas decided he would do what he could to stem the tide or, barring that, provide a cover for the thousands of retreating troops. Pulling the battered divisions of his command together on a rolling hill to the southeast of the gap leading back to Chattanooga, Thomas patched together a defensive line running like a horseshoe from the right of Snodgrass Hill (on the west) to a point one mile distant on the northeast. Thomas calmly sat his horse in the middle of his patched-together defense, spoke in soft tones to reassure his men, and waited for Bragg and Longstreet to come piling in.

He did not wait long. After receiving a message from Rosecrans delivered by James Garfield, a future president, that his "position must be held until night," Thomas fought out the last act of the Battle of Chickamauga in much the same way that Rosecrans had fought out its opening: shifting troops first to his left, where the pressure was the heaviest, and then back to his right—to meet Longstreet's headlong charge. Initially there were no less than three attacks. Then a constant and low pounding ensued, as line after line engaged his position. Finally Thomas attempted to head off the inevitable collapse of his cobbled-together command by launching three regiments from his right against Longstreet's lines. The men went forward, down Snodgrass Hill and into the rebels.

The rebels were troops from South Carolina, backed up by Oates's 15th Alabama, which had marched north with the victorious men of

Longstreet's command. Oates wanted to charge the position to head off Thomas's attack, but he had little luck getting the South Carolinians to move. "I got up on a log and made an appeal to the State pride of the regiment, and asked the men not to go where I directed merely, but to follow me," Oates said. The regiment responded and went forward, but an opening volley from Thomas's left scattered them, much to Oates's embarrassment. The two regiments recoiled and settled into a long-range, stand-up fight.

That Chickamauga was a fight of soldiers was very clear to Oates, even many years later. Despite his own poor showing and aimless wandering, his leadership was never questioned by his own soldiers. Many of the younger privates, adolescents, looked to Oates not only for leadership, but for a comradely care that a father could not or had not given. Civil War historians have long ignored the fact that Chickamauga, perhaps more than any other battle, was fought not simply by young men, but by young boys that now would be considered little more than children. Johnny Clem, the Union's "Drummer Boy of Chickamauga," was twelve years old when he shot and killed a pursuing rebel while riding an artillery caisson. It was not his first act of bravery. He had already gained attention in northern newspapers as "Johnny Shiloh"—the eleven-year-old fighter with the 22nd Michigan.

The 15th Alabama had its own child-soldiers, including sixteen-year-old Tom Wright, one of the regiment's best fighters. Oates ran across him in the front ranks facing Snodgrass Hill. "He was the busiest chap I ever saw, down on his knees loading and firing, but taking good aim at every shot. I slapped him on the shoulder and said, 'Give it to them, Tommie, my boy; I will remember you.' He looked up with a smile and replied 'All right, Colonel.' " Oates moved away from Wright, but soon returned to find that the "brave little fellow had been shot through the head and lay a corpse. I could not repress my tears, and in the heat of battle I shed a few in passing as a tribute to the sublime courage of that child." Farther on, Oates stumbled upon Jack Cariker, an adolescent from Barbour County, who pointed out a shirker hiding behind a tree. Oates told Cariker to go get the man, who was twice as large as "little Jack." Oates whacked the man with his sword, then whacked him again; the man went back into line.

At sunset, Thomas began to pull his battered rear guard off of Snodgrass Hill, one unit at a time. He started on the right, gingerly pulling handfuls of men out of the line, while pulling back the entire command a few steps as he went. Longstreet piled in again, hoping for one last breakthrough and a victory that would destroy what was left of this part of the Army of the Cumberland. But he had met his match. His old schoolmate, George Thomas, worked slowly, deliberately, using time as an ally, and counting on the fact that Longstreet's men were as exhausted as his. At the end, his last troops out of the line launched a savage counterattack against the rebel lines, then turned and headed north, the darkness shielding their last retreat.

Thomas's final retreat from Snodgrass Hill cost three full regiments, who were surrounded and overwhelmed. Hundreds were taken prisoner, but they had saved the remnant of Thomas's command. Chickamauga seemed to balance the terrible defeat at Gettysburg. The rebel army was exultant, as was Oates, who wrote glowingly of the victory years later:

> That night—Sunday, September 20, 1863—I never felt happier, and visited the camp-fire of every company in the regiment. We had gone through another great battle and the lives of many of us were spared, and we were victorious. I say "we," because I think that nearly every man present who participated in the fight felt about as I did. And no one but an old soldier who had "been there" knows how good we felt. Our losses were pretty heavy, but we had borne a conspicuous part in winning a great victory. The regiment had lost eleven killed and one hundred and twenty-one wounded out of about four hundred and fifty who went into action on Saturday.

Chickamauga was the Confederacy's greatest victory, but as the rebel army celebrated above Snodgrass Hill, Lincoln was making a decision that would spell the end of southern hopes for independence. At the end of October, with the Army of the Cumberland besieged at Chattanooga, Lincoln relieved Rosecrans and replaced him with

Ulysses S. Grant. It was a natural choice. The Galena, Illinois, native was the conqueror of Vicksburg and a man who, Lincoln felt, was enough of an improviser to recoup his western army's reputation. The federals in Chattanooga were starving, demoralized, and embittered by their defeat at Chickamauga, and fed up with Rosecrans, who had been too stunned by his setback to initiate any moves to save his surrounded men.

But if the Army of the Cumberland lacked the will to fight, so too did the Army of the Tennessee, whose commander, Braxton Bragg, was being openly attacked by his subordinates for failing to follow up his Georgia victory. Bragg's most senior commanders finally took matters into their own hands, asking Longstreet to petition Jefferson Davis to relieve Bragg. Davis came west to investigate but did not relieve Bragg and, according to Longstreet, "left the army more despondent than he found it." Things were no better in the 15th Alabama, which was posted first at the base of Lookout Mountain and then, in mid-October, shifted to Brown's Ferry, west of Chattanooga on the Tennessee River. When Grant took command he ordered the capture of the ferry, in order to bring rations overland for the Union soldiers.

On the night of October 24, Grant did this, forming a bridgehead at the ferry and surprising the men of the 15th Alabama. Oates responded to Grant's move by bringing his regiment forward in the dark. He deployed his men in line, gave them their orders in a whisper, and sent them forward. "I waited in breathless silence for them to fire, a much longer time than I thought was necessary; but when they did fire it must have done terrible execution, judging from the confusion of the enemy which followed." The 15th hurdled the Union breastworks in the dark and captured eleven prisoners, but were forced to withdraw. Oates ordered another attack, attempting to gain a foothold inside the federal line. "Company E (Dale County), Lieutenant Glover, of Company B, commanding, had five men killed—all shot through the head, one right after another," Oates later wrote.

Oates called for reinforcements, bringing up five new companies at daybreak. Once the reinforcements were in place, Oates ordered another attack, with Company F leading the way. The men wavered, however, after taking a full Union volley. "I rushed in among the men," Oates recalled, "and ordered them forward, and went forward myself, and when within about thirty steps of the enemy (I could see their heads as they fired from behind some logs) I was shot through my right hip and thigh, the ball striking the thigh bone one inch below the hip joint, slightly fracturing it, ran around it and passed through eight inches of flesh. It struck a blow as though a brick had been hurled against me, and hurt so badly that I started to curse as I fell, and said 'God d—' when thinking that possibly I was killed, and that would not seem well for a man to die with an oath in his mouth, I cut it off at the d— and did not finish the sentence. All this flashed through my mind as I fell."

Oates was taken to the rear by two childhood friends, Jeff Hussey and M. E. Meredith, farm boys from the crossroads. Hussey was shot through the arm. The three hobbled back west, fearing they would be shot from the rear. Oates was laid among the wounded in the front yard of a small cabin that was owned by two women. "I was bleeding copiously and became thirsty," he later testified. "I begged the ladies for a drink of water." The firing was so heavy, however, that Oates had to drag himself across the yard to grab the offered ladle. As the minié balls were skipping into the yard from the surrounding woods, Oates's orderly brought him his horse. William Jordan came forward then, just as Oates was mounting, leading eleven prisoners. Oates took command of them, sent Jordan back to the firing line, and set off toward Lookout Mountain, his boot "running over with blood."

At Lookout Creek, Oates was taken from his horse and treated by the brigade surgeon, but his wound was too serious for him to consider returning to battle. General Law arrived with reinforcements, but Oates told him he was too late—the federals had possession of the ferry. Law sent his reinforcements forward anyway and then detailed eight men to carry Oates over Lookout Mountain. "I arrived at our field hospital just before night, where I found Doctor Davis, the accomplished surgeon of the 15th Alabama, who probed and dressed my wound and made me as comfortable as possible during the night." The next day Oates was sent south by rail to Atlanta, where he arrived during the last week of October. He was accompanied by a wounded drummer boy—Jimmie Newberry.

Realizing that he was grievously wounded and would need months to recuperate, Oates asked to be sent home to Eufaula, but his request

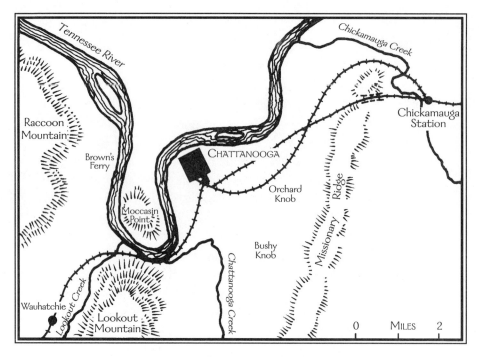

### Chattanooga

The city was a besieger's dream—with Grant's forces bottled up in the city by Confederate lines running from the far north of Missionary Ridge (*on the right*) in an arc to just above Brown's Ferry, on his left. Grant broke the seige by opening the ferry and then attacking up Lookout Mountain and Missionary Ridge.

---

was denied. He was ordered to recuperate at a field hospital. Believing the order irrational, he refused to comply and made his way to Atlanta and then to Macon by train. When a train left Macon for the southwest, Oates, suffering from a fever brought on by the infection of his wound, was on board. He finally made it to Eufaula at the end of the first week of November, 1863, and might well have died had it not been for the Toney family, whose son William had been in Oates's command before being mortally wounded at the Battle of Cross Keys. Under the care of the Toney family, William Oates survived his wound. He was finally at home in Alabama, thirty-one months after he had left.

# 11

## *We Know That Some Must Fall*

IN EARLY AUGUST 1863, exhausted by the exertions of army life, Joshua Chamberlain was felled by malaria, and by mid-August he was so ill that he was sent home to recover. He was happy to be re-united with his family, but was too ill to pay much attention to them. He spent several days in bed, too weak to move. After two weeks, he still felt shaky from the fever of his illness and applied for an extension of his leave, but he was ordered to rejoin his men. He complied with the order, though he was "broken down" and woozy from sickness. On August 26, he was told he would be put in charge of the Third Brigade in recognition of his leadership at Gettysburg. He headed back to Washington and from there back to his old encampment.

One of Chamberlain's first responsibilities as a new brigade commander came on August 29, when he was ordered to march his men into a large field to witness the execution of five Pennsylvanians who had been caught deserting the army. On a hot clear day, the men were brought into the field, placed on caskets, blindfolded, and shot, toppling over into their predug graves. "It was the most affecting sight I have ever seen," the 20th Maine's Will Owen wrote his sister. "I have seen men shot on the battlefield, men with their heads shot off, men with arms and legs gone and passed them all without a thought but to see five men sitting on their own coffins facing 50 loaded rifles that were to be fired at them is a sight that me thinks no one can stand and look calmly at no matter what they have been through, no matter how much misery they have seen. . . . It is an awful thing, but we are living in awful times."

Chamberlain hated this duty, but thought the executions were necessary to keep the army together. The war was coming to a close, he believed, with "the heavy fighting" nearly at an end. He thought there might be one or two more battles, but that was all. For Chamberlain, college life now seemed a distant dream, overshadowed by the war and the story of his defense of Little Round Top. He was now well-known among the army's senior commanders, and a hero. But for all that, Chamberlain was still looked on as something of an oddity, in large part because there were so few professors-turned-heroes in any of the armies. The fact that men like Chamberlain were not supposed to be great warriors, however, clearly caused him problems in the months ahead as successive attempts to promote him to brigadier general failed.

Colonel James Rice, who had fought at Chamberlain's side at Little Round Top, was perhaps Chamberlain's greatest admirer and in the forefront of the attempts to obtain Chamberlain's promotion. He wrote Maine's William Fessenden of Chamberlain's actions at Gettysburg: "My personal knowledge of this gallant officer's skill and bravery upon the battlefield, his ability in drill and discipline, and his fidelity to duty in camp, added to a just admiration for his scholarship, and respect for his Christian character, induces me to ask your influence in his behalf." Adelbert Ames, Corps Commander George Sykes, and Division Commander Charles Griffin added their voices to the growing chorus, but the promotion did not come. Chamberlain was still in charge of the brigade, as its colonel.

Chamberlain did not show his disappointment, but spent his time keeping up a constant barrage of lighthearted letters to his family and learning how to command a brigade. There did not seem to be much to it, especially under Meade, who kept the army firmly immobilized on the Rappahannock, moving them forward only in October, and only then because it looked as if the Army of Northern Virginia was about to steal another march into the north. Meade responded with a desperate lunge at Lee, sending his army in a series of forced marches. Chamberlain and his brigade headed toward Manassas, then north to Centreville, then south again, and then back to Centreville. At Bristoe Station the boom of cannon told Chamberlain that the Fifth Corps had caught Lee before he could swing into the Shenandoah. Lee withdrew, tearing up the Orange and Alexandria Railroad as he retreated, but Chamber-

lain's troops caught his rear guard entrenched in a strong defensive line
at Rappahannock Station.

The short but intense fight at Rappahannock Station was almost as
dangerous to Chamberlain as the battle at Gettysburg. This time, however, Chamberlain's regiment was attacking a rebel line instead of being
attacked by one. Forming his double ranks, Chamberlain led his men
forward over the broken ground, realizing that his troops had lost
any hope of surprise—the rebels were ready. In the midst of the fight,
Chamberlain had his horse shot from under him. After all the marching, Chamberlain's men—in fact, the entire Union army—had failed to
flank Lee's position. General Meade made a wise decision and returned
the men to their camps. After Gettysburg, it seemed, few commanders
on either side wanted a fight. The men slept in line of battle as the late
autumn turned wintry.

On the morning of November 11, after spending the previous night
sleeping in the snow, Chamberlain collapsed, overcome by exhaustion
and the recurrence of the malaria that had plagued him in August. He
was sent north to Washington to recover, but his condition only worsened. After battling a high fever for over a week, he lay near death. Fannie came south to be with him during his last hours. It was a tough time
for Chamberlain—and for the Confederacy; in Chattanooga, Ulysses S.
Grant, who was now the commander of all Union forces in the west,
was planning his next move against Braxton Bragg, while in Washington, Abraham Lincoln was preparing the short speech that he would
give at the dedication of the national cemetery at Gettysburg. As November turned to December, Chamberlain battled his sickness and, as
in August, recovered enough to think of his future. He could now leave
the army, if he so desired, and return home without any recriminations;
he had clearly paid the price that was required. But Chamberlain
thought only of returning to his brigade, and the war.

It was not until just after the New Year of 1864 that he was able to
return to his duties. He was happy to be back in service, though his duties were clearly not to his liking. Rather than being given a brigade in
Griffin's Division, as he had been promised, Chamberlain was told to
remain in Washington as a court-martial officer. His only solace was
that Fannie could be with him, as well as Lieutenant Colonel Charles
Gilmore, now the 20th Maine's ranking officer. But it was still a major

disappointment. As the days turned into weeks, Chamberlain became more and more impatient with his new duties, and increasingly worried that his absence from the army would mean his promised promotion would be overlooked.

He was right, of course, since out of sight often meant out of mind in the backbiting atmosphere that prevailed in the Army of the Potomac. But it was not simply Chamberlain's assignment to Washington that held up his promotion; there was also a hint of resentment, and envy, among some army officers of his record—he was not a "regular" professional soldier like them, but a "volunteer." Chamberlain, of course, was angered by this view, but he did little to counteract it. While he was as ambitious as any officer, volunteer or otherwise, his straitlaced upbringing and utter self-confidence kept him silent. The recognition he deserved would come, he believed, because it must come. Because it was his due.

In this, at least, Chamberlain had much in common with Ulysses S. Grant, whom Lincoln brought east in March 1864 to head the Union armies. Grant was as modest a man as Lincoln could have found, preferring to allow others, most notably Congressman Elihu Washburne, to speak for him. "It is men who wait to be selected," Grant wrote, "and not those who seek, from whom we may always expect the most efficient service." Grant was not just being modest; he actually meant what he said. It surprised him to learn that people viewed him as a hero, or stood in line to shake his hand, or wrote long articles on his strategic thinking. As far as anyone could tell, he had no strategic thinking—but said simply that his old friend William Tecumseh Sherman (in the west) would fight Joe Johnston (the Confederacy's new western commander) and aim for Atlanta, while he, in overall command of Meade's army in the east, would fight "Bobby" Lee and aim for Richmond.

Grant reorganized the five corps of the Army of the Potomac into three, placing Hancock in charge of the Second Corps, Warren in command of the Fifth, and Sedgwick as head of the Sixth—which meant that Chamberlain, back in Washington, now served under Warren, who had sent his regiment to Little Round Top. Grant's army outnumbered Lee's by nearly two to one (more than two to one, actually, counting Burnside's Twentieth Corps, which Grant brought from eastern Tennessee), having filled its ranks with 115,000 men, as opposed to

Lee's force of 61,000. Grant shuttled off to see Sherman in Tennessee, returned, joined Meade's army along the Rappahannock, then sat in his tent to plan the coming campaign.

In mid-March 1864, William Oates—barely recovered from his wound—returned to his command at Bull's Gap in northeastern Tennessee. While Oates now knew it was unlikely the South could win the war, he was still shocked by his regiment's appearance. The soldiers were barely clothed and many of them wrapped rags around their feet to keep out the cold. Worse yet, the 15th, which had once seemed immune to the demoralization that stalked the army after Gettysburg, was plagued by desertions.

One of the deserters was Henry Quentin, a thirty-three-year-old French Canadian who fought at Winchester, Cross Keys, Gaines's Mill, Gettysburg, Chickamauga, and Knoxville, but now decided that he had had enough. He was a good soldier, but he slipped away one night in the snow by simply gathering up his blanket and walking into the woods. Quentin was followed by others: Frank Samuels, Lucius Springs, William Bryley, Henry Faust, William Smith, James Woodham, Cornelius Enfinger, Thomas Morill, William Flowers, William Bullard—and many more, all of them veterans. Oates believed the desertions had two causes: the poor leadership of Alexander Lowther, who took command of the regiment after Oates's departure, and the ill-conceived campaign of James Longstreet, who took his corps north to besiege Knoxville.

Longstreet went to Knoxville under orders, but Lee's "old war horse" did not feel comfortable in independent command and, after besieging the city, retreated east. Longstreet attributed his failure to Evander Law, who, he said, had disobeyed orders. The claim was met by disbelief from Law's Brigade, who stood by their old commander. The charges and countercharges flew as fast as minié balls; the farther the army retreated, the more it seemed beleaguered by its own private war. The growing feud abated somewhat when it was learned that Grant had stormed Bragg's lines at Chattanooga and sent his army fleeing south, but then was taken up again with a new intensity. When it came time to appoint a new commander for Hood's Division, Longstreet bypassed

Law, saying he preferred Micah Jenkins. Law, in a fit of pique, resigned in protest. Oates then joined the fight, leading his regiment to petition for his old commander's return and asking for a transfer from Longstreet's army. For Longstreet this was the last straw, and he ordered that Law be court-martialed. Intent to defend himself, Law came to Oates and Brigadier General Henry "Rock" Benning (whose brigade had attacked Devil's Den at Gettysburg) and asked them to represent him. While the court-martial was never convened (the War Department overruled Longstreet and appointed C. W. Field to lead Hood's Division), the Jenkins-Law feud continued to poison relations between Longstreet and his top commanders. The effect on Longstreet's reputation was much worse—while he was one of the Confederacy's great commanders and one of the most talented military thinkers in either army, the Jenkins-Law feud filled him, as Oates said, "brim full of malice" and fueled resentments against him after the war.

⚜

Finally, blessedly, Longstreet's force was ordered to Virginia, arriving there during the second week of April 1864. General Lee reviewed the troops on April 29. Lee was overjoyed to have Longstreet's command back with his army. He certainly needed them: on May 4, Ulysses S. Grant's army crossed the Rapidan River and marched into the tangled woods of the Wilderness. That same day, Lee entered the Wilderness to intercept Grant, sending Ewell's Corps up the Orange Turnpike and A. P. Hill parallel to him up the Orange Plank Road. Longstreet's Corps was ordered forward from Gordonsville, one day's march to the west. A little after one P.M. on May 5, Ewell spotted Grant's men in his front, deployed his skirmishers, and went forward into the dense undergrowth. Within minutes, his troops made contact, sending an undisciplined fire into the woods and attempting to bring their artillery to bear in the clogged woodland. By late afternoon, Ewell had battled Warren's Corps to a standstill and was fending off attacks from John Sedgwick's Corps, who had brought his command up to reinforce Warren's right. The fighting was done at close quarters, with neither battle line clearly able to see the other. By midafternoon, however, the sheer numbers of Union troops began to be felt. Ewell held on by hitting, withdrawing, and hitting again, pinning Grant on ground of Lee's choosing.

At the end of the first day's fighting, Lee sent messengers back down the roads of the Wilderness with orders for Longstreet to bring his command east. Lee was worried; Winfield Hancock's Second Corps was deployed on the right along A. P. Hill's front, where a concerted push could roll the Army of Northern Virginia back west, giving Grant the inside line to Richmond. Longstreet began his movement at two A.M. on the morning of May 6, but "it progressed so slowly along the devious neighborhood road that it was daylight when the head of the column reached the Plank Road, about two miles in rear of where the fighting ceased the previous evening." Just after the sun dawned on a clear, bright day, Longstreet pushed his men up the Plank Road to reinforce Hill, who was fighting off successive waves of attackers launched by the Union Second Corps. The situation was desperate, with Hill outnumbered and slowly giving ground.

The 15th came upon the left of the road in the first of Longstreet's battle lines, past Lee, whose eyes shone with pride. Lee pointed the men forward to the east. As Oates looked on, the army commander ordered one of his own staff to help a wounded officer, who had just fallen to Oates's left. It would be hard to find anyone in the southern army who did not admire Lee, but no one admired him more than William Oates. "I thought him at that moment the grandest specimen of manhood I ever beheld," he wrote. "He looked as though he ought to have been and was the monarch of the world."

Lee looked at Oates's line coming through the woods and moving to plug the gap that had appeared in Hill's flank. "Whose troops are these?" he asked, his voice carrying above the din of battle.

"Law's Alabama Brigade," came the answer.

"God bless the Alabamians," Lee shouted, and he rose in his saddle in silent salute.

With that, Oates's men went into Hancock's line in a rush. Colonel W. F. Perry, one of Oates's kinsmen from southeastern Alabama, commanded the brigade's charge. "My front rank fired a volley without halting, and the whole line bounded forward with their characteristic yell," Perry later wrote. The Alabamians broke Hancock's first line and descended a slope, but were then forced to halt and reform. They had successfully stopped Hancock's attack, but the Second Corps still lay fully in their front. While resting in the dense woods, the brigade was flanked by one of Warren's brigades on the left and Perry sent Oates's regiment in pursuit. Oates ordered his men to the left, making a full wheel before plunging into the 15th New York Regiment, a converted artillery unit attached to Warren's Corps. Having spent the war guarding Washington, the New Yorkers took one volley, then promptly turned and fled. Perry called Oates's attack "one of the most brilliant movements I have ever seen on a battlefield."

With his flank now secure, Perry ordered Oates's regiment to rejoin the main line, where the brigade was fighting for its life on a small knoll near the Plank Road. Perry ordered his men forward, only to see them come skittering back, taking shelter among the trees. The Union line stood just behind the crest of the hill, its fire aimed purposely upward, where the Alabamians were outlined against the sky. "At this critical moment," Perry later wrote, "the gallant 15th appeared upon the left. Colonel Oates, finding no enemy in his immediate front, swung his regiment round to the right and delivered a single volley up the line which confronted us, and the work was done. The enemy instantly disappeared." The fight was now three hours old, but the day was just beginning: all along the line, from Ewell on the left to Hill and Longstreet on the right, the battle swayed through the Virginia woods.

In these same woods the year before, Robert E. Lee had sent Stonewall Jackson in his famed march to the left of Joseph Hooker's army. Now, outnumbered and outgunned, he concocted a similar plan, telling Longstreet to take four brigades and march them to the right. His object was to fall on Hancock's flank and pummel it back to the Rapidan. Longstreet put Colonel G. Moxley Sorrel, his senior staff officer, in charge of the flank march. "Colonel," he said, "there is a fine chance of a great attack by our right. If you will quickly get into those woods, some brigades will be found much scattered from the fight. Collect them and take charge. Form a good line and then move, your right pushed forward and turning as much as possible to the left. Hit hard when you start, but don't start until you have everything ready." Sorrel went off to prepare the attack.

By midafternoon, as if in anticipation of this explosion, the firing

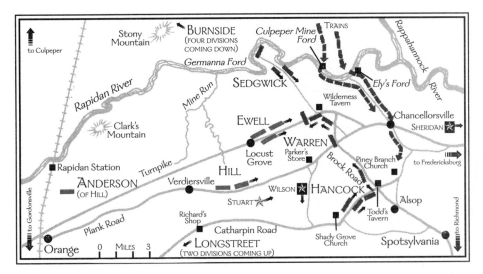

## The Wilderness

Grant's goal was to get through the tangled Wilderness by heading straight south. He did not make it. Hill and Ewell pitched into his army, pinning him in a strung-out line, while Longstreet brought his forces onto the field.

---

died down along the line and men moved forward into the burning woods to retrieve their fallen comrades. Some of the wounded did not make it and were burned to death in the smoldering fires. Both lines now fell into the routine of loading, firing, and reloading that had become common during the war, with neither side gaining a clear advantage. By sundown, Sorrel had completed his flank march—through an old railroad cut, down the Brock Road, and all without being seen—gathering three brigades as he went. Just before sundown, Longstreet joined him. When everything was set, Longstreet gave a nod, and Sorrel moved his men forward toward Hancock's unsuspecting corps. The advance was held up by a brushfire, but Longstreet kept his men moving, taking them farther to the right, and farther into Hancock's rear. They moved effortlessly, pushing the Yankees ahead of them, then let loose a volley—as if to signal the battle's start.

Longstreet's men fell on the Union flank "like a tornado," with brigade after brigade rolling back northwards. The results were all that could have been expected. While the rout was not of the scale or scope that fell on Hooker, Grant's army was being moved slowly into a corner. Hancock's line "began to break slowly, then rapidly." Out in front of the Union corps, the rest of Longstreet's command was ordered forward, pushing steadily to aid in the flanking movement. Jenkins rode up to Longstreet, exuberant about the success of the attack. "I am happy," he said. "I have felt despair of the cause for some months, but am relieved, and feel assured that we will put the enemy back across the Rapidan before night."

As Oates led his men forward, he kept his ear cocked for the battle on the right, now rolling toward him. He could hear the firing distinctly as it roared forward and, like many of his fellow commanders, could almost imagine the battle's end. But then, just as suddenly as the roaring peaked, it died away. The reason only became clear a few minutes later, when word spread through Lee's army that Longstreet was shot, along with Jenkins, and rumored dead. "He [Longstreet] and General Jenkins, whose brigade was the largest in the army, were riding together in front of their advancing lines," Oates later wrote, "when suddenly they came in view of the enemy, turned, and riding back through the dense forest, some of their own men, mistaking them for the enemies, fired on them, killing Jenkins and severely wounding Longstreet, who was lifted onto a stretcher and taken to the rear, which put an end to that movement." Oates was ordered forward in an attempt to retrieve the moment, but it was too late, his attack faltered. The 15th returned to its original lines at nightfall, its ammunition exhausted. All along the front the men of both armies slept where they had fought.

The Battle of the Wilderness continued through the next day, but Longstreet's strong influence was missed. With Fields in command of Longstreet's Corps, Lee would have to depend on his other veteran subordinates. At first light of the next day, Lee pushed Ewell's men into battle on the left, but after several hours of fighting the battle was stalemated. In midafternoon, Georgian John Gordon complained to Lee that Jubal Early had not allowed him to attack Grant's right, which he believed to be "in the air." Lee quickly countermanded the order and sent Gordon's Brigade off on yet another flanking maneuver, attempting on the left what Longstreet had started the night before on the right. Once again, Lee's audacity nearly unhinged the federal army. This time, the victim was the Fifth Corps, whose lines were summarily

crushed in three hours of brutal fighting. Darkness intervened, however, before Gordon could do the most damage. It was, Oates said, "another lost opportunity."

As the firing died, the men of both armies lay exhausted on virtually
the same ground where they had fought for three days. On two of those
days, first on the right and then on the far left, Lee had been presented
with opportunities to destroy at least a part of the northern army. But in
each case, his attacks had ended just as they were about to succeed.
While Grant had taken a severe beating—worse even than the one administered to Hooker the year before—his army was intact and its
morale unshaken. Lee, on the other hand, lost Longstreet, who was
badly wounded, and Jenkins—and 7,500 men. None of them could be
replaced. If anything, the Battle of the Wilderness seemed an eerie re-
play of Jackson's battle against Hooker, when another commander had
fallen when the army seemed just on the verge of a victory. Oates's
brigade commander, Evander McIvor Law, who had seen the battle begin with such promise, was near despair. "We almost seem to be struggling against destiny itself," he said.

At the outset of the campaign, both Lee and Longstreet marked Grant
as a man who would not be as easily fooled as McClellan, as intimidated
as Pope, as stampeded as Hooker, nor pulled to disaster like Burnside.
"We must make up our minds to get into line of battle and stay there,"
Longstreet said, "for that man will fight us every day and every hour
till the end of the war." That is precisely what Grant intended to do.
On May 7, he moved by his own left, marching his army out of the
Wilderness and south, heading for the crossroads at Spotsylvania
Court House. If he got there first he would have the inside line on Lee,
who would be forced to move farther south to defend Richmond. The
race was close. Just as the forward elements of Grant's army were appearing in the woods north of Spotsylvania, Lee's men were rushing to
throw up breastworks near the crossroads.

Back down Grant's long column of marchers heading out of the
Wilderness, the 20th Maine was choking in the dust, heat, and smoke
of the burning woods. They had just finished one of the most vicious
two-day fights they had ever experienced, having fought on May 5

against Hill, who had made a stand in one of the Wilderness's few open fields. The 20th had been taken into battle by their new brigade commander, Joseph Bartlett, who had arrived on the Wilderness battlefield in his gold-laced battle blouse. The brigade had pushed Hill's hard-bitten veterans back into the woods, but they had not been able to withstand the massed fire that had crashed back at them through the trees. Bartlett had moved the brigade in pursuit, but his advance was a mistake, most of the Maine men were cut off and had to fight their way out. They lost eleven dead. The next day, May 6, the regiment had lost another two veterans to long-range artillery fire. The Maine veterans thought the battle worse even than Gettysburg, where you could at least see your enemy. The 20th left one hundred dead, wounded, and missing in the Wilderness before receiving their orders to move south, on the morning of May 8.

The move south from the Wilderness to the crossroads at Spotsylvania through burning, choking woods, was nightmarish. Up ahead, nine miles away at the crossroads, the lead elements of the Fifth Corps were beginning their plunge at dismounted troopers fighting desperately to hold off the blue lines until Longstreet's Corps (now under its new commander, Richard Anderson) could make its appearance. Anderson, whose corps was moving south on a westerly road that paralleled Grant's march south, was pushing his men on at the double-quick, in a desperate attempt to reach the Spotsylvania crossroads before Grant's army beat him there. The 15th Alabama was near the head of Anderson's column. "About 10 o'clock we heard firing to our left and front," Oates wrote. "One brigade of infantry, Kershaw's South Carolina, preceded us. They had reached the village of Spotsylvania Court House none too soon. They took position just in time to meet the first advance of the enemy's infantry as they drove our cavalry."

Anderson's first lines volleyed into Warren's attackers, then reloaded and fired again, the massed fire breaking off into scattered shooting all along the line. Oates was ordered to take his regiment to the left to meet an attempted flank advance. Out across the fields, he spotted one of the southern army's most valiant enemies, the men of the old Iron Brigade, still known by their black felt hats. The 6th Wisconsin engaged the 15th Alabama in a stand-up fight in a woods to the left of the crossroads before Oates's men were ordered back behind the newly constructed breastworks near the courthouse. Both armies now knew the terrible cost of a stand-up battle and felled trees so that the entire ten miles of battleground was protected.

The opening shot of the Battle of Spotsylvania Court House was followed by a pitched and headlong Union attack whose goal was to push Lee aside, leaving the road to Richmond open. The prize now was the Confederacy itself, which was why the contest for Spotsylvania would go on hour after hour, day after day, for fourteen unrelenting days, from May 8 to May 21—amid mud and carnage. By the end, the men from both sides were slipping in the red viscera of their fallen comrades. Out in front of the federal attack on May 8 was James Rice—"as brave and true a man who ever went booted and spurred from the field to report to the God of battles," Chamberlain later wrote—leading his men here much as he had on Chamberlain's right at Little Round Top. He went forward to within one hundred yards of Lee's newly constructed defensive line, which bulged at its northern edge into the form of a mule shoe, so close to the Union line that the flames from each side's guns nearly merged. Rice was struck and went down. Later, as he was dying from his wounds, a surgeon seeking to comfort him asked him which way he wanted to face. "Turn me with my face to the enemy," he said.

The arm's-length fighting was especially exhausting for Oates's men, guarding Lee's left. The firing continued without letup into the night on the second day of the battle, then throughout the third day and on into that night. On May 11, the two lines fought only 125 paces apart, mounting charge and countercharge. Finally, on May 12, to break the stalemate Hancock sent a flying column of twelve regiments forward at the apex of the rebel position—at the tip of the "mule shoe"—an unusual tactic, but brilliantly conceived. The move was so surprising that almost all of Edward Johnson's Division, 5,000 men, were captured, along with sixteen guns, and the rebel line was pierced. For a moment it looked as if the Army of Northern Virginia was doomed. Hancock poured in men to expand the breach, pushing brigade after brigade into his bridgehead. At this, the most critical crisis in his army's history, Lee appeared on the field. With shells and musketry clattering in a crescendo around him, he urged John Gordon's men to build a new line south of the breakthrough to hold Hancock's men in check. Gordon had Lee escorted to safety, then set about the task of retrieving the army, sending attackers into Hancock's line while he built a new set of breastworks to the south. The struggle went on for twenty gut-wrenching hours. Gordon remembered the battle as the most horrifying of the war:

> Mounting to the crest of the embankment, the Union men poured upon the Confederates a galling fire. To the support of the latter other Confederate commands came quickly, crowding into the ditches, clambering up the embankment's side, and returning volley for volley. Then followed the mighty rush from both armies, filling the entire disputed space. Firing into one another across the embankment's crest almost within an arm's reach, the men behind passing up to them freshly loaded rifles as their own were emptied. As those in front fell, others quickly sprang forward to take their places. On both sides the dead were piled in heaps. As Confederates fell their bodies rolled into the ditch, and upon their bleeding forms their living comrades stood, beating back Grant's furiously charging columns. The bullets seemed to fly in sheets. Before the pelting hail and withering blast the standing timber fell. The breastworks were literally drenched in blood. The coming of the darkness failed to check the raging battle. It only served to increase the awful terror of the scene.

The fighting at the mule shoe finally sputtered out, with Lee's army saved from almost certain disaster by the construction of a new defensive line just south of his old position. Grant attacked the line on and off for the next week, but the rebels could not be moved. The battle finally ended on the morning of May 19, but the armies faced each other, in position, for another two days. Finally, on the night of May 21, Grant moved his men by the left again, abandoning his lines at Spotsylvania and heading southeast in pursuit of Lee. His losses were horrific. From the opening of the Battle of the Wilderness on May 5 to the end of the Battle of Spotsylvania Court House on May 21, the Union lost 35,000 men killed, wounded, and missing, a toll that stunned the North. Even

Chamberlain was shocked by the bloodletting. "The hammering business had been hard on the hammer," he wrote to Fannie.

After Spotsylvania, Chamberlain took command of the Third Brigade when Bartlett reported sick and, with the rest of Grant's army, followed Lee's rear guard across the line of rivers toward Richmond. Grant moved his troops south in a great wheel to the left: across the Po River, then alongside Pole Cat Creek, then over the North Anna River, where, with the rest of the Fifth Corps, Chamberlain was ordered to ford his men through the muddy brown water. When the corps crossed the North Anna River, however, it banged up against A. P. Hill's command. Chamberlain rode out to deploy his brigade, stemming the tide of men tumbling back toward the river. He was in front of the line, seeing the rebels come on as artillery shells landed nearby. He excused his own recklessness to the men who tried to pull him out of the line of fire. "It is necessary to know what is going on," he explained in his battle report. On the night of May 26, Chamberlain was ordered to pull his men out of their exposed position along the river and march them south, with the rest of the army, toward Richmond.

Lee now had the inside arc to the Confederate capital. In the race to reach Richmond, he was winning, though barely. Each time Grant moved south, Lee shadowed him, entrenching along Grant's line of march—as if daring the northern commander to attack him. Grant countered these moves by feinting an attack and then moving to his left before striking south again. Lee, on the inside line of march, would attempt to anticipate Grant, marching his exhausted men toward Richmond. Finally Lee interposed himself between Grant and Richmond at a crossroads called Cold Harbor, on the outskirts of the Confederate capital—near the same battlefields where McClellan had been so badly handled. Grant and Lee had been facing off against each other now for one month, and the casualties on both sides were appalling. The nation had never seen such fighting. For the previous three years, battles would come, armies would retreat and rest, and then set out again to battle. But not now. Grant's move across the Rapidan and into the Wilderness inaugurated more than thirty days of endless conflict, with

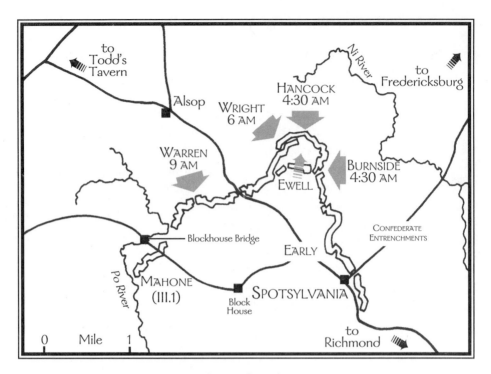

## Spotsylvania

After the Wilderness, Lee raced Grant for the key Spotsylvania crossroads, then faced him in a series of entrenchments. Hancock's attack on Lee's "mule shoe" position during the early morning hours of May 12, 1864—followed by an attack all along the line—crushed Lee's salient, but did not lead to the defeat of his army.

---

both sides becoming expert at throwing up breastworks and building strongpoints wherever they stopped. The armies did not camp and rest, they fought and moved and fought again as their lines snaked south. But the worst was yet to come—a slaughter that would stun the North.

On the night of June 2, the 15th Alabama, with the rest of Law's Brigade, lay in the trenches in front of Cold Harbor, expecting to move to the right at sunrise, as they had done so many nights before. But when daylight came on June 3, the northern army was still present along Oates's front, while the Army of Northern Virginia stretched off to the south. The dawn came on brilliantly and all seemed quiet for a moment, but then Oates heard rifle fire from the woods to the east, followed by the long rolling cheers of blue-clad men. Peering over the rifle pit, Oates realized that the Union lines, which seemed so distant at first, were nearly on top of him, the glint of bayonet steel clearly visible across the field.

> I called out: "Sergeant, give them double charges of canister; fire, men; fire!" the order was obeyed with alacrity. The enemy were within thirty steps. They halted and began to dodge, lie down, and recoil. The fire was terrific from my regiment, the Fourth Alabama on my immediate right, and the Thirteenth Mississippi on my left, while the piece of artillery was fired more rapidly and better handled than I ever saw one before or since. The blaze of fire from it at each shot went right into the ranks of our assailants and made frightful gaps through the dense of men.

In the Alabama trenches, William Jordan fired, then passed his rifle back to a second line to be reloaded and was given a new one—the rotation of muskets going on and on until his front was cleared of charging soldiers. It was just that way all along the lines as Grant sent thousands of men (some of them pinned their names to their shirts so as to be identified when they died) against the rebel entrenchments. "There was greater destruction of life for the length of time and line of any engagement that occurred during the war," Jordan wrote. Oates concurred: "The stench from the dead between our lines and theirs was sickening. It was so nauseating that it was almost unendurable; but we had the advantage, as the wind carried it away from us to them. The dead covered more than five acres of ground about as thickly as they could be laid." Grant lost 12,000 men at Cold Harbor in one bloody day's work, then drew off, heartsick at the human destruction.

After the Battle of Cold Harbor, Joseph Bartlett returned to the army and command of the Third Brigade, but Chamberlain was finally given command of a brigade of his own, six Pennsylvania regiments, in Warren's Corps. These were among the hardest fighters in the army, having sent a regiment of North Carolinians to their graves on the first day of Gettysburg. They were tough men, seasoned fighters, and cared little for their appearance. They looked as tattered as the enemy. On his first day in command, Chamberlain called his regimental colonels together and told them he was familiar with their record and hoped he could measure up to their experiences—a statement that won their immediate loyalty. That same day, Griffin again recommended Chamberlain's promotion to brigadier general, which brought Warren's approval. "I am sure his appointment would add to my strength even more than the reinforcement of a thousand men," Warren wrote in a note to Meade. The recommendation was sent up the line.

Chamberlain was pleased by the show of confidence, but he knew that Warren's support meant little, and Grant's everything—nor, it seemed, did promotions amount to much in the new army. After Wilderness, Spotsylvania, and Cold Harbor, new command arrangements were viewed as little more than niceties. Whole regiments and entire divisions had been swept away in the last forty days, with the result that the army was constantly sorting and resorting its structure, bringing in new men, green and frightened, to fill the gaping ranks. It was not unusual for Chamberlain to be given command of men he hardly knew as regiments were filled up, killed, and refilled.

After Cold Harbor, Grant moved the army yet again, farther south, so that by June 7, Chamberlain's brigade was on the banks of the Chickahominy east of Richmond. Nearly every federal soldier now believed that the movement would be forward, that Grant would hurl the army at Lee, as he had done at Cold Harbor, until the Army of Northern Virginia (its ranks dangerously thin, its men exhausted) disintegrated. But Grant had a different plan. Shocked by the bloody repulse at Cold Harbor, and knowing that only the defeat of Lee's army and not the capture of Richmond would end the war, Grant vaulted south. Starting on June 12, he sent his army in a grand sweep to the left to capture Petersburg, the railroad crossroads town south of the Confederate capital.

Grant drove his army mercilessly, attempting once again to win a race against Lee that would seal his defeat. But standing east of Petersburg were troops under the command to General P. G. T. Beauregard, a long, thin gray line; they were the only soldiers that stood between Grant and victory. The first troops of the Army of the Potomac arrived on June 15, but their attack was disjointed, and Beauregard moved his troops—"old men and boys," Oates described them—into new positions while sending riders north to spur Lee's reinforcements. Again,

on June 16 and 17, Beauregard held his line against the charging federals. At one point his men were nearly overwhelmed. Lee arrived late on
June 17, pouring his veterans into Beauregard's shaken lines. Petersburg was saved.

Chamberlain, with the Fifth Corps, launched an attack on the sev-
enteenth, moving his men forward against a rebel strongpoint, "Fort
Hell," on Beauregard's left, but he could not hold the position. On the
next morning, Chamberlain's brigade was again ordered to attack the
rebel fortifications at the place where they jutted east, which was named
"Rives Salient." He led his men from the front, but the rest of the corps
could not keep up and the Fifth Corps commander, Gouverneur K.
Warren—who had sent Vincent's Brigade, with Chamberlain's regiment, up Little Round Top—did not hurry his men into the breach. It
was a lost opportunity, for Beauregard's defenses and the few men provided from Lee's vanguard almost certainly could have been overwhelmed. Chamberlain could only guess at why he was unsupported
and had little time to speculate. Instead, walking forward at the point of
attack, he was clearly unnerved by the spectacle that greeted him. But
he led his men up into the gray guns and held the crest, Petersburg
clearly visible in the distance.

As Chamberlain was preparing to hold his position against the
overwhelming odds that faced him, a rider galloped forward with orders that he continue his attack. He was stunned by the command,
imagining his brigade wiped away by the certain slaughter. He hesitated and then, for the only time during the war, he refused an order—
deciding instead to scrawl an appeal to Meade: "Circumstances lead me
to believe the General cannot be aware of my situation, which has
greatly changed in the last hour," he wrote. "I have just carried an advanced position held by the enemy's infantry and artillery. I am advanced a mile beyond our own lines, and in an isolated position." He
detailed his position as politely as army formalities would allow, but it
was clear he thought an attack now on the entrenched positions before
him was suicidal. "I have here a veteran Brigade of six regiments, and
my responsibility for the welfare of these men seem to warrant me in
wishing assurance that no mistake in communicating orders compels
me to sacrifice them."

Chamberlain was a good officer, one of the army's finest, but brave as he was, he would not needlessly send his men into a maelstrom. This was not the Army of the Potomac's finest hour, or Warren's, or Meade's, or Grant's (whose Wilderness imprecation to "pitch into them" at every opportunity had been followed, bloodily, for six weeks), but it may well have been Chamberlain's. The messenger returned with verbal confirmation of Meade's orders, that Chamberlain was to step off immediately and attack the enemy in his front. We do not know Chamberlain's reply, and though he was free of cursing or bitterness, he must have doubted the mental acuity of men who would pen such senseless orders. He did his best to comply in order to convince his men that their attack would not be in vain.

He brought his regimental commanders together to give them their assignments. He told them that the rebel lines were just ahead—down a slope, across a stream, then up a hillside on the other side. The only way they could make the charge, he advised, was for each regimental commander to make certain the men did not fire as they moved forward, but to save their first volley for close-in work. He said he hoped the brigade would be supported on the left, which would make their work easier, but he was not sure of it. From where he stood, he could see the Confederate works, complete with trenches and log fronts. The fire from the enemy line, when it was made, was bound to be terrible. There were at least 3,000 men across the valley waiting, fully armed and well protected. They would have a clear shot at anyone, let alone a tightly packed brigade advancing over open ground. Chamberlain realized his brigade had little chance against the fortifications, but he was counting on artillery support from Bigelow's Battery, which had done legendary work at Gettysburg.

At midafternoon, all was prepared. Chamberlain eyed the enemy defenses and was offered a drink of whiskey by an enlisted man. He refused it, then walked down the line of his men telling them what to do: "Comrades, we have now before us a great duty for our country to perform, and who knows but the way in which we acquit ourselves in this perilous undertaking may depend the ultimate success of the preservation of our grand republic," he said. "We know that some must fall, it may be any of you or I; but I feel that you will all go manfully and make such a record as will make all our loyal American people grateful. I can but feel that our action in this crisis is momentous, and who can know but in the providence of God our action today may be the one thing needful to break and destroy this unholy rebellion." He ended then, not having told them that their attack was futile (they could see that for themselves), then moved to the center of the line and ordered his troops forward down the slope and into the rebel fire.

The men moved over open ground in even ranks, taking casualties to nearly within one hundred yards of the rebel defenders, who then rose up and fired with the discipline of veterans who understood the stark terror of massed fire. The brigade's color bearer fell dead only a few feet from Chamberlain, who grasped the flagstaff and shook it, turning and motioning to his men. It was precisely at this moment, as he was urging his men on, that a rebel minié ball entered Chamberlain's right hip, coursed its way through his abdomen, and spun him half around. He whirled from the impact of the blow, then righted himself, planting his sword point in the ground as a steadying guide. He was only upright for a moment before he fell next to his sword. The bullet had caught him as he was turning, almost to the rear, and his first thought was: "What will my mother say, her boy, shot in the back!"

The ball passed through his body, exited his left hip, and left a trail of red on the ground. Within minutes he was faint from loss of blood. As the attack ebbed and then flowed back over him, he urged his men to stand fast. But the attack failed, and his brigade was shattered. It was, as many of them later remembered, a "massacre." Chamberlain was dragged out of range of the point-blank rebel fire, but then was left on the field between the lines. He was spotted, finally, by artilleryman John Bigelow, who ordered four men to retrieve him. Chamberlain was almost unconscious, but protested to his rescuers to take others first. "You are not in command, sir," one said. "Captain Bigelow's order to us was to bring you back, and that is what we must do." Two hours later, Joshua Chamberlain was behind the Union lines at a field hospital, attended by brigade and division surgeons, including one from the 20th Maine, who worked furiously to save his life.

The doctors cut away the fleshy part of the wound, cleaned it out, and then, since the ball that struck him had moved from his right hip to his left and nicked his bladder before exiting, rearranged his battered abdomen. While Chamberlain fought off death, the surgeons were delving into new medical territory. They were no less certain than Chamberlain's senior commanders that he would die. His army superiors immediately began to issue notices of his promotion and citations for bravery. Griffin and Warren came to his bedside, as did several veterans of his old regiment. Warren sent on a note to Meade and Grant, "He expresses the wish that he may receive the recognition of his services by promotion before he dies for the gratification of his family and friends, and I beg that if possible it may be done." Grant agreed and promoted him on the spot—to brigadier general—the only time he did so, for any officer or soldier, during the war. One day after the surgery, Chamberlain wrote a shaky note to his wife:

> My darling wife
> I am lying mortally wounded the doctors think, but my mind & heart are at peace Jesus Christ is my all-sufficient savior. I go to him. God bless & keep & comfort you, precious one, you have been a precious wife to me. To know & love you make life & death beautiful. Cherish the darlings & give my love to all the dear ones. Do not grieve too much for me. We shall all soon meet. Live for the children Give my dearest love to Father, mother & Sallie & John Oh how happy to feel yourself forgiven God bless you evermore precious one
> Ever yours Lawrence.

Several days later, still barely alive, Chamberlain was put aboard a steamer. His obituary was published in the New York papers. But Chamberlain rallied briefly, before a fever set in. Fannie and Joshua's brother John hurried to the Union hospital in Annapolis for what they believed would be his final moments. Remarkably, however, six weeks after being wounded it appeared that the crisis had passed and, while he remained wobbly and weak, he was clearly recovering. It was an especially trying time for Fannie, who thought her husband lucky to be alive. She was happy of course, but his recovery was also a somber time—for she knew that if possible her husband would return to the army, no matter what his condition. In her mind, the months of his convalescence were a race between his recovery and the fall of the Confederacy.

Several weeks earlier, though still in pain, Chamberlain had made his own wishes known in an unusually frank letter to his mother. He had written her that he would return to the war, but not for glory or honor or titles. It was one of the most open admissions of what he wanted in his life. "I haven't a particle of fanaticism in me," he wrote. "But I plead guilty to a sort of fatalism. I believe in a destiny—one, I mean, divinely appointed, and to which we are carried forward by a perfect trust in God. I do this, and I believe in it. I have laid plans, in my day, & good ones I thought. But they never succeeded. Something else, better, did, and I could see it as plain as day, that God had done it, & for my good." Chamberlain returned to Brunswick, and his family, in September—though his mind was still always back to battle and on his divinely appointed "destiny."

While Oates had been placed on the promotion list as a full colonel in May 1863, even before the Battle of Gettysburg, the Confederate Congress had not confirmed his appointment. By the summer of 1864, he still languished as a lieutenant colonel, a fact that grated, especially since it meant that unassigned full colonels (or anyone else senior to him) could legitimately step in to command his regiment. It did not matter, either, that Oates often commanded nearly one-half of Law's Brigade on his many assignments—the Confederate army was run by the book and the privilege of rank by date was given great weight. Oates, it seemed, was always looking over his shoulder at Alexander Lowther, who had once ranked him, but now served as the 15th Alabama's major, its second-in-command. Oates knew Lowther was working to oust him, a fact confirmed after his nemesis returned to the regiment in August from Richmond, waving his new promotion to colonel in Oates's face.

Oates might have stayed with the 15th, but he would not serve under Lowther. Or he could have resigned and gone home, as other officers had, but he instead decided to fight for his command. "I went to see General Lee about it and he gave me a pass and suggested that I see President Davis in regard to the matter. I went to see him. He received me very respectfully. I laid my case before him. He sent a messenger to the Adjutant-General's Office for information, and remarked to me that if it were in his power he would restore the regiment to my command. The answer was returned that Lowther had his commission and it had been confirmed by the Senate. Davis replied, 'I am sorry to say, sir, that he is beyond my reach; I have no power over the matter.' " Davis asked Oates if he would accept reassignment, a question that Oates regarded as purely rhetorical. So it was that, in early August 1864, William Oates reported as commander of the 48th Alabama, which was camped on the north side of the James River.

The 48th was a veteran regiment of Law's Brigade that had suffered heavy losses at Antietam, Gettysburg, the Wilderness, and Spotsylvania. Oates called them "hardy mountaineers," though in August 1864 they were not much to look at. Like the rest of Lee's army, the 48th was exhausted by the long marches and constant fights of the previous month. When Oates took command, they were coming apart. "I at once ascertained what was needed, made requisition, and obtained clothing, accouterments, and everything that was to be had, essential to the comfort of officers and men, and whatever was calculated to increase their efficiency as soldiers." Within one week their fighting spirit was vastly improved, and they were ready to face Grant, who was now slowly extending his own trench lines southward around Petersburg, toward the railroads that provisioned Lee's army.

On August 13, Oates and the 48th were assigned to hold the lines two miles below Drewry's Bluff east of Petersburg, where they were continually shelled by Union gunboats on the James. One shell, as Oates later related, exploded in the trenches, burying an officer, who was frantically retrieved by his men nearby. "He was nearly smothered." There was constant death in the trenches, which were manned in shifts—foreshadowing the trench warfare of the Western Front in World War I, and with many of the same effects. Sickness, cold, fatigue, and battle weariness were the regiment's most constant enemies. On August 16, Union General Winfield Hancock's Second Corps attempted to break the stalemate, advancing up the Darbytown Road near Petersburg, breaking through the rebels' first line of defense. Oates was called in to suture the break before Hancock could sever the north–south road running from Petersburg to Richmond. In the midst of the advance, Oates reported to his corps commander Richard Anderson for orders. The Georgian, who had ably commanded the corps since Longstreet was wounded in the Wilderness, pointed to the lines of Union soldiers advancing over open ground to the east. Anderson said he doubted that Oates could stop the assault. Oates thought otherwise. He marched the 48th and the 15th through a small woods and into a farm, then ordered the regiments to oblique to the right, which would bring them onto Hancock's flank near a farm fence. The odds were enormous—at the very best, all Oates could do was stall the attack. From where they stood, the Alabama men could look for nearly a half mile down the ranks of the advancing federals. "We were not fifty steps apart when both lines opened a terrific fire," Oates remembered. To his left, Alexander Lowther went down, wounded. The federal lines fired again, seemingly unharmed by the Alabamians' own crashing volley. Both sides paused to load, with a smattering of shots breaking the sudden silence. Although he knew he would take fearful casualties, Oates ordered his two regiments over the fence and onto the flank of Hancock's line. Men fell all along the Alabama front.

The sudden appearance of the two Alabama regiments on his far right brought Hancock's entire attack to a crawl, which allowed Anderson precious time to refortify his lines below the bluff. In fact, Oates had Hancock fooled. Believing that Oates could not possibly attack him alone and that other units would soon reinforce the Alabamians from a nearby woods, Hancock moved up several batteries of artillery and shelled the woods line, leaving Oates's men to attack without having to face artillery fire. Oates, seeing his advantage, pressed forward: "Some of my men fell dead or horribly wounded at every step, but the brave fellows . . . pressed forward, driving their enemy until a trench, which had been made by a farmer to turn the water on the hill side, had been reached." There were now only five companies left for Oates to command and no officers, since every one of them was killed or wounded. Even so, Oates ordered his men into the trench, while he remained standing. Inevitably, a minié ball pierced a rifle cloth he was carrying at his side, splaying it out backward. "Colonel, get down in here with us," one of his men called, "they will kill you." Oates vividly recounted what happened next:

A moment later a ball struck me in my right arm, midway between the elbow and the shoulder, breaking it in two, shivering and splintering the bone down to the elbow and upwards to within two inches of the shoulder joint. It struck with such force that it turned me half around and stunned me. I stepped to and leaned against a little apple tree. I was in great pain. One of those large Minie-balls strikes a hard blow.

Oates turned over command of his regiment, then watched them charge the Yankee line, in their "splendid blue uniforms," and come rolling back. "The forty-eighth regiment won imperishable honors on that day," Oates later wrote. "No men, in any battle of the world, ever fought more heroically, on any field, than did the officers and men of that regiment near the Darbytown Road, August 16, 1864. It went into the fight about 300 strong, with some 15 officers. It came out with but 51 men and 3 officers unhurt, and none of them were captured."

Oates made his way to the rear, reported to Anderson, then lay down near a tree. He got up after a while and passed division commander C. W. Field, who expressed regret at his wound. A surgeon came and administered morphine, and finally two men of the 15th Alabama walked up to him to help. A blanket was procured from a Yankee prisoner, and Oates was wrapped in it and sent to the rear with six federal soldiers who had been taken prisoner. "One of them gave me a canteen nearly full of whiskey," he said, "the very thing I most needed, as I was getting sick and very weak from loss of blood. While making the trip I drank all the whiskey. . . . It seemed to me the best I ever tasted." Oates arrived at the field hospital, an acre of land filled with wounded and dying men. The surgeons eventually came to Oates and administered chloroform. Oates could hear the rasp of the saw through the anesthesia as the surgeons cut off his arm near the shoulder.

When Oates awakened he found himself next to Jimmy Morris, a man from his regiment, who was seated at his side and crying—believing his commander dead. Oates shushed him and sent him off for whiskey, then dictated a letter to be sent to his mother and father in Alabama. He told them he was wounded, but that he would survive. An orderly appeared then with Oates's amputated arm and asked him what he should do with it. It must have seemed an odd question. "I told him that I did not care, as it was no longer of any service to me, but that he had better dig a hole and bury it. He did so, just on the opposite side of the tree under which I lay." The next morning Oates was moved south with the rest of the wounded from Law's Brigade to Howard's Grove hospital with other wounded officers. Joining him at the hospital was Captain Simeon Strickland of the 15th Alabama, who had also lost an arm.

The two men fed each other and Strickland helped Oates through his first week of convalescence. "He was the man I needed near, to cheer me and divert my mind from brooding over my great loss. I was a young man of fine physical strength and activity, and to be so impaired by the loss of my right arm made me despondent and at times to feel a regret that I had not been killed. Strickland dispelled my gloom." Oates's wound healed well enough, but soon became infected and the stump had to be broken open to drain. Such secondary hemorrhages were common, and frightful, and caused much death.

One night Oates suffered massive bleeding from his shoulder and slipped into semiconsciousness. "Doctor Mudd got to me, seized my shoulder, and stopped it," Oates later wrote. "My bed was flooded with blood. I saw death close at hand. My whole life passed rapidly before me in panorama, and while I felt regret that I had not been a better man, yet I was not afraid to die, but preferred to live. It was a very consoling thought that I had never committed any great crime." Oates was not expected to live through the night. The hospital doctors held a consultation about what could be done to save the colonel. Everyone believed the wound should be cut open and the artery tied off, except for one—a Dr. J. B. Gaston—who insisted on applying a steady and hard compress. The doctor took off his coat, sat down beside Oates, and "went to work." The next day Oates lay near death, but he somehow survived. Within a week he was out of danger.

There were many men in the hospital now lying near death who had served with Oates. The war had weakened his old regiment, the 15th, nearly destroyed his new one, the 48th, and badly bled out Law's famed Alabama Brigade. One of those at Howard's Grove was James B. Long, who had married Oates's sister. He lay in another ward, sick from typhoid fever. "Though [barely able] to walk fifty steps, I went to see him and found him a very sick man. He requested me to telegraph his wife to come to him. I consoled him the best I could, and persuaded him to wait until the afternoon and see whether there was any change in his condition." Oates went to see him again that afternoon, but he was dying. "I sat by and held his hand while he, in a faltering voice scarcely above a whisper, said to me, 'Don't let my wife and children suffer.' I assured him I never would during the time I lived."

———✦———

Atlanta was captured on September 2. Later in the month, Grant extended his lines farther south and then west around Petersburg, to the South Side Railroad. He was tightening the noose, starving Lee out of the city. In October another attack was made on the Darbytown Road, but it failed and both armies went into their winter camps. In the Shenandoah Valley, troops under Jubal Early were crushed at Cedar Creek and Sheridan lay waste the Confederacy's breadbasket. Early returned to Petersburg a shattered man and faced Lee, who sent him home. But the worst news for the South came in November, when Lincoln was reelected for a second term. Atlanta was looted on November 15. The next day, Sherman cut loose from his line of communications and set out for the sea—"to make Georgia howl." The end was in sight.

Chamberlain returned to the army in November, taking command of a brigade in the Fifth Corps. He hardly recognized the army now, its ranks worn by attrition, many of its veterans gone when their enlistments lapsed. In early December, Chamberlain led his men on a raid down the Weldon Railroad, tearing up tracks for some twenty miles south of Petersburg. The railroad ties were levered out of their beds, then heated and strung out, bent back against each other—into a heap of smoldering metal. The men took great pleasure in their work, creating fantastic sculptures from the bent steel and foraging liberally on the trip, finding applejack for their canteens. Many of them fell out drunk and were left by the side of the road, to be picked up on the move back north. There seemed little danger in this, and the march was diligently carried out. But when the column moved back into their lines, they found that some of their comrades had had their throats cut by roving marauders. Chamberlain's men, enraged by the murders, could not be contained and burned and looted southern homes. "This was a hard sight," Chamberlain admitted.

In December, Chamberlain took time from his brigade to travel to Philadelphia to have a second operation on his wound. He was in increasing pain and was having trouble carrying out his duties. No one in his brigade thought he would return at all. That seemed to be the case, for after his Philadelphia hospitalization he returned to Brunswick to help celebrate the birth of a daughter, Gertrude Loraine—his and Fannie's fifth child. Fannie wanted him to remain in Brewer, of course, but he would not, and announced his intention to return to the army and see the war through to the last battle. His mother protested, writing to him that "surely you have done & suffered & won laurels enough in this war to satisfy the most ambitious," but he was adamant.

Chamberlain returned to the Army of the Potomac in February and was given command of the First Brigade of the Fifth Corps. His chief worry now, it seemed, was watching over himself. John Chamberlain was in New York, and his brother Tom was serving as a divisional provost marshal, which placed him well out of the line of battle. Shortly after his return, he wrote to Fannie that he had made the right decision. "I do not in the least regret my choice," he said, but then reassured her that "I shall not feel obliged to lead any more charges, unless it becomes necessary, and hope to escape any further injuries." In mid-March the army's senior commanders, including Chamberlain, were notified that the army should begin preparing for the spring offensive—and its last battles. They would move against Lee quickly, toward the south, stringing out his defenses to their breaking point, until they reached the railroads heading into Petersburg from the Carolinas.

⊂══━✦━══⊃

Chamberlain received his orders on March 28, and before dawn on March 29, 1865, he had his brigade up and in columns, ready to move off to the southwest toward Dinwiddie Court House. The brigade moved in the brightening dawn, with canteens clanking, over Rowanty Creek and onto the Vaughan Road. Orders soon came to move the brigade to the north up the Quaker Road. Chamberlain was halfway down the column, riding his horse Charlemagne, wearing his faded dark blue field jacket. A courier soon rode down the line and stopped, reporting that the rebels were up ahead, across a small creek and entrenched. Charles Griffin ordered Chamberlain's First Brigade to attack up the road, with the Second Brigade in support on the left. Chamberlain deployed his men and they marched forward, taking fire and wading a creek, but it was not much of a battle. The rebels fled at contact.

Chamberlain kept his men in battle line and moving forward for nearly a mile before emerging from the thin woods into a broad field. But at every step the rebel defenses proved tougher to break. In the far woods, the Confederate line along the Quaker Road was thickly manned and Chamberlain's Brigade was halted by the fire, beginning a slow and sullen withdrawal. The day was hot and cloudy, the ground wet, and the men sweated profusely. Charles Griffin, the division commander, appeared, unworried by the rebel defenses, and ordered Chamberlain to take his brigade ahead and attack. They would be supported on both the right and left by additional troops. Chamberlain re-formed his men at a set of farm buildings in the clearing, then ordered the lines forward, galloping dangerously far in front of his own charging line. He was nearly felled by a minié ball, which struck his horse Charlemagne in the neck and then pierced his sleeve before thumping him, hard, in the chest. He slumped forward, unconscious, over his horse's neck. The federal lines were going to pieces around him, taking destructive fire from the rebel breastworks.

Griffin thought he was dead. "My dear General," he said, when he caught up with him, "you are gone." But Chamberlain was now revived, stunned by the shot he had received, and he spurred his horse forward, trying to revive the Union attack. He whirled back into battle, though men were falling in handfuls around him. "I hardly knew what world I was in," he later admitted. With Charlemagne blown from the wound, Chamberlain dismounted and ran into the farmyard, where he was confronted by a squad of rebels, who demanded his surrender. He shook his head at them. "Surrender, what's the matter with you? What do you take me for?" His faded uniform, nearly gray from the dust and heat, served him well. He convinced the rebels that he was a Confederate officer, then took them in hand and led them into the Union lines as his prisoners.

More reinforcements appeared then, including the 20th Maine, headed by Chamberlain's old friend Ellis Spear. Spear smiled at his old commander and brought out a bottle of wine. For one of the few times in the war, or in his life, Chamberlain drank heartily. He then moved back into line, holding his battered brigade together, and led them back out across the field. By the end of the day, the Confederate positions along the Quaker Road had been destroyed. Chamberlain's actions, and his almost single-handed control of the battlefield, were noticed at headquarters and, this time, he was given the recognition he was due. Warren made sure that even Lincoln was informed of Chamberlain's "conspicuous gallantry" and that the soldier from Maine was promoted to brevet major general of volunteers.

The night of the Union victory at Quaker Road, as the rains came in torrents, Ulysses S. Grant sat in his tent outside Petersburg and studied the maps on the table before him. Another week, or perhaps two, could accomplish the full closure of Petersburg; all that was needed was a series of battles for possession of the roads that led from the south into the city. Grant plotted the moves and then stopped, rethinking the strategy. He leaned over to write out his orders again, this time sending the Union cavalry under General Phil Sheridan on its own, to the far left, to see if it might be possible to end "the matter." Two days later, with the roads still mired in mud, he called Sheridan to his headquarters and told him of his plan, sketching it out on the map in his tent. Chamberlain was to have a key role in this last attack, as his brigade would be on the far left of the Union line, near the White Oak Road, when Sheridan swept his troopers south, then west, and then back north toward Five Forks in a great and looping raid.

Unfortunately, however, while the attack was well conceived, it did not turn out as planned. On the morning of April 1, as his men were boiling their coffee, Chamberlain heard a rolling sound, like a great fire, coming toward him from the west, followed by the roar of massed musketry. Soon stragglers came out of the woods, followed by lines of frightened men. Nearby, he heard the crash of artillery. Parts of the Fifth Corps, somewhere to the front, were in a wild retreat. Nearby, General Griffin rode to Chamberlain on his lathered horse, his eyes burning with anger. "General Chamberlain," he cried in alarm, "the Fifth Corps is eternally damned." Chamberlain mounted his horse and ordered his men into line, standing aside to allow the retreating troops to make their way to the rear. The rebels were coming at them through the woods, and thousands of blue-clad men were moving back in disarray.

Chamberlain quickly organized his brigade in a thick battle line, putting a nearby brigade to his left, then sent out skirmishers. Yet another brigade was deployed as a reserve. Over on the far right, General Gibbon had brought the Second Corps out of its camps to meet the onslaught of Lee's men, who had begun the attack near dawn. Soon the rebel line appeared in Chamberlain's front. His line moved slowly to stop the attack. After only a quarter of an hour, Chamberlain's men were pushing forward, reversing the southern tide. The woods broke up Chamberlain's line, but he pressed his command forward, back over the ground where the rebels had launched their attack, and to within sight of the rebel breastworks. On the right, Gibbon's men were also moving forward.

With his men carrying their muskets at right-shoulder arms, Chamberlain halted his line to reform it, with the breastworks clearly visible across the clearing to his front. He believed that here, near the White Oak Road, the Union army finally had the final victory in its grasp. He ordered the men forward, making sure their lines were fully aligned, their flags unfurled, against the rebel works. A Confederate officer watched Chamberlain in the distance, then hunkered down to meet the Union assault: "I thought it was one of the most gallant things I had ever seen," he later wrote. Chamberlain's men closed the gap, taking fire, never wavering, until they were nearly on top of the rebel positions—then went in at a run, with Chamberlain on Charlemagne, in front of the charge. The firing was heavy for a moment, but then ceased as rebels clambered back out of their defenses and headed north and west. The Confederate line was broken, its colors captured. Chamberlain considered moving his men in a wheel to the right, but paused, waiting for orders from his corps commander, General Warren. Out ahead, screened by the woods, Sheridan's men were skirmishing around Five Forks.

With his men resting on their arms, Warren now hesitated, not knowing whether to send his men to help Sheridan, to await further orders, or to attack the rebels at Five Forks. He contracted his lines, fearing a rebel attack like the one that had burst on him that morning. As night came on, Warren was as uninformed as anyone in the entire army. He did not know whether Sheridan needed his help or not. At dawn, Chamberlain put his men on the road straight west toward Five Forks. He reached Sheridan's position, a long line of dismounted

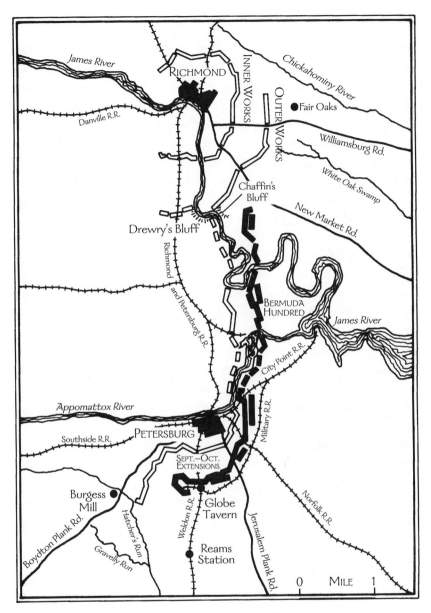

## Richmond and Petersburg

Richmond was ringed with rebel entrenchments (*in white*), but Grant had his eye on Petersburg, which contolled the rail lines coming into the Confederate capital. Grant dug siege lines (*in black*), then cut the rail lines from east to west, extending his forces farther and farther around the southern city. When the last rail line was cut, Lee had little choice; he retreated west, following the line of the Appomattox River.

cavalrymen, four miles south of the crossroads, at midmorning. The rebels were still in Warren's front and digging in, but Warren did not attack—a fact that made Sheridan enraged. When Charles Griffin appeared with his division, Sheridan ignored Warren and placed Griffin's troops and Chamberlain's, which were nearby, in a line facing directly north, and ordered them to attack and turn the rebel flank.

The attack began at four P.M. with Chamberlain, now acting under Sheridan's orders, moving his men forward toward Five Forks. In the thick brush, Chamberlain's Brigade lost touch with the rest of the army, but he plunged ahead anyway, searching for the rebel line. After one-quarter of a mile Chamberlain heard firing on the left, so he halted his brigade and investigated. Topping a rise, he saw that much of the rest of his division was now involved in a stand-up fight with a rebel line. He moved his men forward in support, to the head of a gully, and then into a field beyond, coming in on the flank of the rebel line. The firing grew in intensity. Chamberlain kept going, emerging finally at the right rear of the southern defenses. The fire reached a crescendo as Chamberlain's men poured volleys into the rebel entrenchments in front while federal troops poured volleys into their flank.

Surrounded now by fire from two sides, most of the rebels in the advance guard south of Five Forks surrendered—nearly 1,500 men. Chamberlain quickly rounded up his prisoners, sent them to the rear, then reformed his own battle lines facing the crossroads. Everything now, with darkness coming and the rebels surprised, was done at the double-quick. Moving his battle lines forward, Chamberlain came upon Sheridan, who was shouting and riding from one end of his line to the other, urging his men forward. "Push out to Five Forks," Sheridan shouted at him. Chamberlain was now as frantic as "Little Phil," believing that it might be possible to pile into the remaining rebel works to overwhelm their lines and surge into Petersburg itself from the south.

Chamberlain moved his men back north, linking up with other units of the Fifth Corps as he went. As firing increased on his front, he urged his men forward, toward the Ford Road, which now appeared to be the key to the rebel position. Up until now, the battle had been nothing but confusion, but it finally took shape here, south of the crossroads, under Sheridan's guiding hand. Miraculously, three divisions were finally in line and working together for the first time that day—and pressing forward toward the rebel barricades. Chamberlain saw the rebels' breastworks come alive; in places the gray-clad men actually stood to face the advancing federals.

"Griffin came down from the right, dashed ahead of me and jumped his horse over the works," Chamberlain wrote, describing the Union onslaught into the Confederate position. He took his own horse into the rebel lines, then saw his men follow him. Only on the far right were the rebels able to withstand the attack, but even they finally splintered away. Only a few remnants of rebel regiments now stood in their line, but they faded back toward Petersburg. At this moment, Sheridan took advantage of the power given him by Grant and relieved Warren—just at the moment of his corps' greatest triumph. "After nightfall," Chamberlain later wrote, "the corps was drawn in around Five Forks, for a brief respite. We were all so worn out that our sinking bodies took our spirits with them. We had reasons to rejoice so far as victory gives reasons; but there was a strange weight on the hearts of us all."

That night, also, there was a weight on the heart of Robert E. Lee, who knew that the defeat at Five Forks meant he would have to abandon his positions around Petersburg and take his army west. The next morning he sent a dispatch to Jefferson Davis, telling him that he could not hold his lines and that the government should make preparations to leave Richmond. That night Lee sent his forward elements through Petersburg and west on the road that followed the Appomattox River. His intention was to make his way to Danville, receiving provisions for his army along the way, then head south for a link-up with Joe Johnston's army, then facing Sherman in North Carolina. He would play out the string as long as possible—for he knew that as long as the southern army remained in the field, the Confederacy survived.

⸎━◆━⸎

But the end came quickly. What was left of the Army of Northern Virginia arrived at Amelia Court House on April 4, then headed west again, to Sayler's Creek, on April 6. There was a brief and vicious fight where one whole part of Lee's army was swallowed up. The rebel commander put the disaster behind him and headed west again. On the night of April 8, Lee arrived at Appomattox Court House, intending to find provisions. But there were none to be had.

Lee's army was surrounded at Appomattox, with its way west—where the southern commander hoped provisions awaited his troops—barred by Grant's forces. After receiving reports that a way out of the encircling Union army was impossible, Lee approached Longstreet to ask his opinion. The First Corps commander, now recovered from his near-fatal wound at the Wilderness, wrote of the emotional encounter in his memoirs:

> He was dressed in a suit of new uniform, sword and sash, a handsomely embroidered belt, boots, and a pair of gold spurs. At first approach his compact figure appeared as a man in the flush vigor of forty summers, but as I drew near, the handsome apparel and brave bearing failed to conceal his profound depression. He stood near the embers of some burned rails, with graceful salutation, and spoke at once of affairs in front and the loss of his subsistence stores. He remarked that the advanced columns stood against a very formidable force, which he could not break through, while [the Union army] was at my rear ready to call for all the work that the rear-guard could do, and, closing with the expression that it was not possible for him to get along, requested my view. I asked if the bloody sacrifice of his army could in any way help the cause in other quarters. He thought not. Then, I said, your situation speaks for itself.

Lee responded that he feared the northern commander would demand harsh terms. Longstreet thought this unlikely, but told Lee that if Grant's demands were "humiliating," Lee should "break off the interview and tell General Grant to do his worst." Lee straightened up at this advice, strengthened by Longstreet's words. But he knew that he would have to meet with Grant; his men were on the edge of starvation, were clothed in the bare remnants of their once-thick gray uniforms, and down to their last bit of ammunition. What horses were left of their cavalry—or to pull their artillery caissons—were skin and bones. The Army of Northern Virginia now consisted of less than 30,000 soldiers, but only 9,000 of them were armed. Lee mounted his horse to see Grant while his troops "marched to form the last line," but was delayed while a flag of truce was arranged. Riders were dispatched from all fronts to delay a fight, after which Grant agreed to meet Lee and arrange for the surrender of his army.

William Oates learned of Lee's surrender in Abbeville, where he was awaiting orders to report to Joe Johnston, whom he hoped would be able to use his services. Joshua Chamberlain was at Appomattox and saw the flag of truce announcing that Lee and Grant were meeting. He was jubilant, but disbelieving. Just two weeks before, he had been south of Petersburg in what seemed an endless siege. Now the gray men across the way were heading home.

"We could not look into those brave, bronzed faces, and those battered flags we had met on so many fields where glorious manhood lent a glory to the earth that bore it, and think of personal hate and mean revenge," Chamberlain wrote. "Whoever had misled these men, we had not. We had led them back, home. Whoever had made that quarrel, we had not. It was a remnant of the inherited curse of sin. We had purged it away, with blood offerings."

# PART THREE

# 12

## The Passing
## of the Dead

J OSHUA CHAMBERLAIN'S ROLE at Appomattox appears to be almost otherworldly. He had received Grant's last battle orders, to prepare to advance to meet a rebel attack from the thin gray lines that faced him. Just moments later, in the midst of these preparations, Chamberlain was the first to notice Lee's white flag of truce breaking through his ranks. "Now I see the white flag earnestly borne, and its possible purport sweeps before my inner vision like a wraith of morning mist," he later wrote. "He comes steadily on, the mysterious form in gray, my mood so whimsically sensitive that I could even smile at the material of the flag—wondering where in either army was found a towel, and one so white." Next, a Confederate staff officer appeared out of the mist with a plea. "I am just from Gordon and Longstreet. Gordon says: 'For God's sake, stop this infantry, or hell will be to pay!' I'll go to Sheridan." The officer wheeled and went pounding off, hoping to delay an unnecessary clash between the two armies.

Chamberlain could not bring himself to believe that the war was ending, but did not send his men forward. "I was doubtful of my duty," he wrote. "The flag of truce was in, but I had no right to act upon it without orders. There was still some firing from various quarters, lulling a little where the white flag passed near. But I did not press things quite so hard." Chamberlain believed he might have been wrong not to order an assault, however, for soon after the Confederate officer passed to "go to Sheridan," a rebel shell exploded nearby, killing an officer of the 185th New York regiment—perhaps the last soldier killed in Virginia. The exploding shell did not dampen the urge for peace, however, and Chamberlain's men surged forward to see the passing of Lee and Grant.

"I had mounted," Chamberlain wrote years later, "and sat looking at the scene before me, thinking of all that was impending and depending, when I felt coming upon me a strange sense of some presence invisible but powerful—like those unearthly visits told of in ancient story, charged with supernal message. Disquieted, I turned about, and there behind me, riding in between my two lines, appeared a commanding form, superbly mounted, richly accoutered, of imposing bearing, noble countenance, with expression of deep sadness overmastered by deeper strength."

Once again, quite by accident, Chamberlain was privileged to play the role of history's observer. "It is Robert E. Lee! And seen by me for the first time within my own lines. I sat immovable, with a certain awe and admiration. He was coming, with a single staff officer, for the great appointed meeting which was to determine momentous issues." Lee was followed by Ulysses S. Grant:

> He, too, comes with a single aide, a staff officer of Sheridan's who had come out to meet him. Slouched hat without cord; common soldier's blouse, unbuttoned, on which, however, the four stars; high boots, mud-splashed to the top; trousers tucked inside; no sword, but the sword-hand deep in the pocket; sitting his saddle with the ease of a born master, taking no notice of anything; all his faculties gathered into intense thought and mighty calm. He seemed greater than I had ever seen him—a look as of another world about him. No wonder I forgot to salute him. Anything like that would have been too little.

Americans of the nineteenth century enjoyed viewing epic tableaux painted in stark relief, of great heroes on understanding steeds, and honorable men with the look "of another world" about them, who were always deciding issues that were not of passing interest, but "momentous." Grant's meeting with Lee was not simply viewed as the most important encounter of the war, it was a benediction—their actions and the southern surrender was ordained by a higher, unseen power. This is how it seemed to Chamberlain. "Neither of them [Grant and Lee], in truth, free, nor held in individual bounds alone; no longer testing each other's powers and resources, no longer weighing the chances of daring or desperate conflict. Instruments in God's hands, they were now to record His decree."

Lee met Grant in the home of Wilmer McLean and signed the surrender of the Army of Northern Virginia. When he returned to his lines, southern soldiers crowded around in silent sadness, reaching out to touch the flanks of his horse. Longstreet painted the most affecting picture, of a man saddened before his broken, disbelieving warriors:

> As General Lee rode back to his army the officers and soldiers of his troops about the front lines assembled in promiscuous crowds of all arms and grades in anxious wait for their beloved commander. From force of habit a burst of salutations greeted him, but quieted as suddenly as they arose. The road was packed by standing troops as he approached, the men with hats off, heads and hearts bowed down. As he passed they raised their heads and looked upon him with swimming eyes. Those who could find voice said good-by, those who could not speak, and were near, passed their hands gently over the sides of Traveller.

A veteran called out from the crowd: "General, are we surrendered? Are we surrendered?"

Lee turned and spoke to his soldiers: "Men, we have fought the war together, and I have done the best I could for you. You will all be paroled and go to your homes until exchanged."

That night, after the surrender, Longstreet approached Chamberlain's camp and asked that rations be sent to his soldiers. They were "starving," he said. Chamberlain complied and then was summoned to headquarters, where he was told he would be in command of the official surrender. The assignment came as a surprise, and Chamberlain was puzzled that he was named for the honor. "Taking the assignment as I would any other," he wrote, "my feeling about it was more for the honor of the Fifth Corps and the Army of the Potomac than for myself. In lineal rank the junior general on the field, I never thought of claiming any special merit, nor tried to attract attention in any way, and believed myself to be socially unpopular among the 'high boys.' I had never indulged in loose talk, had minded my own business, did not curry favor with newspaper reporters, did not hang around superior headquarters, and in general had disciplined myself in self-control and the practice of patience, which virtue was not prominent among my natural endowments."

It was these qualities in Chamberlain, in fact, that Grant was looking for at Appomattox, where a surrendered army was at the mercy of its conquerors. The Union commander was especially worried that his army might celebrate their victory, leading to new clashes with their antagonists. Simple dignity, an important quality in the son of a Galena tanner, was called for, especially after the bloodletting of the previous years. In this, Grant had been instructed by Lincoln, who counseled all of his commanders over the last months to "let 'em up easy." Grant wanted to follow that instruction to the letter, if for no other reason than to set the precedent for the hard years ahead. Grant surely sensed in Chamberlain something of his own quiet character, and most especially their common belief that, since justice was universal, all achievement is eventually recognized. Chamberlain had his own view of why he was picked to receive the official surrender: "Tout vient à point pour qui sait attendre—'Everything comes in good time to him who knows how to wait,' " Chamberlain said.

Chamberlain was not only willing to conduct a dignified surrender ceremony, without even muffled drums, he believed that he needed to go one step further. The next morning, as the gray ranks marched forward to stack their arms and flags, Chamberlain ordered his soldiers, arrayed in the field behind him, to "shift arms"—a stark and unmistakable marching salute of the southern army. General John Gordon, chosen by Lee to lead the last march of his depleted ranks, was astounded by Chamberlain's gesture and the clear snap of flesh on wood that resounded across the war's last field. Chamberlain later wrote:

> Gordon at the head of the column, riding with heavy spirit and downcast face, catches the sound of shifting arms, looks up, and, taking the meaning, wheels superbly, making with himself and his horse one uplifted figure, with profound salutation as

he drops the point of his sword to the boot toe; then facing to his own command, gives word for his successive brigades to pass us with the same position of the manual,—honor answering honor. On our part not a sound of trumpet more, nor roll of drum; not a cheer, nor word nor whisper of vain-glorying, nor motion of man standing again at the order, but an awed stillness rather, and breath-holding, as if it were the passing of the dead.

The rebel soldiers stacked their arms, furled their flags, and turned for home. General Lee signed their paroles, testaments of service, which many of them framed and placed on the walls of their cabins and homes to be pointed to with pride in the years ahead. Most departed Appomattox only with memories, though some walked south with mementos that they would never surrender. William Oates remembered one of these men: Jonathan Archibald, fifty years old at Appomattox—and wounded twice, once at Antietam and again at the Wilderness. After the 15th marched with Longstreet's Corps to the surrender, Archibald took the regimental colors from the staff of the regiment, "hid them under his shirt, brought them home with him," and was buried with them when he died in his seventies.

It was a remarkable surrender. After Lee's men stacked their arms, they visited the Union camps to meet their adversaries and exchange stories. They were given food, coffee, and blankets. A number of southern commanders refused to furl their battle flags, keeping them as mementos for later years or burying them in the nearby woods—where the Yankees would not find them. Nor were all southerners willing to accept the verdict of the war. Just after the surrender, Joshua Chamberlain spotted a southern officer who "seemed so disturbed in mind" that Chamberlain stopped to comfort him. Chamberlain pointed out the good "bearing" of the men on both sides to the southerner, adding that this proved that "brave men may become friends." The southerner bitterly disagreed. "You're mistaken, sir," he said. "You may forgive us but we won't be forgiven. There is a rancor in our hearts which you little dream of. We hate you, sir!"

But this bitter reaction was the exception. Few southern soldiers wanted to fight on and, while there was much reminiscing between the soldiers of both sides about the battles they had fought, there was little talk of who was right and who was wrong. For almost all southerners, the national debate was ended, decided by arms—and the verdict was final. Years afterward, Chamberlain penned his own thoughts on the surrender and what it meant, echoing Lincoln's view that the war was penance for the sin of slavery. Now the debt was paid—"purged," as Chamberlain wrote, "by blood offerings." On the afternoon of April 9, the Army of Northern Virginia ceased to exist and within two days all of its men had turned for home. The only army left on the field was the Army of the Potomac, which stayed at Appomattox for the next week. On the night of April 14, Chamberlain received orders to prepare his men for the long march back to Washington.

On that same evening, Good Friday, Abraham Lincoln, still buoyed by the news of the southern surrender, decided to attend a performance of the comedy *Our American Cousin* at Ford's Theater. Lincoln had not wanted to go, but felt that he had to, since people expected to see him there. He resigned himself to the evening, thinking it might be a good break from his worries; he had spent the previous week thinking about Reconstruction, about how to bring the former Confederate states back into the Union. After a meeting with General Grant, who had come to Washington after Lee's surrender, Lincoln set off for Ford's Theater. In the carriage on the way to the theater he turned to his wife in apparent exultation: "I never felt better in my life," he said. But Lincoln was late for the play, and when he entered the theater (in the middle of the first act) the audience rose and the orchestra played "Hail to the Chief." Lincoln acknowledged the audience and took his place in the presidential box overlooking the stage. At a little after ten P.M.—in the middle of Act III—the performance was interrupted by an explosion, followed by the scream of Mary Lincoln. The president had been shot. John Wilkes Booth, the assassin, leaped onto the stage and cried "Sic Semper Tyrannis"—thus always to tyrants—Virginia's state motto. Lincoln was carried to a room across the street, where he died the next morning, Saturday, April 15.

The commanders of the Army of the Potomac learned of Lincoln's assassination just a few hours after his death, but Joshua Chamberlain did not hear of it until the next day, Easter Sunday—while marching east with his troops to Farmville, on the road to Richmond. A cavalry officer rode up to him with a telegram. "It was no uncommon thing to receive a military telegram in those days," Chamberlain later wrote, "but something in the manner and look of this messenger took my attention." The messenger announced that the telegram was personal, so Chamberlain walked away from his troops to read the message. "The President died this morning. Wilkes Booth the assassin. Secretary Seward dangerously wounded. The rest of the Cabinet, General Grant, and other high officers of the Government included in the plot of destruction."

Chamberlain's first emotion was not shock, but fear that his men would seek vengeance against southerners. He ordered that a double guard be put around his troops with orders that no one was to leave the division's encampment. A woman from a nearby house came to ask Chamberlain about the news.

"It is bad news for the South," he said.

"Is it Lee or Davis?"

Chamberlain replied: "I must tell you, madam, with a warning, I have put your house under a strict guard. It is Lincoln."

The next day, Chamberlain continued to march his division toward Richmond, which lay smoldering, set afire after Lee had abandoned it. Everyone was on alert, fearful that the government was being attacked by unseen, traitorous forces. "Strange forebodings pressed upon my mind," Chamberlain wrote. "It seemed as if the darkest things might be yet to come; as if, now, that men of honor had given up the fight, it had fallen to baser hands." But none of Chamberlain's men took revenge on southerners. Instead, they all seemed plunged into despair. Chamberlain called on a chaplain to speak to his men while they were camped west of Petersburg. At first the minister called for retribution against the assassins, urging Chamberlain's men to "sweep such a spirit out of the land forever, and cast it, root and branch, into everlasting burning," but then, eyeing the disapproving Chamberlain uneasily, he counseled the soldiers not to turn their rifles against their former enemies. "Better to die glorious, than to live infamous," he said. "Better to

be buried beneath a nation's tears than to walk the earth guilty of a nation's blood. Better, thousandfold, forever better, Lincoln dead, than
Davis living."

After camping near Richmond, Chamberlain moved his command
north on the road to Washington. Even though the war was now over, it
never seemed far away. Chamberlain was awakened one night near
Hanover Court House by his tethered horse, worriedly pawing a skull-
filled earth.

Upon arrival in Washington at the beginning of May, Chamberlain's men were ordered to camp on Arlington Heights, across the river
from the White House, on the grounds of the Lee mansion, Robert E.
Lee's home before the war. He was told to prepare his division for
the Grand Review of the armies. Chamberlain spent the next two weeks
contemplating doing something special to distinguish his own troops,
but decided that they should march as they had fought, in the simple
soldiers' uniforms they had worn in battle. Joining him in Washington
was Reverend Adams, who came south from Brunswick to join in the
celebration of the Union victory. He brought a message that Fannie and
the Chamberlain children were in good health. Adams joined Chamberlain in the Fifth Corps encampment on Arlington Heights, followed
the regiment to its campground in Washington, then accompanied
a group of Maine dignitaries into Washington to watch the Grand
Review.

The first day of the Grand Review, more than one month after Lincoln's death, was reserved for the passing of the Army of the Potomac,
more than 130,000 men in all, accompanied by wagons, artillery, draft
horses, and pontoons. During the Grand Review, Chamberlain was invited to survey the Fifth Corps from a position on the dais with Lincoln's successor, Andrew Johnson, and other official dignitaries—an
unexpected pleasure and great honor. As the Fifth Corps marched
down Pennsylvania Avenue to the White House, Chamberlain paid
special attention to his old First Division. Their passing seemed to
mark for him yet another opportunity to pen a religious allusion, one
that he found increasingly meaningful as a result of all he had seen. In
fact, the more he thought about it, the more he decided that the events
of the previous month corresponded to a kind of national passion play,
complete with trial (Five Forks), pagan enemy (the Confederate army),

apostles (Grant, Meade, and Warren), the martyred (his dead comrades), the honored vanquished (Lee), and even the expiating crucifixion—Lincoln's death.

He wrote: "For me, while this division was passing, no other thing could lure my eyes away, whether looking on or through. These were my men, and those who followed were familiar and dear. They belonged to me, and I to them, by bonds birth cannot create nor death sever. More were passing here than the personages on the stand could see. But to me so seeing, what a review, how great, how far, how near! It was as the morning of the resurrection!" Reading Chamberlain's prose now, more than one hundred years after the event, it is easy to put down his musings as the predictable response of a religious man to great events. But Chamberlain was not the only one who believed that the Republic's having passed a momentous crisis seemed to be fated by a higher power. Just days after his murder, Lincoln, perhaps the most earthy and single-minded of the North's fighters, was being transformed from a good president to a great president, and thence to something even greater. In 1862, when Lincoln had visited the army, Chamberlain had thought him a good horseman, but that was about all. Another Maine man, a private, had described the president as "homely as a stump fence." But now he was Jesus: "the sacrifice at Washington."

Chamberlain wanted to return to Maine as quickly as he could, but he stayed behind in Washington after the Grand Review, he later claimed, to take care of the business of his division. He attended victory dinners throughout the end of May and into June, and spent his days mustering his men out of the service. But while Chamberlain was busy with military matters, he had also stayed in Washington in order to allow his brother and the other soldiers of his former regiment, the 20th Maine, the opportunity to celebrate their victory in their home state without his presence. He feared that his return would take attention away from their accomplishments. Chamberlain was aware that he was more than just an oddity, a professor-turned-warrior; he was famous. He was even being mentioned as a possible candidate for higher office, perhaps as governor of Maine. Chamberlain had a national reputation, won largely because of his exploits at Gettysburg, his heroism at Petersburg, and the fact that he had been chosen to accept the Confederate surrender.

In the middle of July, the 20th Maine was ordered to return to Portland. One week later, Chamberlain was pleased to learn that his brother Tom, now a captain, and Ellis Spear, who had been promoted to lieutcnant colonel, had returned with the regiment and received a hero's welcome. While Thomas Chamberlain had not served in the midst of battle to nearly the same degree as his famous brother, he had served well and honorably in the posts he was given. Ellis Spear went out of his way to ascribe Tom's activities and success as due to his own talents, and not to any preferments that he might have indirectly received from Joshua. He was promoted to a high rank, Spear said after the war, "on the force of his own character" and had fulfilled his duty "with marked ability and success." At the end of July 1865, Joshua Chamberlain finally set out for home. He arrived there unannounced at the beginning of August, two years and eleven months after he had left.

☙———◆———❧

The Civil War was a cataclysm of unimaginable proportions. By the time Lee's last "serried ranks" of soldiers stacked their arms at Appomattox, just over 200,000 men and boys, North and South, were dead in battle. Disease, drowning, accidents, murder, suicide, and execution carried off another half million. The total of deaths was well over 600,000—623,000 is the best estimate. Another 471,000 soldiers were wounded, many of them permanently crippled. One in ten northern soldiers was killed or wounded, one in four southerners. Many thousands lay unidentified in shallow graves on hundreds of battlefields. Many thousands left home and were never heard from again. Many, we suspect, took the opportunity that war afforded to leave unhappy marriages or mean circumstances. One million men and women died or were maimed in the Civil War. Thousands of them were little more than children.

The national numbers are reflected by the regiments commanded by Oates and Chamberlain. Of the 1,612 men who served in the 15th Alabama, 297 were killed, 599 wounded, and 459 died of disease. Only 159 men survived more than two battles without receiving a scratch. The 15th Alabama surrendered 172 men at Appomattox. While the toll for the 20th Maine was not nearly so bad, it is just as shocking. The

20th Maine took 1,621 men into battle, of whom 147 were killed, 381 wounded, and another 146 died of disease. But these casualty figures do not reflect the true carnage of the war; in its last weeks, the 20th Maine was filled with new recruits who never saw combat, but were counted on its final rolls.

The final true tally of the war's cost was far worse than even these numbers suggest. The Civil War was more brutal than any other conflict in which Americans have fought. There were hundreds of thousands of unseen casualties—what one current journalist, in referring to World War II, called our national "family secret." Wars shatter lives beyond repair and each American family has a story of how a son, brother, or father cannot hold down a job or becomes an alcoholic or, something simpler, cannot sleep with the light off. This was true also of those families whose sons, brothers, and fathers survived the Civil War.

Thomas Davee Chamberlain returned to Portland as a hero, but he did not make a smooth transition from war to peace. He did not know what to do with himself. He tried to become a successful businessman, working with his brother John in Brooklyn, New York, as a clerk and then as the business's sole proprietor, but he decided to return to Maine and was a merchant in Bangor for a time. Nothing seemed to hold him. He worked in the state pension office, but also found that unsatisfactory. He was seen in public, many times, drunk. He was an embarrassment to his family and a worry to his aging mother. He moved to Florida, but his brother Joshua was told that he was lazy and could not be counted on to work hard. He died of lung disease at the age of fifty-five. Joshua Chamberlain's brother John worked with the Christian Commission on some of the conflict's bloodiest battlefields. He died in 1867 of tuberculosis. Joshua Chamberlain was convinced he had contracted the disease during the war.

William Oates saw many of these same casualties, some of them lingering for years after the war. He wrote of a captain of one of his regiment's companies and "an officer of great courage" who had returned home to Glennville, Alabama, to find his plantation ruined and his slaves gone. He tried to make his farm pay over the next years, but the war had broken him. He could not go on. The Confederate defeat, the destruction of his plantation, the flight of his slaves, the desolation that he felt—the loss of everything that he knew—"made him feel sad and lonely," Oates wrote in his memoirs. Within several years of Appomattox the captain, who had once been in the front ranks of his regiment during its attack at Lookout Mountain, was taken to "an insane asylum." He never emerged. Oates saw him there years later and tried to make himself known to his old comrade. It was no use. The man did not recognize his old friend and comrade. "His mind seems to be entirely gone," Oates wrote.

The war hardened American society in ways that would have seemed shocking just years before. Men who should not have been in uniform were pushed into the ranks. Twenty-seven-year-old Alpheus Brooks was one of these. Brooks was a good man, but he was not a good soldier. He kept deserting. Oates later wrote that everyone knew Alpheus's real problem was that he was "very weak-minded"—the nineteenth century's phrase for being mentally retarded. Alpheus did the best he could to fight the war, but he was afraid. After deserting in 1864, when Oates was no longer with the regiment, he was court-martialed and shot. Oates was heartsick when he heard the news. Brooks should have been disciplined, he said, but never executed. But few men suffered more than Augustus Harvey. Harvey was a twenty-year-old private when he was wounded at Second Bull Run. He tried to make his way back to Alabama, but his wound would not heal and he stopped in Fort Gaines, Florida, to ask for help. He died in the street, unaided, because the townspeople were convinced that he had smallpox. He did not. He lay in a gutter for many hours before dying.

But the war's biggest impact was on the freedmen. Appomattox ended slavery, but it did not end the trial of the South's black population, which were suddenly dependent on their own meager resources to feed themselves and their families. Until then only a quarter of southern blacks had had any taste of freedom and, while the end of slavery was an accomplished fact in much of the South by April of 1865, Appomattox sparked a social revolution. The South's black population was not only now officially free, it was on the move; hundreds of thousands of former slaves took to the roads in search of husbands, wives, fathers, and mothers who had been separated by war or bondage. No one, North or South, knew what would happen with these former slaves, how they would get land or begin to feed themselves, once the movement had ended.

Both former slaves and the northern blacks, however, had played their part in the war. This was less true in the South than in the North, though in February 1865 the Confederate Congress finally passed legislation that allowed for the impressment of slaves in the Confederate army, using them as laborers, drivers, and cooks, and allowing more white soldiers to reach the front lines. But it had been too late; the South had not been able to enlist black soldiers quickly enough to make good on its armies' losses. The same was not true in the North, which had 178,895 blacks in its ranks at the end of the contest. Black soldiers fought in 39 major battles and 410 minor engagements, suffering 68,178 casualties. America's black population could claim a stake in the nation's future, then, not simply because they were deemed to have the same inalienable rights as everyone else, but because they had made the same sacrifice as others to win them. "Now that God has smitten slavery unto death," Edward Beecher, Harriet Beecher Stowe's brother, proclaimed after Appomattox, "He has opened the way for the redemption and sanctification of our whole social system." But Beecher's views were optimistic. Frederick Douglass gave a more realistic assessment: "Verily," he said, "the work does not end with the abolition of slavery, but only begins." Nowhere was this more apparent than in Alabama.

For William Oates, Lee's surrender confirmed what he had known for some time: that unless there was some extraordinary intervention, the South would lose the war. It was this knowledge, perhaps, that made him unusual among Confederate veterans. While he had his share of resentments—which he issued often, in long and stinging criticisms of northerners—at the end of the war he was ready to put aside his disgust at the outcome of the conflict and begin to build a new life. If anything, his war service now propelled him into the front ranks of Alabama's leaders, a fact he was well aware of when he began to rebuild his law practice in Abbeville. For the time being, however, he was busy with family responsibilities, having decided to take his sister and her children into his own modest home. He spent his first year back in

Alabama seeing to the requirements of his family, helping those from his regiment who now returned to reconstruct their former lives, and trying to determine how best he and southeastern Alabama's other veteran leaders could begin to rebuild the Eufaula Regency.

How Oates was able to eventually retrieve his fortune remains largely unknown, but at least part of his immediate postwar success and his ability to feed his now enlarged family was due to his comparative youth and to his legal and business abilities. With Alabama bereft of any currency since the Confederate dollar was now worthless, he undoubtedly traded his services for food at the same time that he worked as one of Abbeville's unofficial municipal officers. He was one of the small town's few lawyers and its leading citizen, so it is only natural that he would be consulted to settle disputes, as he had been before the war.

There are few descriptions of Oates in Alabama in the immediate post–Civil War period, but it is clear he did everything he could to take up where he left off—as a talented lawyer, man of property, and political activist. It did not take much to convince Oates that one of the most important ways to begin rebuilding Alabama was to resuscitate the Democratic Party. Just prior to the war, Oates was viewed as one of Henry County's talented Democratic Party operatives and one of its most loyal members. He used this, as well as his reputation as a talented lawyer, to restore his old contacts and wide-ranging friendships. Both before and during the war—when he returned home to recover from his wounds—Oates had made powerful friends in southeastern Alabama, not the least of which was the Toney family of Eufaula, which he regularly visited. Coupled with his friendships among the Eufaula elite, Oates's contacts served as a strong political base on which he could build his law practice and political career.

When not involved in adjudicating arguments in Abbeville or serving as his community's unofficial municipal officer, Oates was on the move. He took the most time to look after the affairs of the soldiers in Henry County, those of the Henry Pioneers, which he had first recruited and which formed Company G of the 15th Alabama. These men knew him best and admired his leadership during the war. But he also traveled to visit soldiers in Pike, Barbour, and Dale counties, as well as those up the road in Eufaula. At the beginning of the conflict these men had formed the Eufaula City Guards, which served as Company K of the 15th Alabama—and were the core of the regiment. Oates also visited his family at Oates's Crossroads and deepened his political contacts throughout all of central and eastern Alabama.

In the years ahead, Oates took advantage of his service and his ties to those who served with him in the war. While he might stray from these roots on occasion, most especially when elected to statewide or federal office, he regularly returned to Henry County to ensure that his political support was intact. Daniel McClellan, Frank Merritt, Thomas Acree, William Carr, James Miller (Abbeville's shoemaker), William Holley (who, during the war, knew where to find whiskey), Seaborn Hughs, James Morris (Abbeville's Baptist preacher), William Parish (a good Democrat), A. B. Skipper (Abbeville's postwar sheriff), David Merritt (the town's deputy sheriff), George Wiggins ("a highly respected citizen"), Barney McArdle, Allen Kirkland, Robert McKnight, Samuel Woodham ("an intense Confederate"), Charles Kincey, Bryant Melton—this list, and many more besides—was the core of Oates's political family.

Oates extended this core group to include others who had served in Evander Law's Alabama Brigade, men from the larger cities of central and southern Alabama. He visited Montgomery often, to keep contact with the state's political leaders. But his real base was still in Eufaula, where he had first received his legal training. Anyone in eastern Alabama who wanted to be active in politics had to take note of Eufaula's importance. Oates revived his old contacts in the city and made new political friends. Among them was Jesse Carmichael, who lost his right hand at Antietam. Carmichael returned home to his family farm and "began anew the battle of life." As Oates recounted: "With his one hand he worked, made crops, supported his little family, and read law of nights by pineknots for about two years, and then his father, who was Probate Judge of the county, took Jesse as a clerk in his office, where he became familiar with the forms and laws of procedure in that court." With Oates, Carmichael helped rebuild the Democratic Party in Eufaula and he remained one of Oates's most steadfast supporters.

Oates's undeniable claim to political leadership in Henry County in the years immediately following Lee's surrender was based on his exemplary war service and on the reputation he had built up in Abbeville in 1859 and 1860. It was bolstered by the reputation of John Oates, who was as respected for his political and legal abilities as his older brother. Just prior to his death at Gettysburg, for example, John Oates made his way back to Abbeville on a recruiting mission and found David Merritt in jail for the murder of one John Talley. John Oates somehow got Merritt out of jail and "took him to the army." Merritt deserted in January 1865 when "he heard unpleasant reports about his domestic relations" (as William Oates delicately phrased it), then, after the surrender, stood trial for Talley's murder. He was represented by William Oates and was acquitted.

Merritt's case is only one example of how William Oates took special care to look out for those who had served with him in the war. Throughout his career, Oates would unashamedly place wartime service and Democratic Party loyalty above almost any other consideration. Even in matters of personal principle, Oates looked out for those who had been tested in battle. When Isaac Culver "became involved in a personal difficulty"—the murder of a "colored man named Buford Whitehurst"—Oates sprang to his defense, though it was clear, even from Oates's description, that Culver was in the wrong. It is not a compliment to the judicial system of Alabama in the 1860s that Culver was acquitted, but it is symbolic of Oates's own loyalties that he notes that Culver was "defended by his old captain as his lawyer." That Culver served in the 15th Alabama, if only for seven months, was enough for Oates.

Oates's postwar writings—his memoirs, letters, and official papers—tell of his difficult political work, his struggle to revive his community and state, and his work to realize his own ambitions. Rarely did Oates talk of the enormous economic and political obstacles facing the people of Abbeville and Eufaula, or of those in the rest of the state. But the obstacles to a return to normalcy and to economic prosperity were daunting. Everywhere Oates turned he could see the onset of poverty and hopelessness.

⚬══◆══⚬

Alabama was devastated. Though the numbers are imperfect, an estimated 34,000 of its men were killed in battle or died of disease, while 20,000 were disabled for life. Nor could those who returned expect to take up the lives they had left behind. There were now 20,000 widows in the state and 60,000 orphans; almost all of Alabama's railroads were destroyed (along with trestles, stations, water tanks, machinery, depots, and repair shops), as well as its foundries, livestock, municipal centers, and all of the state's investments. Selma had been sacked by a detachment of Union cavalry, and the contents of the town that could not be borne off by the blue-clad raiders were destroyed. Nearly all of Decatur, in northern Alabama, had been burned.

In the war's aftermath, federal soldiers who were required to occupy the South's major cities, towns, and rail junctions systematically stripped the region of its surviving resources. In Decatur, anything that could be moved, and that had not been destroyed in the fire, was shipped north. The countryside was scoured for food to feed the occupying army and Union soldiers took what they needed. Lawlessness was endemic, with many Union soldiers believing that the fruits of war were now theirs to be enjoyed. The practice of taking food when it was needed was a continuation of the wartime strategy of 1864 and 1865, which dictated that Union soldiers could live off the land. This policy, however, exacerbated rural poverty, and large tracts of the major southern states, including Alabama, that had once been under cultivation were abandoned.

It is almost impossible now to understand the full depth of the southern crisis. It was not simply that the former Confederate states needed to rebuild their industries and resuscitate their farms; by the summer of 1865, civil order itself had collapsed. The Union troops posted in the state were undisciplined and hated by the native population. Nothing was yet decided about the circumstances under which the states of the old Confederacy could be readmitted to the Union, and no one in Alabama had built a strong enough political base to form even the semblance of a government. Nor were local or state authorities quick to impose social order; not only did they lack the funds to do so, but many of the state's most important political authorities were uncertain whether their own claim to office would be upheld. This political confusion was the result of the debate over Reconstruction and the attempt by the federal government not only to reimpose its sovereignty, but to ensure that the social gains won by the Civil War would now be institutionalized as law among the states of the former Confederacy.

Reconstruction remains one of the most confused and contentious eras of American history. On the one side were those who supported a moderate course aimed at readmitting the southern states to the Union on lenient terms. Their moderate program was opposed by a majority of Republicans in the U.S. Congress. These Radical Reconstructionists believed that the South should be subdued, the freedmen's rights imposed on its governments, and former rebels disenfranchised. There was a certain amount of political cynicism embedded in the strategy; many Republicans endorsed the radicals' tactics because they believed they would ensure the triumph of the Republican Party in the South. On the other side were moderate Republicans and northern Democrats, including President Andrew Johnson, who believed that once southern states had sworn loyalty to the federal government and repealed their ordinances of secession they should be restored to the Union.

The debate over what form Reconstruction should take became the most important political question in the years immediately following Appomattox. The question was a part of nearly every public forum—not only in Congress, but also in the former states of the Confederacy, where pro-Unionists who once opposed secession attempted to gain political ascendancy over their political competitors. In almost every southern state, the political competition between former Confederates and Unionist elements led to open warfare, which included the use of intimidation, public threats, and even murder. This was true in Alabama, which was the scene of an internal civil conflict nearly as contentious as the Civil War itself.

The first attempt at restoring the power of Alabama's government was made soon after Appomattox, when a call went out for a general convention to rewrite the state constitution in line with Andrew Johnson's moderate Reconstruction policy. But by the middle of 1865, it was clear that more would be required. Radicals in Congress imposed a federal proclamation outlawing all existing southern state governments. In Alabama, this was followed by the summary arrest of all government officials who had served in the Confederate Congress—even the patriarch of the Eufaula Regency, John Gill Shorter, was detained and questioned by federal authorities. The mechanisms of state and local law enforcement quickly disintegrated. In remote Abbeville and in other parts of Alabama, local law enforcement was almost nonexistent.

By the late summer of 1865, for instance, Henry County was plagued by gangs of Confederate deserters who had gone over to the Union cause. The most notorious of these was the 1st Florida Cavalry, a Union regiment whose soldiers, as far as Oates was concerned, were worse than deserters, but were traitors who used their northern uniform as a license for plunder. The 1st Florida commander Joseph Saunders, a former millwright and Confederate officer from Dale County, had resigned his commission in the Confederate army and fled to northern Florida, where he organized his band. Saunders allied his gang with Union troops on Florida's coast, procured uniforms, and began "military operations"—stealing food, horses, and anything else they could lay their hands on, under the pretext of "confiscating" potential war material. The situation became particularly critical when the farmers of Henry and Barbour counties were bringing in their first postwar crops. In desperation, a number of Oates's neighbors lay an ambush for the cavalry regiment below a bridge culvert. On this occasion "when crossing Pea River at Hobby's Bridge," Oates wrote, "some of the people who felt outraged at their conduct were concealed near the bridge and fired on the squadron, killing some and wounding others."

The kind of vigilante justice meted out by the citizens of Abbeville was by no means unusual. The traffic in whiskey and guns was booming and people were frantically attempting to find ways to feed their families. In northern Alabama, especially, the specter of a poor harvest, even starvation, turned people to desperate measures. The situation was complicated by those Alabamians who considered themselves Unionists, had voted against secession, and had spent the war trapped between the two armies; northern soldiers did not distinguish one southerner from another and Confederate loyalists viewed them as traitors. Now the tories, as they were called, took their revenge, looting the homes of Confederate soldiers, who then retaliated by lynching some of the tories. Order was restored only when the provisional governor ordered county militias to check the violence and arrest the perpetrators.

A second civil war had begun in many other parts of the state, fueled in part by the recruiting of black soldiers to serve in some of the Union units, which exacerbated the political situation—so much so that for the next half decade a large portion of Alabama's white citizens openly flouted federal authority. The bitterness caused by the presence of Union troops in the state, the lack of political power in the hands of white southerners, the social stresses caused by the emancipation of the former slaves, and deteriorating economic conditions continued to worsen relations between the North and South. "The issue was decided," Oates had written after Lee's surrender. But clearly it was not.

As the political situation in the South continued to deteriorate, the debate over Reconstruction was reaching a crescendo in the North. The issue was so important, in fact, that people running for public office knew that their ultimate success often depended on how they answered a number of key questions. Should southern leaders be put on trial for treason? Should the freedman be allowed to vote? When should the southern states be readmitted to the Union? Knowing that he had been mentioned as a prospective gubernatorial candidate, Joshua Chamberlain did not hesitate to speak out on important state and national issues, and he was adept at talking about the conditions for the readmittance of the southern states—a subject on which he was viewed as an expert. Chamberlain agreed with the moderate Reconstruction program of Andrew Johnson, but he understood that such a position was becoming increasingly unpopular. Northerners wanted the South punished.

During the year that followed his return to Brunswick, Chamberlain made a number of speeches on Reconstruction before citizens' groups in Portland and Augusta and his views on the issue became widely known. "Secession must be repudiated with its debts and claims, its spirit and principle," he told one audience. "We must have guarantees good and sufficient against any future attempt to destroy this government whether in the exercise of a pretended right by open war, or by the more artful and insidious assaults against the principles on which this Nation is founded." Chamberlain's opinions on the South were applauded by the vast majority of northerners, many of whom believed the South should be punished for causing the war. But, in fact, while Chamberlain's remarks were artful and heartfelt, they were also skillfully ambiguous. Chamberlain was careful not to come down firmly on the side of the moderates and knew it would do his political prospects no harm to condemn any move that would "destroy this government"—especially since the southern states were in no condition to do so. Nor did he bother pointedly to define the "principles upon which this Nation is founded," leaving such words for his listeners to define, each to his or her own political tastes. On one particular subject, however, Chamberlain refused to waver: he believed that the states of the former Confederacy must meet a strict test of national loyalty before their readmission; until then, he said, they should be held in "strict probation."

Chamberlain enjoyed his notoriety and was proud that his name was being mentioned for higher political office. But there were doubts that he had the physical stamina necessary to fulfill the duties of being Maine's governor. During the summer of 1865, within weeks of his return to Brunswick from Washington, he was once again plagued by fits of depression that were only temporarily relieved by spending more time with his wife and children. Unhappily, Chamberlain seemed to feel more discomfited by uncertainty over the future than he did by the day-to-day routine of teaching rhetoric and modern languages as a professor at a sleepy New England college. At times it seemed to him that he simply would not be happy no matter what he did; he enjoyed the financial security brought by his teaching position, while at the same time he loathed the boredom that Bowdoin's predictability brought. His physical disabilities, caused by his nearly crippling abdominal wound, played into this dilemma, since they meant that the life he had led as an army officer was now simply out of his reach. Nor was his frustration at being back in Maine a problem that set in over time. Within a few short weeks of his return home, Chamberlain worried that he would be forgotten by the larger, outside world and that he would die unnoticed in Brunswick.

The August 1865 visit of Ulysses S. Grant to Bowdoin helped to set his mind at ease and filled him with more energy and optimism than he had felt since Five Forks. Grant had always liked Chamberlain, though the two had only met twice before, and he had followed Chamberlain's military career carefully. Nevertheless, it came as a surprise to Chamberlain that Grant not only accepted his invitation to attend Bowdoin's August commencement (Chamberlain apparently did not know that Bowdoin graduate General Oliver Otis Howard had already arranged the visit), he agreed to be a guest at the Chamberlain home. When the general arrived in Brunswick, Chamberlain was there to greet him.

Grant's visit was all Joshua and Fannie could have hoped for. The hero of the Union was modest, unassuming, and willing to give Chamberlain a central place beside him during his short visit and Bowdoin's commencement ceremonies. Chamberlain arranged for the general to receive an honorary doctorate and organized the postcommencement ceremonies at which Grant was honored. Grant was nearly overwhelmed by the adoring crowds, but played his part well, as he had done many times since Appomattox, standing quietly and smiling, shaking hands with a crowd of well-wishers, then meeting with businessmen to hear their projects and waving away those who asked him to speak. He was the man of the hour and no one in Brunswick, or anywhere else in the country, doubted for one moment that he would someday be president. Grant knew this also; he coveted the office, and his schedule of public appearances following Lee's surrender and the Grand Review looked suspiciously like a campaign tour. He journeyed to Philadelphia, New York, Chicago, Boston, and then up the coast to Portland.

Grant's visit and his place at Chamberlain's side—as well as his obvious camaraderie with his former division commander—convinced Maine's Republican leaders that the professor from Brewer was just the man they needed in the statehouse. He was not only a war hero, he was probably the most popular man in the state, outside of Grant, of course. That Chamberlain's political views might be in doubt, or unknown, hardly seemed to matter, since having him at the head of the Republican ticket in 1866 would assure the state Republican Party's success at the ballot box. Even Grant seemed to approve. How else to interpret his relaxed banter, easy smile, and stern but soldierly handshake with the Bowdoin professor? Chamberlain acquitted himself well; while he was clearly not used to such politicking, he quickly became adept at it, standing beside Grant whenever the opportunity arose to shake hands with the same businessmen and political leaders who shook hands with the great man.

Chamberlain was euphoric, but it did not take long for his mood to grow dark again. Grant's departure sparked a return of the old doubts and uncertainties and the deep unease he felt for the future. Then tragedy struck when Fannie and Joshua's fifth child, their seven-month-old daughter, died suddenly at the end of the summer. Dr. Adams conducted the funeral, with the grieving Joshua and Fannie in attendance.

Fannie, especially, was overtaken by grief, and her husband could do little to help her. This was the third Chamberlain child to die in infancy—the first, a boy, died in 1857 shortly after birth, the second, a girl, died on September 26, 1860, four months after she was born. The deaths of three children in a comparatively short time, in spite of the fact that two other children, Grace and Wyllys, lived on in apparently good health, placed enormous strains on the marriage, especially given Chamberlain's continuing medical problems. It seemed that just as he and Fannie were about to live a normal life together, events or fate intervened to set them apart. When not worried about the future, anxious about his modest role at Bowdoin, or concerned about his children's health and well-being, Chamberlain was occupied in a constant and losing battle against the pain caused by his wounds, which sapped his strength. Soon after Grant's departure, Chamberlain was even forced to petition the general to put him back on the active list so that he could afford to have another surgical treatment, a request that caused Chamberlain deep embarrassment.

Fannie and Joshua Chamberlain celebrated their tenth wedding anniversary on December 7, 1865. Chamberlain gave his wife an expensive gold-and-diamond bracelet that contained, in double bands, twenty-four hourglasses, each inscribed with the name of a battle in which he fought. The band also contained the shoulder boards of a major general, with two inset diamonds. The gift was opulent by any measure and intended to show Fannie her husband's love. But even with the celebration of their anniversary, the marriage remained strained, with Fannie overtaken by the death of a daughter, the sameness of her life, and her husband's continuing bouts with restlessness and pain. She knew he was thinking of running for governor and had been talking to Republican Party leaders about his prospects. As their later correspondence shows, Fannie strongly disapproved, hoping that her husband would this time overcome his unease with the life of a professor and stay close to home.

Chamberlain went on without her approval, since he welcomed the chance for the new adventure political office seemed to hold. He told Fannie he was not in any position to turn down the offer, which he considered an honor, and that he sincerely believed he might do the state some good as its leading political official. He made it sound as if he were not looking forward to spending time in Augusta as the state's chief executive, perhaps to mollify her open disapproval. When he was called to a meeting to discuss his candidacy he went willingly, but only after glancing over his shoulder at his waiting wife. "I hate these things," he said. But he did not.

The meeting with Republican leaders in Augusta went according to its ordained script. The party leaders told Chamberlain they would like him to head their ticket and that, in view of his wartime record, he would almost certainly be elected. He agreed with them—he would stand as the Republican Party's nominee during the upcoming election. He returned to Brunswick soon after and announced his candidacy to his wife.

# 13

# *The Bone of Contention*

JOSHUA CHAMBERLAIN did not know it, but the real reason for Grant's visit to Maine was not to see him, or to receive an honorary degree at Bowdoin, or even to touch base with a potential political constituency. Rather, Grant came to speak with Oliver O. Howard on the subject of the Freedmen's Bureau, which was established in early 1865 to oversee the southern slave population's transition from bondage to freedom. Abraham Lincoln had appointed Howard head of the bureau because of the Maine soldier's deep commitment to helping the former slaves. It was a thankless task, made worse by the political infighting over the course of Reconstruction and the question of just how much power the bureau should have. Howard met Grant in Boston prior to the general's trip to Portland to gain his support for one of his favorite projects—turning over large tracts of untilled southern land to the former slaves to work.

Whether Chamberlain was aware of these political maneuvers is uncertain, but there is little doubt that he listened closely to Grant's opinions on Reconstruction to see if they accorded with his own. But Grant did not make his views known, especially when it came to setting peacetime policy. With his eye on the presidency, he feared that one misstep could cost him the White House. Grant left Maine, went to Canada, returned to Illinois, then took a trip to the Carolinas to check on the condition of Union troops in the southern states, but also to see for himself how the freedmen were faring. His report on his trip praised Howard, but he criticized bureau "abuses" and implied that giving former slaves more land would heighten black-white tensions. He was against expanding the bureau's power: "The presence of black troops, lately slaves, demoralizes labor, both by their advice and by furnishing in their camps a resort for the freedmen for long distances around."

Grant's report accorded with Andrew Johnson's moderate policy of "restoring" southern governments to their prewar status instead of the congressional posture of "reconstructing" them under harsh conditions. This was a shift for Grant, who had been one of the first Union generals to use a policy of "confiscation" of slaves as a weapon of the war. Now he feared that the Freedmen's Bureau could be used as a tool by Radical Reconstructionists to disenfranchise the South's white population. Grant not only held no animus for the rebel leaders, he took the position that they were the "thinking men" of the South and the only ones capable of restoring social order in the region. Grant feared that violence in the South would escalate if the freedmen were given equal rights and criticized them as "imbued with the idea that the property of his late master should, by right, belong to him." Grant's report to Johnson placed him at odds with the radicals in Congress who, shortly after his report was presented to the president, barred former rebels who attempted to take their seats in the House and Senate, and then passed legislation that endorsed black freedom and gave former slaves the right to vote.

Chamberlain's own views of the freedmen, and the tentative manner in which he navigated the shoals of the nation's great social questions over the next four decades, reflect the unease felt by many northerners over the question of black rights. Like many northerners, Chamberlain wanted to punish the South, but not if that meant enfranchising the newly freed slaves. Chamberlain added that his views were consistent with Union war aims; Lincoln fought to preserve the Union first, and then to abolish slavery. Before Antietam, Abraham Lincoln surely would have agreed with Chamberlain's views. The president had been hesitant to shift the focus of the conflict from a simple fight over secession to a complex and dangerous struggle to end slavery—to transform the War for the Union into a Civil War, with all that that implied. The distinction had been important for Lincoln: the War for the Union was a political contest with limited ends, while the war launched by the Emancipation Proclamation was aimed not only at the defeat of southern armies, but the destruction of southern civil institutions, a *civil* war in every sense of the term.

Lincoln had not wanted the war to spark a social revolution, but by late 1862 he believed he had little choice. It had become more difficult to convince northern boys that they needed to kill southerners to just bring them back into the Union, and a chorus of voices had been raised to let the South "go in peace." Harnessing the abolitionist movement could silence these voices and save the Union—something that Lincoln had been willing to do, even if saving the Union came at the price of southern social harmony. We would like to believe that Lincoln wanted to bequeath equal rights to America's black population, but that was not part of his formula. His goal was to reunite the nation, and he used any instrument at hand. Chamberlain followed his example. The war was fought to save the Union and end slavery, and that was all. The freedmen were on their own.

William Oates forever denied that the war was fought over slavery. "For slavery alone, or the money value of the slaves, two-thirds, and probably three-fourths, of the Confederate soldiers would not have risked their lives and fought as they did," he wrote. Instead, he said, southerners went to war to win their independence. They were a different people entirely from those in the North, with different traditions and beliefs. Oates did not dismiss the problem of slavery, though his argument was a deft, if flawed, sleight-of-hand: "It was complimentary to [poor white southerners] that they had the intelligence to foresee that universal emancipation would come a rivalry with them in industries, unpleasant contact, mixed schools, negro officeholders, indignities, miscegenation, and general demoralization."

It was while penning this view that Oates first hinted at what might have been the real cause for his replacement as colonel of the 15th Alabama back in 1864 and the actual reason why—in spite of his stellar record as an officer—he was never confirmed by the Confederate Congress as a colonel. After Lincoln issued the Emancipation Proclamation, Oates had begun to worry that his men would face a wave of "black lines of battle." The South would not lose the war, it would be drowned in a sea of blue uniforms. The only way to respond, he had reasoned, was for the southern government to enlist slaves. He had argued that the Confederacy should "make soldiers of them, which could easily have been done, because the bonds of friendship between white boys and negroes was strong." In February 1863, Oates went to Richmond to discuss his views with members of the Confederate Congress, an institution that he bitterly labeled "that august body of incompetents."

His first stop in the Confederate capital had been in the offices of Congressman James Lawrence Pugh, his Eufaula mentor who represented southeastern Alabama in Richmond, just as he had once represented it in Washington. Pugh greeted him affectionately, but had been shocked by his proposal. For Pugh, Oates's proposition was irrational on its face. "Why," he had said, "negro soldiers would not fight, and they would desert to the Union side to obtain their freedom."

Oates had thought otherwise:

> I replied that was quite true, unless freedom was granted them; and that the law of their enlistment should provide that every negro soldier who received an honorable discharge from the service should be forever a free man, and should be entitled to a bounty of 80 acres of the public land as his homestead; and let the same law provide for the general emancipation of his wife and children. I was fully satisfied that with such provisions as these in the law the negro men would volunteer in great numbers; and that with proper drill and discipline, and with experienced white officers to command them, they would not desert, and would make efficient soldiers. I knew that to make soldiers out of them they must be emancipated, and if the Confederacy did not do it, the Union would.

"If we free the negroes to make soldiers of them," Pugh had replied, "that is simply throwing aside the bone of contention, and we had as well stop the war at once." Slavery was what the war was about, and no argument that Oates could make would change it, not even the fact that Confederate soldiers believed they were, in Oates's words, fighting for "home rule, local self-government, for separate national independence."

Oates's February 1863 trip to Richmond had assuredly destroyed whatever chance he had for higher rank. It had been the first time anyone had suggested that the South enlist its slaves as soldiers, but not the last. Confederate General Patrick Cleburne, one of the South's most talented officers, had ruined his candidacy to head the western armies by suggesting emancipation in a paper circulated among commanders of the Army of the Tennessee in early 1864. His paper reached Richmond shortly thereafter. His readers were thunderstruck. "If slaves will make good soldiers, our whole theory of slavery is wrong," Howell Cobb, one of the Confederacy's leading statesmen, had responded.

Even when the Confederate Congress agreed to allow the enlistment of slaves in noncombat roles in early 1865, they did not emancipate them: "A negro who did not have sense enough, under that law, to have deserted to the enemy at the first opportunity would have been [too] much of an idiot to have made a soldier," Oates later reflected. "No sensible negro would have volunteered under that law, if honestly explained to him, unless it was for the purpose of availing himself of the opportunity it would have given him to desert to the other side, where he could, beyond doubt, have obtained his freedom." The Confederate government's inability to enlist black soldiers, Oates felt, led to its defeat. "After slavery was practically dead the Confederacy clung to its putrid body and expired with it."

After the war Oates did not believe in giving the freedmen equal rights and he was not a progressive in race relations. Like Chamberlain, he could not abide "the absurdity of universal manhood-suffrage." But his views on black-white relations were unusually discerning for his time. He was deeply embittered by the South's inability to bridge its racial divide and disillusioned by the thought that the Confederate government would choose slavery over victory. There is in his writings and public speeches a sadness that the racial and political violence that plagued the South in the decades following the Civil War could have been prevented, but wasn't. "When the Union armies triumphed and the Confederacy was destroyed the negroes were enfranchised, and directed by a horde of plundering carpet-baggers and native scalawags, general bankruptcy came and general ruin threatened all the homes in the South. It was a realization of the grave apprehension of the poor white men in the Confederate ranks."

Oates's views reflect those of many southerners after Appomattox, who reacted to emancipation's social revolution by prosecuting what amounted to a second civil war. But this one, unlike the first, was

fought largely between southerners. Living in what was virtually a devastated nation, under the rule of what many of its inhabitants believed
was an occupying army, and with many of its young men now struggling in a labor market that included the newly emancipated freedman,
the guns of southern men were increasingly turned on each other, black
*and* white. Ironically, the most intransigent rebels lived in those parts of
the South that had shown the most uneasiness with secession. When
the policies of Radical Reconstructionists began to take hold in the
South, pro-Unionists and anti-Unionists in these white counties openly
fought each other in a bid for political power.

◦━━✦━━◦

Alabamians who supported the Union were called "tories," southerners who supported the Confederacy but became Republicans were
called "scalawags," and those who came into Alabama from the North
to make investments, buy land, run for political office, or organize the
Reconstruction administration were called "carpetbaggers." But the
most hated people in Alabama in the years immediately following
the end of the war were the freedmen, who were viewed as ready-made
oppressors in the hands of the occupying northern army. As far as
many white Alabamians were concerned, the Freedmen's Bureau, the
occupying Union army, and the former slaves were working in concert
to wrest control of the South from its citizens and place it in the hands
of the radical Republicans. Proof of the conspiracy was the fact that the
Freedmen's Bureau seized Confederate property and sold it; regulated
contracts between black laborers and white farmers, voiding those it
thought to be unfair; ordered the state government to give freedmen the
vote; and tried cases involving former slaves when the civil courts
proved prejudiced.

Alabama had been under the rule of a military administration since
the last day of the war, but white resentment peaked when John Pope,
the "miscreant" of the Second Battle of Bull Run, became the state's
military governor in March 1867. Pope inaugurated the program of the
radical Republicans, which he supported, and by June had recast the
state's polling districts to give blacks more power, barred former Confederate officials from holding office, and established military commis-
sions to punish anyone interfering with voter registration. The voting

regulations caused an outcry among the state's Confederate loyalists and discomfort among moderates in Washington, but Pope moved forward with his Reconstruction program by calling a convention to rewrite the state's constitution. Of the one hundred delegates who convened in Montgomery that October, thirteen were black and a large number were northerners.

Alabama Democrats, a large portion of them who had served the Confederacy, believed that the constitutional convention was illegally called. They argued that a large number of former Confederates were barred from participating in the delegate selection process and that therefore the convention was not representative of Alabama's white population. These dissenters, a clear majority of the white population, dubbed the Montgomery meeting the "Unconstitutional Convention," "Pope's Convention," the "Circus," or, more viciously, "Swayne's World-renowned Menagerie"—so named for General Wager Swayne, the assistant commissioner of the Alabama Freedmen's Bureau. During one of the first convention sessions, the disenfranchised Democrats pointed out, the chaplain prayed for the "Unioners," then followed this blessing by asking God to bring down "cusses on rebels." This was followed by acts aimed at humiliating the former rebels; one of the convention's first acts was to dissolve Jones County, because it was named for a Confederate colonel. After these preliminaries, the convention proceeded to break up Alabama's black belt counties into smaller units, thereby giving black Alabamians, and the Republican Party, greater delegate strength in upcoming legislative elections.

The convention's sessions proceeded without outside interference until its delegates voted for an increase in pay; then John Pope intervened. It would not look good, he said, for the delegates to be seen caring more for their pocketbooks than the state's business and he counseled moderation in the convention's future conduct. Pope's concern, however, was that the delegates' actions might threaten the future of the state's Republican Party. He did not want them to go too far.

The convention's most important debate, however, was on who would be allowed to vote in state elections and how far the restrictions on former Confederates should be taken. It was a very delicate question: if there too many restrictions, the convention would be condemned as a puppet of Republican interests; if there were too few, the coming vote would result in a Democratic Party victory. A number of radical delegates believed that the best way to ensure that only "loyal" voters would come to the polls was to decree that anyone who voted for secession, any former members of the Confederate Congress, all Confederates above the rank of captain, any who had served in the Confederate government, and any Alabama state official who served during rebel rule should not be allowed to vote—about thirty-five percent of Alabama's white population. "We have a rod over their heads and we intend to keep it there," one delegate explained.

After four days of divisive debate, the convention voted to adopt a loyalty oath designed to identify unreconstructed rebels and keep them from voting: "I accept the civil and political equality of all men; and agree not to attempt to deprive any person or persons, on account of race, color or previous condition, or any political or civil right, privilege or immunity, enjoyed by any other class of men; and furthermore, that I will not in any way injure or countenance in others any attempt to injure any person or persons on account of past or present support of the government of the United States, the laws of the United States, or the principles of the political and civil equality of all men, or for affiliation with any political party." For old-line Democrats, unreconstructed rebels, and supporters of the former Confederacy, the most offending phrase was contained in the oath's first line.

In response, many former Confederates refused to take the oath and were effectively "disenfranchised." The convention's actions hardened anti-Reconstruction sentiments among many white Alabamians. Being disenfranchised became a point of pride and a symbol of opposition to the northern occupation. The widespread dissent did not bother Pope, however, who circulated lists that contained the names of any Alabamians who had ever held public office in the Confederate state or national governments.

The proceedings of the Alabama convention attracted considerable public attention among northerners, who viewed Alabama as the most important test of whether the radical program of Reconstruction outlined by Congress would work. Many northerners, including New York publisher and radical abolitionist Horace Greeley, doubted that it would. He advised the adoption of a more moderate program that would induce southern cooperation with the federal government and lead to the early readmission of southern states into the Union. Greeley condemned Alabama's proposed constitution as unworkable and counterproductive. John Pope went ahead despite these criticisms, however, believing that he could get the constitution approved in a statewide referendum. Such ratification was virtually assured, he believed, especially given the voter registration policies he had put in place. Pope confidently scheduled a vote on the new constitution, and for representatives to the state legislature, for the first week of February 1868.

In fact, while Pope remained confident, he was actually facing a series of insurmountable obstacles—including widespread defections among northern Alabama's Republicans, who resented the freedmen's newfound equality. They had fought, they said, to bring Alabama back into the Union and they did not want to have their power diluted by black votes. Nine members of the convention, almost all of them from northern Alabama, signed a petition protesting the constitution. Twenty-six convention delegates went so far as to hold a separate anti-constitution caucus that condemned the proposed governing document, saying that it would place the state "in the hands of a few adventurers under control of the blacks."

Throughout January, the anti-convention Conservative Party (which was really the core of the old Democratic Party machine of Alabama, but under a new name) organized opposition to the constitution's ratification. Alexander White and former Governor L. E. Parsons led the effort, turning the vote on Alabama's future into a referendum on the freedman's rights. To organize opposition to the vote, as well as to strengthen the Conservative Party, White and Parsons formed the "White Man's Movement" in Dallas County in west-central Alabama and wrote a series of resolutions that they peddled to local political meetings around the state. The resolutions played on white Alabama's fear of racial integration. The movement's manifesto proclaimed that American institutions were established by white men, that the U.S. government was a white man's government, that only white men should rule America, and that the freedmen should never be given the right to vote—let alone "equal" rights.

At a Conservative Party executive committee meeting held in Montgomery a short time after the manifesto was published, it was decided that the party would not field candidates for the state legislature, as doing so would imply endorsement of the constitution. That was the only public decision made by the party executive committee, but unofficially the Conservatives decided to boycott the election altogether, hoping that so few voters would cast ballots, less than the required fifty percent, that the election would be nullified. To add to this, Conservative Party leaders also decided to wage a campaign of fear at the state's polling places by openly threatening those who came to vote. Conservative Party leaders were not certain their tactics would succeed, but they believed the numbers were on their side. At the beginning of February 1866, there were 160,000 registered voters in the state, 88,000 of whom were freedmen. Even with the strict "disenfranchisement" regulations put in place by Pope, everyone knew the vote would be close. Moreover, it was clear that the constitution would fail if agents of the White Man's Movement—who served as the Conservative Party's henchmen—were able to scare away black voters.

Just days before the election, Alabama's new military governor, General George Gordon Meade, who had taken over for Pope four weeks earlier, attempted to encourage a vote for the constitution by striking some of the most unpopular northerners from the ballots for state office. Meade's strategy was to make the constitution more palatable, but Radical Reconstructionists in Congress disagreed with his strategy. Meade was directed to allow the election to go forward with the northerners on the ballots. Meade responded, in an act of desperation, by firing unpopular Freedmen's Bureau official Wager Swayne and replacing him with General Julius Hayden. Hayden then disqualified a number of embarrassingly pro-Republican candidates from state ballots before Washington could overrule him. Meade and Hayden then urged the statewide pro-Union clubs, called "Loyal Leagues," to do whatever they could to drum up support for the constitution.

But it was too late. When the polls closed after four days of voting, it was clear from the poor turnout that the constitution had failed to win ratification. While only 1,005 voters voted against the constitution, the returns showed that less than fifty percent of registered voters actually voted in the election. According to law, the vote was nullified. The failure was a victory for Alabama's white Conservative Party, but it also showed that opposition to the Radical Reconstruction program was widespread.

General Meade certified that the election was fair and honest and that the constitution was "lost on its merits," but the radicals were not satisfied. They were convinced that the vote had been stolen. In fact, the evidence supports their view. A survey conducted by the state's Radical Executive Committee (a Republican Party organization supporting the Radical Reconstruction viewpoint) was forwarded to Washington, with a detailed list of statewide political abuses that included "outrageous acts," "force," "persuasion," and "threats" conducted by the White Man's Movement agents. In Henry and Dale counties, the report showed, there was actually no election at all, since none of the state-appointed registrars agreed to serve at polling places during the vote. Their refusal was a direct result of the campaign of political intimidation laid out by Conservative Party leaders in Montgomery.

The results in Henry and Dale counties were also due to the efforts of William Oates, whose name was included in a report of eyewitness testimony around a polling place, where voters were fearful of casting ballots because of the "outrageous acts committed by a Mr. Oats." The reference was probably, but not certainly, to William Oates. In Barbour County, also, the agents of the revived Eufaula Regency made it plain that any vote by a white male would result in "social ostracism." In Montgomery, only 41 of 4,200 registered white voters cast ballots. The Conservatives were buoyed by their victory and published a broadside that amounted to a declaration of war against Alabama's Reconstruction authorities:

> We reiterate the advice hitherto offered to those of our southern people who are not ashamed to honor the service of the "lost cause" and the memory of their kith and kin whose lives were nobly laid down to save the survivors from a subjection incomparably more tolerable in contemplation than in realization. That advice is not to touch a loyal leaguer's hand; taste not of a loyal leaguer's hospitality; handle not a loyal leaguer's good. Oust him socially; break him pecuniarily; ignore him

politically; kick him contagiously; hang him legally; or lynch him clandestinely.

By the time the voting on the constitution took place, the White Man's Movement was openly assisted in its program by one of Alabama's most potent new political associations, which made no apology for carrying out its program of beatings, terror, and, as suggested in the Conservative broadside, lynching—the Ku Klux Klan.

⟐━✦━⟐

While the Ku Klux Klan was the most notorious organization of its kind, it was not the only one. Within months of Lee's surrender at Appomattox, militia companies of former Confederate soldiers had been formed to monitor the activities of federal troops and the freedmen. In the wiregrass region of Dale, Henry, Barbour, and Pike counties, these militia organizations were secretly organized and rode at night, often in disguise. Different militia companies patrolled different parts of the state, but they all used similar tactics. Horse thieves were hung in southern Alabama as a warning to "uppity" blacks, the "Black Cavalry" was formed in eastern Alabama to disarm black militias, and the "Men of Justice" was formed in northern Alabama to remove freedmen from land given them by the Reconstruction authorities.

The Ku Klux Klan built a strong following using these militias as a base of support. The Klan had been started by former Confederate soldiers of northern Alabama and southern Tennessee, but soon spread south. In the late 1860s and early 1870s, the Klan became the unofficial military arm of Alabama's Conservative Party and drew support from disenfranchised Confederate officials. Its members formed dens, were given fanciful and alarming disguises, and were awarded strange titles. Early in 1867, the "Grand Cyclops" of the first KKK den in Pulaski, Tennessee, called for a national convention of the organization in Nashville. The first KKK convention divided the former Confederate states into a single "Empire," which was ruled over by a "Grand Wizard" assisted by a staff of ten "Genii." Staff officers in each of the states were given the titles of "Hydra," "Furies," "Goblins" and "Night Hawks." The KKK adopted a constitution whose purpose was to "protect the weak, the innocent, and the defenceless from indignities, wrongs, and outrages of the lawless, the violent, and the brutal; to relieve the injured and oppressed; to succor the suffering and unfortunate; and especially the widows and orphans of Confederate soldiers." The first Grand Wizard of the Ku Klux Klan was Nathan Bedford Forrest, the renowned Confederate cavalry commander who was known throughout the South for his exploits as the "Wizard of the Saddle."

The KKK was prominent in northern Alabama by the spring of 1867, but it soon spread south and west, becoming especially powerful in western Alabama in 1868, its rise spurred on by opposition to the February vote on the new state constitution. Its chief apologists claimed that the Klan was not powerful or effective and dismissed it as no more than a "club." But even in its earliest years, the KKK had a profound influence on southern politics. The organization followed strict rules of secrecy; a southerner who wanted to join was asked if he was ever a Union soldier, if he agreed with Reconstruction, if he was a member of the Union League (in Alabama, the Loyal League), if he opposed black equality, and, most importantly, if he favored the rule of a "white man's government." The strict admissions test and the organization's secrecy rules meant that it was only rarely penetrated by federal, state, or municipal authorities.

The effectiveness of the Klan in carrying out the program of the Conservative Party in Alabama is indisputable. By the time of the February 1868 vote on the state constitution, thousands of freedmen had been sufficiently threatened by the KKK that they refused to go to the polls, despite the efforts of federal soldiers to protect them. Alabama blacks faced the threat of violence every day. In Sumter County, west of Montgomery, the Klan murdered—one by one—the white leaders of the Loyal League, and then turned on half a dozen freedmen who attempted to keep the league alive. Klansmen regularly visited the homes of blacks who supported the Radical Resconstructionist program, to administer beatings. "There are but few white males in our county belonging to the Republican party," a Calhoun County, Alabama, resident testified later, "and those few are ostracized and cursed . . . in some instances their houses have been surrounded by disguised bands in the night time, threatening their lives if they do not desist in their political course." The height of Klan violence in Alabama came in 1870, when the Klan lynched one white man and four blacks in broad daylight in Cross Plains, in the heart of the black belt just west of Montgomery.

The KKK's reign of terror spurred Congress to appoint a Joint Select Committee on the Klan's activities. James Pugh was one of the committee's star witnesses from Alabama. At first Pugh denied that the Klan operated anywhere in southern Alabama; in this, it is clear, he was accurate. But he purposely soft-pedaled the program of political intimidation practiced by Alabama's Conservative Party: "I have become satisfied that the white people have made a great mistake in not accepting universal suffrage," he testified, "and I believe that they would have done so if it had not been for the offensive use that was made of negro suffrage by a class of persons who were sent down there to control it in the work of reconstruction."

In spite of the decades of racial prejudice that followed Reconstruction, there is an odd ring of sincerity in Pugh's tone that reverberates through post–Civil War Alabama history. A close study of the political record of southeastern Alabama shows that, for the next forty years, Pugh and his followers in the Eufaula Regency, including William Oates, wrestled with the problem of black suffrage. Living in the part of the state where anti-secessionist sentiment was most pronounced and large cotton plantations least in evidence, southeastern Alabamians attempted to come to terms with their racial problems by enlisting black votes when they could, and keeping blacks away from the polls when they could not. Oates and his political followers were racially prejudiced, of that there is no doubt, but they were also political realists who were obsessed by the need to rebuild a political machine that served their purposes. Pugh, still the Regency's titular leader, refused to allow Klan violence to infect his community, calling them "thieves and plunderers" and "the very worst enemies of our people." His protest was sincere.

William Oates was not a member of the Klan and there is strong evidence to suggest that he opposed its program. But he was not above engaging in political intimidation, especially when it came to making certain that ballot boxes contained more Conservative Party (or Democratic) than Republican ballots. That the Klan's terror campaign did not reach into Henry County was due in large part to the fact that Oates found the KKK's program of lynchings distasteful and its ham-handed methods counterproductive. Oates was more interested in political power than in racial purity, a distinction in views that placed him in stark opposition to central Alabama's clique of race baiters. In 1863, Oates would have had the South recruit black soldiers as "the last hope" of the Confederacy; in 1868, Oates would have recruited black voters if it would have saved the state for the Conservative Party. Of course, Oates was not any more successful in convincing the party establishment to drop the barriers to black voting in 1868 than he was in trying to convince James Pugh to recruit slaves in 1863—but he had clearly set out along that road.

The William Oates of 1868 was different from the William Oates of 1863 in one important respect. While he still believed that southern nationalism was a worthy enough project to justify recruiting black supporters, he was more realistic than he had been five years before. His opinions on slavery had cost him command of the 15th Alabama near the end of the war, and he was not about to allow his opinions on campaigning for the black vote to ruin his political career. If the Conservative Party could use the fear of racial "mixing" to gain white votes, Oates was willing to go along. In truth, Oates was also quite willing to use Alabama's prevalent racial prejudices for his own purposes. So when the Conservative Party called for a convention of delegates to be held in Montgomery in June 1868, Oates attended as a delegate from Henry County. The call for the convention, published in Alabama's leading newspapers, is instructive of the Conservative Party's underhanded appeal to white prejudice: "A convention of the white people of Alabama, without distinction of old political parties, opposed to negro domination and Radical misrule in government, is called to meet in the city of Montgomery on Wednesday, June 4."

During the years that William Oates was attempting to revive his political fortunes in Alabama, Joshua Chamberlain was beginning his own political career in Maine. In the spring of 1866, Chamberlain became a candidate for governor. His challenger for the Republican nomination was an old-guard Maine conservative, Samuel E. Spring, who thought Chamberlain was too soft on the South, would not support the party's program of Radical Reconstruction, and was too much of an unknown to trust with the party leadership in the statehouse. But Chamberlain's status as a war hero, his friendship with Grant, and his high public profile proved too much for Spring, who lost the nomination to Chamberlain at the party convention in June. Chamberlain did little campaigning for the governorship, not only because that was the custom of the time, but because he believed his war record would be strong enough to carry him to victory. He made appearances at political clubs and local civic organizations, but he carefully left his opinions on the most important political questions unstated; he often fell back on reminiscing about Maine's central role in winning the war—a popular topic.

Soon after Chamberlain's nomination, Leonard Woods retired as Bowdoin's president and Chamberlain was asked to serve as the college's interim executive officer. His candidacy for governor prohibited him from succeeding Woods as Bowdoin's president, but he gladly agreed to oversee the college until a change of administrations was put in place. He also graciously accepted Bowdoin's award of an honorary doctor of law degree and promised both faculty and students that he would maintain close and cordial relations with them should he be the state's new governor. Chamberlain was feted at almost every turn and was even considered for a colonelcy in the regular army—an offer proffered by his old Fifth Corps commander, Gouverneur Kemble Warren. Tempted though he was to resume his military career, he knew it was out of the question; his physical problems were simply too debilitating to make regular army service a possibility. He therefore turned down Warren's offer and began his gubernatorial campaign in earnest, taking care to show that he supported important aspects of the Radical Reconstruction program. Despite this, many of the state's mainline political powers continued to voice their doubts about his candidacy and criticized him for not taking a harder line on the south. The *Bangor Whig*, the state's most conservative newspaper, for instance, refused to endorse his candidacy until Chamberlain made an unequivocal statement in support of the harsh measures imposed by Radical Reconstructionists. Chamberlain did so, repeating that he believed he had always agreed that disloyalty needed to be punished and that he was a good Republican who supported the party's program. But Chamberlain could not keep himself from being honest about his views on the freedmen; he said that he thought it inadvisable to give the former slaves the right to vote.

Chamberlain's opponent in the September election was Eben F. Pillsbury, an anti-Lincoln Democrat who had criticized the slain president during the war. Pillsbury campaigned on a platform that war heroes did not always make the best governors and that the state needed a steady hand at the helm. But the voters were not convinced by his arguments. Chamberlain's war record was enough for him to gain popular support, and if he did not seem to fully agree with the radical measures passed in Washington to punish the South, it did not show at the polls. When all the ballots were counted, the results showed he had gained the largest majority of any candidate for a state office in Maine history—nearly seventy percent of all votes cast, a landslide.

After the election, the 20th Maine's chaplain, Alfred C. Godfrey, wrote his former commander, warning him that public life would be different than commanding a regiment. Chamberlain should use caution, Godfrey said: "Well, Gen, honors have come down on you gloriously and I am glad of it. The way the world reckons it is a great thing to march up the hill of honor as fast as you have. It was decidedly double quick movement. You have reached the top of the highest hill in the State of Maine. Great place to see and be seen. Don't get dizzy-headed. Be as true in Me. as you were in Va. And no man can take you down." But Chamberlain was hardly dizzy with success. For while the governor-elect might have been one of the most celebrated men in Maine, his personal life was disintegrating. After the election, Fannie—who refused to accompany her husband on his few campaign trips—now told him that she would not follow him to Augusta, the state capital. She was adamant; she would stay in Brunswick with her friends.

Fannie had done her best to meet her husband's growing needs and had coped with his fame as best she could. When Chamberlain went off to war she steadfastly supported his decision; she stood by him when he was near death and helped nurse him back to health. After the war, when Chamberlain entertained his wartime colleagues at their home near Bowdoin, she welcomed them, entertained them, stood by her husband's side as he spoke with them, smiling at all the right times. But after many years of wondering when her own time would come, it was clear that she had had enough. She had greeted in sullen silence the news that Joshua was going to Augusta to meet with Republican leaders to talk about a political career, and undoubtedly had chuckled at his protests that he found such meetings tiresome. She knew her husband better than anyone; while he had proved to be an idealist and believer in steady, traditional principles, she knew he was an enormously ambitious man. It came as no surprise to her either that he accepted the Republican nomination for governor or that he was elected. And it apparently came as no surprise to him that Fannie now refused any further participation in his public life.

The source of tension between the two is unclear. While many of Fannie's letters to her husband no longer exist, it is clear from his correspondence that he knew his wife did not fully support his political career. One suspects that there was always a feeling on Fannie's part that Joshua Chamberlain became her suitor for larger purposes, primarily because she was the adopted daughter of the community's most prestigious minister. She never said this, not once, but the Reverend Adams had at one time implied it, almost openly. Adams did not, after all, warn Chamberlain about Fannie, but warned her about *him*. On the other hand, Joshua was forced to wait three long years for her while she was in Milledgeville, a parting that might have contributed to his belief that he could leave his wife for nearly the same amount of time to go to war. Whatever the case, by the time Joshua Chamberlain became governor of Maine, at the height of his fame and power, his marriage was deeply troubled; Fannie Chamberlain, who had supported him faithfully during the war, now felt discarded.

❦

Joshua Chamberlain was inaugurated for his first one-year term as governor of Maine during the first week of the new year of 1867. It must have been a proud moment for him; his inaugural address to the state legislature was a ninety-minute speech on what he hoped to accomplish in his new office. After asking the delegates to ratify the Fourteenth Amendment—making freedmen citizens—Chamberlain outlined three areas of concern: expanding the program of internal improvements that would attract new businesses to the state, establishing a new agricultural college to educate the state's young, and grappling with the issue of capital punishment, which, he argued, should either be carried out because it was part of the state's laws or rejected altogether. Chamberlain's primary goal, however, was to attract new settlers and industries to the state at the same time he worked out a program that would keep Maine's businesses and youngest citizens from leaving the state. "I trust it will not be deemed an undue boldness if I venture to put the question whether it would not be advisable for the State to open her hand just wide enough to give a limited guaranty by her endorsement to such of her public enterprises as she might select, with such restrictions and securities as should ensure her against any reasonable likelihood of loss, or the necessity of asking a single dollar of the people in the way of taxation." In other words, the new governor advocated what amounted to the nineteenth-century equivalent of supply-side economics, lowering taxes on businesses if they would agree to stay in Maine. Despite the loss in tax revenues his program would cost the state, Chamberlain made it clear that he would not make up the difference by increasing taxes on Maine's citizens.

Chamberlain's inaugural speech also leaned heavily on his war experience and was almost certainly written with an eye to reassuring Republicans that he would support the Radical Reconstruction agenda. Now that he was in office, the new governor wisely decided he was not going to offend his supporters, especially since he could do little to reverse the harsh measures of Congress in his current position. Nevertheless, he left little doubt about his own loyalties:

> We are struck with amazement, and thrown upon our guard when we see those who with scorn and contumely spurned the Constitution, and defied the Government, and sought with violence and cruelty to destroy the Union, now demanding, with equal effrontery and the same spirit of violence, without an apology for the past, without a guaranty for the future, the unconditional restoration of their rights under the Constitution, their place in the Union and their prestige in Government.

The *Bangor Daily Times* praised Chamberlain's speech, but only after issuing a backhanded swipe at his oratorical skills: "What it lacks in brevity it makes up in perspicacity—the only valid excuse that can be adduced for length in State essays." Other newspapers weighed in with their own judgments, nearly unanimously praising Chamberlain for being "broad, liberal [minded] and comprehensive." In nearly all cases, the praise was accompanied by a reminder that Chamberlain was the same "brave" and "dauntless" soldier who had honored the state during the recent war. No one was about to forget this, of course, even though the new governor was embroiled in controversy from the moment he took office.

At issue was the growing power of the temperance movement, which had gained prestige among a small but powerful minority of Maine voters. As governor, Chamberlain urged the legislature to immediately repeal temperance laws that called for the imprisonment of anyone caught selling liquor and he advocated that a special police force founded for that purpose be suspended. The legislature followed his lead. Chamberlain's views on the temperance movement came as a surprise, since it was widely known that he was nearly abstemious. When he called the legislative acts unconstitutional and followed this up by remarking that the Prohibition movement had gained too much power, the state's churches and temperance clubs condemned him. Chamberlain ignored the criticism, but trimmed his sails—while he still opposed what he viewed as the excesses of the temperance activists, he refused to engage them in a public debate. Instead, he deftly turned the attention of the public and the legislature to a new issue: the completion of a hydrographic survey of the state's waterways, the publication of which, he hoped, would attract new industries.

By far the most controversial of his acts came in his defense of the death penalty. He appeared particularly stubborn in the face of rising public sentiment against capital punishment. Maine had traditionally maintained the death penalty as part of its statutes, but it had also as traditionally never used the law to actually execute anyone. Chamberlain changed that. He pardoned two murderers, but then insisted on sending another, a former slave named Harris, to his death. He responded to the outcry of protest against his action by saying that any law on the books ought to be used. This explanation puzzled many of his supporters, who had difficulty determining whether he actually supported or opposed the death penalty, or whether he was actually serious—that he really believed that an enacted law, no matter how discredited, should be followed. His reasoning struck many as obscure, but it appears he was acting out the principle he had enunciated in his Bowdoin master's oration on "Law and Liberty." It was the principle of obedience to the law that needed to be upheld, Chamberlain argued, and not necessarily the law itself. "If we cannot make our practice conform to our law," he argued, "[we should] make our law agree with our practice."

Surprised by the vehemence of the criticism leveled at him, Chamberlain tried to explain the execution of Harris by saying his own views on the subject were not pertinent, in any event, since it was his job to enforce the laws the legislature had passed. This was almost too much for some of his supporters, who were looking for a much simpler answer, and better leadership. Not everything could be based on principle. Did he or did he not agree with the practice of capital punishment? Chamberlain answered only that he sought "wisdom and strength from above." Of course that was not good enough; it seemed the more the public demanded an explanation of his views in simple and straightforward language, the more impatient Chamberlain became. "Many are bitter on me about capital punishment," he confessed in a letter to his mother, "but it does not disturb me in the least." But it did. (Chamberlain then went on to tell his mother that he agreed with the death penalty because he believed it deterred crime, something which he did not tell his fellow citizens.)

At times Chamberlain appeared to confuse the workings of "Providence" with the workings of simple politics. He slipped over the line when it came to arguing his position on capital punishment, falling back on his training as a mechanistic Calvinist. His views struck some voters not only as obscure, but as arrogant. It was one thing to argue that the universe acted in accordance with His perfect laws, with humans as "instruments" in His hands, and quite another to assume that any act that was carried out must be, by definition, a part of His plan. Chamberlain confused "His law" with *the law,* and the Calvinistic belief in "the elect" with his own role as "the elected."

Maine's voters had little patience for talk of principles, preferring simple answers to simple questions. But after the public response to the Harris execution, Chamberlain's political skills improved quickly. After a few rocky months in office, he proved increasingly adept at dealing with the state legislature, grew accustomed to the daily requirements of governing, and enjoyed the innumerable state speaking tours his role now demanded. Like Oates, Chamberlain carefully cultivated his friendships with his former soldiers, using them as his primary base of political support. He counted on their loyalty to return him to the state-house for three successive terms and used them as a protective cloak for his most difficult political decisions. He was especially adept at arguing for public relief of war widows and orphans, which became a favorite means of assuring the strength of his political network.

Chamberlain enjoyed being governor and wished his wife could have enjoyed it with him. Instead, Fannie stayed in Brunswick while he spent much of his spare hours in Augusta staying in a boardinghouse. He visited his home as often as he could, but it was not enough for Fannie. His marriage continued to deteriorate, and by 1868 he and Fannie were thinking about getting a divorce. The central issue seems to have been Fannie's insistence that her husband settle down and stay closer to home. But she was also dissatisfied with his fame and suspicious of his ambition. It was difficult being married to a hero and even more difficult being married to a governor. Joshua Chamberlain was celebrated nearly everywhere he went, while she was ignored. It seemed especially grating that her complaints about him were dismissed as unimportant, while his about her were believed; she was still viewed by him as being "headstrong," "temperamental," "impatient," "impulsive," "willful," and "flighty"—descriptions that she resented. At one point, in late 1868, her dissatisfaction with her husband became so profound that she spread reports that he had struck her during an argument. He responded to these claims by writing an angry letter to her from Augusta:

> Now last night after I had gone to bed, Mr. [Johnson] came in with a very distressed demeanor & begged me not to be angry with him but he saw such great & ruin impending that he must tell me. Miss [illegible] it seems is freely telling people that you told her (& a Mrs. D also as well as everybody else) that I abused you beyond endurance—pulling your hair, striking, beating & otherwise personally maltreating you, & that you were gathering up everything you could find against me to sue

for divorce. Mr. Johnson says this is doing immense harm, whether the *fact* is so or not & the bitter enemies who now assail me on public grounds will soon get hold of this & will ruin me. He is in great distress & begs me to do something—what he does not know.

You must be aware that if it were not you who were so clearly implicated in this business, I should make quick work of these calumniaters [sic]. I fear nothing for myself. But you must see that whatever comes upon me; comes upon you too with even more effect & for your safety I must again offer the suggestion that you act with wisdom and discretion.

If it is true (as Mr. Johnson seems to think there is a chance of its being) that you are preparing for an action against me, you need not give yourself all the trouble. I should think we had skill enough to adjust the terms of a separation without the wretchedness to all our family which these low people to whom it would seem that you confide your grievances & plans, will certain bring about.

You never take my advice, I am aware. But if you do not stop this at *once it will end in hell.*

Fannie Chamberlain was a desperately unhappy woman. There is no firm evidence that Chamberlain abused her, as she claimed, but the lack of it hardly proves his innocence, and his letter to her cannot count as a denial. Unfortunately, we do not have her response, only the indirect evidence that the two eventually put aside the episode and apparently spoke of it no more.

In spite of Fannie's charge of physical abuse, and the apparently deep troubles in their marriage, it is clear that Chamberlain showed his wife deep affection. He did not rule out getting a divorce, but she would have to insist upon one. His letters to her continued to express his love and his care for her well-being. Still, he was exasperated by her and seemingly powerless to give her the kind of life she wanted. He was especially troubled by her habit of confiding what he considered to be their private affairs to her friends. He was puzzled and bewildered by her unhappiness and tried to understand it, but he had the unfortunate habit of treating her like a child. Joshua Chamberlain must have reminded Fannie of her adopted father, who had the same habit. Finally, in frustration at their deteriorating relationship, Chamberlain abandoned the field altogether. They lived apart for long periods during his terms as governor, until they apparently agreed on a mutually satisfactory arrangement, the details of which were never recorded. They remained together, married, but the relationship changed forever: Fannie agreed to cooperate in playing her role as the proper and loving wife, while Joshua allowed her her independence.

# 14

# *The Same Dark Question*

T HE CIVIL WAR was a cataclysm for the South, destroying its commerce and industry and sowing the seeds of social revolution; but the war also left a legacy of bitterness and hatred in the North. This legacy was played out in the halls of Congress, with the president and Congress moving toward a crisis over national Reconstruction policies. The confrontation had been building since Appomattox and the assassination of Abraham Lincoln, but it reached crisis proportions in late 1867 and early 1868. On one side of the debate was President Andrew Johnson, who had initiated a program of "Restoration" in the months immediately following Appomattox. Johnson's moderate program required the southern states to renounce their secession ordinances, abolish slavery, and ratify the Thirteenth Amendment. Congress, controlled by a strong core of Republicans who vehemently disagreed with this policy, responded by refusing to recognize the southern governments that were formed under Johnson's policies, passed a strong Civil Rights Act, strengthened the Freedmen's Bureau, and passed the Fourteenth Amendment, making black Americans citizens. Johnson opposed the Congressional Radical Reconstruction Program, but he had little choice but to enforce congressional laws. Congress easily overrode each of his vetoes and imposed increasingly harsh Reconstruction measures on the South.

The Radical Reconstructionists were frustrated by Johnson's attempts to interfere with their program and in early 1867 began to look for a way to remove him from office. Early that year, congressional radicals enacted legislation requiring Johnson to pass all of his orders to the army through its senior commander, Ulysses S. Grant. The radicals then followed this with a bill prohibiting the president from firing any cabinet officers without congressional approval. The bills were intended to set a trap for Johnson; the Radical Reconstructionists knew he wanted to fire Secretary of War Edwin Stanton, who agreed with their program. When he did, they would remove him as president.

Johnson, an impatient, tactless, and intemperate man, played into their hands. Instead of making common cause with Republican moderates who were secretly opposed to the program of the most radical of the Reconstructionists—the "firebreathers"—he alienated them: he openly encouraged southerners to actively oppose the congressional Reconstruction program, he replaced several military commanders in southern states with conservatives, and he let it be known that he wanted to be the Democratic Party's nominee for president in 1868.

Johnson believed that most northerners supported his moderate policies. But that was a miscalculation. When he fired Edwin Stanton as secretary of war in the summer of 1867, House Republicans filed eleven charges of impeachment against him and brought him to trial in the Senate for "high crimes and misdemeanors." The claim was that he had purposely violated the law and "flouted the will of Congress." Johnson had few supporters, even among the army leadership, which he had tried to cultivate. "He attempts to govern after he has lost the means to govern," William T. Sherman said in disgust, "he is like a General fighting without an army." Even Ulysses S. Grant, the living symbol of the Union victory and a moderate on most Reconstruction issues, maintained a diligent silence on Johnson's policies. When Johnson was impeached, Grant forged new friendships with congressional Republicans in order to enhance his future political fortunes. He was not about to speak out in defense of the unpopular president.

Johnson vowed to fight for his presidency, organized his defense, and presented his case in the Senate in April 1868. But he mounted a weak defense; instead of saying he believed the president had the right to fire a cabinet member, he claimed that the law did not apply to Edwin Stanton because he was appointed by Lincoln. His arguments again offended moderates, who wanted him to openly oppose radical policies. Many congressional moderates now openly castigated him as "obstinate, self-willed, and combative." But even these moderates knew that Johnson could not be convicted and removed from office because of his offensive personality and that Radical Reconstructionists would have a difficult time proving he had actually committed any crime. The moderates—and Johnson—also knew that his removal as president would make Benjamin Wade, the president pro tem of the Senate (and the next in line of succession), the new chief executive. Wade was acceptable to most Radical Reconstructionists, but there were a few holdouts who opposed his pro-labor, high-tariff, anti-business economic policies. If these radicals sided with congressional moderates, then Johnson would remain in office.

By early May 1868, it was becoming more and more apparent that Johnson would not be convicted: not only were many members of the Senate uncomfortable with replacing him with Wade, it was becoming obvious that his trial was brought on by Radical Reconstructionists who wanted to guarantee Republican hegemony in the South. By the middle of May, a group of a half dozen influential moderate Republicans—who had been willing to go along with the radicals up until the final vote—now decided to switch sides, preferring, as they said, "the present situation [with Johnson as president] to the change proposed [with Wade as president]." These moderate Republicans knew that their vote to acquit Johnson would be controversial with their constituents and might even cost them their political futures. When the final ballots were cast, Johnson was retained in office by a single vote, cast by Maine Senator William Pitt Fessenden. In fact, the result was not as close as it seemed.

When Fessenden cast the ballot that acquitted Andrew Johnson, his fellow senators, legend has it, were thunderstruck and pleaded with him to reconsider his position. Unshaken, Fessenden said that while he disliked Johnson and abhorred his policies, he would not be remembered as the first man to convict a sitting president. In truth, Fessenden had decided long before the final vote that he would cast his ballot for acquittal, a calculated decision that was part of a series of secret negotiations between radicals who opposed Benjamin Wade becoming president and moderates who supported Andrew Johnson. As part of the agreement, Johnson promised he would end his opposition to the radicals' Reconstruction program. The only thing left to be decided had been whether it would be Fessenden or someone else who cast the vote leaving Johnson in the White House.

Joshua Chamberlain supported Fessenden's vote and defended the senator against his most vocal critics in the Maine political establishment. But even Chamberlain was surprised by the public outrage over Fessenden's vote among the general public. The more he defended Fessenden, the more Chamberlain himself was criticized for being soft on southern Democrats and former Confederates, and the more he was associated with Johnson's moderate Reconstruction policies. Chamberlain defended himself and Fessenden in public meetings held around the state and successfully deflected the most vocal criticism, but this cost him dearly with his core supporters, including veterans groups. The crisis passed, but it was clear that Chamberlain might have permanently harmed his own chances for political advancement. Worse still, he had inadvertently set himself against some of the state's most respected Republican leaders, especially Maine Congressman James G. Blaine.

Chamberlain's decision to support Fessenden was a matter of principle based on his own suspicions of the radicals. While Chamberlain did not have the political experience commanded by Fessenden, who was a lifelong politician, the two were alike in many respects. Both feared the growth of radical Republican power, both sensed that the public was growing weary of the constant Reconstruction controversy, both believed that the Republican Party needed to take a new course to maintain its public standing, and both were convinced that the most important issues facing the nation were economic—and had little to do with the outcome of the war. Even more important, however, both Fessenden and Chamberlain (and many other Republicans) were now beginning to swing back to the moderate center of the political spectrum in search of issues that would maintain Republican supremacy in the decades ahead.

While many of the programs passed by the Radical Reconstructionists would remain in force until federal troops finally left the South in 1876, the heyday of punishing the South for starting the war had already passed—a fact that Fessenden and Chamberlain astutely recognized. By the end of 1868, key Republicans, and even some radicals, began to agree and decided that the less controversy there was over Reconstruction, the better it would be for the Republican Party. So while both men were excoriated for refusing to condemn Johnson in the immediate aftermath of his trial in the Senate, their long-term political views were well in step with mainstream Republican leaders, who were more interested in holding on to political power than in punishing the South.

The Johnson controversy mirrored the deep disagreements over Reconstruction policies throughout the nation. Exhausted by the bloodletting, many northerners were intent on allowing the arguments over slavery and secession to fade into the past. These moderates believed that the southern states should be allowed to reenter the Union as long as they remained loyal to the federal establishment. For the most part, moderate northerners believed that the war had been fought primarily to maintain the Union and not to end slavery. Others disagreed and were suspicious that the South would remain "unreconstructed," and that the social revolution wrought by the end of slavery would be reversed if former rebels were allowed to take their place in the political establishment. These northerners, most of whom formed the core of the abolitionist movement, believed that, having won the war, it was now up to the federal government to win the peace by ensuring equal rights in the South—by force if necessary. The abolitionists' views were shared by a hard core of Radical Reconstructionists, who also understood the unprecedented opportunity that had fallen into their hands. Reconstruction, they thought, gave them an opportunity to crush the Democratic Party and thereby ensure that the South's political future would remain in their hands.

Many of these same divisions were present in the South. Most southerners believed that the war had settled the question of secession, and they were willing to once again be loyal citizens of the American republic. While the slaves were now free, these southerners viewed the change in their status as nominal and that the relationship between the races would be dictated by southern whites—as it always had been. On the other hand, those southerners who had abhorred secession and fought against their region during the war believed that they would be rewarded for their loyalty by their northern allies. While a distinct minority, these Unionists looked on themselves as the new political power in the region, and while few of them viewed Reconstruction as a means of giving the freedmen equal rights, they knew they would have to depend on black votes to maintain political power.

It was inevitable that these contending views would clash. The first clash came in the North, during the Johnson impeachment crisis. Though Johnson was allowed to stay in office, the radicals had successfully passed most of their program. It was now possible for northerners who wanted to punish the South to ally themselves with those who believed that the North's triumph on the battlefield guaranteed the former slaves equal rights. The most serious conflict over the treatment of the former Confederate states, therefore, took place in the South itself, where the radical program of Reconstruction was carried out by what southerners looked on as a northern army of occupation.

After the impeachment crisis passed, the Republican Party establishment looked to Ulysses S. Grant to be the party standard-bearer in 1868. Grant was the perfect national candidate. Not only was his position on Reconstruction ambiguous enough to satisfy Republican radicals, he also commanded enormous popular support. Chamberlain endorsed Grant, spoke out in favor of his candidacy, and publicly campaigned on his behalf when he was nominated—at the Republican Party convention in Chicago—and celebrated with the rest of his party when he was elected. Nevertheless, Chamberlain was mindful of the fact that the new president and he had had indirect and distant disagreements in the past—especially over Grant's endorsement of Gouverneur Warren's dismissal at the hands of Grant crony Phil Sheridan during the Battle of Five Forks in the last days of the war. Sheridan, supported by Grant, had humiliated Warren by summarily dismissing him for not being aggressive enough during the battle. The action was viewed by Union soldiers as high-handed and unnecessary. Warren was a favorite of the troops and had a stellar record as one of the heroes of Gettysburg, while Sheridan was looked on as an abrasive interloper. It was difficult for the Maine governor to put his loyalty to Warren aside or support Grant's friend Sheridan.

The controversy over Warren's dismissal during the Battle of Five Forks, and the clamor among his troops that his service be recognized and Sheridan condemned, is now little more than a historical footnote. But at the time, Warren's treatment aroused considerable political comment and involved the reputations not only of Grant, Meade, and

Sheridan, but of Warren's division and brigade commanders—many of whom were now among the Union's most important political leaders. There was, in fact, much more at stake than whether Sheridan was justified in dismissing Warren. Over a period of nearly two decades, from Lee's surrender at Appomattox until the Warren Court of Inquiry published its final findings, the debate over Warren's actions became an important political battleground as Warren's defenders were perceived as calling into question Sheridan's judgment on a host of issues, the most important of which was his defense of Radical Reconstruction policies.

After the war, Sheridan had been appointed the military commander in Louisiana and Texas. When congressional opposition toward Andrew Johnson was beginning to build in 1867, Sheridan had reacted to anti-Reconstruction sentiments in New Orleans by breaking up anti-Republican political rallies, promoting the registration of black voters, firing the head of the New Orleans police, placing Union troops in city police uniforms, and dismissing the anti-Reconstruction mayor of New Orleans. Sheridan had then dismissed the entire New Orleans City Council for opposing the Radical Reconstruction program and ordered federal troops to keep former Confederates from voting on the state constitution. While Sheridan had defended these actions by saying he was only "faithfully carrying out the law," his program not only ensured that most of the state's voters (sixty-five percent) were black, but that the state's new political administration would be dominated by Republicans.

President Andrew Johnson had reacted to Sheridan's program by transferring him out of Louisiana. Grant had protested the transfer and defended Sheridan. While Grant was a moderate on Reconstruction, he supported Sheridan's actions in Louisiana not because he agreed with them, but because of his friendship with "Little Phil." He had urged Johnson to reinstate his friend, but the president was adamant. "His rule has, in fact, been one of absolute tyranny," Johnson told Grant, "without references to the principles of our government or the nature of our free institutions." Given his fiery temperament, Sheridan was remarkably low-key about his dismissal, saying that he welcomed "the order that lifted from me my unsought burden." But he remained one of the South's most vitriolic critics: "If I am disliked," he told an aide, "it is because I cannot and will not cater to rebel sentiment. . . . I did not care whether the Southern States were readmitted tomorrow or kept out for twenty years. The more I see of this people the less I see to admire."

Sheridan moved to a new command in the West and bided his time—knowing that Grant's campaign for the presidency would undoubtedly succeed and that when his old commander was elected, his career and reputation would be resuscitated. And that is precisely what happened. Grant swept to victory in the presidential contest of 1868 against Democratic challenger Horatio Seymour. When Grant became president, William Tecumseh Sherman became the nation's new army commander and Sheridan was promoted to the second spot, behind Sherman. When Sherman retired, Sheridan took his place. By most measures, Sheridan led a life of accomplishment. If he was outspoken and controversial, he was also unapologetic about his own views of the most important question of the day. But Sheridan's increasing power did not dampen Chamberlain's opinion of him, a view he first made public in 1869, during Grant's first year in the White House—in other words, precisely at the time when they might endanger his chances for higher public office.

In July 1869, Chamberlain traveled to New York City to attend the founding convention of the Society of the Army of the Potomac, one of the most powerful postwar veterans groups. As governor of Maine and one of the war's nationally known heroes, Chamberlain was much in demand. He was given a prominent place at the convention and agreed to serve as one of the meeting's featured speakers. The fact that the society contained the army's top generals, including Phil Sheridan and Ulysses S. Grant, did not intimidate him. He had decided that at a key moment in his speech he would pointedly remind society members that they should not only honor those who gave their lives for the Union, but that they should rehabilitate those officers who had run afoul of Grant, Sherman, and Sheridan. While Chamberlain couched his statement as a defense of those who had faithfully served the Union during wartime, they were aimed squarely at Sheridan, and their political tone was unmistakable.

"Nor do they forget to-night those officers, once the favorites of fortune, whom misunderstanding, impatience, or jealousy has stricken from our rolls," Chamberlain said in even tones. He was surprised when his words led to rustling from the back of the hall, which seemed to roll forward, until all in attendance were standing in a mass ovation. The crowd of veterans knew that Chamberlain could only be referring to Warren. Encouraged by the raucous acclamation and ignoring the damage that such an open break with the army's powerful triumvirate might cause, Chamberlain plunged ahead: "Pardon me, comrades," he said, "if I venture here to express the hope, knowing all the pains and penalties of so doing, that tardy justice (if that can be called justice which is tardy) may be done to officers whose character and service in behalf of the Republic, deserve something better than its hasty and last- ing rebuke." It was a biting sentence aimed squarely at those who now stood at the peak of political power.

Chamberlain knew very well that there were extreme "pains and penalties" for his words, including the very strong possibility that Ulysses S. Grant would hear of them. The president was certainly pow- erful enough to prevent Chamberlain from being considered for a Sen- ate seat from Maine or, if he left the governorship, to ensure that he be slighted in all considerations for the awarding of government post. There was much more at stake in Chamberlain's defense of Warren than loyalty to an old friend and commander or his own aversion to the nation's highest ranking military officers—"the high boys," as he called them. Chamberlain placed his entire political future as a Republican at risk by questioning the foundation of its Reconstruction policies and by implicitly criticizing Sheridan's—and Grant's—dismissal of Warren. In defending Warren, Chamberlain was reaffirming his conservative roots in Brewer, his family's admiration for the South, and his long-held and deeply felt suspicions of federal power.

Despite his stinging rebuke of Sheridan and, by implication, Grant, there was never any clear break with the president, who continued to speak favorably of Chamberlain. Yet, when it came time for Chamber- lain to run for a fourth term as governor, few in Maine's Republican Party wanted him to. The party hierarchy, those who had been in posi- tions of power during the Civil War and the years after, offered the nomination of at least three prominent Republicans, including former governor Israel Washburne, and each of them turned it down. No one wanted the job, in large part because of the party split over the temperance issue, but also because the state's economy was sagging and no one had any idea how to revive it. With no one else available, the party again turned to Joshua Chamberlain, though this time with much less enthusiasm than they had been able to muster in 1866 during his first campaign. Chamberlain reluctantly agreed to run again and to serve if elected, but only because he had his eyes set on Maine's big prize—a seat in the U.S. Senate.

This was a calculated decision on Chamberlain's part. He knew he did not rank very high in the affections of Maine's senior political leaders, especially in the eyes of the state's powerhouse, James G. Blaine, but he also knew that if his bid for a fourth term failed he could return to Bowdoin, which had promised him a job whenever his tenure as governor ended. Or, if not elected, he could begin to patch together the support he would need to be elected senator. Running for a fourth term provided a way to keep his hat in the political ring.

Chamberlain was duly nominated by the Republican convention and set out on his fourth political campaign. But if the Bowdoin professor believed his tour of the state in search of votes would be a triumphal procession, a curtain call at the end of his time as the state's chief executive, he was mistaken. The public was not particularly excited by Chamberlain's predictable speeches, which still contained the essential themes of heroism and duty. Many of those who greeted him now were less excited by meeting a hero of the war and more inclined to seek answers to their pressing economic problems.

Much of the tepid response to Chamberlain's nomination for another term had to do with his increasingly serious confrontation with the leaders of the state's temperance movement. The movement had begun in the 1820s, but it did not gain widespread popular support until after the Civil War, when its small core of organizers was strengthened by abolitionist activists. Many of these former abolitionists looked on the movement as a means of showing the new political power of women. The temperance movement, in fact, served as a testing ground for the growing movement for women's suffrage, and many of the most prominent women abolitionists became leaders in all three movements. The Prohibition Party was organized in 1869, in the same year as the National Woman Suffrage Association; the larger, and more powerful, National Women's Christian Temperance Union was formed in 1874. The temperance movement was especially strong in Maine, which had prohibited the sale of liquor for a short time prior to the war.

Chamberlain made no secret of his views on the question: he thought the strict prohibition of liquor was too harsh and that leaders of the temperance movement were too radical in their demands. He had even, unwisely, refused to speak to a temperance convention back in 1868, but confidently thought that his principled stand, which dictated that people ought to be left alone to do what they wished—and his warning that the leaders of the movement were too extreme—could still appeal to Maine voters. But everywhere he went in the days leading up to the final balloting for his fourth term, Chamberlain was reminded that his "principled stand" had exploded the myth of Republican unity. His refusal to court the prohibitionist vote or give them a chance to speak during the Republican convention in Augusta caused a walk-out by some convention delegates and led to the formation of an anti-liquor party that cut into his support. Instead of speaking forcefully about his own temperate views and his history of abstinence, which might have gone a long way toward assuaging the Republican prohibitionists, Chamberlain lectured the movement's leaders, saying that it was not up to the state to enforce abstinence. Most voters agreed with his views, but he then, characteristically and disastrously, went a step too far, adding that the only real solution to the problem was for the general populace to rediscover the importance of the "spiritual element."

Maine's voters were as hardworking, patriotic, and devout as any in the nation. They would have gladly accepted Chamberlain's explanation that it was not the job of the government to intervene in their private lives, but they were insulted that he thought he could use his office to lecture them about the "spiritual element" in their lives. Just a few short years before, Chamberlain's overblown phrases would have seemed like pearls of wisdom delivered from a savior of the Union, but now these same comments seemed priggish and overbearing. The situation was exacerbated by the Democrats, who had revitalized their party during Chamberlain's tenure as governor and now nominated Franklin Smith—a successful businessman and accomplished legislator—as their standard-bearer.

Smith was an articulate and bold campaigner with broad visionary ideas. He proved to be a formidable opponent and for a time it actually seemed as if Chamberlain would lose the contest. The Democrats enlisted the aid of their strongest newspapers and hoped that the entrance into the race of a prohibition candidate, the divisions in the Republican Party, and voter apathy would lead to victory. But despite growing voter suspicions, Chamberlain won the balloting, albeit by a narrower margin than ever before. Chamberlain seemed chastened by the vote and the criticisms leveled at him by friend and opponent alike, so he worked to make his inaugural address the opening of what he hoped would be a final year of accomplishment and progress. "What this state needs is capital—money in motion, whether gold or currency," he said. "Our material is stagnant, our industry crippled, our enterprise staggered for want of money, which is power."

Chamberlain issued a special plea for an expansion of public services, including the enlargement of public mental health treatment, and monies for new commercial enterprises. He also unwisely issued a warning to the temperance movement, which he criticized once again for its extremism. He was pleased with the effort, proud of his three years of accomplishment—and largely unaware that his anti-prohibitionist sentiments had set the stage for a legislative deadlock. Rather than pushing his economic program, the legislature (in which supporters of temperance had enough votes to block his agenda) made certain that the fourth Chamberlain administration in Augusta passed without any movement on his economic program.

The only incident of note in Chamberlain's final year as governor, in fact, was a visit he made to Portland to welcome the British warship *Monarch* to Maine's shores. Escorted by a powerful array of American warships, the *Monarch* came to Portland to deliver the remains of American philanthropist George Peabody, and nearly the entire city turned out for the occasion. Chamberlain was still fascinated by military affairs, and so used the *Monarch*'s visit as a chance to visit the ship, hobnob with its captain, and welcome the British crew to a series of well-orchestrated public events. The round of dinners, celebrations, and official ceremonies thrilled Portland's citizens and surprised the British. It also gave Chamberlain a last opportunity to enjoy his time as governor in a year when he had been surrounded by controversy and by a loss of public support.

Although there was never any question that Chamberlain could have won the votes for renomination for a fifth term in June 1870, Republican leaders let him know that another term in office was out of the question. Chamberlain was not disappointed. He was not only tiring of the job, he realized he had reached the end of his talents as governor. New blood was now needed to revitalize the party's sagging fortunes and repair its relations with the state legislature. If Chamberlain was embittered by the Republicans' refusal to nominate him for a fifth term, he did not mention it, and he was mollified somewhat by the knowledge that Democratic Party leaders had actually approached him about standing for election as governor at the head of their party. It was an offer he quietly but politely refused, though he retained an inner glow in feeling that he might still carry a political banner to victory. Besides, four terms in Augusta had worn Chamberlain down. Perhaps more important, Chamberlain realized that while he had much to be proud of in his public life, his failures had been rooted in his inability to compromise. He needed time to pull his life together, plan for the future, and perhaps even begin the slow process of building a new political base that would take him to the U.S. Senate.

Chamberlain shared a number of personal drawbacks with other veterans of the Union army: a tendency to overplay the heroism of his own role, his constant focus on the sacrifices made by his generation of Americans, and his sense that he held a monopoly on principle. In time these qualities would grow tiresome to even his strongest friends and supporters. But even his political opponents had to admire his stubborn stance on political questions he believed in, and admit that while his four terms as governor would not be remembered as a period of stunning progress and growth, he had done an admirable job of providing the state with the political stability it needed in the aftermath of war. Also, Chamberlain could be well satisfied by those accomplishments that he had attained in his four terms in Augusta, including the establishment of what would become the state university, the settlement of new immigrants in northern Maine, the completion of a hydrographic survey (to be used to attract new businesses), and the reorganization of the state militia.

We expect great things of great warriors and are often disappointed when they fail to be as great off the battlefield as they were on. Chamberlain suffered in the voters' eyes primarily for this reason. Chamberlain was not a revolutionary, after all—which is why he was elected in the first place. Years later, when the political controversies that seemed so important in the late 1860s had passed, Bowdoin College President DeWitt Hyde argued that the Bowdoin professor and war hero should not be remembered for what he did, but for what he did not:

> As a statesman, he was in advance of his time. Called to solve the problems entailed by the Civil War, his administration as Governor was marked by patience and fairness; he refused to use the power that people gave him for ends other than the people's good: and when the leaders of his party advocated the impeachment of the president; the protracted agitation of sectional differences; and immediate suffrage for the emancipated Negroes; he stood firmly, sagaciously and self-sacrificingly for more moderate and pacific measures—measures which subsequent history has shown to be far more beneficent than those which in the flush of military victory, the heat of party strife, and the fire of personal ambition, unfortunately prevailed.

Hyde's description is telling. For those same qualities that Hyde viewed as his strengths, others viewed as weaknesses. While Maine's citizens gave their governor great latitude because of his stature as a national war hero, at key points over his four terms in office Chamberlain had committed the cardinal political sin—of needlessly making enemies of those whom he could have recruited as political allies. It was primarily for this reason that Republican leaders decided the party should shift its attention to a more pragmatic leader.

The same kinds of shifts were occurring elsewhere throughout the North, as Civil War veterans serving in public office found that their claims to former glory were not enough to ensure the success of their legislative programs. Even Ulysses S. Grant, whose popularity was undeniable, had difficulty translating his public standing into fundamental legislative progress. Americans not only seemed less willing in 1870 to cast their vote on the basis of past glory, a new political agenda—geared toward a gilded age of economic expansion and massive new immigration—was eclipsing the issues of national unity and race that had energized a generation of Americans. Once again, American women played a central role in defining the nation's most important questions.

In September 1869, Harriet Beecher Stowe published "The True Story of Lady Byron's Life" in the *Atlantic Monthly*. Her article sparked a storm of protest, cost the magazine over 15,000 readers, and subjected her to widespread vilification. Like Chamberlain, Stowe had been allowed to read Byron and the Bible as a child. To the Beechers, the Chamberlains, and thousands of other Americans, the great Lord Byron could do no wrong, despite the shocking allusions to the attractions of incest that pervaded his poetry as well as the rumors of sexual scandal that stalked him. He was handsome, strong, brilliant, and mysterious; that he was pursued by hosts of unseen demons made him more so.

Educated New Englanders like the Beechers were fascinated by Byron's life of aristocratic dissipation, vicariously shared in the thrill of a strangeness they could never practice, and mimicked his droll attitude toward the exceeding tedium of everyday life. They followed his exotic journeys, gloried in his romantic notions, and imagined they were a part of his legion fighting for Greek freedom against the infidel Turks. Even when Byron divorced his wife, New England bluebloods excused the act by pointing to a series of scurrilous reports on her behavior: she was shrill, capricious, overly demanding, and ungracious; her refusal to speak bluntly of the reasons for his abandonment were taken as further proof of her wifely inabilities.

Stowe visited Lady Byron in 1856 and learned the truth of their divorce, but put away the story until 1868, when Countess Guiccioli published a hagiography of the poet that blamed Lady Byron for the marital breakdown, accusing her of being a shrill prude. Stowe responded by baring, in the pages of the *Atlantic Monthly*, Byron's incestuous liaison with his half-sister Augusta Leigh and his neglectful, abusive, self-centered, and unhinged behavior toward his wife—which left his wife in "an abyss of infamy" that "her marriage was expected to cover."

Stowe told her readers that she admired Byron despite these faults and she praised his genius, but this made not a whit of difference to the literary lions of her day, who spent the next months denouncing her. Perhaps predictably, few of Stowe's critics actually took issue with her claims (they had heard rumblings of such indiscretions), but were instead offended that she should mention the great poet's foibles at all. Even the late Lady Byron was vilified—for having uttered the truth about her unhappiness and thereby besmirching the reputation of the century's greatest poet.

There was a trap in this. Lady Byron would be disparaged in either case—by refusing to defend herself she was tacitly confessing her "shrill prudishness," and in talking openly of the problems she was breaking one of society's most sacred taboos. Women of Stowe's age were wrapped in a code of silence about the details of their private lives, including marriage and what were delicately referred to as a woman's "conjugal responsibilities." Stowe, and the leaders of the women's movement, commented openly in the popular literary magazines of the day on the division of America into private and public spheres, with women inhabiting the former and men the latter, spheres that allowed for a virtual segregation of the sexes. The end of slavery assured a torrent of articles by and about women's rights. In *Hearth and Home*, one of the most popular family magazines of the era, Stowe wrote: "This question of Woman and her Sphere is now, perhaps, the greatest of the age. We have put Slavery under foot, and with the downfall of Slavery the only obstacle to the success of our great democratic experiment is overthrown, and there seems no limit to the splendid possibilities which it may open before the human race." In publishing "The True Story of Lady Byron's Life," Stowe was purposely attempting to destroy the barrier between private and public spheres by engaging in the most revolutionary act possible: making the private public. One of Stowe's biographers, Joan Hedrick, calls her article on lady Byron the *Uncle Tom's Cabin* of woman's sexual slavery.

Fannie Chamberlain's life evinced the very sexual segregation that Stowe was attempting to bare. Although it was, in part, her own choice not to accompany Joshua Chamberlain when he went to Augusta to pursue his public career, Fannie remained in charge of the endless work of raising children and meeting the requirements of maintaining a household, responsibilities that her husband had apparently little difficulty in abandoning. Worse yet, Chamberlain was less concerned with her unhappiness than he was that she might make her dissatisfaction public. The attacks on Stowe abated, just as the terrible confrontations between Chamberlain and Fannie finally ceased with the apparently mutual agreement to live separate lives. The women's rights movement, invigorated by "The True Story of Lady Byron's Life," could not be stopped, however. Now that the abolitionist movement had succeeded in freeing the slaves, women believed it was their turn. Stowe had made this point explicitly in her introduction to her article on Lady Byron: "You will see that the position of a married woman [Lady Byron] under English common law, is, in many respects, precisely similar to that of the negro slave. The common law, while it allows to a husband the free privilege of living apart from his wife, if he does not choose to be with her, allows to the wife neither privacy nor retreat from her husband if he proves disagreeable to her."

The fact that the North was taken up with such controversies, only three years after Appomattox, shows the degree to which it had recovered from the war. Unfortunately, the same was not true of the South, where the Reconstruction struggle had not abated. In Alabama, the old Democratic Party was about to gain the power it had ceded after Appomattox.

◦▬◆▬◦

In spite of its defeat at the polls, Alabama's constitution was eventually accepted by the U.S. Congress and in July 1868 the state was readmitted to the Union. As a result of the state's readmission, the hardline anti-Reconstruction Conservative Party now reverted to its original form—as the Democratic Party—and turned its attention to rebuilding the state, regaining its prewar political power, and reversing the gains the freedmen had made since the end of the war. Like almost all southern Democrats of that era, Alabama's Democratic Party leaders believed that if they could turn back the clock on the gains of the freedmen, or at least disenfranchise the "black Republicans" in their midst, they could build a social system based on the separation of the races. It was toward this end that they worked diligently during the first half decade of the 1870s.

The pro-Republican and radical state administrations in Montgomery had focused their efforts on fighting the growing threat to their rule in central and western Alabama, where open warfare with white supremacists and unreconstructed Democrats was an almost daily occurrence. That was not the case in Henry County, where the people led lives circumscribed by the harsh routines of planting and harvesting. The fact of segregation had already come to Henry County, where the hardscrabble economy, the sparse population, and the minority black population living in the midst of poor white agricultural communities made improvement in the political and economic status of the freedmen almost impossible. For the next four generations, Alabama's wiregrass farmers were consumed with the struggle of pulling a living from the land, while their political leaders attempted to build an industrial infrastructure that would make their lives easier.

In the opinion of men like William Oates, steeled by the experience of war and hardened by their hatred of men they viewed as northern interlopers, the only way to lead Alabama to economic recovery was to regain political power. This meant not simply defeating the Republicans at the polls, it meant taking away the black vote—the Republicans' base of support. Oates spent much of the 1870s attempting to do just that. After rebuilding his law practice in Abbeville, he worked to make sure the Democratic Party regained its ascendancy in Henry County; it was a job that he found comparatively easy. As with Chamberlain in Maine, Oates's veteran contacts were a base of steady political support. Using this network, and the friendships he had gained through years of service to Pugh, Bullock, Buford, Gill Shorter, and others of the Eufaula Regency, Oates was named as a delegate to the Democratic national convention in New York in 1868, where he became widely known and respected among Democratic Party figures, including former Union General Winfield Scott Hancock.

By 1868, the "one-armed hero of Henry County"—as his supporters dubbed him in a series of political rallies—was known to every party loyalist and voter. Oates transferred the methods that his mentor in the Eufaula Regency, James Lawrence Pugh, used in Barbour County to Abbeville, where, from the beginning of the 1870s on, few candidates for any office could be elected without Oates's approval. He was single-minded in supporting the state Democratic machine and pushed his own party organization in Henry County to make certain that every polling place and ballot box was monitored. His methods and vigilance on behalf of the party became a standard that was used throughout the state. "In those dark days of reconstruction, when but little hope was left for the true patriot, he was vigilant and bold, upholding the Democratic flag in the thickest of the storm," the *Mobile Advertiser* later crooned. "Alabama should be proud of such men as Oates. Without the advantages of a finished education, and beginning life in poverty, he has carved his way with his good left arm, the only one left him by the fortunes of battle, to a proud position at the bar and a foremost place in the esteem of the people of East Alabama."

In 1870, Oates was elected to the state legislature, which was still dominated by Republicans. That year also marked the first time since the end of the war that a Democrat won the race for governor. The results of the voting show that Alabama reverted to its prewar political traditions, with Democrats carrying southern and northern Alabama, where white voters left the Republican fold in droves when the party candidate ran with a black candidate for secretary of state. The Republicans carried the former Whig counties of central Alabama. The Democratic candidate, Robert Burns Lindsay, called himself a "white man's candidate." When the ballots were counted, Lindsay had won by less than 2,000 votes, but only a thin sliver of thirteen counties remained Republican and the Democrats seemed on the verge of recapturing their hold on the state government.

But the radical Republicans refused to concede the election and for a brief time two governors served in Montgomery—one, a Republican, supported by the radical-dominated state Senate, and the other, a Democrat, supported by the Democrat-controlled state House. The Alabama Supreme Court, a radical stronghold, ordered the House not to recount the votes, fearing a Democratic victory. The political crisis nearly led to violence, as the state Senate called in the militia to support Republican claims. But the state Democratic-controlled House refused to give in. After three weeks of political tension and paralysis, when the state seemed on the verge of an internal civil war, a federal circuit court ordered Lindsay to take office.

Oates served in the state legislature as a member of the House Ways and Means Committee. His committee assignment was the most challenging job he had yet had, especially in light of the state's financial situation. In 1868, 1869, and 1870, successive Republican administrations had attempted to boost their popularity by raising state property taxes. Their intent was not only to raise badly needed funds for railroad and educational investment, but also to put pressure on the state's remaining large landholders, who were particularly hard hit by the new levies. The owners of large plantations, which were now being worked by paid black laborers, were forced to declare bankruptcy. The land holdings were then split up and sold off, or turned over to new tenants, many of whom were small white landowners or freed slaves. As a result of the Republican tax policy, Oates's service on the House Ways and Means Committee was filled with frustration. There was simply no way for the committee to balance the state's books, raise needed revenue, or, given Republican control of the state Senate, ease the tax burden on Alabama's largest white landholders.

Oates remained in Montgomery for only a single term, after which he was forced to return to Abbeville after losing his seat to a resurgent Republican. For the first and the last time in his career, his own Henry County political machine failed him. He was not alone. The year 1872 marked the final Republican statewide resurgence, which was based on the state's depressed economy and disgust that Lindsay had failed to pass any substantive economic measures. Lindsay's poor showing was also the major reason Oates was forced out of the legislature, for try as he might, Henry County's most prominent war hero simply could not overcome the economic fears of his own constituency.

Oates might well have been somewhat philosophical about his 1872 defeat. He knew that Democrats would return to office in time, and his name was continually mentioned for statewide posts. He was put forward in both 1870 and in 1872 for governor at the Democratic state party convention, and he was mentioned often as a congressional candidate and even a possible contender for the U.S. Senate. Like Chamberlain, he coveted a Senate seat, believing it to be the highest office he, or anyone from Alabama, could ever attain. But his failure to hold his House seat in the Alabama legislature in 1872 was ironically well timed. He was now saddled with extra responsibilities: his father had died after a long illness in 1871, and he had returned to Oates's Crossroads to close up the family home and move his mother into his own house in Abbeville, where they joined the family being raised by his sister Mary Long.

Oates's absence from state politics was only temporary, however, and in 1875, at the end of Reconstruction, the forces of the Republican administration were finally defeated in Alabama for good. Oates was brought back to Montgomery as a prominent member of a new constitutional convention, called to sweep away the vestiges of the northern occupation. He was not only a strong believer in segregation and intent to institutionalize it as part of Alabama law, he harbored a deep bitterness against scalawags, whom he viewed as traitors to the southern cause. He rejoiced in the fact that ten years after the war, the southern Democratic Party was once again triumphant throughout the old Confederacy.

The official end of Reconstruction came with the election of Rutherford B. Hayes in 1876, in one of the most dramatic elections in the nation's history. The Republican Hayes was a strong candidate, with a stellar war record, but he was challenged by Samuel Tilden, who had won his reputation as the Democratic reform governor of New York. In the general election, Tilden won an apparent victory, outpolling Hayes by 300,000 votes. But there were disputed returns from Louisiana, South Carolina, Florida, and Oregon; the twenty electoral votes of these states could tip the balance toward Hayes. Because the Constitution did not establish a means of resolving disputed vote counts, the election was thrown into the House of Representatives. The House created a special commission to resolve the dispute, and in January 1877 they announced their decision, awarding each of the disputed electoral votes to Hayes. The decision made him president.

In fact, the commission's decision was the result of a series of complex political maneuvers between Democrats and Republicans. During a meeting at a Washington hotel, southern Democratic Party leaders agreed to award Hayes all of the disputed electoral votes in exchange for a withdrawal of federal troops from Louisiana, South Carolina, and Florida—the only southern states where they still remained. In addition, southern leaders received Republican promises that the Democratic Party would now control federal patronage jobs in the South and federal aid for new internal improvements in their region.

The harshest terms of Reconstruction had been slowly ending over a number of years—in Alabama, its end actually began as early as 1868, when the Democratic Party won a number of state legislative seats despite Republican control of black votes. But the fact that federal troops continued to occupy three states of the old Confederacy rankled Democratic Party leaders, despite the gains they had made. The agreement over the Hayes election finally ended their region's political stigmatization and allowed the Democratic Party to regain the power it had wielded prior to the election of Lincoln. The withdrawal of the last federal troops in the South brought an official end to the Reconstruction era and was celebrated throughout the region. In the North, on the other hand, critics castigated the Republican leadership (calling Hayes "His Fraudulency") for placing electoral politics above political principles. Hayes's election, they argued, was a setback to all that had been won by Lee's surrender at Appomattox. Not only did the Hayes deal allow former rebels to resume their place at the head of southern state governments, it was a betrayal of the freedman.

Joshua Chamberlain disagreed. He did not like the fact that "negroes" were being abused, he said in a speech in Boston in the immediate aftermath of the Hayes election, but their lot was not unlike that of any other minority. "We must do the best we can for the negroes," he said, but then wondered whether all the bloodshed during the Civil War had really been sacrificed so that "negroes might have no one to stop them in going to the polls." He made it clear that he disagreed with federal interference in any state matter and warned his listeners that they, like the men of the South, might also one day be subject to federal rule. "Look to it, men of New England," he said, "or you may bitterly rue the day. Some other issue may arise and we be the ones who want our rights rejected." Besides, America was a free country, free for all of its citizens, but "first [for] the men who made it so, then those who are cast upon it." He then turned his attention to the violence and charges of corruption that had marred a number of southern elections and were the subject of much attention in the North:

> Yes, I say it. The men who made a country what it is, given it character and built their very lives into its history are to have the foremost hand if we would keep the country true to its

mission, true to its ideal. The voting business in the South will
regulate itself. As for the presence of rebel Generals in Congress, you yourself took back the States which they represent,
and besides they have sworn to support the Constitution and
laws of the United States.

Chamberlain's biographers have cited these words as evidence of
the "kinship" he felt with the southerners he had fought. The South
had overturned Appomattox, it was believed, and fought the dream
of equal rights at every turn. Certainly that was true of Oates—who
worked diligently for the separation of white and black in every aspect
of southern life. But if Appomattox was betrayed, many northerners
took a hand in it simply by looking aside. Chamberlain was one of
them.

# 15

## *God's Ways Seen by Men*

WILLIAM OATES and his fellow commanders in the Confederate armies believed that, while they had been defeated, their cause was just. They had an abiding faith that the South would rise to its former glory and that its institutions would take on the same characteristics they had had on the eve of Fort Sumter. Slavery was gone, swept away forever, but that did not mean the unique character of the old Confederacy need also die. "I am one of those who do not believe the cause is lost," Oates wrote E. P. Alexander, the Army of Northern Virginia's artillery commander, not long after the war. "I believe that it is only stifled by force & will again be revived & ultimately triumph." Even during the darkest days of Reconstruction, southern leaders believed that if they could remain united, they would emerge as the leaders of a rejuvenated South that would one day wield the kind of political influence that it had during the three decades prior to the Civil War. But some few officers in the former southern armies disagreed, not only counseling moderation and patience, but even aiding the Reconstruction authorities. One of these was James Longstreet, William Oates's corps commander in the Army of Northern Virginia. Longstreet's "betrayal" of the southern cause—and the southern response to his actions—helped to define how southerners viewed themselves after Appomattox and built the myth of the "Lost Cause" that remains part of the southern legacy.

Longstreet, who took up residence in New Orleans after Appomattox, was initially viewed as one of the South's future leaders. As such, he knew that his opinions would carry weight with his former soldiers.

In 1867, disturbed by the mounting violence that greeted the government's Reconstruction policies, he wrote a letter to the *New Orleans Times* urging his fellow southerners to "accept the terms that are now offered by the conquerors." If there be any lack of good faith, Longstreet added, "let it be upon others." Many of Longstreet's comrades who served with him in the Army of Northern Virginia agreed with his views. Robert E. Lee, the new president of Washington College in Virginia, had said virtually the same thing a number of times since the end of the war.

Several weeks later, Longstreet sat down to write a second letter expanding on the themes of the first. His gravest fear was that recrimination and hatred between the sections would be reignited and that a second Civil War would follow. He therefore urged cooperation with the Republican Reconstruction authorities, which would alleviate the growing sectional bitterness and dampen the worst effects of the South's military defeat. His views were well stated, moderate in tone, and intended to bring former enemies into a new era of reconciliation. This second letter gained wide circulation in the North after it was reprinted in the *New York Times*.

Even more than the continuation of sectional bitterness, Longstreet feared that without southern cooperation, the entire fabric of southern civilization would be undermined by Republican rule. He was especially alarmed by the prospect of a Republican alliance with southern blacks, a potent political combination that he believed would disenfranchise southern whites for a generation or more. Longstreet wrote a third letter on this subject. In it, he went beyond the cooperationist sentiments expressed in his first two letters and spoke bluntly about the South's racial problems—which he viewed as the core issue of the time. When Longstreet took this letter to his friends and business associates for their opinions, each of them pleaded that he keep his views to himself. John Bell Hood was the most outspoken: "They will crucify you."

Undeterred by this warning, Longstreet left New Orleans for Mississippi to visit his uncle, one of the South's leading authors and educators, Augustus Baldwin Longstreet. The senior Longstreet had raised his nephew as his son, providing a needed mentor for the younger man. After looking at the letter, he issued a blunt opinion, urging that the letter not be published. "It will ruin you, son, if you publish it," he said. But Longstreet returned to New Orleans and on June 8 his letter appeared in the local newspaper:

> It is all important we should exercise such influence over that vote, as to prevent its being injurious to us, & we can only do that as Republicans. As there is no principle or issue now that should keep us from the Republican party, it seems to me that our duty to ourselves & to all of our friends requires that our party . . . should seek an alliance with the Republican party. . . . If the whites won't do this, the thing will be done by the blacks, and we shall be set aside, if not expatriated. It then seems plain to me that we should do the work ourselves, & have it white instead of black & have our best men in public office.

The reaction to Longstreet's letter was immediate and furious. He was denounced as a traitor to his race, his section, and the Democratic Party. He was vilified. When Longstreet wrote to Lee seeking an endorsement of his views, even his old commander turned him aside. "I cannot think the course pursued by the dominant political party the best for the interests of the country," he answered Longstreet, "and therefore cannot say so, or give my approval." Lee, who died in 1870 at the age of sixty-three, was willing to agree with Longstreet that southerners should stoically accept their fate, but he was unwilling to go much further. Disappointed by this response, Longstreet weathered the cyclone of criticism in silence. Set on his course, Longstreet traveled to Washington in January 1869 to attend the inauguration of his old friend Ulysses S. Grant. Several days later, Grant named him surveyor of customs in New Orleans. Watching these events from afar, Harvey Hill, one of Longstreet's admirers, shook his head in wonder and wrote, "Our scalawag is the local leper of the community."

By 1870, Longstreet openly supported Republican Reconstruction policies, had made friends with New Orleans' most prominent Republicans, and supported the Radical Reconstruction governor of the state. He was named head of the New Orleans city militia as a reward for his pro-Republican stance. His earlier moderate views were now forgotten;

for many southerners it appeared that he had become one of the occupiers. While he attempted to defend himself from his accusers, saying that he was only attempting to moderate the harsh terms imposed on the South by the North, his pleas were ignored and he was socially and politically ostracized. Longstreet's apostasy became a focal point for southern views of the war, and his betrayal of southern nationalism made him a convenient target for those who were searching for reasons for why the South had lost the conflict.

On January 19, 1872, on the anniversary of Lee's birthday, Longstreet's old nemesis from the Army of Northern Virginia, Jubal Early, attacked the former First Corps commander, blaming him for the loss of the Battle of Gettysburg. Longstreet, he said, had failed to attack as ordered at sunrise on July 2. Had the attack been made at dawn as Lee intended, Early claimed, the South would have won a brilliant victory. One year later, Early's claim was buttressed in a paper delivered by William Pendleton, Lee's nominal artillery commander. Longstreet's failure "to assault at daylight was the cause of the loss of the battle," Pendleton said. The Early-Pendleton claim was taken up by others. Longstreet was vilified as being "stubborn" and "dilatory," and his failures as a commander were recalled, printed, emphasized, and talked about. By the mid-1870s, Longstreet's failure to obey Lee's orders on the morning of July 2, 1863, had become part of the southern historical canon. Early made "the sunrise attack order" the centerpiece of a series of lectures he gave throughout the old Confederacy, where his talk drew huge crowds and fueled endless comments.

There was only one problem in all of this, of course, and that was that Lee did not issue a "sunrise attack order" on July 2. No one has ever been able to find a record of such an order and the key participants in the battle, including important members of Lee's staff, said that he never issued one. Lee aide Charles Venable thought Pendleton's claim to knowledge of such an order ludicrous; Pendleton was simply not taken seriously by Lee and so was not in a position to know whether such an order was given. "I cannot but attribute his statement with regard to Gettysburg to an absolute loss of memory said to be brought on by frequent attacks resembling paralysis," Venable wrote. But it was Walter Taylor, another of Lee's aides, who identified the real issue in the Longstreet controversy: "I regard it as a great mistake on the part of those who, perhaps because of political differences, now undertake to criticize & attack your war record," he wrote to Longstreet.

But these defenses of Longstreet were lost in the public clamor for more information on Gettysburg, the sunrise attack order—and Longstreet's disagreements with Lee. Early and Pendleton responded by using the Southern Historical Society, which they had established to air issues on war, as a forum for Longstreet's enemies. The society's immensely popular magazine the *Southern Historical Society Papers* became the primary means of weeding out the South's political apostates and institutionalizing what came to be known as the myth of the "Lost Cause." The liturgy of the Lost Cause was known to all loyal southern soldiers, and never needed to be stated explicitly: that the South's cause was just, had nothing to do with slavery, that the southern armies had never been defeated but were simply overwhelmed by sheer numbers, that southern men were brave and true crusaders, that Robert E. Lee could make no mistakes—and that if it had not been for James Longstreet's disobedience of Lee's sunrise attack order on July 2, the South would have won the Battle of Gettysburg and, with it, the Civil War.

Within two short years of Early's first mention of a sunrise attack order, Longstreet's failure at Gettysburg was accepted as a fact by a vast majority of southern people. It remains a central and accepted pillar of the southern understanding of the war to this day. In the 1870s, however, the specious claim became so popular, support for it so widespread, and the anti-Longstreet cabal so strong that even those former commanders of the Army of Northern Virginia who had no direct knowledge of the events of July 2 entered the fray. In many ways, political legitimacy was measured by a soldier's willingness to accept Early's claim about the sunrise attack order as fact—even among those who knew it was not true. So it was that former General John Gordon, the post-Reconstruction governor of Georgia and leader of the state Ku Klux Klan, could claim that Lee died believing the Longstreet was responsible for the defeat at Gettysburg.

⚬══✦══⚬

Many of Lee's former aides were initially stunned by the claim against Longstreet, but they were loath to defend a scalawag. One notable voice in defense of the former First Corps commanders was that of Lafayette McLaws, who believed that Early's and Pendleton's allegation amounted to a slur on Lee's character; the army commander, McLaws wrote, never would have issued such an order and, if he had, would have seen it carried out. Lee was many things, but sloppy was not one of them—he certainly had tighter control of his army than Longstreet's critics believed. But McLaws was just one among a handful of voices. Longstreet himself took much longer to reply. In 1877, he shattered Early's claim in a series of articles published in *Century* magazine and in the *Philadelphia Weekly Times*. Unfortunately, in defending himself, Longstreet characterized Lee's plan of attack at Gettysburg as strategically unsound. Lee was too audacious at Gettysburg and adopted a plan of attack at variance with the one he said he would follow before the invasion. Lee, Longstreet implied, had led the army into its stumbling defeat.

Early and his followers struck back by soliciting comments on Longstreet's actions at Gettysburg and publishing them as misleading excerpts in the *Southern Historical Society Papers*. After Longstreet's ill-fated attempt to defend himself by deflecting attention to Lee's deficiencies, Early knew that few southern soldiers would refuse to criticize Louisiana's most notorious Republican. When the call went out for papers, some of the leading Confederate military figures responded with vitriolic condemnations of Longstreet's military abilities. One of those solicited for comment was William Oates, who decided that he would ally himself with Early and his followers as a chief Longstreet critic. His article appeared in the October 1878 issue of the *Southern Historical Society Papers*.

Oates's condemnation of Longstreet was not a surprise to Early or his followers. They knew that the former Alabama colonel did not like Longstreet, thought him conceited and stubborn, and resented the fact that he had promoted Micah Jenkins over Evander Law, an Oates favorite, at Knoxville. But given this background, Oates's attack on Longstreet was not nearly as scathing as it might have been—or as Early would have expected. While Oates blamed Longstreet for his failure to move quickly, for arguing with Lee about the battle, and for not paying the obeisance necessary to Lee's sacred memory, he refused to issue the obligatory and, by now, standard anti-Longstreet diatribe.

In a remarkable passage in his article, Oates implicitly endorsed one of Longstreet's complaints about Lee's plan of battle: "It may have been best," he conceded, "for Lee to have flanked Meade out of his strong position and have forced him to attack and thus to have acted on the defensive." It is hard to miss Oates's implication that that is precisely the strategy Longstreet himself had recommended. To compound this sin, Oates delicately offered that Lee might have been mistaken (though he would never use that precise word) in ordering Pickett to attack on the afternoon of July 3. "Lee, with all his robust daring and adventurous spirit," Oates wrote, "should not have ordered the impossible, as was apparent to a skilled observer." Which was Oates's backhanded way of giving voice to his own views about Lee's headlong style of battle: that Lee too often did order the impossible. As for the identity of Oates's "skilled observer," the former Alabama colonel was silent—though it is possible he was thinking of Longstreet; it was Longstreet, after all, who suggested to Lee that a charge over nearly one mile of open ground against an entrenched enemy could not and would not succeed. But the most remarkable aspect of the article was not that Oates put such views on paper, but rather that Early and his editors would actually allow them to find their way into print.

Unlike the other disputes of the postwar period, including the debate over whether Warren should have been dismissed by Sheridan, the Longstreet controversy has continued well into the twentieth century. For three generations and more—until the centennial anniversary of the war in 1960—Lee's sunrise attack order remained an unquestioned pillar of southern faith. But the importance of the Longstreet controversy has less to do with Gettysburg than with the rewriting of the war's history by southerners that was necessary given the Confederacy's belief that God had blessed their cause.

The belief in God's will as the arbiter of men's actions was central to the southern cause. That was especially true when the South was winning; not since Adam was created in the Garden of Eden "did a holier cause engage the hearts of the nation. Is not the hand of God in all this?" one writer had asked during the war. Nor, at first, had defeat undermined this faith. Even after Gettysburg, Lee had cited a beneficent Providence as the architect of events: "We do not know what is best for us. I believe a kind God has ordered all things for our good."

This was precisely the point. After 1872, southern writers took up Lee's theme, arguing that a beneficent Providence dictated the South's travails in order to assure its salvation.

But devout southern soldiers, strengthened both by battle and by the evangelical movement that had swept through their armies, could not accept that God would actually order their *defeat*. It was the fact of the southern defeat, even more than the ruined railroads and burned cities, that so deeply affected the southern people and that led them in a search for real or imagined scapegoats and generations of lynchings, cross burnings, mob violence, public whippings, and character assassinations. But the southern defeat also led to the abandonment of the southern faith in Lee's assurance that God authored the flow of history. After 1870, Calvinism collapsed in the South, and southerners flocked to evangelical and Pentecostal churches in a search for personal salvation in a movement as important as any of the nation's great awakenings.

A hard core of Calvinist believers remained, however, marrying their conception of the Lost Cause with their certainty in God's plan. Many southern officers insisted that they could see in the South's defeat a sure sign of His blessing, and in so doing they also canonized Robert E. Lee. Virginian John Daniel was the first to note Lee's Christlike qualities in a speech he gave in 1870, but many other southern ministers and historians followed his lead. Appomattox, they said, was Lee's "Gethsemane," where, like Christ, he prayed on the way to his crucifixion. They imagined the suffering Lee—"What he suffered his lips have never spoken"—attempting to put aside the bitter cup and then rising in expectation of meeting Grant to surrender his army. Lee mounted Traveller and then set out to face "the Cross of Calvary beyond." He entered the McLean family parlor, Golgotha, to meet Grant.

There is more than mere literary allusion in this view. Many southerners of the nineteenth century—indeed, many Americans from all regions—were so imbued with the symbolism of their religion that everyday events took on an otherworldly cast. Viewed from the jaded perspective of the twentieth century, these religious musings appear almost naive, but they were very real to those Americans who survived the nation's bloodiest conflict. The search for a reason for mass death, for an explanation for the piles of young men laid to rot among the country's most beautiful fields, was constant and necessary. Americans imbued their war with meaning, and southerners their defeat with a larger purpose. Within one year of Lee's surrender, Fanny Downing's "The Land We Love" was one of the most widely read poems in the South:

> Man did not conquer her, but God
> For some wise purpose of his own
> Withdrew his arm; she, left alone,
> Sank down resistless neath his rod
>
> God chastens most who he loves best,
> And scourges whom he will receive.
> The land we love may cease to grieve,
> And on his gracious promise rest! . . .
>
> Though howling waves around thee toss,
> Rest calm in thine exalted strength,
> Sublime though ruined, till at length,
> The crown of heaven replace thy cross!

The only problem with the notion of Lee as Jesus, carrying the cross of the South, was the fact that Lee led his army into the maelstrom at Gettysburg. But even that was now taken care of. It is now part of the myth of the Lost Cause that not only was Lee not responsible for the defeat at Gettysburg, he would have assuredly won the battle—if only he had not betrayed by the South's Judas, James Longstreet.

❦

After finishing his fourth and last term as Maine's governor in 1870, Joshua Chamberlain returned to his wife and family in Brunswick. While he was temporarily without a job, he still hoped that the Republican Party would one day nominate him for the U.S. Senate. But with his old nemesis, Maine Senator James G. Blaine, now firmly in control of the state party apparatus, Chamberlain knew his chances for higher political office were dim. So when Bowdoin College President Samuel Harris resigned his post to pursue a professorship at Yale, Chamberlain was in a perfect position to assume the job. The Bowdoin Board of Directors knew Chamberlain was their best candidate: he had not only served on the Bowdoin Board of Trustees since 1867, he had a national reputation, which would help the college raise money. Chamberlain was energized by the opportunity and, after taking the position in time for the 1871 school year, immediately set about instituting a series of educational reforms that he had been thinking about for more than twenty years—ever since the day he had been offered his first teaching post at the school. While Bowdoin had maintained a reputation for offering New England's young men a classical education and was considered one of the region's leading private colleges, Chamberlain feared that the nineteenth century, with its emerging focus on science, would pass the college by. With the approval of the board, Chamberlain added a badly needed science curriculum to the college's offerings. Bowdoin's graduates were skeptical of such innovations, Chamberlain knew, so he moved to allay their concerns.

"I do not fear these men of science," he explained during his inaugural address as president of the college, "for after all they are following in God's ways, and whether they see Him now or not, these lines will surely lead to Him at the end. Sooner or later, if not now, they will see and confess that these laws along whose line they are following, are not forces, are not principles. They are only methods." Chamberlain was being somewhat disingenuous—he knew full well that men of science were pursuing their discipline not because it accorded with their view of God, as he implied, but because the physical evidence dictated their course. "I would say that Laws are God's ways seen by men, while Principles are God's thoughts to himself," Chamberlain said. The new age dictated new thinking, Chamberlain believed, and "we must understand it, if we can."

Chamberlain's words marked a significant change in his own thinking and set him apart from many of the college's leaders and alumni, who were schooled in the Calvinist tradition. His avowal that "laws are God's way seen by men" reflected an intellectual leap for a person who, in nearly everything he wrote, believed it quite possible that God intervened to reward and punish. In many respects, he was moving toward Oates's conception of the universe, as a mechanism of nature that was perfect in its movements. But Chamberlain's attempt to broaden the college curriculum was also a purely pragmatic decision on his part; Bowdoin had always had difficulty making ends meet, and his first year as president was no different. His predecessor had been an indifferent fund-raiser and Chamberlain and the Bowdoin board, faced with a significant financial shortfall, needed to broaden the college's financial base.

There were other reforms that Chamberlain wanted to institute as Bowdoin's president. He considered allowing women to enroll as students, for example, and explained his views using the same reasoning he had applied to broadening the curriculum. Women were in need of a higher education, he said, so as to allow them to "rise to the harmonies of spiritual science." God's plan included woman because "she is the heaven appointed teacher of man, his guide, his better soul. By her own right, however, she inherits here, not as the sister of man, but as the daughter of God." While Chamberlain made certain Bowdoin's all-male character did not change, he also made it clear that he had different, more progressive views than his predecessors.

In spite of his new views on education, Chamberlain remained a man married to the concepts of duty and honor and was dedicated to making certain they were impressed on the young men of Bowdoin. He also remain convinced that America was a part of a greater plan and that the Civil War was only the first in a series of conflicts in which American men would become involved. The nation, he said, had "new interests to guard and keep." It was for this reason that, during the 1872 school year, he decided to institute compulsory student drill led by an official instructor of military sciences. The student body was formed into four drill companies and required to purchase West Point–style uniforms. The state also lent Bowdoin four cannon for artillery drill.

Significantly, the same Bowdoin alumni who had grumbled about the introduction of new science courses now calmly accepted Chamberlain's ideas on the need for military discipline. But after the first year, when the newness of the drill began to wear off, the idea of marching and saluting between, before, and following classes—and during special events—began to wear thin. With the exception of six lone students, everyone in the student body decided to petition the board to order an end to the drilling. The major complaint was economic—none of the students believed that a compulsory exercise should result in an extra uniform fee—while others complained that the drilling took time from their studies. When the board decided to ignore the student complaint, the students organized a protest. In the spring of 1874, large numbers of students began to boycott the mandatory drill sessions, and those who attended shouted profanities at the drill instructor.

In an attempt to bring the protests under control, Chamberlain suspended a number of students. The students were not intimidated by this, however, and on one spring day in 1874 the entire junior class voted to boycott the drill sessions. Graffiti protesting the drills and Chamberlain's actions followed; soon a full-scale "drill rebellion" was under way. Many of the students' parents sided with their sons and put pressure on Chamberlain to reverse his disciplinary strictures and return the college to its more fundamental educational goals. But Chamberlain would not back down, and with the "drill rebellion" in full stride he suspended the entire freshman, sophomore, and junior classes for ten days and vowed that every student would be barred from Bowdoin unless they signed a pledge to end the rebellion. They refused.

Only a few members of the faculty supported Chamberlain's position. Many people criticized him for being strident, priggish, and dictatorial. Chamberlain responded by arguing that the drill requirement was nothing compared to what he had had in the army, which brought rumblings that the college president was too busy reliving his past to pass judgment on a new generation of students. Chamberlain grew prickly, noting the importance of military instruction to the building of character and laying down his own view that the breech of discipline in the drill rebellion was akin to the highest sort of dishonor. This did not go down well with parents who believed that Bowdoin should stick to teaching the classics, leaving the sermonizing for the pulpit. The drill rebellion gained widespread attention in northern newspapers, where Chamberlain's actions were castigated as being out of step with the postwar society.

The Bowdoin board supported Chamberlain in public, but in private there were growing doubts that his position was giving the college the kind of attention it needed. The board was taken by surprise by the depth of feeling among the students and general public. The college had never had such controversy before and did not want it now. Many board members were fearful that Chamberlain's stubbornness was costing Bowdoin its hard-won reputation. Eventually, several Maine newspapers picked up these doubts and used the rebellion to criticize Chamberlain for a number of his decisions while governor: "The same sickly longing for the exercise of autocratic power that once sent a thrill of disgust and horror through the State by needlessly and obstinately insisting on legal homicide which was demanded neither by the laws nor by public sentiment, has made the halls of Bowdoin tenantless."

When it became clear that none of the suspended students from any of the three classes would return to the school under the conditions dictated by Chamberlain, the Bowdoin board intervened, informing Chamberlain that from now on the drill would not be required and that every student who had been suspended, except the worst offenders, would be allowed to return to classes. Chamberlain could hardly have missed the pointed criticism issued by the board in its final report on the incident: "The President of the college must deal both with Faculty and Students face to face with unswerving directness of statement, and in the manner of doing the duties of his station, because they are duties and not because his station is superior."

Chamberlain considered resigning his post as president, but to leave Bowdoin in the immediate aftermath of the drill rebellion seemed to him to be an admission of defeat. So while he proposed leaving the college in a letter to the board, they asked him to remain in his post; they could not spare him. Chamberlain had proved to be a talented fund-raiser and his name continued to bring notoriety to Bowdoin despite its troubles. Chamberlain was complimented by the board's request and candidly admitted that he had overreacted to the student rebellion. "Some difficulties I have met with were unexpected," he confessed to the Bowdoin board, "and, I think, unnecessary, and some doubtless the result of my own too sanguine and self-reliant spirit. However that may be I am willing to leave to time the justification not only of what I have done, but of what I have attempted and not been able to carry through." Chamberlain remained president of Bowdoin throughout the 1870s, but he focused his attention on raising money for the school and left the college's student policies in the hands of others.

In 1878, at the age of fifty, Joshua Chamberlain could look back on a life of accomplishment. He was a renowned soldier, scholar, politician, and college president; these were successes he could hardly have dreamed of as a stuttering boy growing up in Brewer. While there were moments of crisis in his life—the near-breakup of his marriage, the controversies of his governorship, the drill rebellion at Bowdoin—there were a number of triumphs that reminded Chamberlain of the accolades he received as the "Hero of Little Round Top." Perhaps the most surprising came within a year of his being named Bowdoin's president, in 1872, when he had been mentioned as a possible running mate for newspaper publisher Horace Greeley, who was leading a breakaway group of Republicans disenchanted with Grant's presidency. When Grant won the Republican nomination despite this opposition, the Democratic Party turned to Greeley as their candidate. Chamberlain had been named as a possible vice presidential nominee. Eventually, Greeley named a Cincinnati businessman with firm Democratic Party credentials to the second spot, but it was clear that Chamberlain would have helped the Democratic ticket. His prestige as a great soldier would have brought distinction, votes, and the patina of Republican respectability to Greeley's candidacy.

It is unlikely that Chamberlain ever would have seriously considered being Greeley's running mate, and reports that he was on a "short list" of possibilities were probably no more than rumors. A report that the two men had actually met, and that Greeley offered Chamberlain the job, is suspect: the Democratic Party convention was held in Cincinnati and Chamberlain was nowhere nearby. Most important, it seems highly unlikely that Chamberlain would have associated himself with the meteoric but unstable publisher and reporter—who praised Lincoln, then opposed him; rabidly supported Lincoln's war policy, then put himself forward as a peacemaker; and finally even announced that he would put up the money for Jefferson Davis's bail when the rebel president was arrested following Appomattox.

That Chamberlain's name was even mentioned with Greeley's must have been an embarrassment for the former Maine governor, who prided himself on his friendships with Republican loyalists. Despite their political differences, Chamberlain continued to maintain a cordial relationship with Grant, and it is unlikely that he would have considered running against his old commander. Nor could Chamberlain have rejected the loyalty shown him by Republican leaders during his time as governor, when his views on the freedmen, his support of Fessenden, and his criticism of radical Republicans ran counter to the party's policies. From Chamberlain's point of view it is just as well that he did not take the rumors seriously, for Greeley lost the election in a landslide.

Other honors had come to Chamberlain during his years as Bowdoin's president, a position he remained in throughout the 1870s. In 1876, he had delivered a much publicized oration on Maine at the nation's centennial celebration in Philadelphia, extolling Maine's virtues and advocating—as he had done as governor—the state's attractions for new businesses. In 1878, he had served as U.S. commissioner for education at the Paris Universal Exposition, an appointment he had received from President Hayes. After five months in Europe, he had returned to the United States and presented a report on his trip to the U.S. Congress, advocating that the country adopt a number of European educational innovations.

At the age of fifty, Joshua Chamberlain could also be proud of the family he had raised. While it is unlikely that the tensions in his marriage had dissipated, the agreement he and Fannie had come to during his time as governor had saved their relationship. While Fannie had not accompanied him on his trips to Philadelphia or Paris, she seemed to take some enjoyment from her place as the wife of a college president and had remained the proper hostess for his many dinners. One of Chamberlain's proudest accomplishments was the enrollment of his son Wyllys at Bowdoin in 1877—an appointment made on the basis of scholarly achievements. Chamberlain's daughter Grace entered her teenage years as her father's favorite and the two became very close. The Chamberlain children were able students and well disciplined, and had an awe of the famous men and women who visited their home. There was only one disappointment. By the end of the 1870s, it was clear Chamberlain would not be named as the Republican nominee for a seat in the U.S. Senate, and the more time passed, the more his name faded from public view.

By 1880, Joshua Chamberlain's public career was over, but William Oates's was just beginning. That year, Oates ran for Congress as a Democrat from Alabama's Third Congressional District and won the seat handily. The overwhelming victory was not merely a sign of his growing popularity, but evidence that the Alabama Democratic Party had regained its monopoly on power. By this time, the last remnants of the Alabama Republican Party were fighting for survival and the real elections for state legislators, governor, Congress, and even the U.S. Senate were held in Democratic Party caucuses or at the party's state convention. Oates was the first to admit, in public, that the Democrats prevailed in Alabama through the crudest of electoral means—often by stuffing ballot boxes. The party machine was at its most powerful in southeastern Alabama, where Oates held sway. Years later, he criticized these corrupt practices as unjust, though only because they were no longer needed. "When ballot box stuffing first began," he said, "I approved it as a necessity. But it has survived its usefulness. It is a horrible example of dishonesty to set before the young men of the State."

By 1880, underhanded political methods were no longer needed to ensure a Democratic victory—except in those cases where a talented Republican, a maverick party member, or third-party spoiler threatened the privileged rule of what Alabamians proudly called the "Bourbon restoration." The Bourbons—or old-line Democrats—took as their goal the governance of the state along the same political lines that were followed prior to the Civil War and took their name from the Bourbon king who followed Napoleon with the promise that he would restore the monarchy "as if the revolution had never happened." Oates claimed that he was not a part of Alabama's Bourbon establishment and resented the description, but he continued to have connections with some of its most prominent members, including the remnants of the Eufaula Regency.

In the years of the Bourbon restoration, when there were real troubles at the ballot box, Oates relied on "Barbour County Fever" to control recalcitrant Democrats and the odd Republican. This was the name given to a series of tactics endorsed by the Eufaula Regency that included forcing black Alabamians to "pledge" that they would always cast their ballot for a white man, publishing blacklists of black politicians, and loudly and publicly berating Republican candidates with crowds of well organized Democratic Party loyalists. The "fever" proved more effective than any other act of intimidation and quickly spread through the state. Republicans could do little to counter the campaign. One historian later described Barbour County Fever as "any process for making life miserable for white Radicals."

Even if they won an election without depending on these corrupt practices, southern Democrats were often greeted skeptically in Washington. From his first day in Congress, Oates had to defend himself against charges that his election was the result of underhanded white-supremacist methods. He resented the charge and later drafted a speech he wanted to give in the House defending his state. Oates wrote out his remarks in longhand with great care, making numerous corrections and deletions. He spent hours on the text, intending it to be both a personal political testament and a true picture of white-black relations in Alabama. While Oates eventually decided that he should not give the speech, it remains an unapologetic and startlingly honest assessment of how southerners viewed the Deep South's political process:

> Northern men do not understand the Negro question at all. They can't see how it is possible that a Democrat can be elected to Congress in a district where there is a majority of colored population except by intimidation or fraud. The *Chicago Inter-Ocean*, a Radical Republican newspaper, says that I am representing a Republican district elected apparently without opposition, but that it was in consequence of intimidation of Republican voters. It says, "the Alabama member admits that he owes his own seat to fraud." This is a malicious falsehood.
>
> The reasons for the reckless assertion are that in round numbers the census shows over 15,000 colored Republican in [my] district, and that so large a number would not abstain from voting if they had not been intimidated. . . . Every man who is familiar with elections in the South of late years knows that the votes of more than half of the Republican Negroes are on the market. The state, county, and municipal elections are notoriously so. They are for sale, and cheap at that. . . . I admit that once in our history cheating and miscounting were practiced in a good many localities, but that now is of rare occurrence. It is a thing of the past. There is no necessity for it except when campaign funds are exhausted. No force or intimidation is employed anywhere in the South. Colored Re-

publicans are frequently paid to stay at home and work on election day. But more frequently they stay away from choice or indifference. The whites do the same thing which accounts for the smallness of the vote polled.

Despite these protests, Oates and other southern Democrats knew that ballot box stuffing, intimidation of voters, and the strict enforcement of segregationist policies were the primary last-resort means for ensuring that the Democratic Party remain in office throughout the South. From the end of Reconstruction forward, for the next four generations, the Republican Party virtually disappeared from the southern political landscape while the most important political contests in the South were decided inside the Democratic Party, just as they had been before the election of Lincoln.

❦

True to his Democratic roots, as well as his constituents, Oates spent his earliest days in Washington fighting for southern rights, which included a repeal of the notorious "cotton tax," which had been placed on Alabama and other southern states during Reconstruction. The tax robbed Alabama of millions of dollars of much-needed capital at a time when agriculture and industry were destroyed. But the most important issue from Oates's point of view was the tax was levied as punishment for southern secession. Oates looked on it as a reparations payment; he believed if he could get the tax repealed and the funds returned, he could lift the onus for starting the war from southern shoulders. While Oates never succeeded in this (and never really expected to), the issue identified him with the southern cause and increased his popularity in his home state.

Returning to Alabama after his first two years in Washington, however, Oates realized that his future political success was going to be as dependent on his ability to fit in with the Washington social scene as it was on his own political talents. The simple truth, he realized, was that a bachelor rarely gained political influence in Washington. It was primarily for this reason that Oates married Sarah "Sallie" Toney, the daughter of the planter Washington Toney, on March 28, 1882. Oates had strong ties to the family, which had nursed him while he recovered in their home after being wounded during the war. It was then that he first saw his future bride. Sarah Toney was only twenty years old at the time of her marriage to Oates, having been born the same week that the then-colonel was listening to the guns of Antietam thundering across the Potomac.

His marriage to Sarah Toney was Oates's final step away from his father's crossroads farm. While little is known of the details of Oates's relationship with his wife, a legend sprang up about how "the one-armed hero of Henry County" was first introduced to her when she lay in her crib—and vowed then and there that she would one day be his wife. The story is obviously apocryphal, but it had great meaning among Alabama voters, who saw in such prophecies a confirmation of the talents of their leaders. Apparently there were also other suitors, but Sarah decided, while still a teenager, to marry her war hero and live with him in Washington. The ceremony was held at "historic Rose-land," the Toney home, and was attended only by close friends and members of both families.

The local Eufaula newspaper featured the marriage as a major news item, as did the *Montgomery Advertiser*, which praised the new congressman and repeated his legendary courtship of Sarah. "There were a number of daughters in the household and some of them of mar-riageable age, but it was the winsome babe of the family who won the heart of the wounded soldier." The stories were accompanied by short biographical notices of Oates as a lawyer who "stands in the front rank of the Alabama bar, proud, prudent and preemptory and at the same time tender hearted and courageous"—important qualities for a man who needed to make "a far more gallant and successful charge [for the hand of Sarah Toney] than he ever did upon the bloody fields of Vir-ginia." Everyone testified that Oates "made a good marriage," having captured the hand of a talented and beautiful woman, who was twenty-seven years younger than he at the time. The descriptions we have of Sarah are predictable, and meet all the stereotypes of the perfect south-ern matron:

> The charming bride is the pride of this community. Her liter-ary accomplishments have ripened into gems of poetry and won for her a wide circle of admirers. The distinguished poet

Galagher declared her birth-day carol to her mother one of the rarest gems he had seen. Her gifts as a scholar are not however, her chief attractions. Beauty, grace and loveliness are so bewitchingly blended in her person and character that one hesitates which to admire the most. May blessings strew their path through life.

Oates and his new bride left for Washington immediately after the wedding and within weeks of his arrival in the capital it was clear that the congressman from Alabama, then entering his second term, had made a very useful match. Sarah Toney provided the social graces that Oates needed to gain power and prestige in a city that valued personal friendships and judged a congressman's worth as much by his talents as a host as it did his as a legislator. His wife gave William Oates the legitimacy he needed to be respected and helped to draw him into the inner circles of the congressional club that he had not joined during his first term. Oates's constituents and his political allies in Alabama not only appreciated the patina of worldliness shown by Sarah, but compared it to the plebeian habits of unsophisticated northerners. Years later, the *Montgomery Advertiser* reviewed Sarah Oates's conquest of Washington:

> Her taste for entertaining was developed under the tutelage of the Toney traditions and the well known generosity of that family, has no parallel in the State. The social reminiscences of old Roseland are historical and the famous house parties given there within the past half hundred years, have been upon the scale of ante-bellum entertainment. Ladies played at cards, or hearts, as they chose, and gentlemen rode to hounds and servants prepared great feasts, which were as bountiful as those ever given at Violet Hill, Primrose Terrace, and other Alabama homes.

Oates's power grew in the House of Representatives, though not simply because of his marriage to the charming Sarah Toney. He was soon considered one of Washington's most accomplished constitutional lawyers and he gained recognition among his colleagues as an innovative legislator, the result of his mastery of House rules. He was one of the first southern Democrats to perfect the art of the filibuster; at one point he demanded that the House hear his protests on the cotton tax and, when they refused, tied up House approval of a tax measure by speaking for eight exhausting days and nights. He soon after launched a second filibuster, once again on his favorite subject the cotton tax, that lasted an entire week. In an era of waning federal power, Oates was an unapologetic conservative and helped to create the foundations of the states' rights doctrines that would be used to defend southern segregationist policies into the twentieth century.

The official record of Oates's years in Congress is sparse. The work of Congress in the late nineteenth century was not nearly as important to the nation as it is now, and many members spent their time in strict constituent services. America was also in the midst of a vast industrial revolution that would leave the Deep South, and Alabama, impoverished. Oates, and many other southerners, were deeply concerned that the South would be left behind in the rush for economic riches, but they were loath to abandon the region's traditional mistrust of outsiders, federal largesse, and social change. What Oates's official record of his years in Congress does note is what Alabamians considered his greatest achievements. They reflect the standard political beliefs of southern conservatism:

> He opposed the alien ownership of land, combated unrestricted immigration into the United States, urged the amending of the national bank laws, approved the liberal coinage of silver, spoke for the incorporation of the Nicaragua canal company, but objected to the United States' endorsement of the bonds of that or any other corporation; he opposed the experiment of the interstate commerce law, worked vigorously, although unsuccessfully for the return of the $68,000,000 cotton tax to the southern people, favored liberal appropriations for the improvement of natural waterways, but opposed appropriation for canals, was responsible for the non-enactment of the direct tax refunding bill . . . endorsed [President Grover] Cleveland's measures for congressional repeal of the silver purchasing clause of the Sherman silver law; he pressed the appointment of Hon. Hilary A. Herbert as secretary of the navy.

Oates served in Congress in what has been called the "era of the brigadier generals," when the leadership of the nation, and especially of its statehouses, was firmly in the hands of Union and Confederate veterans. The young men who fought the war had come of age, and it was nearly impossible for any political candidate to come into office without having served in the national armies. This was especially true in the South, where a host of former Confederate officers dominated the political landscape—so much so, in fact, that the list of postwar southern governors reads like a roll call of the leadership of the Army of Northern Virginia: rebel cavalry commander Wade Hampton served as two-term governor of South Carolina, General John Gordon as governor of Georgia, J. E. B. Stuart's right hand, Fitzhugh Lee (Robert E. Lee's nephew), was governor of Virginia, brigade commander Benjamin Humphreys was governor of Mississippi, Brigadier General Edward Perry was governor of Florida, and Brigadier General A. M. Scales was governor of North Carolina.

In the North, also, as a generation of young men reached their middle years, they were rewarded for their military service. Presidents Grant, James Garfield (who escorted William Rosecrans from the field at Chickamauga), and Rutherford B. Hayes could not have gained a national reputation without having served in the war. The same could be said of Winfield Scott Hancock, who ran for president in 1880 but lost. Unlike the South, however, the North tired of its heroes within twenty years of Appomattox and elected a new generation of leaders who had not served in the war, and by 1876 most of the North's great soldiers had already retired from public life. Nevertheless, some northern soldiers—whose most prominent political service was now behind them— were occasionally recalled to office or special duty to provide needed stability in times of turmoil or political crisis. This was true for Joshua Chamberlain in 1880, during a political controversy involving the Greenback Party.

c⬦⬥⬦ɔ

When the Union went to war in 1861, it helped to raise money for the effort by issuing non-interest-bearing government notes to serve as currency in the place of gold. The "greenbacks," so named because the backs of the notes were printed in green ink, were popular among laborers and farmers in the Midwest and South, where there was always opposition to a "hard money"—or gold or silver payment—economy. The federal government attempted to take the $450 million in bonds out of circulation at the end of the war, but the greenback currency remained popular with the people, and acceptance of greenbacks, or "soft money," in payment of debts continued.

The rise of the Greenback movement resulted from the tremendous expansion of the American economy, mass industrialization, and the refusal of the federal government to dampen the effects of a boom-and-bust economy. The rise of a class of professional financiers and the growing sophistication of a pervasive banking industry sparked suspicion among small landowners, independent entrepreneurs, and workers who traditionally mistrusted all speculation and what they called the "big money" interests and who found it increasingly difficult to keep up with the unpredicted surges in economic growth. The solution to this unpredictability, they felt, was the continued issuance of greenbacks, in addition to the acceptance of payment of debts in gold and silver, which would increase the money supply and provide a ready source of easily obtainable capital.

The Greenback political movement prospered in poor economic times because farmers and laborers had few resources to fall back on during a depression. As the economic picture brightened, the strength of the Greenback movement faded. The closing decades of the nineteenth century were so turbulent economically, with booms followed by deep economic panics, that they also became politically volatile. By the early 1870s, Democratic soft-money and Republican hard-money activists were engaged in a bitter political feud that was brought to a head by Congress's decision in 1873 to discontinue using silver as a means of payment. At first the decision seemed to favor the soft money or greenback advocates, but in time the price of silver fell so precipitously that small farmers and businessmen believed that Congress had conspired to make silver almost worthless—thereby constricting the money supply and driving down the prices on farm products. The "Crime of '73" convinced many rural Americans that big government backed by rich industrialists and New York financiers were in league to impoverish the people. People began to advocate the coinage of "free silver"—driving up its worth and making it more available to hard-pressed farmers.

The Greenback Party was formed in 1874 by a rising tide of rural discontent to redress the "Crime of '73." The party's platform called for the acceptance of debt repayment using gold and silver, and the issuance of greenbacks. The party gained strong early support among rural states like Maine, where easy money seemed to promise easy growth. The Greenbackers had so much strength in Maine, in fact, that in 1878 they supplanted the Democrats as the state's second most powerful party and succeeded in denying a majority to the Republican candidate for governor. As a result, the election was decided by the sitting Maine legislature, where enough Republicans, fearing the upstart Greenbackers, threw their support to the hard-money Democratic candidate, Alonzo Garcelon, an ally who had a better chance of winning than their own candidate. Garcelon became governor. In September 1879, the same thing seemed about to happen once again: this time, the Republican candidate, Daniel Davis, received 68,000 votes, the Greenbacker Joseph Smith received 47,000 votes, and the Democratic incumbent, Alonzo Garcelon, received almost 29,000 votes. With the Republicans in control of both houses of the Maine legislature, it appeared certain that the Republican, Davis, would be inaugurated as governor.

But in the election of 1879, a number of newspapers controlled by the Democrats accused their hard-money allies, the Republicans, of election corruption. Alonzo Garcelon—who finished third in the race—mounted a statewide political movement to call for a recount and an investigation. A commission was appointed and its report cited skewed returns in those districts where a number of Republicans had won because of bribery and fraud. In a new "count-out," the commission awarded the contested legislative seats to the Democratic candidates. The Republicans were enraged; it looked to them like the election was being stolen from them by the governor's commission and awarded to a party that, in the name of political expediency, had forgotten its hard-money principles. The state was thrown into a political crisis. The count-out gave the Democrats enough new power in the legislature that a combined Democrat-Greenback ("Fusionist") vote would put the

Greenbacker, Smith, in the governor's mansion. The pro-Davis Republicans responded by pointing out that a number of Fusionist district ballot boxes were also tampered with—and by mounting statewide "indignation meetings." The debate over the count-out grew increasingly bitter.

Maine's most powerful politician, Republican Senator James G. Blaine, entered the crisis, fearing that the election of a Greenbacker would lead to the overthrow of the state's powerful Republican machine, which would be a critical blow to his chances of securing the Republican nomination for president. Blaine came to Augusta at the height of the crisis to help organize the "indignation meetings" and mold a strategy to intimidate the Democrats. Looking on from Brunswick, Joshua Chamberlain followed the events in Augusta very closely. In his opinion Blaine's actions were purposely designed to stir up the state's political tensions. With armed political gangs forming in Augusta on each side of the issue, Chamberlain wrote Blaine that "what we now need to do is not to add to popular excitement which is likely to result in disorder and violence, but to aide in keeping the peace by inducing our friends to speak and act as sober and law-abiding citizens. I hope you will do all you can to stop the incendiary talk which proposed violent measures, and is doing great harm to our people."

By late 1879, Governor Garcelon was under mounting public pressure to call out the state militia to disarm the political gangs and restore order in the state capital. Instead, he called for a hundred volunteers to protect the governor's office—which only served to further inflame the situation. He attempted to arm these volunteers from the state's stocks of weapons and ammunition in Bangor, but Republican forces refused to turn over the material. Finally, Garcelon found 20,000 rounds of ammunition, which arrived in Augusta on December 30. Garcelon's army was supplied with the needed ammunition just in time: across the street from the capitol, a crowd of Blaine's riflemen was gathering to begin an assault on Garcelon's forces. It was only when a clash became imminent, in early January, that Garcelon decided that an Augusta street battle would destroy his governorship. He therefore signed an executive order on January 5—"Special Order No. 45"—that called on the state militia, and its new commander Joshua Chamberlain (who had recently been appointed major general in the state militia, and its commander), to take control of Augusta until the political crisis had passed. For the next twelve days, in an environment bordering on civil war, Chamberlain acted as the state's chief executive.

With more self-confidence and assuredness than he had shown in the years since Appomattox, Chamberlain moved quickly to resolve the deteriorating situation. Beginning on the evening of January 5, Chamberlain made a number of bold moves to help end the crisis. Even though he had the power to arm the militia and bring it to Augusta, Chamberlain instead decided to put on his own militia uniform and come to Augusta himself, unarmed and without calling on help from any of Maine's troops. He met first with Augusta Mayor Charles Nash, to gain the cooperation and control of the capital city's police, then persuaded Governor Garcelon to withdraw his troops from the capital building. Next he gained control of the state's election papers and placed them under guard, and stationed police at all of the state's major administrative offices.

Chamberlain, functioning from a small office in the capitol, was under enormous pressure. After Chamberlain took control in Augusta, the president of the Maine Senate, James D. Lamson, told him that the Fusionists now supported him, Lamson, rather than Joseph Smith, who had run on the Greenback Party ticket. Lamson now insisted that he should be recognized as the de facto governor, since he represented the winning party. Chamberlain dismissed Lamson's claim, even though he liked Lamson and thought his claim had some merit. Chamberlain then met with U.S. Senator Lot Morrill, a Blaine partisan, who wanted to know if Chamberlain had any military plans in the case of an outbreak of violence. Chamberlain was correctly ambiguous, not wanting to tip his hand to Blaine, and he sent Morrill away with a warning that the Republicans would be making a mistake by turning to violence to force the election issue. Armed gangs supporting each of the candidates continued to control the streets of Augusta, and tensions mounted with every passing day. Blaine's small army of men was headquartered at his home in Augusta, while Greenback and Democratic supporters, also fully armed, stayed at a local hotel. Chamberlain sent word to his son to send him his two Civil War pistols.

"The excitement is now terrific in bitterness," Chamberlain wrote the chief justice of the Maine Supreme Court on January 12. "The fusionists swear they will resist with blood and fire if the Court sustains the Republican program." Blaine was just as adamant, and sent one of his assistants, Thomas Hyde, to Chamberlain with a warning—if the Fusionists were not put out of office, Hyde said, then Blaine's men would "pitch the fusionists out of the window." Chamberlain shook his head at Hyde, whom he had known for many years, and told him: "Tom, you are as dear to me as my own son. But I will permit you to do nothing of the kind. I am going to preserve the peace. I want you and Mr. Blaine and the others to keep away from this building." Chamberlain's strategy was to bide his time, keep civil order, and maintain a strict political neutrality. He would not say who he thought should be governor, believing instead that the contending sides should abide by the decision of the state supreme court. He would keep the peace until that happened.

By the beginning of the second week of the crisis, Chamberlain was receiving death threats from every side, and the former governor was forced to sleep at different residences each night for fear of being kidnapped. Augusta's mayor assigned a bodyguard to escort Chamberlain through the city. One night, while leaving his office, Chamberlain was told that there was a gang of men outside on the capitol grounds who were waiting to kill him. Chamberlain went out through the dark and cold to meet them, calmly buttoning up his coat as he approached, saying:

Men, you wish to kill me, I hear. Killing is no new thing to me. I have offered myself to be killed many times, when I no more deserved it than I do now. Some of you, I think, have been with me in those days. You understand what you want, do you? I am here to preserve the peace and honor of this State, until the rightful government is seated—whichever it may be, it is not for me to say. But it is for me to see that the laws of this State are put into effect, without fraud, without force, but with calm thought and purpose. I am here for that, and I shall do it. If anybody wants to kill me for it, here I am. Let him kill!

Chamberlain then threw open his coat as an old veteran who knew him stepped from the crowd: "By God, General, the first man that dares to lay a hand on you, I'll kill him on the spot."

And with that, as Chamberlain watched, the gang moved away.

At the height of the crisis, the Fusionists turned against Lamson and threw their support back to the Greenbacker Smith. But Smith, having recaptured the Fusionist leadership, overplayed his hand by announcing, on January 16, that he was "revoking" Chamberlain's authority and that no one should obey his orders. When Smith sent one of his assistants to demand Chamberlain's surrender, the Augusta police turned him away. Later on that same day, the state supreme court finally passed down its decision—undoing the recount and validating the original election of a Republican legislature. The following day, January 17, the legislature met and elected Republican Daniel Davis as governor.

With crowds of armed men in the streets and the Fusionists vowing revenge, Davis took control of the government and sent a message to Chamberlain thanking him for his service. "In common with all the citizens of this State I have watched with great anxiety the events of the past few days, and rejoice with them in the good results of the wise and efficient measures adopted by you for the preservation of the peace and protection of the property and institutions of the State," Davis wrote. Chamberlain responded with nonchalance to the threats still pouring down on him. "I consider my trust, under Special Order No. 45, as at an end." He then closed his office in the capitol, put on his coat, and walked out through the angry crowds. But the violence that everyone expected did not occur. Within days, the armed gangs that had patrolled Augusta's streets had dispersed and the state returned to normal.

Chamberlain was pilloried from every side. He was blamed for the election of Davis. He was the "Republican Renegade," the "Most Dangerous Man in Maine," the "Serpent of Brunswick," or the "Tool of Blaine." In fact, Chamberlain had so successfully maintained his neutrality that few had guessed that he had been impressed by the Greenbacker, Lamson—and believed that he would make the best governor. He was less impressed by Davis, and even less so by his old nemesis, James G. Blaine. Blaine, on the other hand, resented Chamberlain's high-handed methods and the attention his role as head of the militia had brought him. While Blaine was pleased that Davis became governor, he made sure that Chamberlain's political career was ended. Of all the criticisms leveled at Chamberlain, the most hollow was that the

"Hero of Little Round Top" was the "Tool of Blaine." When Blaine was named secretary of state in the Garfield administration, Chamberlain was not asked to fill his seat, nor was he rewarded with a Republican nomination for the seat when it became available. That honor went to Eugene Hale, one of Blaine's strongest supporters.

Chamberlain was disappointed, but he did not feel betrayed. He had never been a Blaine man and never would be, and consoled himself that he had done the right thing during the "Twelve Days" when the Maine state government was under siege from contending political factions. If anything, Augusta Mayor Charles Nash, who had seen Chamberlain through the political crisis, was more upset than the former governor. A year after the crisis, he wrote to tell Chamberlain of his disgust with the Republican Party's refusal to name Chamberlain as their Senate candidate: "The ingratitude—yes, indecency—of men from whom a year ago I fondly hoped better things has disheartened me somewhat. I will be on hand and do everything possible in my humble way." But there was nothing to be done. Chamberlain would never win his party's nomination for a Senate candidacy.

# 16

# *What Do You Do About Yours?*

M ANY OF THE GREAT SOLDIERS of the Civil War were now passing away. The most renowned, and mourned, was Ulysses S. Grant, who died in 1885. Chamberlain played a prominent role in the events surrounding his burial in New York. Winfield Scott Hancock organized the funeral and made sure to give Chamberlain's carriage a place in the front rank of the mourners. The honor surprised him. "I would not have chosen that position," Chamberlain wrote Fannie from New York, "because it was too much." Hancock did not think so and directed Chamberlain to stand near the door of Grant's tomb during the final ceremony.

Grant's funeral brought together the generation of American soldiers who had fought the nation's bloodiest war; one of Grant's pallbearers was former Confederate General Joseph E. Johnston, who had become a good friend. Fitzhugh Lee, the Confederate cavalry commander, helped Hancock with the funeral arrangements. Grant lay in state in New York City Hall for one day while 250,000 mourners came to pay their respects. On the next morning, the funeral procession marched up Broadway from City Hall, then headed west to Riverside Drive, five miles in all, to a new tomb overlooking the Hudson River. The procession was viewed by one million Americans, who crowded the city streets. Thousands more watched from the bluffs above the Hudson during the interment. All of the great Union commanders were present: Sheridan, Sherman, Daniel Sickles (whose line was broken on Gettysburg's second day), and Chamberlain. "It was the last of the great scenes," Chamberlain told Fannie. "At least for this generation."

Chamberlain had good reason to be surprised by his position of prominence in Grant's funeral. The two had always been friends, but they did not see eye to eye on many important matters, including the question of Gouverneur Kemble Warren. In 1880, after years of attempting to clear his name, Warren had been granted a hearing before a special court of inquiry to answer charges that he had been overly cautious in his actions at Five Forks in April 1865, for which he was relieved of command by General Phil Sheridan. Chamberlain had always supported Warren, even though he knew that Grant disapproved, and by 1880 he was known as a committed Warren loyalist and Sheridan critic. In his final act in the drama, Chamberlain had testified on behalf of Warren before the court of inquiry in Washington. To prepare for his testimony, Chamberlain had spent hours reviewing the case and making notes on it, attempting to re-create from memory and army dispatches exactly what had happened south of Petersburg in April 1865. Reviewing the materials had given Chamberlain an opportunity to hone his occasional addresses on Lee's surrender and to begin a manuscript on the battle of Gettysburg. He had always wanted to write a book about the war, but his schedule had never allowed him the time to commit his thoughts to paper.

Prior to his testimony, Chamberlain had met and talked with Phil Sheridan and Winfield Scott Hancock, but Sheridan's greeting was cool and distant. Chamberlain had not been bothered by this: he testified in calm and unexcited tones, denying that Warren had ever purposely circumvented or ignored an order, and impressed the court with his belief that the confusion of battle and conflicting orders from others above Warren—by which he could only mean Meade, Sheridan, or Grant—were confusing and ambiguous. In November 1882 the court had exonerated Warren from any wrongdoing in his actions and stated that Grant and Sheridan were wrong to discipline him for his inaction. Warren had not jeopardized the Union victory, the court held, and furthermore he had acted properly and according to orders. It was a stinging rebuke of the higher command of the Army of the Potomac. Warren was vindicated, but more important for Chamberlain and his comrades, Sheridan had been embarrassed by the court's findings. There was no solace in this for Warren himself, however, who had died three months before the findings were released.

In the years before Grant's funeral, Chamberlain, along with Oates, had been indirectly involved in yet another, similar investigation—that of Union General Fitz-John Porter. McClellan's old commander had been arrested and court-martialed for disobedience of orders during the Second Battle of Bull Run, then convicted and dismissed from the army. But the findings were politically charged, as Porter was a well-known Democrat, a "McClellan man," and a reputed enemy of Ulysses S. Grant. Many old soldiers, including Chamberlain, believed that Porter's dismissal was one of the greatest injustices of the war, perpetrated by John Pope to cover his own incompetence. Porter applied for relief and in 1878 President Hayes had appointed a board of inquiry, similar to the one later convened in the Warren case, to look into the charges. After hours of testimony and review, the court had exonerated Porter and recommended that Hayes restore him to duty. Hayes needed an act of Congress to do so, and one finally came, in a bill passed in 1886. Chamberlain had publicly supported Porter, and Oates had given two speeches defending him in the House of Representatives and then had voted for his reinstatement to the rank of colonel.

Chamberlain had remained a supporter of Grant despite their disagreements, which never seemed to be so serious that it harmed Chamberlain's standing in his eyes. But Grant surely must have known that Chamberlain viewed him in much the same way as his former antagonists in the South. "Grant was a strategist; he was not an economist," Chamberlain wrote in his account of his former commander's qualities. "He saw what was to be done, and he set himself to do it, without being much controlled by consideration of cost or probabilities. . . . He never seized the moment to turn disaster into victory. He seemed to rely on sheer force, rather than skillful maneuver." But damning as this judgment was, Chamberlain knew full well that without Grant, the war might not have been won. "His concentration of energies, inflexible purpose, unselfishness, patience, imperturbable long-suffering, his masterly reticence, ignoring either advice or criticism, his magnanimity in all relations, but more than all his infinite trust in the final triumph of his cause, set him apart." As Grant was laid in his tomb in Riverside Park, Chamberlain stood nearby in mute testimony to the man who was America's second greatest general—second only to Robert E. Lee. Whom he had defeated.

Following the lead of others in his generation, Chamberlain thought he saw opportunities in the South, and after Grant's funeral he bought land near Ocala in central Florida and organized a land development company, the Homosassa Company. Managing the Ocala holdings— orange groves, a lumber business, a hotel, and other real estate being developed for settlement—took much of Chamberlain's time. Florida natives cited Chamberlain's activities in the state as an inducement for the building of vacation homes and the opening of businesses. "Large tracts of land have been acquired in this vicinity by a company of capi- talists, surveys have been made, avenues cut through the hammock, and every effort made to attract permanent settlers as well as transient visitors," a Florida promotional broadside noted. "Probably there is no better or richer soil in the State for most of the semi-tropical crops." Chamberlain spent his time looking for capital to develop the region, then sent his son Wyllys to Ocala to handle the company's legal mat- ters. Chamberlain's most pressing need, however, was to link his Ocala holdings to the rest of the South—and he spent considerable time look- ing for a way to build a railroad joining Ocala to the Gulf and to destina- tions to the north and east.

Chamberlain was careful not to stake his future entirely on his Ocala development company, however, and accepted offers from other firms to lend his name to their investments. By 1885 he was serving on the boards of several investment and financial firms and became so busy managing his own business network that he settled in New York and opened a Wall Street office. From there he monitored his purchases and responded to frequent correspondents: editors seeking articles on his Civil War experiences, managers of Florida orange groves, the president of the Florida railroad company in which he had a small inter- est, and the board of directors of a textile mill. Chamberlain purchased an apartment in town, where Fannie visited him.

In 1888, he traveled to Gettysburg to attend the twenty-fifth an- niversary of the battle. Much to his surprise, he was elected president of the Society of the Army of the Potomac. Chamberlain traveled to Get- tysburg again in October 1889, to attend a reunion of the 20th Maine and to dedicate Maine's battlefield markers. "Service was the central fact," he told his regiment. "That fact and that truth, these monuments commemorate. They mark the centres round which stood the manhood of Maine, steadfast in noble service." Most of Maine's most important officials were present for the dedication and the meetings that followed, but Chamberlain was the center of everyone's attention. A meeting of all of the state's regiments was held at the Gettysburg Court House on the cool October evening following the dedication of the 20th Maine memorial. Chamberlain, his hair long and mustache now gone to gray, was the featured speaker. He cited Maine's great contributions to the war and concluded by criticizing those who had referred to the four years of fighting as the War Between the States. He made it plain that he would not have anything to do with that interpretation. Those words seemed to imply that the rebels had a just cause; for him, the war was an unjustified insurrection of rebels against a legal government. "It was a war in the name of certain States to destroy the political existence of the United States."

By 1890, Chamberlain, at the age of sixty-two, continued to be much in demand as a speaker, though his speeches were sometimes difficult to follow, as he continued to use the complex and high-blown constructions he had perfected as a stuttering youth. "His writing and addresses show a tendency to reaches of thought somewhat abstruse," one sketch of his life gingerly noted. "They are, however, suffused with a certain poetical idealism, and in religious conceptions with a spirituality almost mystical. But on themes relating to practical life and action he comes to the front with a power that is thrilling." He received little if any compensation for his constant attention to the needs of his fellow veterans or for his speeches, but despite being short on funds he nevertheless traveled incessantly to dedicate new memorials and raise money for veterans and their widows. Chamberlain even carried on a correspondence with former Confederate General John Gordon for a time, proposing that the two combine their addresses into a full presentation for American audiences, but nothing came of the idea. Chamberlain certainly could have used whatever income a twentieth-century-style speaking tour would have brought them, for by the beginning of his sixty-fifth year, the development business he had spent so much time trying to build in Ocala was nearly broke.

"I am coming to realize better than ever what you have seen so

long," Wyllys wrote to his mother at the height of Chamberlain's financial difficulties, "father cannot ever be relied upon to look out for himself, but always for the other fellow." While Chamberlain was short of
cash and his companies were suffering—the early 1890s were a time of
considerable impoverishment for many people—he was nowhere close
to penury. The life of an aging soldier might not be the most financially
rewarding, but it did have its advantages. Chamberlain was not forgotten and was still recognized and honored for his service during the war.
In 1893, Congress voted him the Medal of Honor for "distinguished
gallantry" in saving the Army of the Potomac's right wing at Gettysburg. Letters of congratulations poured in from soldiers all over the
country.

By the late 1880s, a worldwide overproduction of agricultural com-
modities had pushed American farm prices down. This, coupled with a
slowdown in the expansion of the economy, a lack of easy credit, scarce
currency, and high interest rates, caused American farmers and laborers to suffer through their worst economic crisis. Increasingly, America's small farmers were falling into debt. To meet the growing crisis, a
convention of farmers' alliances, a growing rural movement, was held in
St. Louis in early 1890. That meeting was followed soon after by an
even larger convention in Ocala, Florida. The Ocala convention included a cross-section of the nation's emerging reformist element, including delegates from the Southern Farmers' Alliance, the Colored
Alliance, the Northern Farmers' Alliance, and the Knights of Labor.
These groups comprised a strangely cohesive coalition of resurgent
land-hungry western Republicans, disaffected southern Democrats,
rural land reformers, and poor rural blacks.

The delegates issued what came to be known as the "Ocala Demands," calling for the nationalization of railroads, the regulation of
telephones and telegraph lines, a graduated income tax, "free and un-
limited coinage of silver," an eight-hour day, women's suffrage, and
the direct election of U.S. senators (then chosen by state legislatures).
The Ocala meeting was the opening wedge in a broad-based national
"populist" reform movement that saw its ultimate realization in the pas-

sage of landmark progressive legislation in the early twentieth century. The populist movement soon swept the country and, while it was strongest in western agricultural states, it fielded candidates for governor in every major state of the "Solid South" and sought to supplant the power and appeal of old-line Bourbon political leaders like William Oates. Oates viewed the populists as latter-day carpetbaggers, Democratic Party renegades, and northern "me-tooers" who cloaked their yearning for power in the slogans of political reform.

Alabama's leading populist was an Eufaula neighbor of Oates's by the name of Reuben F. Kolb. A native of North Carolina, Kolb was now a plantation owner and local Democratic Party organizer. He befriended poor southern farmers, who were thrilled by his political skills, his call for agricultural reform, and his demand for a greater voice for Alabama farmers in Montgomery. A latter-day Edmund Ruffin, Kolb spread the gospel of agricultural reform throughout southeastern Alabama. Crop diversification and land rehabilitation, Kolb preached, could end the constant impoverishment of Alabama's soils—and he pointed to his own plantation as an example. There, he had taken land out of cotton production and started raising watermelons so big that they were known as "Kolb's gems."

Kolb soon vaulted into the vanguard of the Alabama agricultural movement and earned himself a place in the party's innermost councils. He was named Alabama agricultural commissioner and immediately launched a tour of the state's rural areas, where he preached his gospel of agricultural reform, established farmers' institutes, and initiated a popular touring display of Alabama agricultural products called "Alabama on Wheels." Like postwar Republicans, Kolb drew his strongest adherents from North Alabama farmers—the old Unionists—and from central and eastern Alabama's black sharecroppers. Kolb denied that he was a breakaway Democrat or that his program would undermine the Democratic Party, but he had attended the St. Louis Farmers' Alliance convention, endorsed their reformist views, and signed on to the Ocala Demands. He also pledged, with other populists, that he would "support for office only such men as can be depended upon to enact these principles into . . . law, uninfluenced by party caucus."

What appealed to Alabama farmers most, however, was Kolb's

support for the new Populist Party program to help rural farmers. The party's "subtreasury" plan called for the creation of agricultural warehouses where farmers could store their grain and produce until prices increased. The subtreasury, Kolb argued, would act like a farmers' bank and ensure loans to small landholders. Small farmers could borrow money against their stored products and would not be forced to sell underpriced harvests until the national market stabilized. The program was an ingenious attempt at market regulation that Kolb soft-pedaled as a reform. Democrats, however, knew that it attacked their party's most basic principle, which condemned any government interference in any part of the state's business.

William Oates mistrusted Kolb, hated the "soft money" program of the Populists, and believed that the Farmers' Alliances marked the greatest threat to Democratic Party supremacy since Reconstruction. He was especially disturbed by Kolb's anti-caucus pledge, since its acceptance would mean the end of the party system that had ensured his election as a U.S. congressman. He not only benefited from the caucus system he had helped to build but, more important, as head of a new and growing rural movement, Kolb threatened to derail Oates's political plans—which included a run for the governorship and then, he hoped, a seat in the U.S. Senate. By inserting himself in Democratic Party politics and moving forcefully against the caucus system, Kolb could very easily end Oates's political career. When Kolb announced that he would run for governor in 1890, Oates hurried back to Montgomery from Washington to assess the political situation and Kolb's popularity. Oates visited party leaders throughout the state in an attempt to gain their support for stripping Kolb of his Democratic Party credentials.

The state Democratic machine sprang into action, with Oates serving as a behind-the-scenes organizer. Alabama's U.S. senator, John Tyler Morgan, led the way in condemning Kolb's apostasy and called him a "selfish and reckless schemer." Kolb's greatest deficiency, Morgan claimed, was his reliance on outsiders (mainly northern reformers) and his attempt to subvert the Alabama Democratic Party machine. The sin was unforgivable. "[Kolb has] employed Knights of Labor, and all that, Republicans and their allies—the greenbackers—and all that, to serve a great, generous, honest, and noble party, a dirty, mean, low, sneaking trick!" Morgan wrote to one Democratic Party leader in Selma.

Kolb responded to this challenge by establishing populist newspapers and election committees throughout the state, which vowed to take the levers of Democratic Party power out of the hands of "tricksters and bosses" and put it back into the hands of the people. Kolb's candidacy was probably doomed from the beginning, since the head of the Democratic Party made certain that delegates to the state party convention were chosen on the basis of the last election, a practice that virtually guaranteed the party machine could choose its own candidate. In response, Kolb contested the delegate selection process in a number of machine-controlled jurisdictions. In Eufaula, his backers attempted to force their way into a local party meeting wielding umbrellas, wooden staves, and knives, and then engaging in a street brawl—one of the few times a Democratic Party dissenter had actually challenged the strength of the Eufaula Regency on its own ground.

Kolb's tactics were even more successful than he had imagined. When the party convention finally met in Montgomery in May, Kolb led all other delegates with 237 votes. After the thirty-third ballot, the party's leaders convinced all but one of the other contenders, a man by the name of Thomas Goode Jones, to stand aside. Jones was nominated by a majority of the delegates on the thirty-fourth ballot and elected governor in August.

After losing his bid for the governorship in 1890, Kolb realized there was little chance he would ever gain higher office as a Democrat. So, in 1892, maintaining that he was a steadfast Democrat and saying that he would remain so until his dying day, Kolb attended the Populist Party convention in Cincinnati. He returned to the state to barnstorm for support for his new party-within-a-party, a group he called the "Jeffersonian Democrats." As a testament to his enormous popularity and the talents he had shown by nearly capturing the nomination in 1890, Democratic Party leaders responded by launching an all-out campaign to stop him.

The 1892 election was one of the most vicious in Alabama state history. The Democratic Party establishment used its newspapers to launch a campaign of intimidation against Kolb followers. Kolb responded by forming Citizen's Alliance groups, a strike force of reformers organized to outintimidate his party machine opponents. The alliances organized rallies that were quite similar to Maine's "indignation meetings." During one Montgomery rally, in the heart of the hard-core Democratic district, they even burned Governor Jones in effigy. But Kolb was consistently outmaneuvered on the county level; whenever local party meetings gave him a majority of delegates, the Jones faction would stage a walkout, hold their own meeting, and elect new delegates. These new delegates were promptly recognized as "legitimate" by party leaders. So when the party held its convention, Kolb was assured of losing the nomination again, in spite of his enormous statewide support. What happened next could have been predicted as early as 1890: Kolb took his delegates off the convention floor and out of the party, announcing that he would run as a third-party candidate.

The election was marked by its racial stridency. In the middle of the campaign, the Democrats announced that when they won the vote they would immediately pass election laws "as will better secure the government of the State in the hands of the intelligent and virtuous." Not willing to rest on such subtleties, the Democratic press published vituperative attacks on the "nigger rights section" of the Populist platform, drawing people's attention to the presence of northerners in the Populist Party, and predicting that Kolb and his followers would soon "fuse" with that most hated of all political species, the Republicans. Kolb denied the accusation, of course, recognizing that such attacks might drive a wedge between his rural supporters in southeast Alabama and his white support in northern Alabama.

Reuben F. Kolb probably won the Alabama governor's election of 1892, even though the final balloting did not show it. When all the votes were counted, Jones was reelected by 11,435 votes. The people of Alabama knew better, but since the state constitution did not contain a provision for a recount or a recall (it was written by Democrats in 1875), Jones was duly inaugurated as governor. The message was clearly heard by Alabama's voters: the Bourbons would not be unseated by legal means. Nevertheless, despite the election victory, the Democratic Party machine lost much of its luster. Yet in many respects the Democratic campaign succeeded in raising doubts about Kolb's continued support for "white rule" in the South. There was still no doubt that Kolb would run again two years later in 1894. This time, however, his opponent would be William Oates—the "one-armed hero of Henry County."

The rise of the Populist Party in America was in response to economic hardship, industrialization, the impoverishment of the small farmer, and political corruption. In the mid-1890s the economic recession that had plagued rural America in the first part of the decade worsened and Alabama's farmers faced their worst economic crisis since Reconstruction. Large landholders were being turned out of their homes and small landholders were forced into sharecropping. The price of cotton, vegetables—of everything produced on the farm—had started to fall. The depression that started in rural America reached into the nation's factories, including those in Alabama, where new iron smelting and steel producing works had grown up in Birmingham. Coal miners went on strike across the state during Jones's term as governor, and he had responded by calling out the troops, thereby ensuring the miners' continued support of Populist Party aims. But even as the Populists gained strength against the entrenched interests of the Democratic Party stalwarts in Montgomery, the rural base of Kolb's support began to wane.

Two factors eventually led to the defeat of the Populist Party in the South: the easing of economic conditions and the successful campaign of Democrats to tar the Populists with support for black rights. The specter of a race war that had been raised before secession and used throughout Reconstruction remained the card that white southern Democrats would use again and again whenever there was a threat to their political control. Even so, the waning popularity of the Populists was no guarantee of an easy Democratic victory in 1894, and as the political season opened nearly everyone believed that Kolb might this time, and against all odds, win his governor's seat.

Oates returned to Alabama after resigning his congressional seat with only one thought in mind—to pave his way to the Senate by winning the governor's mansion. He started by gaining the endorsement of the Democratic state convention, where he won a hard-fought victory against a "free silver" candidate. Smeared with charges of corruption in the delegate counting, Oates ignored the claims and defended his nomination on the principle that he had served as a loyal Democrat for over two decades. But there was no doubt that he was in for the political fight of his life. The fact that Oates was from Henry County worked against him for the first time, since Kolb was also from the southeastern part of the state and could claim the allegiance of a tight constituency of small farmers near Eufaula—no longer a Regency stronghold. Knowing he faced a tough campaign, Oates followed his nomination by organizing a series of rallies complete with speeches, free barbecue pork and beef, endless kegs of beer, and hours-long orations, all followed by more hours of shaking hands. He brought his friends with him, old veterans who had served with the 15th Alabama and still supported their courageous captain.

"Your valiant one-armed hero can work the veteran racket more adroitly and successfully than any fellow of the state who shows a scar or empty sleeve as a passport to office," a Kolb supporter commented to a Democrat during the campaign. But there was a touch of admiration in the statement, for the "veteran racket" was an accepted part of southern politics and had been since Appomattox. Even Kolb, himself a hero of the war, had to admit that Oates was far more popular than the previous Democratic nominee—who did not have as obvious a claim to heroism as the "one-armed hero of Henry County." Oates used this veteran's support to his advantage, whipping his old regiment into line early in the campaign, then sending his supporters out to tell the voters that Oates had once fought for their rights and would do so again. Oates's campaign was shrewd—while he was a hard-core Democratic conservative, he rarely espoused doctrines that might have alienated small farmers, such as during the convention when he unwisely said he thought Alabama's children did not need to be educated past the primary grades. "If educated beyond this point," he said, they would never "work another day in the sun."

Oates demonstrated versatility as a political campaigner. He went into every part of Alabama to sell his program, arguing that the state needed to be placed on a sound fiscal basis, that its industries needed to be revitalized, and that new railroads needed to be built. Oates's followers turned out wherever he spoke, spreading oats from wagons over the crowd, and wearing oats in the bands of their hats. Kolb responded by making a corncob his campaign icon and throwing seeds of corn into the crowd wherever he appeared. Neither man was above poking fun at the other—and using it to advantage. Oates skewered Kolb as a man who spent his time campaigning for governor, and urged the newspapers that supported his candidacy to refer to R. F. Kolb as Run Forever Kolb. But the heart of Oates's appeal was his service to Alabama's voters through fourteen years in the House of Representatives.

Oates was a conservative candidate and never wavered from his belief that southern nationalism could only be defended by electing Democratic officials. While he refused to acknowledge that the Democratic Party was a white man's party, he also refused to distance himself from the white supremacist language of the party's most strident supporters. He talked about "law and order," a phrase used to remind voters of the chaos that had plagued Alabama during Reconstruction. Democratic officials, however, openly used their wedge issue—race—as a political card to draw white voters away from Kolb and back into Democratic ranks. As a result, the election of 1894 stands as one of the most viciously and closely fought in the state's history, as well as far outstripping any subsequent election for race-baiting.

In one incident during the campaign, the "unmentionable" fact of southern history was actually spoken in public. It occurred during a question-and-answer session that Oates endured as a candidate in an appearance before the state legislature. Now consigned to a historical footnote in Alabama history, barely mentioned by state historians, the "scandal" is still whispered about today around Montgomery. It was alluded to, in passing, in anecdotal references to the 1894 campaign by commentators writing in the 1950s when race was once again the state's most pressing issue. One of these sources, Virginia Foster Durr, a civil rights activist, characterized the question put to Oates as the most embarrassing question that could ever be put to a white man then living in Alabama. During Oates's question-and-answer session with the state legislature, Durr tells us, a man stood up in the back of the chamber and thrust his question, his condemnation, in Oates's face.

"Well," the man asked, "what about all those nigger children you've got in the backyard?" The question, breaking all the taboos, must have brought the chamber to an absolute hushed silence.

Oates, unfazed, shouted back: "What about them? I feed them. I clothe them. I house them and I educate them. What do you do about yours?"

The question might have been asked of any white man in Alabama, or in Virginia, or South Carolina, or anywhere in the South, where, as its most famous Civil War diarist, Mary Chesnut, wrote, the women of the plantation were forced every day to look on the faces of their husbands' offspring. We do not know the name of the black woman, or women, who bore Oates's children, nor do we know the children's names or what happened to them. But it is hard to deny the fact of their existence, since Oates himself admitted as much. So they are there, in history, as a part of his story, and they were to have an effect, years later, when Oates himself transformed his view of Alabama and rethought what its future should be. But in 1894, the fact that Oates had fathered illegitimate black children had little or no effect on the race for governor; he was not the only one who had done so.

Though Oates was a master campaigner and party organizer, he was a much less accomplished orator than Kolb, who responded to Oates's campaign by setting up his own breakneck schedule of stump speeches, free barbecues, and political rallies. Kolb could not escape the race issue—which the Democrats emphasized at every turn. Kolb attempted to distance himself from his black supporters, just as Republicans had tried to do two decades before. In fact, Kolb had little choice, since he realized that the black belt ballot boxes in central Alabama were in the hands of the Democratic Party machine anyway. He campaigned in areas where he knew he could gain a majority vote, though he realized that even among those Democrats who wanted a change, his name no longer sparked the same loyalties that it had two years previously when he had run against Jones.

◦═══◆═══◦

In the end, the Democrats won the election, defeating Kolb 111,875 votes to 83,292. Oates celebrated the victory by planning a huge reception in Montgomery. But Oates's election brought immediate charges of corruption: "The inauguration of William C. Oates on December 1 is the last peaceable inauguration of a man counted in by ballot box stuffers," the *Columbiana People's Advocate* editorialized. "The honest, intelligent, and patriotic citizens of Alabama have set the seal of condemnation on ballot box thieves and their beneficiaries; the old guard who have heretofore voted dead negroes and pointer dogs to overturn the votes honestly cast by white men in white counties in north Alabama had better pack their 'duds' and move to greener pastures." Kolb would not concede that he was defeated and on December 1—the same day as Oates's inauguration—he held a counterinauguration, making his own governor's address on the capitol grounds.

Oates ignored Kolb and took office as the state's new governor. The inaugural festivities matched his pride in having risen to the highest office in the state and were a paean to his background as the commander of the 15th Alabama. The *Montgomery Advertiser* even promoted the new governor for the occasion, and Colonel Oates became General Oates. "This event was one of pronounced distinction and elaborateness. The floral decorations were most effective and artistic. When the bugler's blast announced the opening of the twenty-first annual ball of the Montgomery Greys, given in honor of General and Mrs. Oates at the armory Friday night, there was a brilliantly tinted and pretty setting formed for the tableaux. Mrs. Oates was gowned in white duchess satin silver spangled and trimmed in rose point lace."

There was talk of revolution in Montgomery, of armed men who would come and remove Oates from office and place the Populists in power. Kolb knew, however, that such an insurrection was not only impossible, it would lead to the senseless slaughter of Kolb's forces. While Kolb continued to keep up the pretense of serving as governor, he knew he had little recourse but to concede that he had lost. In spite of the charges of corruption swirling around Oates, Kolb had still received 50,000 fewer votes as a candidate against the "one-armed hero of Henry County" than he had against Jones two years earlier. Kolb knew that the Jeffersonian-Populist movement was losing strength in the state and would continue to do so, especially if economic conditions improved. He also feared that the movement he had led would align itself with the Republicans in a last-ditch effort to win the statehouse, a strategy he knew was doomed.

While Kolb could be satisfied that he had opened Alabama politics, and its dominant party, to new thinking, he also realized that the response to his candidacy was the strengthening and reuniting of the solid Democratic Party, which would remain untested in Alabama politics for the next seventy years. During the campaign of 1894, Democratic Party organizers had begun a "disenfranchisement movement" that struck thousands of black voters from the state voting rolls. Literacy tests, poll taxes, and "character" assessments were now used throughout the state as an excuse to keep blacks from the ballot box. This new strategy was also aimed at poor white farmers, who had formed Kolb's base of support. An apocryphal story about the openness of such corruption soon made the rounds:

"You would refuse to register Jesus Christ himself," one voter claimed to a Democratic organizer.

"That would depend on his party," the Democrat responded.

William Oates gave Alabama steady, if unimaginative, leadership for the next two years. But his time as a political official was over. Having argued that loyalty to the Democratic Party and its leaders was one of his first principles, Oates could hardly launch a run for the Senate against John Tyler Morgan—who had tirelessly campaigned on his behalf in 1894. While he put his name forward as a Senate candidate in 1896, his efforts were halfhearted and his candidacy was set aside by the Democratic machine in favor of a "free silver" candidate. While Oates would be keenly disappointed in his inability to gain the Senate seat he so desired, he was undeniably proud of having become governor, the highest elected state official in Alabama, after starting life as a poor boy at Oates's Crossroads.

<hr />

Joshua Chamberlain did not take easily to old age. It seemed to him a betrayal. He was shunted from public life and public attention, spending his days now in the old Hawthorne house near the Bowdoin College campus or in his offices in New York looking after his investments and managing his property. His wound continued to flare up painfully, keeping him inactive for weeks at a time. His children were gone; Chamberlain's son Wyllys attempted to make a living as a lawyer in Ocala, but there was little business. His father had to send him money until he came north. Chamberlain's old veteran friends were dropping from sight—retiring to silence or dying one by one. Fannie was increasingly ill and was plagued by the recurrence of migraines. By the middle of the 1890s, it was clear that she might soon go blind. There was little her husband could do to ease her pain or improve her health. Chamberlain spent as much time with her as he could, but still struggled to remain active in national affairs and make a contribution despite his age.

Chamberlain was still a member of a number of corporate boards, including real estate, development, and bond companies, but he was tired of the constant bickering of corporate allies and enemies and wanted to do something more useful. In 1892, therefore, he accepted a position as president of the Institute of Artists and Artisans and spent much of the decade procuring subscriptions and raising money for the art school. As Chamberlain conceived it, the institute would focus on instruction in every art form, including painting, sculpture, architecture, and illustration, as well as in metalworking, jewelry, ceramics, and interior decoration. Chamberlain then established a summer art institute on the Maine coast near his summer home at Domhegan.

In addition to his work for the Institute of Artists and Artisans, Chamberlain took on the presidency of *New England* magazine and edited a huge multivolume work, *Universities and Their Sons*. He continued to speak before civic groups and at major conventions. The difference now was that many of the people he met were born after the war. Their knowledge of the conflict was far less extensive than those to whom Chamberlain had spoken over the past thirty years. He was undisturbed by this evidence of the passage of time, feeling that his views might be even more important now than they had been in the first decade following Lee's surrender.

Chamberlain was aware of the details of William Oates's career and followed it closely. He was certainly aware of his old adversary's political successes, as well as the controversy that surrounded his election as governor of Alabama. It would have been difficult, indeed, for Chamberlain to have ignored the news about Oates; a number of Chamberlain's closest friends and former military comrades spoke to Oates often. Oliver O. Howard stayed in constant touch with Chamberlain and almost certainly gave him a detailed account of Oates's own views on the war—which became national news and sparked a new controversy in 1895.

⚬══◆══⚬

William Oates had been invited to a number of Confederate reunions and had attended some, but he always seemed to be elsewhere when the veterans of both blue and gray met at Gettysburg. We can only guess at the reasons for his absence, but certainly one of them must have had to do with the fact that the Army of Northern Virginia lost the battle—a fact that Oates was not inclined to celebrate. This was not true of other battles, of course, and over the years Oates, like Chamberlain, took the opportunity to attend reunions and give speeches. He remained especially close to Alabama's veterans and made a point of appearing at regimental dinners and army society meetings. But he had never given a major address at such a gathering, nor put his thoughts on the war and its aftermath on paper. That changed on the evening of September 20, 1895, when Oates was invited to be one of the major speakers at the dedication of the Chickamauga and Chattanooga National Military Parks.

The first ceremonies dedicating the battlefields took place on Snodgrass Hill on September 18, the anniversary of the battle, where George Thomas (the "Rock of Chickamauga") had made his stand thirty-two years before to save the northern army. A speaker's platform was erected, looking out over the newly placed monuments that dotted the fields. A band played patriotic songs in the Georgia dusk, while crowds of veterans, their wives, and their families stood in expectation of hearing from the battle's aging commanders. General John Palmer of Illinois spoke, followed by John Gordon of Georgia, then General John Schofield of New York and James Longstreet of Georgia.

The next day the crowds moved to Chattanooga to place monuments on the hills overlooking the city, where Rosecrans's army was trapped after the loss at Chickamauga and where Oates was severely wounded. A reunion of the Army of Northern Virginia took place on the night of September 20, bringing the dedication ceremonies to an end. Oates was the scheduled featured speaker. Oates enjoyed himself immensely at the reunion, walking over the battlefields and meeting with veterans of the old army units.

John Schofield set the tone for the occasion by firmly putting aside any suggestion that the war had left matters unsettled. In the clear tones that attended all such gatherings, Schofield uttered what everyone then accepted as the basic truth of the war: "It was left to you, my comrades, gallant soldiers of the South and North," he told the crowd gathered at Snodgrass Hill, "to debate the questions which the forefathers left unsettled, and finally to decide them after four years of very earnest argument."

That was not the way William Oates saw it. For him, the war may have settled "the questions the forefathers left unsettled" in favor of the North, but he was unwilling to concede that therefore the South had been wrong. He made this clear as he rose to address the veterans of the Army of Northern Virginia on that night:

> This great gathering and the fraternal feeling manifested will give to the historian, for the record, something new under the sun. This great occasion is a greater honor to the Union veteran than to the Confederate, because he was the conqueror, and yet he indulges no vain or offensive boast over his fallen rival. It is a high compliment to the Confederate that his prowess and patriotism are thus acknowledged. It is patriotic and sensible on the part of the Union veteran because it commends the side he fought for to the more generous consideration of the younger generation of Southerners.

And so Oates, at least at the beginning of his speech, paid ritualistic obeisance to the soldiers of both sides of the conflict. The crowd responded with nods of approval and the high-ranking Union officers behind him on the platform politely applauded.

But then Oates went on to say: "It is complimentary to the Confederate veteran in this way to acknowledge defeat though accomplished by overpowering numbers, and to strike hands with his late adversaries as honorable men." There was a rustling in the crowd, but Oates plunged ahead, reviewing the Constitution, describing southern life and manners, and then returning again to take a hard slap at Schofield and others who believed that Right had triumphed: "It is sometimes asserted that the war was a necessity merely to settle the construction of the Constitution. I think that is a mistake. It indicates a want of recollection as to the true causes of the war, or those who assert it have convenient memories or a genius for inventing theories of conciliation for our defeat." Oates had had enough of reconciliation. But the worst was yet to come, as the Alabama governor launched into his views on slavery and how mistreatment of the slaves was punished in the Old South. Here the speech degenerated, as Oates was subjected to catcalls from his audience. "I knew a man to be tried the year before the war began for killing his slave, and he was convicted and sent to the penitentiary."

A voice suddenly cried from the back of the crowd: "He should have been hung, damn him."

Oates looked up, unperturbed: "Well, there are a good many people who deserve hanging and never get their deserts," he said.

The audience was now entranced by Oates's speech. They were shocked by his defense of slavery and the southern cause, but also titillated that here, at least, was not a standard speech of reconciliation of brother and brother that they had heard so many times before. Oates told his listeners that the war need not have happened at all, if it had not been for "a great and growing political party, confined alone to the Northern States, whose slogan was hostility to the institution of slavery." The war, he argued, was not about slavery alone, but about the southern states' obligation to defend "their ancient and well defined right to govern their own internal affairs in their own way." They were kept from doing so, Oates added, "by attrition, under the guise of law and constitutional administration." There were cries of "No" among the crowd, and people came to their feet in protest.

Oates was undisturbed. "I know that some of you Union men do not relish what I am saying, but hear me through; I will tell you the truth and give you nothing but facts." And on he went, through the battles and the valor of southern arms. But his point was made—there were some Confederates who would not be reconstructed, and he was one of them. At the end of his speech there was a smattering of applause, mostly from those who agreed with him. But others, especially on the platform, walked away. Only one veteran and commander did not. Oddly, in light of everything we know about the man, Oliver O. Howard came forward, smiled at Oates, and extended his hand.

The Oates speech made national news and sparked a minor controversy among Civil War veterans. The former Confederate colonel had done something no other Civil War veteran had ever dared—he had ripped the scab off the wound of the war. Oates said in public, and to northerners, what southerners had been saying in private, and in southern magazines, for years: that the South had never been defeated, but only overwhelmed; that its cause was not a betrayal of the Union, but just; that the war was not fought to defend slavery, but southern rights; and that the lot of the bondsman was actually a blessing—and not a curse. Oates's speech was a clear reminder to his northern listeners that, three decades after Appomattox, real differences remained between southerners and northerners that could not be healed by a show of reconciliation at a handful of battlefield reunions.

Oates weathered the storm of criticism that descended on him after his remarks at Chickamauga, serving out his single two-year term as governor. In 1896, he retired to private practice as a lawyer, spending his days in Abbeville, Eufaula, and Montgomery and occasionally traveling to Washington for political meetings. His health was good, though he was occasionally plagued by respiratory maladies. He vacationed in New Hampshire, wrote long letters on current events to the *Montgomery Advertiser*, and even traveled through Europe. Like Chamberlain, he believed his days in the public eye had ended.

In 1898, an insurrection in Cuba brought both Chamberlain and Oates back into public affairs. Chamberlain wrote a series of articles on the growing Spanish-American crisis for the *Bangor News*, claiming that Spain's destruction of the U.S. battleship *Maine* was not an accident. Like many other Americans, he believed that the United States could not stand by and let its honor be questioned. As the country moved toward war, Chamberlain began to think of ways in which he might participate and offered his services as a military adviser to Maine Governor Llewellyn Powers. "I feel that I shall most certainly avail myself of your counsel and assistance," Powers responded. Chamberlain then penned letters to Secretary of War Elihu Root and Maine Senator William Frye, asking for an assignment—perhaps as commander of U.S. troops. "I cannot but think that my day is not yet over for the service of my Country," he wrote. "You gentlemen in Congress and in the offices of the Government are in your right place: I desire to be in mine."

Chamberlain never got the call for military service he thought he deserved, but William Oates, the retired governor of Alabama, did. On May 28, 1898, after Congress had declared war on Spain, President

McKinley appointed him a brigadier general of volunteers, thereby jumping him in rank from his original lieutenant colonel in the Confederate army to a higher command in the U.S. army. There was little public comment on the move, and other ex-Confederates were appointed to military positions at the same time, but Chamberlain did not fail to notice that "Col. Oates, I see" was given a high rank, while he was given nothing. Oates moved quickly to try to convince the president to give him command of Alabama troops, but his request was caught up in a battle of red tape with the War Department. Oates was sent to Mobile, where he reported to brigade commander John Gordon, then returned to Montgomery to await further orders. He was sent, finally, to Tampa, where he met his commander, Major General Coppinger, who, Oates wrote, "wore a dirty, rusty-looking over-shirt, baggy seated trousers to match, and a slouchy army hat," and who just happened to be the son-in-law of James G. Blaine, Chamberlain's old political competitor.

Oates had an argument with Coppinger over command of troops and returned to Montgomery in a huff, where he fired off a protest letter to the secretary of war. He argued that Coppinger was incompetent, adding that compared to the other corps commanders he had served under, such as Stonewall Jackson and James Longstreet, Coppinger would not have even made a good courier. Summoned to Washington, Oates was finally told to report to the army training camp at Harrisburg, where he would be met by the camp commander General James Duncan Graham. There, Oates was given command of a brigade of soldiers from Pennsylvania, Connecticut, and New York and set about training them. In their quiet hours, Oates and Graham became friends and rode over the Pennsylvania countryside, talking about the war. "I found General Graham very much of a gentleman," Oates said.

It is one of the ironies of history that Oates's time in Harrisburg was at Camp Meade, under the command of the brother-in-law of the Union's commander at Gettysburg, George Gordon Meade. But an even greater irony came when Oates left the camp for South Carolina, then returned to find that his brigade was assigned to Brigadier General Adelbert Ames, the original commander of the 20th Maine. Ames had had a checkered postwar career, serving as the provisional governor and then senator from Mississippi during Reconstruction, where he spent hours pleading with his old comrades, including Chamberlain, to pay more attention to the plight of blacks in the South. These pleas fell on deaf ears and the unreconstructed Mississippi legislature forced him out of the state. During the Spanish-American War his former service was remembered by McKinley, who appointed him as brigadier general of volunteers.

Oates was given a new brigade, but the war with Spain ended before he saw action. One of his enduring memories, however, was of being at the head of the Peace Jubilee Parade held in Philadelphia to celebrate the American victory. "The sight of an old maimed Confederate soldier commanding Union troops raised in the Northern States was such an evidence of a reunited country that it produced applause from one end of the line of march to the other, a distance of seven miles," he said. Oates took his command to Atlanta, where he was joined by his wife, and then was mustered out of the service. Oates's reflections on his time as a brigadier general of volunteers were not extensive, but he could not remain silent about what he considered the most important war in which he had fought. He served the Confederacy as colonel, he said, and the United States as a brigadier general—and he was "right both times."

In late 1904 and early 1905, as both men were reaching an age when the contentions of the past might be expected to have faded from view, William Oates fought one last battle with Joshua Chamberlain. Oates had been contemplating the placing of a monument to the 15th Alabama at Gettysburg, at exactly the spot where he believed his regiment had stood—on the far right of the rebel line and within twenty yards of the federal line. Oates traveled to Gettysburg in the summer of 1904 to inspect Little Round Top and to point out to park commissioners the line his regiment took on the afternoon of July 2, 1863. Oates walked up Little Round Top to the exact spot where, he said, his regiment held its most forward position. But the commissioners who accompanied him said they had evidence that his regiment did not, in fact, advance so far as he believed. In support of their position, they produced a letter from Joshua Chamberlain that contradicted Oates's memory.

Oates did not believe he would have any trouble gaining approval for his monument, but after the 1904 inspection, he knew he would have to argue his point with his old antagonist. Chamberlain simply would not agree that the 15th Alabama had gotten anywhere near as close to his own line as Oates believed—and he was adamant on the point. The issue was taken up with Colonel John Nicholson of the War Department, who attempted to adjudicate the two claims. In fact, the difference in distances involved was minor—about fifty to seventy-five yards. But that did not mean the issue was unimportant, for Chamberlain claimed that the placement of a monument to the 15th Alabama where Oates wished it to be would have placed the rebel regiment inside his lines and exaggerated the success of their attack.

Frustrated by his inability to convince the War Department to approve the monument, Oates finally wrote Chamberlain directly. Oates attempted to be conciliatory, but it took his every effort, and the words are strained and cold:

> Col. Nicholson has sent to me your letter to him of the 16th . . . which I have carefully perused, and take pleasure in writing directly to you on the points involved. General, neither of us are as young as we were when we confronted each other on Little Round Top nearly 42 years ago. Now, in the natural course the memory of neither of us is as good as then. You speak in that letter of having corresponded with me and that you had received two letters from me. I will not dispute your word for you are an honorable gentleman, but I have no recollection of ever writing a letter to you, except at the present moment, nor do I remember ever to have received one from you. I have heard and read much about you—among other things, the very complimentary notice of your soldierly and gentlemanly conduct at Lee's surrender, in [General John B.] Gordon's book of Remenicinces [sic], but never had the honor of meeting you after the war.

Oates went on to review his claim that a monument of the 15th Alabama Regiment should be placed at Gettysburg at a point of its farthest advance. Oates said that he did not want to quibble as to exactly where that point might be: "If you, General, will write to the Commissioners, or to its chairman, and say that you have no objection to erecting it there, I assure you that there will be no inscription upon the shaft derogatory to your command and if mentioned it will be complimentary, for well do I know that no regiment in the Union Army fought any better or more bravely than your regiment at that spot."

Chamberlain, however, would not agree. He reviewed Oates's application for the placement of the monument and found fault with Oates's memory—claiming that he had previously written Oates, and that he had no objection to a monument to the 15th Alabama. Nevertheless, he said, he could not agree to the placing of a monument on ground designated by Oates, since the 15th Alabama did not reach that close to the Union lines or, as Oates claimed, "doubled back" his left so that it almost touched his right. The attack of the 15th Alabama, Chamberlain implied, was simply not that successful. The letter was testy:

> In [your] letter I find your impressions place me at a disadvantage in your estimation on two very different grounds; first, in that your former correspondence by way of letter made so little impression on you that you are led to deny having such correspondence; and secondly that you ascribe to my influence with the Government authorities their refusal to permit the erection of a monument to the 15th Alabama on the ground where they fought. These suggestions compel me to look over my vouchers to see if I have possibly been mistaken on topics of so much importance as to involve my word of honor.

These were fighting words since, in that time especially, a man's "word of honor" could not be questioned lightly. Chamberlain then went on to protest that he had "no objection whatever to the erection of a monument by you on the ground attained by the 15th Alabama or any portion of it, expressing only the wish that this ground be accurately ascertained." Chamberlain argued that Oates was simply wrong in his assumption about how close his regiment had come to the 20th Maine, or at what point it had penetrated his lines, if it did at all—and therefore Chamberlain simply could not agree to the placing of the monument on the ground that Oates designated.

That is where the issue ended, with no more correspondence between the two. There was much more to the controversy, however, than Oates could have known. It now seems unlikely, in light of the historical evidence, that the Gettysburg Park Commission was inclined to place any monument honoring the 15th Alabama at Gettysburg, even had Chamberlain agreed with Oates on the details of the battle. After Chamberlain wrote to Oates, he sent a copy of his letter to John Nicholson of the War Department's Gettysburg National Park Commission. Nicholson wrote back: "I wish to congratulate you upon the dignified, manly, soldierly and gentlemanly way in which you have replied to him," Nicholson wrote. "It is very clear that General Oates has not the slightest idea of admitting the views of any one in the controversy except himself." Nicholson added that the monument debate was being turned over to the chairman of the commission. Several months later, the commission turned down Oates's request for a monument to the 15th Alabama on Little Round Top.

Oates was deeply disappointed. He wanted the regimental monument to serve as a memorial not only to those who fought there, but to his brother and his close personal friends, and had spent hours designing the monument and writing its inscription:

> To the memory of Lt. John A. Oates
> and his gallant Comrades who fell here
> July 2nd, 1863. The 15th Ala. Regt.,
> over 400 strong reached this spot, but
> for lack of support had to retire.
>
> Lt. Col. Feagin lost a leg.
> Capts. Brainard and Ellison,
> Lts. Oates and Cody and
> 33 men were killed, 76 wounded
> and 84 captured
>
> Erected 39th Anniversary of battle,
> by Gen. Wm. C. Oates who was
> Colonel of the Regiment.

The Chamberlain-Oates controversy over the 15th Alabama monument not only shows how the war lived on long after its guns were silenced, but exemplifies the very real wounds that remained between its antagonists. The generation that had fought the war was dying, and yet they had not forgotten the past. Even forty-two years after the events, the battle was fresh in the minds of Chamberlain and Oates, despite the care they took in complimenting each other on their successful careers. "I should be glad to meet you again, after your honorable and conspicuous career of which the trials and tests of Gettysburg were so brilliant a part," Chamberlain told the former Alabama commander in his last letter.

Yet, despite this formal cordiality, Chamberlain and Oates never gave any indication that they would have really liked to meet each other; they never talked, never addressed the same crowd or served in the same legislature. The only time they faced each other directly was at opposite sides of the most important conflict of their day. But despite this, their lives, careers, families, experiences of war and peace, and successes and failures are remarkably similar. Both grew up in modest surroundings, in rural communities, where education and God were ever-present realities. Both were self-made men who became amateur soldiers. Both excelled in battle, both served as governors of their state, both yearned for a seat in the Senate—both were denied. Had they met, they would have had much to talk about. A list of the topics on which they might have found common ground would be lengthy and an almost perfect reflection of their society's most important principles: both mistrusted big government, believed in an elected elite of "the best men," thought political stability the engine of economic growth—and had large ideas about the course of the American Republic.

At the end of his public career, Oates retired to a life of uneasy leisure before agreeing to serve as a graves commissioner investigating the locations of lost Confederates. He attended a reunion of his regiment, spoke at veterans' dinners, and vacationed with his wife. In 1901, he served his state one last time, as a delegate to a new constitutional convention, called to make certain that the threats to his party's supremacy would never become a reality. The "disenfranchising convention" of 1901, as it is referred to by historians, was organized around the principle of what was then called the "soldiers' clause," designed to make certain that only voters approved by the white-dominated Democratic Party would be registered. Oates watched the proceedings with increasing skepticism and worry and finally, now, in the waning years of his life, decided that he must speak up to disagree.

Rising to his feet at an important moment in the convention's proceedings, Oates condemned the move to disenfranchise Alabama's black voters, speaking in clear and certain terms of his worries for the state's future as two societies—one white and one black. The time had come to end corruption in Alabama politics, he said. "White men have gotten to cheating each other until we don't have any honest elections," he said. It must have occurred to Oates's political friends that the former governor had had some firsthand experience in this and that he was now suddenly changing his stripes. But they listened anyway to his argument that inevitably the corruption in the state political system would lead to an explosion and that the state's black population, cowed as it was, would eventually, inevitably, demand its rights. The delegates listened politely and voted overwhelming to reject his proposition. Because of the vote of the 1901 convention, Alabama's black population was effectively neutralized as a factor in all future elections—until other brave men and women, fifty years later, began the long process of reversing that political tradition.

Oates returned home and continued to practice law, and wrote his book on his experiences during the Civil War. *The War Between the Union and the Confederacy* is a massive and detailed work—perhaps the finest first-person account of the war ever written. In his preface to his book, Oates repeats his earlier claim to being a simple man, without educational achievements, protesting that he had "no pretense to scholarly attainments" and lacked "the advantages of a classical education." Yet Oates's simple education serves him well, certainly as well, or better, than Chamberlain's more formal years of scholarly achievement. His book is fascinating, his sentences tightly written, his command of drama nearly unequaled by other battlefield writers. He shows an amazing breadth of knowledge of other battles and a prodigious memory for those with whom he fought. *The War Between the Union and the Confederacy* is one of the clearest expositions of why so many southerners went to war in 1861, and why those who remained alive forty years later looked on their experience and their cause with pride. In every respect, Oates concluded, the conflict between North and South "was the mightiest war that ever rolled its purple flood across the track of time."

In his last years, Oates aged gracefully. He was a constant and imposing figure in Montgomery and a regular attendee at Democratic Party functions. He continued his many journeys around the state, checking in on old veterans who had served with him from the Shenandoah to Petersburg. When his health permitted, he would make certain to attend the funerals of his old comrades—a gray-bearded figure with a cane. Even in his old age, rumors about Oates's private life continued to circulate among the political gossips of Montgomery. The rumors included one that helps to fill the gaps in his life following the end of the Civil War. Historians now know that the rumor that William Oates fathered two (white) children just after Appomattox are true—though he never admitted to that in public. In 1865, an unnamed woman gave birth to a son, Claude. Two years later another unnamed woman gave birth to a son, Josh. Both were educated at the University of Alabama, with their father paying the tuition. Josh Oates became a lawyer and Claude a doctor, and Oates helped to set them up in business in Texas. But neither of them ever had anything else to do with him, and he never, ever mentioned them to anyone.

Oates's health failed slowly. In his last years, his old war wounds pained him. He died on September 9, 1910, at the age of 77.

⌖

"Your husband and children 'rise up and call you blessed'—as the old scriptures represent the crowning grace of woman," Chamberlain wrote to Fannie on her eightieth birthday. She died a few weeks later, on October 18. Chamberlain remained in retirement, spending more and more time with his writings, and completing his account of the last days with the Army of the Potomac. His work was later released as *The Passing of the Armies*. Unlike Oates's longer work, Chamberlain's memoir is overlaid with literary allusions, biblical references, and a sheen of romanticism that almost overawes his narrative. It does not compare well with Oates's work—but then, Chamberlain did not attempt to tell the story of the war through its battles. Rather, his account is a defense of his view that God had somehow intervened in the conflict—and blessed its victor. The value of *The Passing of the Armies* is in the glimpse it gives us of Chamberlain and of those thousands of other Union soldiers who believed that their army was an instrument in the hands of God: "This army will live, and live on, so long as soul shall answer soul, so long as that flag watches with its stars over fields of mighty memory, so long as in its red lines a regenerated people reads the charter of its birthright, and in its field of white God's covenant with man."

Chamberlain was surrounded in his last days by the men of Bowdoin, who often came to visit him. He visited Gettysburg one last time in May 1913, but fell ill early in 1914 and could not rise from his bed. He died on February 24, at the age of eighty-five—six months before the reverberations of a new and more deadly war sounded from Europe.

# Montgomery and Brunswick

**W**AR CREATES SHARED HISTORY. Even after Appomattox, William Oates and Joshua Chamberlain found that in spite of having fought in opposing armies they had the most important thing in common—they had the war. The Civil War brought the nation together, and made it one, as nothing had before—or has since. Both men sensed this, and this unity is their lasting legacy, their gift to us.

There is no doubt that there is something disturbing in these two lives. Neither is the hero we may have expected to find: glorious in war, forgiving in peace, progressive and fair-minded. Writing history is an exercise in myth-breaking—we should not expect Oates to defend the freedman, nor Chamberlain to be an abolitionist. Oates packed ballot boxes, Chamberlain lectured and berated his wife. Oates worked to undo black gains during Reconstruction. Chamberlain defended the effort.

To be sure, the men who fought the war and gave their lives fought honorably and courageously for their ideals. Oates and Chamberlain were two such men whose courage cannot now be doubted. But they were not perfect—and we do them a disservice to think them so. Nor is it enough to say that they were products of their time. Many other men and women fought hard for their ideals, opposed the tyranny of white-hooded murderers, worked diligently every day to bring about a new ideal of equality, and died for their beliefs. Chamberlain and Oates are worth remembering both for what they did and for what they didn't—and for what they can teach us about . . . us. The Civil War did not end at Appomattox, the South did not rise again, the Lost Cause was not honorable, the South did not redeem itself through Reconstruction, the North did not serve the nation by turning its back on its newly emancipated citizens. For all of those who "went with their state" because it was the "honorable thing to do," many, many others walked out of the South in disgust and headed north to fight secession, and slavery, and racism.

William Oates was buried in Oakwood Cemetery in Montgomery. His funeral brought Alabama's political establishment together to pay homage to his life. He was extolled in print by the leading newspapers of the state. Among the mourners were the few veterans left of the 15th Alabama. But Oates wanted to be remembered for his accomplishments that went beyond the war. He penned his own epitaph, which appears on his gravestone:

Born in poverty,
Reared in Adversity,
Without educational advantages
Yet by honest individual effort he
Obtained a competency and the confidence
Of his fellow men,
While fairly liberal to relative and to the
Worthy poor.
A devoted Confederate soldier,
He gave his right arm for the cause.
He accepted the result of
The war without a murmur,
And in 1898–9 He was a Brigadier General
of United States Volunteers in the War with Spain

On the back side of the monument is the simple inscription:

A Soldier in two wars,
Captain, Colonel and General
Legislator, member of Congress and Governor.

Chamberlain's monument is in Pine Grove Cemetery, next to the Bowdoin campus, where he had spent so much of his life. Muffled drums accompanied the cortege and speeches were given at his memorial. The official mourners were surviving members of the Grand Army. The services took place in the First Parish Church, where his father-in-law had preached and where Harriet Beecher Stowe—who had died at her home in Connecticut in 1896—had seen her vision of the chained slave. Chamberlain's monument is simple, with his name and the date of his birth and death.

The reputations of both men suffered after their deaths. Oates was consigned to oblivion, the knowledge of his life and exploits limited to historians, scholars, and Civil War aficionados, who believed his role in the Battle of Gettysburg never received the attention it deserved. Chamberlain too was forgotten, in part because of an attack on him by Ellis Spear, who wrote that Strong Vincent played a more epic role in the struggle for Little Round Top and that Chamberlain had not ordered the bayonet charge that swept the 15th Alabama from the field.

Six decades later, Chamberlain's wartime heroism was resuscitated by an avalanche of books, articles, and movies on his life that set off a debate among Civil War historians on his true worth. He is now rightly remembered for that moment on July 2 when his little regiment saved the Union. Oates and Chamberlain were not the only ones who have faded from America's memory. Other great soldiers have also been forgotten, their sacrifice and service eclipsed by the memories of more horrible fights in bloodier wars.

John Bell Hood, Oates's division commander, fared poorly. He spent the last years reliving his mistakes as the head of the Confederacy's western armies, which he had led to an ignominious defeat at Nashville. He returned to New Orleans, where he died of yellow fever in 1879. Jubal Early, who convinced Oates to add his voice to the *Southern Historical Society Papers*, died bent over and embittered in Lynchburg in 1894, while Longstreet, the man he reviled, spent his last years managing his hotel in Gainesville. Longstreet died in 1904, a Republican to the end. The colorful and strange Richard Ewell died in Spring Hill, Tennessee, plagued by criticisms that his failure to attack on the first day at Gettysburg had cost the South victory. Richard Taylor, the head of the Louisiana Tigers that had fought with Oates at Gaines's Mill, penned one of the war's lasting memoirs. Taylor was undoubtedly one of the best-educated men of the nineteenth century. He died in New York City, one month after his book's publication, in 1879.

Oates's favorite commander and the head of the Alabama Brigade, Evander McIvor Law, returned to Alabama after the war, moved to Florida, and became a successful attorney. He died there in 1920 at the age of eighty-six.

Chamberlain's comrades did not have as many difficulties finding their way after the war as Oates's, though only a handful were able to reach the level of success and accomplishment they had enjoyed in a dozen battles in the four years they spent in uniform. George McClellan finally won an election—as governor of New Jersey, where he died in 1895. George Gordon Meade administered the Reconstruction policies in the South's fifth military district, but left the post to become commissioner of Fairmount Park in Philadelphia. He believed he was never given proper credit for the victory at Gettysburg. He was right: it was a masterpiece. He died in Philadelphia of pneumonia in 1872. Union General David Birney, the son of Alabama planter James Birney, died during the war from illness. His final words were a plea: "Keep your eyes on that flag, boys."

Joseph Bartlett, who vied with Chamberlain for leadership of a division in Warren's Fifth Corps, went on to become minister to Sweden in 1867, after which he resumed his career as a successful lawyer in New York City, where he died in 1893. George Sykes, who commanded the Fifth Corps at Gettysburg, stayed in the army, died in 1880, and was buried at West Point. Phil Sheridan was promoted to full general, wrote a two-volume history of the war, and died at his home in Nosquitt, Massachusetts, in 1888—never a popular man. Charles Griffin, who pushed for Chamberlain's promotion, lived for only two years after Lee's surrender. He remained in the army, but refused to leave his post in Galveston when yellow fever rampaged through the town. The disease killed him in 1867. Daniel Butterfield, whose bugle call for the 20th Maine became "Taps," ended his career in the army, died in 1901, and was buried by a special order of the service at West Point, which he had not attended. Oliver O. Howard, Chamberlain's Bowdoin counterpart, lived a life of great accomplishment, as an educator, head of the Freedmen's Bureau, defender of the rights of American Indians, and founder of Howard University. He died in Vermont in 1909.

Adelbert Ames, the first commander of the 20th Maine, was breveted major general for gallantry and became one of the army's staunchest defenders of equal rights. After serving as provisional governor of Mississippi during Reconstruction and as a commander in the Spanish-American War, Ames retired to Ormond, Florida, where he died at the age of ninety-seven in 1933. He was the last surviving general who served in the Civil War.

# *Acknowledgments*

I BEGAN THIS BOOK thirty-five years ago, when I was nine years old. I grew up in a small town in Wisconsin—there were no bookstores in the town, no book reviews, and if book clubs existed I did not know of them. The world of words seemed far away or, in my case, only as close as the condensed *Reader's Digest* books that my mother ordered. They came in cardboard wrappings in the mail and when she was done with them I leafed through their pages, looking at the drawings that invariably accompanied the text. One of these books was John Pullen's *The Twentieth Maine*. I read the book in fascination as a young boy.

The second book I read on the war was a part of the "I Was There" series for children. These were fascinating books, which featured as their main characters a young boy and girl who overheard (from a nearby closet or closed trunk) the major events of history: the signing of the Declaration of Independence, Lincoln's assassination at Ford's Theater, Washington crossing the Delaware. I read *I Was There . . . at Gettysburg* and imagined that I was hidden away, like the young heroes, in the cupola of the Lutheran Seminary on Seminary Ridge—and saw John Buford looking down at General Reynolds as the gray ranks advanced beyond.

My sister Anne bought me the *American Heritage Civil War*, abridged for children, which I still own. She does not remember doing this, but I can recall the precise moment that she handed it to me. I was fascinated by the maps, which showed miniature soldiers marching over slopes and through fields. I studied the Civil War diligently through high school and college, where I met my wife, who is a direct descendant of James Longstreet, a man I admire. We have his calling card, with its red battle flag, framed in our home.

For two decades I read everything that I could on the war, but it was only in reading and rereading Shelby Foote's *The Civil War: A Narrative* that I thought of putting to paper the story I had first heard in my childhood—that two men, and not one, made the Battle at Little Round Top. I postponed the task, however, until 1994, when my agent, Gail Ross, urged me to write the story I had come to know so well. I am indebted to Gail for pushing me to write this book, and to Jane von Mehren of Viking Penguin, who ushered the final product to completion with gracious expertise and advice. My thanks also to Kristine Puopolo of Viking Penguin for her detailed work in editing the manuscript.

I am indebted to the men and women of Vietnam Veterans of America Foundation—and most especially to Bobby Muller and John Terzano, with whom I have worked for many years—for giving me the time and facilities to complete this book. America's Vietnam veterans have taught me that while there is little of value that comes from war, it creates enormous opportunities for reconciliation among peoples who might not otherwise know peace—and that war is the creation of shared history.

I am indebted to those historians who first blazed this trail, but most especially to the biographers of Chamberlain and Oates who set the stage for this work. I am also indebted to the historians of the National Park Service at Gettysburg, Fredericksburg, and Chickamauga, to those fine men and women at Bowdoin College who keep the memory of Joshua Chamberlain alive, and to those from the Alabama State Archives who spent countless hours tracking down documents, diaries, journals, letters, and regimental anecdotes. My thanks go especially to Robert Krick, who is the historian at Fredericksburg National Military Park; to Jim Ogden, the historian at the Chickamauga and Chattanooga National Military Park; and to Dr. Norbert Kerr at the Alabama State Archives. I wish to especially thank my researcher at Bowdoin College, Keisha Larkan, a young history student of considerable talents who helped me to find a treasure trove of invaluable documents on Chamberlain. My gratitude also goes to the researchers at the Abbeville Library in Oates's hometown, and to Charlton Oates Pingel—who sent me valuable genealogical information on the Oates family—but who is not, surprisingly, a descendant of Colonel Oates.

I wish to thank my sister Anne Balderson, who first introduced me to the Civil War, and my sister Lois Brown, who urged me to write. My wife Nina Mikhalevsky and our children, Madeleine and Cal, proved ever patient with my endless monologues and odd need for absolute silence.

Finally, I have dedicated this book to the graduates of Northwestern Military and Naval Academy, in whose ranks I was proud to stand. The men and women of Northwestern honorably served their nation for 106 years, through six wars and countless peacetime challenges. My time with them at the Academy is, for me, the best proof that our great national experiment will work—that men and women of all races, colors, creeds, religions, and ethnic backgrounds can live together in understanding in a nation that was "conceived in liberty."

# Notes

PROLOGUE

## The Rocky Hill

1 *The 15th Alabama had been on the move: The War Between the Union and the Confederacy*, William Oates, Morningside Press, Dayton, OH, 1985, pp. 195–96. First published in 1905 by The Neale Company, Philadelphia (hereafter, *Oates*). See also *From Manassas to Appomattox*, General James Longstreet, Mallard Books (reprint), New York, 1991, p. 337; and "Lee's Invasion of Pennsylvania," General James Longstreet, in *Battles and Leaders of the Civil War* (vol. 3), Castle Books, New York, 1956, p. 249.

2 *The 15th had reached Snicker's Gap: Ibid.*, p. 195. See also "The Struggle for 'Round Top,' " General E. M. Law, in *Battles and Leaders of the Civil War* (vol. 3), pp. 318–19.

3 *William Oates thought his Alabama regiment: Ibid.*, pp. 198–99.

3 *"This is a most magnificent country"*: *Histories of the Several Regiments and Battalions from North Carolina in the Great War, 1861–1865*, University of North Carolina Press (vol. 22), p. 28. See also *High Tide at Gettysburg*, Glenn Tucker, Morningside Press (reprint), Dayton, OH, p. 162.

Dorsey Pender's letters to his wife provide some of the most pointed anecdotal evidence on the campaign. "He had the soft brown eyes of a dreamer but hits like a hammer in an attack. His love letters to his wife, written almost daily even during intense campaigning, show a deep religious faith and a compassion and softness altogether out of harmony with the fierce ruthlessness of the battlefield," Tucker says. Pender was mortally wounded on July 2.

4 *Like the 15th Alabama*: "Report of Col. Joshua L. Chamberlain, Twentieth Maine Infantry," in *Official Records of the Union and Confederate Armies* (vol. 27, series 1), Government Printing Office, Washington, D.C., 1889, p. 622 (hereafter, *OR*). See also "Headquarters Third Brigade," in *OR* (vol. 27, series 1), pp. 621–22; and "The 20th Maine at Little Round Top," H. S. Melcher, *Lincoln County News*, Saldoboro, ME, March 13, 1885.

4 *"The shot and shell flew pretty lively"*: Maine to the Wilderness: The Civil War Letters of Pvt. William Lamson, 20th Maine Infantry, ed. Roderick M. Engert, Publishers Press, Orange, VA, 1993, p. 68.

Lamson's letters, written to his sister, Jennie, provide interesting vignettes of camp life in the 20th Maine. Lamson served until May 5, 1864, when he was wounded and taken prisoner during the Battle of the Wilderness. He died soon thereafter. It is thought he was buried near the battlefield, but the location of his grave is not known.

5 *"Your army is free to act"*: "Hooker's Appointment and Removal," Charles F. Benjamin, in *Battles and Leaders of the Civil War* (vol. 3), p. 241. See also *OR* (vol. 27, series 1), p. 61.

6 *Early on the morning of July 2*: "The Struggle for 'Round Top,' " General E. M. Law, in *Battles and Leaders of the Civil War* (vol. 3), pp. 318–19.

Law testifies that he first received his orders at three A.M. and moved immediately to Gettysburg. Other commentators say that the order came later, at four or even five A.M. The differences are important, since some contemporaneous commentators say that Law's Brigade spent eleven hours on the road to Gettysburg, which places them on the battlefield at two, three, or four on the afternoon of July 2—and therefore marks the starting point of their march and countermarch through the woods behind Seminary Ridge. Oates's description of the brigade's movement is probably the most accurate: Law received his orders at three A.M., broke camp, and began their movement at four A.M. Law then spent nine hours on the road, arriving at about noon—or perhaps soon thereafter—on the afternoon of July 2. Oates is correct if his eyewitness testimony, that he saw Lee and Longstreet conferring on the rise to the east, on Seminary Ridge, is true—they were conferring between noon and one P.M.

7 *At nearly the same moment*: "Report of Col. Joshua L. Chamberlain, Twentieth Maine Infantry," *OR* (vol. 27, series 1), p. 622.

Chamberlain's movement to Gettysburg is more difficult to fix. The most detailed and accurate report was given by Fifth Corps commander Major General George Sykes in his official report (*OR*, vol. 27, series 1), pp. 592–658. Sykes understates the exhausting pace set by the corps, which traveled for four days starting at Frederick, Maryland (on June 29), and ending at Gettysburg at eight A.M. on July 2. Chamberlain's own account of the march ("Through Blood and Fire at Gettysburg," *Hearst* magazine, 1913) is typically ambiguous; he said only that "all day we had been marching North from Maryland."

8 *"the best marching done in either army"*: From Manassas to Appomattox, p. 365.

9 *Hood's Division took the lead*: Ibid., p. 366.

9 *It was three-thirty when the artillery opened*: Ibid., p. 369. As always, there is widespread disagreement with the time of the opening bombardment of July 2. It may have been quite later than Longstreet had thought—as he himself intimates, saying that he ordered the artillery to open its "practice" rounds at three P.M. That can only be true if the march and countermarch (of ninety min-

utes) began at one P.M. Which it did not. It is more likely that the first shots were fired at closer to three-thirty (as Law suggests) and the first troops stepped off, from the right, at about four P.M. This would accord with McLaws's Division's step-off time, one hour later, of five P.M., when William Barksdale sent his Mississippi Brigade directly east, toward the Peach Orchard.

CHAPTER 1

*I Went Out Among Strangers*

13 *The elder William Oates came to Montgomery:* "Data: William C. Oates," Alabama Department of Archives and History, Montgomery, Alabama; see also *The Papers of Governor William C. Oates, 1835–1910* (hereafter, *Oates Papers*), Administrative Files (1 file).

Genealogists and historians have the same problems: while America's state-houses and courthouses contain the most detailed and usable records of any nation, the records themselves disagree, often on the most important and funda-mental facts—birth dates and deaths, children, marriages, and residence. It is not different in the case of the Oates family, whose chief forebear was once thought to be Stephen Oates. That is the case for the Oateses of southwestern Alabama, but not for the Oateses of *southeastern* Alabama. Stephenson Oates is the actual fore-bear of William C. Oates. He was born in Dobbs County, North Carolina, in 1764 and died there in 1817.

The information on the Oates family of Pike and later Henry counties was provided to me by genealogist Charlton Oates Pingel of Enon, Ohio, who fol-lowed William Calvin Oates's family because they were often confused with hers—which came from southwestern Alabama, and are no relation. There is no doubt, however, that William Oates's father came to Alabama in 1828.

14 *Edmund Ruffin, a slaveholder and plantation owner: Ordeal of the Union: A House Dividing, 1852–1857*, Allan Nevins, Scribner's, New York, 1947, p. 179.

14 *By the early 1850s . . . J. Foster Marshall: Ibid.,* pp. 182–83. Marshall's address to the State Agricultural Society of South Carolina in 1857 was issued as a pamphlet and gained wide circulation in the South.

15 *Adams's policy was unpopular in the South: Civil War and Reconstruc-tion in Alabama,* Walter L. Fleming, Reprint Company, Spartanburg, SC, 1978, pp. 4–10. Fleming is from the "Dunning School" of historians, who spent much time critiquing Reconstruction from a southern viewpoint; but his account of the Alabama nullification controversy is authoritative.

16 *There were 85,000 whites and 41,000 slaves:* "Families and Free Popula-tion," *1840 U.S. Census* (Alabama), U.S. Census Bureau, 1840, National Archives. The breakdown is by county, and then within the county by house-hold. The records are detailed, though not so much as later, and invaluable.

17 *Alabama was being gradually transformed: Civil War and Reconstruc-tion in Alabama,* p. 3.

17 *and later accounts describe William Oates as a "planter"*: Alabama Department of Archives and History, *Oates Papers*, "Governor's Vertical File—Oates, SG6998," Administrative Files.

The statement describing William Oates as a planter appears in Governor Oates's Governor files—it is mentioned in an untitled obituary on Governor Oates, probably from the *Mobile Register* of 1910.

17 *Their oldest child, William: Henry's Heritage*, Dr. Hoyt Warren, Henry County Historical Society, Abbeville, 1980, pp. 36–39. Charlton Oates Pingel, "Letter to Mr. William Norden," December 20, 1986 (in author's private collection).

In a discussion on her work on the Oates family, Pingel mentions the same names of William Oates's siblings, their date of birth, and their last known residence. She notes that much of the family material, including family records, has disappeared over time. There is an Oates family Bible that has been passed on to an unknown descendant, the particularly important parts of which have been passed down through generations of researchers. The sisters and brothers of William Oates were pieced together by a careful reading of *Henry's Heritage*—which contains a wealth of biographical material on the early Henry and Pike County settlers—and by genealogists. As always in such research, women are not listed separately, but as wives, making such investigations nearly impossible to do with absolute certainty.

In one record, Sarah's name is noted as "Prudence." Every other record, and her son William's own biographical sketch completed for the Alabama Archives, gives her name as Sarah.

18 *The young William Oates: Oates*, p. 277.

19 *The "Second Great Awakening". . . was sparked . . . by James McGready: The Road to Disunion*, William W. Freehling, Oxford University Press, New York, 1990, pp. 289–90.

19 *"Will I ever see anything more like": American History: A Survey*, Allan W. Brinkley, McGraw-Hill, New York, 1990, p. 188.

20 *In Rochester, New York, Charles Grandison Finney: The Road to Disunion*, p. 290. Also see *Harriet Beecher Stowe: A Life*, Joan D. Hedrick, Oxford University Press, New York, 1994, p. 103.

21 *Beginning in his early teenage years:* "William Calvin Oates, Biography," in *Oates Papers*. Oates handwrote two such biographical sketches for himself, undoubtedly at the request of the Alabama Department of Archives and History; these two biographies, his sparse official letters, his book, a smattering of autobiographic sketches, and a sketch of his trip to Europe are all we have by his hand. The two biographies agree in all details.

22 *"The facilities for obtaining an education"*: Ibid.

22 *"I went out among strangers"*: Ibid.; and "Gov. Oates's Early Education," William C. Oates II, *Montgomery Advertiser*, June 1, 1930 (hereafter, "Oates Autobiography").

Just before his death, William Oates penned a short autobiography, in his own hand, to his son, so that he would "at least know the outlines of my career." There are only two extant copies, one of which is in the hands of a descendant. The most complete version for the public, however, was printed by his son, in the body of a letter that he wrote to the *Montgomery Advertiser*, which appeared under the headline "Gov. Oates's Early Education." It appeared on June 1, 1930.

23 *The episode that Oates remembered: The Heyday of Spiritualism*, Slater Brown, Hawthorn Books, New York, 1983, pp. 98–104.

24 *The investigation brought even larger crowds: Ibid.*, pp. 103–5, 115.

26 *American spiritualism swept through New York: Ibid.*, pp. 128–32. See also *Radical Spirits: Spiritualism and Women's Rights in Nineteenth-Century America*, Ann D. Braude, Beacon Press, Boston, 1989.

26 *On a hot June day in 1851:* "Oates Autobiography." See also "Introduction" to *Oates*, Robert Krick (no pagination).

The journey taken by Oates has led historians on a tangled chronological chase. Robert Krick has the best account, though Glenn LaFantasie's short biography of Oates, in *Gettysburg* (Bantam Books, New York, 1992), is also quite useful. Using the Oates material, historians must work back—from the Civil War—to determine just when Oates departed Alabama and when he returned home. In addition, Krick mentions that this was the second time that Oates left, the first time after having been beaten by his father.

Oates himself was strangely ambiguous in the dates for his departure and where he went and when. The material is so sparse, in fact, that it is quite possible that Oates's "wanderings" through the Southwest were more abbreviated than either he implies or that later authors assume. Researchers invariably get the feeling that there is something wrong with the account—that Oates was either purposely hiding something or that he was exaggerating his own youthful encounters. The one witness to these events, John Oates, left no records of his meeting his brother in Texas. Even so, it is possible to find corroborating material that confirms Oates's account—in the medical records of the yellow fever epidemic that swept through the Gulf Coast during his journey. This account is taken primarily from Krick and those few chronological markers left by William C. Oates.

31 *Oates said later the important lesson:* "Introduction," Robert Krick, in *Oates* (no pagination).

Chapter 2

*Shadows Luminous in the Sunset Glow*

39 *Lawrence Joshua Chamberlain was given his name:* Chamberlain Family Bible, Brewer Public Library, Brewer, Maine. See also *In the Hands of Providence*, Alice Rains Trulock, University of North Carolina Press, Chapel Hill, pp. 26–27.

40 *The Chamberlains came to America: Ibid.*, p. 25. See also *Genealogical and Family History of the State of Maine* (vol. 1), New York, 1909, pp. 131–33.

40 *Chamberlain's regiment marched and countermarched: Ibid.*, p. 26.

40 *Chamberlain's mother, Sarah Dupee Brastow: In the Hands of Providence*, p. 28.

42 *Nevertheless, in his teens Joshua Chamberlain agreed:* "Early Memoirs, J. L. Chamberlain," Joshua Chamberlain, Joshua Chamberlain Papers, Bowdoin College Library, Brunswick, Maine.

42 *"Just do it": In the Hands of Providence*, p. 33. Depending on the biography, the words are "Just do it," or "Do it, that's how," or "Move it." Chamberlain repeated the story often as a way of explaining his later exploits as the result of his disciplined upbringing, and his account also differs.

43 *Nevertheless, the ethic of the time: The Christian Home in Victorian America, 1840–1900*, Colleen McDannel, Indiana University Press, Bloomington, 1986, pp. 111–19.

44 *In the early 1840s, Joshua Chamberlain's father: In the Hands of Providence*, pp. 32–33. The hardship visited on the family as a result of the financial troubles of Chamberlain's father was a good deal more harsh than Trulock describes. See *JLC: A Sketch*, Chamberlain Association of America, in Joshua L. Chamberlain Papers, Maine Historical Society, Augusta.

44 *The senior Chamberlain staved off bankruptcy: JLC: A Sketch*, pp. 4–6. Trulock's biography, taken to be a definitive work, does not mention the senior Chamberlain's financial problems. See also *To Gettysburg and Beyond*, Michael Golay, Crown, New York, 1994, pp. 12–13.

44 *As a child, Joshua had developed: Ibid.*, p. 7. *To Gettysburg and Beyond*, pp. 14–15, *In the Hands of Providence*, pp. 40–41.

45 *"Now in the declining day of the sower":* "Early Memoirs," pp. 66–67.

47 *Over the course of the next year: In the Hands of Providence*, pp. 36–37.

48 *"They seem to understand my duty pretty well":* "JLC to My Dear Pastor," May 5, 1848, Bowdoin College Collection, Brunswick, Maine.

49 *When the townspeople complained: In the Hands of Providence*, pp. 39–40. See also "Early Memoirs," pp. 55–56, 63.

50 *"I know well my father will be proud":* "Early Memoirs," p. 40.

50 *Cleaveland and Smyth were joined:* "Early Memoirs," pp. 42–44.

51 *He finally sought help from Alpheus Packard:* "Early Memoirs," pp. 63, 66.

52 *"may have reached into the whole of [my] life":* "Early Memoirs," p. 66.

52 *"In the depths of every heart, there is a tomb": The House of the Seven Gables*, Nathaniel Hawthorne, Ticknor and Fields, Boston, 1851.

54 *When school opened at Bowdoin in late August:* "Early Memoirs," pp. 63–65.

CHAPTER 3

*Written in Blood*

56 *Abolitionism came to Alabama: The Road to Disunion*, pp. 113–17.

Freehling bases his account on Betty Fladeland's *James Gillespie Birney: Slaveholder to Abolitionist*, Cornell University Press, Ithaca, NY, 1955. Birney's letters, which contain detailed accounts of his travels in Alabama, were collected in two volumes in 1938, by historian Dwight Drummond. See especially Birney's "Letter on Colonization, Addressed to the Rev. Thornton J. Mills," New York, 1834. Most accounts of Birney treat him as a revolutionary abolitionist; Freehling was the first historian to comprehensively document his prior life as a plantation owner in Alabama, thereby dispelling the myth.

57 *After his last public address: Ibid.*, p. 117.

59 *In July 1837: Ibid.*, p. 117.

59 *Watching the events of the summer of 1837: Harriet Beecher Stowe: A Life*, p. 105.

Beecher's letters to her husband, father, and sisters are collected in *The Life and Letters of Harriet Beecher Stowe*, Annie Adams Fields, Houghton Mifflin, Boston, 1897.

60 *The "Lane Debates," as they were called: Ibid.*, pp. 102–4. The most useful modern analysis of the effect of religion on the abolitionist movement, its ties to the "Second Great Awakening," and Harriet Beecher Stowe's rebellion against Calvin appears in *Patriotic Gore*, Edmund Wilson, Farrar, Straus, and Giroux, New York, 1962, pp. 3–58. Wilson's was the first comprehensive account that tied the events of the war, the nation's postwar writings, and religion together.

60 *Weld reacted quickly to the board's decision: The Beechers: An American Family in the Nineteenth Century*, Milton Rugoff, Harper & Row, New York, 1981, pp. 201–12.

62 *"What on earth are you doing, Henry?": Patriotic Gore*, p. 12.

63 *By 1841, their financial situation was perilous: Harriet Beecher Stowe: A Life*, pp. 138–41.

64 *just when the Stowes' financial situation: Ibid.*, pp. 190–92.

Hedrick places Charley's death as a key turning point in Harriet Beecher Stowe's thinking about slavery, linking the two through a study of infant mortality: "The capriciousness of a Calvinist God, to whom there was not recourse but submission to his disciplinary rod, was monstrously paralleled by the cruelty of an overseer who held the human destiny of slaves under his whip. Infant mortality among slaves was twice that among the white population and slaves possessed their own children only at the whim of the master, who often sold them into distant bondages."

65 *Finally, in early 1850, Calvin: Ibid.*, pp. 194–96.

66 *But she still felt uneasy, even "haunted by the idea": Ibid.*, p. 197.

67 *The passage of the Fugitive Slave Act: Ibid.*, pp. 203–5.

68 *One day, after a disagreement with Harriet: Ibid.*, pp. 204–5.

69 *Not only was he an interested political observer: In the Hands of Providence*, pp. 42–43.

69 *Fannie Adams was the adopted daughter: In the Hands of Providence*, pp. 43–47.

70 *"Your father has not much faith in our relation":* "JLC to Fannie Adams," June 7, 1852, Joshua L. Chamberlain Papers, Maine Historical Society, Bangor, Maine.

71 *Chamberlain courted Fannie throughout early 1851: In the Hands of Providence*, p. 48.

71 *In the middle of the service: In the Hands of Providence*, p. 43. See also *Harriet Beecher Stowe: A Life*, pp. 210–17, and *Patriotic Gore*, pp. 31–32.

There is no independent testimony that places Joshua Chamberlain in the church on the day of Harriet Beecher Stowe's revelation. He apparently never even wrote of the incident, or perhaps had never heard it. That he was present for the conception of, arguably, America's greatest novel seemed not to impress him at all. Mrs. Stowe was in the church on March 2, 1851, sitting in pew number 23, which is marked today by a small plaque.

## CHAPTER 4
### *A Fair English Education*

72 *For Simms, the devil was now made manifest: The Road to Disunion*, pp. 241–42. See also *The Edge of the Swamp: A Study in the Literature and Society of the Old South*, Louis D. Rubin, Jr., University of Louisiana Press, Baton Rouge, 1989, pp. 103–26; and *The Letters of William Gilmore Simms*, ed. Mary C. Simms Oliphant, University of South Carolina Press, Charleston, 1952.

There is some disagreement that Simms was actually responding to *Uncle Tom's Cabin*, a contention that has caused a minor literary flap. Freehling makes the claim that it is so, based on Simms's letter (which intimates only that Simms was very aware of Stowe's work, which was then appearing in serial form), and is much clearer in the actual reading of *Woodcraft*.

73 *"I no guine to be free no way":* *Woodcraft*, William Gilmore Simms, Dodd Publishing, New York, 1852, p. 52.

73 *"To work industriously and steadily":* *The Cotton Kingdom*, Frederick Law Olmsted, New York, 1860, reprinted as *The Slave States*, Paragon Books, New York, 1959, p. 251.

75 *Oates's first stop was the town of Cottonwood:* "Oates Autobiography."

76 *Together, the three had launched: Henry's Heritage*, pp. 52–55.

76 *"There were over fifty girls":* "Oates Autobiography."

78 *"I now studied in my room and went to the Academy": Ibid.* Oates also details his stay at Lawrenceville in his 1892 biography, written for the Alabama Department of Archives and History, *The Papers of William C. Oates, 1835–1910*, Administrative Files.

79 *He said that Lawrenceville had "put" it in his head:* "Oates Autobiography."

79 *Eufaula was also the home: Henry's Heritage,* pp. 61–62.

Biographies of the major members of the firm can be found in the various papers of the Alabama Department of Archives and History. Oates also provides a brief sketch of each of the major members of the firm in his personal files as governor. The most complete and detailed biographical information on the Eufaula Regency and its rise to power is in *Alabama, Her History, Resources, War Record and Public Men,* William Brewer, Reprint Company, Spartanburg, SC, 1975. Also of invaluable assistance was *A History of Alabama to 1900,* L. D. Miller, Paragon Press, Birmingham, 1901.

80 *Pugh had studied law under: Henry's Heritage,* p. 143.

80 *Edward Courtney Bullock was the firm's legal expert: Henry's Heritage,* pp. 128–31.

82 *"Judge Dougherty was holding the Circuit Court":* "Oates Autobiography."

83 *Yancey, especially, came to define the increasingly intransigent: The Life and Times of William Lowndes Yancey,* John Witherspoon Du Bose, University of Alabama Press, Montgomery, 1892, pp. 192–213.

83 *Simply by suggesting that the international slave trade: The Impending Crisis, 1848–1861,* David M. Potter, Harper & Row, New York, 1976, pp. 397–98.

84 *There were many turning points in the debate: Southern Commercial Conventions, 1837–1859,* H. Wender, Johns Hopkins University Press, Baltimore, 1930. See also *The Emergence of Lincoln: Douglas, Buchanan, and Party Chaos, 1857–1859,* Allan Nevins, Scribner's, New York, 1950, pp. 404–6.

85 *"Give me a case of oppression": Southern Commercial Conventions,* pp. 291–97.

85 "We shall fire the Southern heart": *National Intelligencer* (newspaper), July 20, 1858.

## CHAPTER 5
### *To the Harvest Home of Death*

86 *"quarrelsome, petulant, hot-headed, turbulent": Jefferson Davis: The Man and His Hour,* William C. Davis, HarperCollins, New York, 1991, p. 263.

86 *By 1858, however, Davis was a spectral figure: Ibid.,* pp. 74–75, 264–65.

86 *Then, in 1837: Ibid.,* pp. 264–65.

87 *The Mississippi legislature cheered these words: The Emergence of Lincoln,* p. 414.

88 *The high point of Davis's Maine trip: Jefferson Davis: The Man and His Hour,* pp. 265–66.

88 *Fortunately for Bowdoin graduates: In the Hands of Providence,* p. 9. See

also *The Papers of Jefferson Davis* (vol. 6), ed. Lynda Lasswwell Crist and Mary Seaton Dix, Louisiana State University Press, Baton Rouge, 1985, pp. 375–76.

89 *In the late summer of 1858 . . . Woods's views: In the Hands of Providence*, p. 400.

89 *By the time Davis and Fessenden: In the Hands of Providence*, pp. 59–60.

90 *In the autumn of 1852: Ibid,* pp. 48–49.

90 *The trouble began with his graduation:* "Early Memoirs," pp. 70–71.

91 *The problem began when: In The Hands of Providence*, pp. 48–53.

91 *It was particularly galling: Ibid.,* p. 51.

93 *"overspread with loneliness and gloom": Ibid.,* p. 49.

93 *"the jar in the cellar way": Ibid.,* p. 411. The letters from Joshua Chamberlain to Fannie Adams are well kept and collected, but many of those from Fannie to Joshua have not been preserved. The Chamberlain–Adams letters for this period are in the Joshua Chamberlain Papers at Bowdoin College or at the Maine Historical Society.

94 *Part of the campaign:* "JLC to Fannie, May 28 (1852)," Maine Historical Society, Augusta, Maine. See also *In the Hands of Providence*, p. 46.

94 *"I know in whom": Ibid.*

95 *When her husband James barred: Elizabeth Cady Stanton–Susan B. Anthony Correspondence: Correspondence, Writings, Speeches*, Ellen Carol Du Bose, Schocken Books, New York, 1981, pp. 157–59.

96 *"I know you do not make the laws": Appeal to the Christian Women of the Southern States*, Angelina Emily Grimké (privately published pamphlet), New York, 1836. See also *The Grimké Sisters from South Carolina*, Gerda Lerner, Houghton Mifflin, Boston, 1967, pp. 138–43.

96 *"If a ruffian attacks her children": Harriet Beecher Stowe: A Life*, p. 230. The original of this letter, written to the *New York Observer*, is in the Beecher Family Papers at the Sterling Memorial Library at Yale University.

96 *"True, we have not felt the slaveholder's lash": Harriet Beecher Stowe: A Life*, p. 226.

97 *Finally, he suggested that they leave: In the Hands of Providence*, pp. 46, 49.

99 *The subject, "Law and Liberty," was a distillation:* "Early Memoirs," pp. 72–73. Chamberlain was called to the pastorate in Belfast, Maine, and Wolfeboro, New Hampshire. Chamberlain graduated from Bangor, but he was not an ordained minister.

99 *The two were married by the Reverend George Adams:* "The Records of the First Parish Church," Brunswick, Maine. In addition to the church records, Dr. Adams's diary of his ministry is also available for inspection, as is his correspondence. Letters from Fannie Chamberlain's relatives concerning the marriage are available at the Maine Historical Society.

101 *In the summer of 1859, abolitionist John Brown: John Brown: A Biography Fifty Years After*, Oswald Garrison Villard, Houghton Mifflin, Boston, 1910, pp. 426–27.

101 *Married to Dianthe Lusk: Ibid.,* p. 18.

102 *"God is my judge": Ibid.,* p. 588.

102 *"Remember, dear wife and children all": To Purge This Land with Blood,* Stephen B. Oates, Harper & Row, New York, 1970, p. 347.

103 *On the eve of the Civil War, most southerners opposed secession:* See *The Secession Movement in Alabama,* Clarence Phillips Denman, University of Alabama Press, Montgomery, 1933; "The Secession and Cooperation Movements in South Carolina," Chauncey Samuel Boucher, Washington University *Studies* 5 (1918); "Alabama Secedes," William Brantley, *Alabama Review* 7: 7; *The Growth of Southern Nationalism,* Avery O. Craven, Louisiana State University Press, Baton Rouge, 1953.

104 *William Oates was among the moderates: Oates,* pp. 52–53. Oates did not attend the secession convention as a delegate, but there is a strong possibility that he was among the large numbers of observers. As noted in the text, he attended the inaugural ceremonies for Jefferson Davis.

106 *"I could not fire the first gun of the war": The Civil War: A Narrative* (vol. 1), Shelby Foote, Random House, New York, 1958, p. 49.

## CHAPTER 6

### *If Honor It Be*

109 *One of these was Company G: Oates,* pp. 67–68.

109 *"My company was raised in the north end": Ibid.,* p. 67.

110 *"We were entitled to commutation for clothing": Ibid.,* p. 68.

110 *Cantey's Rifles contained an assortment of both odd: Ibid.,* pp. 569–797.

Oates's appendix to his history of his regiment contains the most detailed Civil War account of regimental losses, and anecdotal information, in existence. Oates accounts for nearly every recruit of Cantey's Rifles, and nearly every soldier of Law's Alabama Brigade.

113 *Longstreet, age forty, was large, like a block:* See *Lee's Lieutenants: A Study in Command* (3 vols.), Douglas Southall Freeman, Scribner's, New York, 1942; *Lee and Longstreet at High Tide,* Helen Dortch Longstreet, University of North Carolina Press, Chapel Hill, 1940; *Lee and His Lieutenants,* Edward A. Pollard, E. B. Treat, New York, 1867; *James Longstreet: Soldier, Politician, Officeholder, and Writer,* Donald Bridgman Sanger and Thomas Robson Hay, Louisiana State University Press, Baton Rouge, 1952.

The best and most compelling description of Longstreet appears in *Lee and Longstreet at Gettysburg,* Glenn Tucker, Morningside Press (reprint), Dayton, OH, 1982.

113 *Thomas Jonathan "Stonewall" Jackson:* See *Lee's Lieutenants: A Study in Command; Stonewall: A Biography of General Thomas J. Jackson,* Byron Farwell, Norton, New York, 1992; *Stonewall Jackson,* Col. G. F. R. Henderson, Longmans, Green, London, 1899.

The most compelling description of Jackson appears in *Conquering the*

*Valley: Stonewall Jackson at Port Republic*, Robert K. Krick, Morrow, New York, 1996.

114  *One day they were marched out:* Oates, p. 76.

114  *"Some of the mounds where the slain were buried":* Ibid., p. 76.

115  *"I regarded this as a criminally foolish order":* Ibid., pp. 77–78.

115  *"Now why do you suppose":* Destruction and Reconstruction, Gen. Richard Taylor, Appleton, New York, 1889, p. 159.

115  *"The road to glory cannot be followed":* Stonewall in the Valley, Robert G. Tanner, Doubleday, New York, 1976, p. 152.

115  *Trimble was a fighter:* See *High Tide at Gettysburg*, pp. 175–78. Trimble was one of the great strategists of the war, though much ignored by later historians. Before Gettysburg, Lee paid him the highest compliment that he could—he called him in to seek his advice on the coming campaign.

117  *A Union division appeared out of the afternoon sun:* Oates, p. 82.

117  *He was convinced the war would last:* In the Hands of Providence, p. 52.

118  *"The slave-holding spirit was not contented with toleration":* Ibid., p. 60.

118  *"The flag of the nation had been insulted":* Ibid., p. 60.

119  *On one hot summer afternoon:* Ibid., p. 61.

119  *Like Chamberlain, Howard was a devout Congregationalist:* Autobiography, General Oliver O. Howard, Appleton, New York, 1907.

120  *His new resolve was confirmed:* In the Hands of Providence, p. 58.

120  *The firing was far off at first:* Oates, p. 96.

121  *Knowing that he was outnumbered:* Stonewall in the Valley, pp. 209–15.

122  *Banks was laconic:* The Civil War: A Narrative (vol. 1), pp. 435–36.

122  *"wholly unnecessary and a cruel punishment":* Oates, p. 97.

122  *"He inspired his men with blind confidence":* Ibid., p. 98.

123  *Ewell ordered Trimble's Brigade forward:* Ibid., pp. 98–99.

123  *"Now the firing opened heavily":* Ibid., p. 99.

125  *"No one could conjecture where we were going":* Ibid., p. 100.

125  *"We would march a mile or two":* Ibid., p. 101.

126  *Ewell's Division was up at dawn:* Conquering the Valley, pp. 155–61.

126  *"Away we went for about a mile":* Oates, p. 102.

128  *"He who does not see the hand of God":* I Rode with Stonewall, Henry Kyd Douglas, University of North Carolina Press, Chapel Hill, 1940, p. 78.

129  *"In three months, Jackson had marched":* Oates, pp. 105-6.

130  *Johnston attacked McClellan's two isolated corps:* The Civil War: A Narrative (vol. 2), pp. 446–49.

131  *"Personally brave and energetic to a fault":* To the Gates of Richmond: The Peninsula Campaign, Stephen W. Sears, Ticknor & Fields, New York, 1992, p. 57.

132  *But Jackson was asleep, exhausted from the month-long Valley Campaign:* Ibid., pp. 191–201.

132  *but Oates probably comes as close as any historian:* Oates, p. 124.

133 *"The bombshells bursting, their fragments flying": Recollections of War Times*, W. A. McClendon, Paragon Press, Montgomery, AL, 1909. Oates quoted McClendon extensively in his own account of the Seven Days' Battles. A copy of the original, without pagination, in McClendon's hand, is in the possession of the author. It was originally written on the stationery of a railroad company.

135 *The relentless march apparently had an enormous psychological impact:* "Hanover Court House and Gaines's Mill," Major General Fitz-John Porter, in *Battles and Leaders of the Civil War* (vol. 2), pp. 339–40. See also "Lee's Attacks North of the Chickahominy," Lieutenant General Daniel Harvey Hill, in *Battles and Leaders of the Civil War* (vol. 2), pp. 358–60.

136 *"I was so tired and worn out": Recollections of War Times*, p. 19.

CHAPTER 7

### *Kill the Brave Ones*

137 *On this, the third of what turned into seven days of fighting:* "The Opposing Forces in the Seven Days' Battles" (compiled by eds.), in *Battles and Leaders of the Civil War* (vol. 2), pp. 313–17.

The total losses for the entire seven days have been calculated at, Union: 1,734 killed, 8,062 wounded, and 6,053 missing or made prisoner; Confederate: 3,286 killed, 15,909 wounded, and 940 captured or missing.

139 *By the time of Shiloh, Grant was a household name:* The most telling sketch of Grant is in *Grant Takes Command*, Bruce Catton, Little, Brown, Boston, 1968, pp. 24–25.

140 *Chamberlain's letter to Washburn: In the Hands of Providence*, p. 61.

141 *"I have always been interested in military matters":* "Joshua Lawrence Chamberlain to Governor Washburn," July 14, 1862, Maine State Archives.

141 *There were detractors among Chamberlain's colleagues at Bowdoin:* "Josiah Drummond to Israel Washburn," July 22, 1862, Maine State Archives.

141 *The anti-Chamberlain movement was led: To Gettysburg and Beyond,* Michael Golay, Crown, New York, 1994, pp. 63–64.

142 *The 20th Maine was a typical regiment: The Twentieth Maine,* John J. Pullen, New York, 1957, pp. 1–17.

143 *Ames was a striking man: Ibid.,* p. 14. See also *In the Hands of Providence,* pp. 12–14; and "The Story of the Raising and Organization of a Regiment of Volunteers in 1862," Brigadier General Ellis Spear, U.S.V. War Papers, Military Order of the Loyal Legion of the United States, no. 46, March 4, 1903.

144 *John Pope brought groans of despair to everyone: The Civil War: A Narrative* (vol. 1), p. 643.

144 *"I have come to you from the West": Ibid.,* p. 643.

145 *"I want Pope suppressed": Ibid.,* p. 589.

146 *The most important change: Oates,* p. 121.

Cantey was posted to the Gulf Coast for the remainder of the war. His transfer was ostensibly due to poor health, but he served with distinction in his new posting. He survived the war by only three years.

146 *we have only Oates's word about Lowther: Ibid.,* pp. 87–89.

147 *Petty jealousies, stark ambitions, stubbornness: The Civil War: A Narrative* (vol. 1), p. 590.

A. P. Hill did not fare well under Jackson either and had to be released from arrest by Lee a number of times. A. P. Hill was a volatile personality, but a valued strategist. Oddly, he seemed sick just as a battle was about to come on—except at Sharpsburg, where he performed admirably. Hill may well have suffered into middle age from the effects of a sexually transmitted disease, contracted while he was a West Point cadet. He and Henry Heth were best friends, and were both cited for their "lax conduct" during the cadet years after spending a furlough in New York. The best insight into Hill's character is given in *General A. P. Hill,* James I. Robertson, Jr., Random House, New York, 1987, pp. 14–18.

147 *On August 9, in a textbook deployment: Oates,* pp. 128–30.

148 *"While the artillery duel was progressing"; Ibid.,* p. 131.

149 *"I have no recollection of any considerable battle": Ibid.,* p. 132.

150 *He wrote these thoughts down: The Civil War: A Narrative* (vol. 1), pp. 704–10. See also *Lincoln,* David Herbert Donald, Simon and Schuster, New York, 1995, pp. 366–69.

150 *"In great contests each party claims to act": Lincoln,* pp. 566–67. Donald rightly points out that Lincoln gave a much more pointed summation of these views in his Second Inaugural Address, it being, as Donald puts it, "less gnostic."

150 *"The innocent for the guilty": Harriet Beecher Stowe: A Life,* p. 305.

151 *One night in February 1862: Patriotic Gore,* pp. 91–98.

151 *"My paramount object": The Collected Works of Abraham Lincoln* (vol. 5), ed. Roy P. Basler, Rutgers University Press, New Brunswick, NJ, 1953, pp. 388–89. Donald's analysis of the passage in *Lincoln,* p. 368, is worth reading.

153 *"On the morning of the 25th": Oates,* p. 133.

153 *"There was a pile of bacon": Ibid.,* p. 135.

155 *"I stood at the end of the woods": Ibid.,* p. 142.

155 *"We advanced to within hailing distance": Return to Bull Run,* John J. Hennessy, Simon and Schuster, New York, 1993, pp. 179–80.

155 *"The carnage in our ranks was appalling": Oates,* p. 145.

156 *"On the morning of the 29th": Ibid.,* p. 145.

157 *Finally, with all of the troops he wanted on hand:* "The Second Battle of Bull Run." Major General John Pope, in *Battles and Leaders of the Civil War* (vol. 2), pp. 467–71.

158 *Coming from Lee this was more than a suggestion: The Civil War: A Narrative* (vol. 1), p. 633. Thus giving rise, it seems, to the view that Longstreet was always tardy in attacking; but in this case, at least, his "slows" and stubbornness paid off—when he went in, the next day, he hammered Fitz-John Porter and won the battle.

159 *"Old Pete" then ordered his men forward: Ibid.*, p. 638. When asked by a messenger if he could not now attack, Longstreet is reported to have answered, finally: "Certainly."

160 *Oates saw Longstreet's advance: Oates*, p. 146.

## CHAPTER 8
### All That I Am Called To

161 *On July 24, Confederate General Braxton Bragg: The Civil War: A Narrative* (vol. 1), pp. 574–78.

161 *"Let it be borne in mind": Ibid.*, p. 577.

162 *In that instant, with McClellan riding to his new command:* "From the Peninsula to Antietam," General George B. McClellan, in *Battles and Leaders of the Civil War* (vol. 2), pp. 545–46.

163 *"Neither confiscation of property, political executions of persons": Landscape Turned Red*, Stephen W. Sears, Ticknor & Fields, New York, 1983, p. 36. The "Harrison's Landing Letter" later appeared as a political circular in McClellan's campaign for the presidency in 1864.

164 *Chamberlain tried to keep the men in formation: In the Hands of Providence*, p. 67.

164 *Army life agreed with him: Ibid.*, pp. 80–81.

165 *Ambitious and talented, Butterfield: Ibid.*, pp. 87, 99, 108. See also *High Tide at Gettysburg*, pp. 71–73.

165 *The "Lost Order" detailed Lee's location:* "The Finding of Lee's Lost Order," Brigadier General Silas Colgrove, in *Battles and Leaders of the Civil War* (vol. 2), p. 603.

166 *Across the way in the darkness: Oates*, pp. 161–62.

167 *"I was not in the battle of Sharpsburg": Oates*, p. 163.

167 *"Fighting Joe" Hooker's bluecoats came out of the misty dawn: Landscape Turned Red*, pp. 191–92.

The records of the Iron Brigade, including *Service with the 6th Wisconsin*, by Rufus Dawes, can be found in the manuscript collection of the Library of Congress. The actions of the 15th Alabama are best summarized in the after-action report of Colonel James A. Walker, of Trimble's Brigade. That report is in vol. 19 (part 1, series 1) of the *Official Records* (pp. 976–97). The numbers of killed and wounded of the brigade are given in vol. 19 (part 2, series 1) on p. 640.

169 *D. H. Hill angrily watched them go and threatened to court-martial Feagin: Oates*, p. 179.

169 *The battle now shifted east and south:* "Sharpsburg," Major General John G. Walker, CSA, in *Battles and Leaders of the Civil War* (vol. 2), pp. 677–79.

170 *This time it was "Bull" Sumner who came on: Landscape Turned Red*, pp. 216–18.

170 *The rebels might have defended the sunken road all day:* "The Invasion of

Maryland," General James Longstreet, in *Battles and Leaders of the Civil War* (vol. 2), pp. 667–70.

171 *The battle then shifted south:* "With Burnside at Antietam," David L. Thompson, Co. G, 9th NY Volunteers, in *Battles and Leaders of the Civil War*, (vol. 2), pp. 660–62.

172 *Antietam became known as "artillery hell": Battle Tactics of the Civil War*, Paddy Griffith, Yale University Press, New Haven, CT, 1987, pp. 169–71.

Napoleon attempted to use the artillery charge in Europe, but never perfected it; John Pelham came closest to mastering the technique, using it to great effect at Fredericksburg. Griffith rightly points out that, despite eyewitness testimony on artillery effectiveness, the use of the arm was much more effective in close-range, defensive duels with enemy infantry. Despite its deficiencies—and the inordinate amount of time it took Civil War commanders to learn to use it effectively—artillery deployment could be decisive; it certainly was at Antietam.

173 *"The echoes of the artillery in the parting salutes": Oates*, p. 162.

Despite this, Oates's comment articulated several pages earlier is worth noting: "The Confederacy was beaten when the ardor of the people began to flag, when the spirit of volunteering ceased, and the disposition to seek soft and safe places appeared instead. But I could not see it. I was too young and full of hope and Confederate patriotism." In other words, Oates places the defeat of the Confederacy at the moment when the Confederate Congress was forced to pass the first conscription law—in April 1862—a full one year before the Union enacted its first conscription act. Oates says desertions rose from that date.

174 *Lee calmed the shaken parson:* "Report of Brig. Gen. Jubal A. Early," *OR* (vol. 19, series I, part 1), no. 269, pp. 972–74. See also *In the Hands of Providence*, pp. 74–75.

175 *"I wish you could be beside me":* "JLC to Fannie Chamberlain," October 26, 1862, Joshua Chamberlain Papers, Library of Congress.

175 *Adelbert Ames, the commander of the 20th Maine: Adelbert Ames: General, Senator, Governor*, Jessie Ames Marshal, Dodd, Mead, New York, 1964, pp. 101–3.

176 *"Col. A drills us sergeants every day to see who is fit":* "Tom Chamberlain to Sae Chamberlain," from *The Twentieth Maine*, pp. 34–36.

176 *"I wish you could hear Lawrence": Ibid.*

177 *Fannie wrote Joshua: In the Hands of Providence*, p. 62.

177 *In the midst of the conflict: Ibid.,* pp. 420–21 and 86. Trulock notes: "Fannie did not have to ask his permission for her travel plans as she customarily did: Chamberlain told her he did not expect her to stay in Brunswick in the winter but realized that the children and Aunty would."

178 *one of Harriet Beecher Stowe's more poignant works: Patriotic Gore*, pp. 35–37.

180 *The Great Revival of the Army of Northern Virginia: Christ in the Camp*, Rev. J. William Jones, Sprinkle Publications (reprint), Harrisonburg, VA, 1986, pp. 258–64.

180 *"In General Trimble's, and the immediately neighboring brigades"*: *Ibid.*, p. 524.

181 *In one of the most enduring: Ibid.*, p. 218.

182 *Burnside's plan was simple enough:* "Sumner's Right Grand Division," General Darius Couch, in *Battles and Leaders of the Civil War* (vol. 3), pp. 109–13.

182 *Nine separate attempts were made:* "The Pontoniers at Fredericksburg," Major Wesley Brainerd, 50th New York Engineers, in *Battles and Leaders of the Civil War* (vol. 3), pp. 121–22.

182 *"It is impossible fitly to describe"*: "The Confederate Left at Fredericksburg," General Lafayette McLaws, in *Battles and Leaders of the Civil War* (vol. 3), p. 87.

184 *"No troops on earth"*: *Oates*, p. 166.

184 *The Yankees responded: Ibid.*, p. 167.

187 *Back across the Rappahannock:* "Sumner's Right Grand Division," General Darius Couch, in *Battles and Leaders of the Civil War* (vol. 3), pp. 115–16.

187 *The men of the 20th Maine saw Humphreys's vain attack: In the Hands of Providence*, pp. 95–96.

187 *"God help us now"*: *Ibid.*, p. 95. See also "JLC Letter to Governor Washburn," December 17, 1862, Pejepscot Historical Society, Maine.

187 *"We reached the final crest"*: "My Story of Fredericksburg," Joshua Lawrence Chamberlain, *Cosmopolitan*, January 1913.

188 *"We had to pick our way over a field"*: *Ibid.*

189 *"It was a very droll time . . . at the White House"*: *Harriet Beecher Stowe: A Life*, pp. 305–6.

The story of Lincoln's statement to Stowe is undoubtedly apocryphal, as there is no record of it in Stowe's correspondence. Certainly she would have recorded it in the letter written to her sister shortly after her meeting with Lincoln—penned at the beginning of December—and she did not. The story has gained such currency that Edmund Wilson, in *Patriotic Gore*, took it as established fact.

David Herbert Donald, in *Lincoln* (p. 542), says this: "Harriet Beecher Stowe was a firm supporter of Lincoln. She remembered how kindly the President had received her at the White House back in 1862, when, according to a family story, he exclaimed, 'So this is the little lady who made this big war?'" Donald puts the question mark after the statement, the first time it has been written in that way. Donald undoubtedly is correct, that the statement from Lincoln is part of the Beecher family mythology, and therefore it is undoubtedly not true.

## CHAPTER 9

### *Men Standing Bright as Golden Grain*

191 *The 15th Alabama spent New Year's Day: Oates*, p. 174.

191 *"The soldiers under him think they are better"*: "A Letter from Noah B.

Feagin," Jan. 30, 1863, Alabama Department of Archives and History, 15th Alabama Regimental file.

192 *Feagin's trial was a minor affair: Oates*, p. 179.

193 *Law's Brigade moved south in March: Ibid.*, p. 175.

194 *"You must hold your ground General Pender": Chancellorsville*, Stephen W. Sears, Houghton Mifflin, Boston, 1996, p. 294.

194 *In February he had taken a leave: In the Hands of Providence*, p. 108.

195 *"My dear little Daisy":* "JLC to Daisy Chamberlain," Special Collections Room, Bowdoin College, Brunswick, ME.

197 *The war could not be extended, Lee believed: From Manassas to Appomattox*, pp. 327–33.

199 *He did so by creating three corps of three divisions each: Ibid.*, pp. 332–33. See also *High Tide at Gettysburg*, pp. 10–14.

Perhaps, as Glenn Tucker suggests, the outstanding question in the reorganization of the Army of Northern Virginia is why Lee passed over one of his most capable senior officers in favor of A. P. Hill and Richard Ewell. As Tucker notes, D. H. "Harvey" Hill "had one of the best fighting records in the army," and could hardly have been more difficult to get along with than A. P. Hill. The ostensible reason for Harvey Hill's exile to North Carolina was his loss of Lee's order at Sharpsburg. Lee could hold a grudge. If Jackson's absence wounded Lee's army, Harvey Hill's exile to North Carolina killed it.

199 *"He was singularly devoted to duty": Oates*, p. 401.

199 *McLaws was one of the few genuinely modest men: Lee and Longstreet at Gettysburg*, pp. 14–17.

200 *The appointment of Hill and Ewell: The Civil War: A Narrative* (vol. 2), p. 435.

Longstreet mentioned that A. P. Hill's post should have gone to D. H. Hill, but he was not Longstreet's first choice. Longstreet's choice for corps command was McLaws, and he maintained that position even through his later feuding with the Georgia general.

201 *On the dark night of June 28: From Manassas to Appomattox*, p. 324.

Harrison was a "player"—an actor—and was found after the war by a number of Confederate officers. Harrison was not alone in his activities. One of the unknowns of Gettysburg is the number of men Lee sent north to scout routes. There may have been quite a few. A number of Pennsylvania farmers recognized men in Confederate ranks whom they were sure they had seen before—weeks before—traveling the countryside and asking questions. General Lee did not do anything that was not well planned.

202 *Early on the morning of July 1:* "Reports of Maj. General Henry Heth," *OR* (vol. 27, series 1, part 2), p. 637.

203 *To get a better perspective on the fight: High Tide at Gettysburg*, p. 106.

Buford did not survive the war, but died of typhoid fever, in December 1863, after being promoted to major general.

204 *At ten-fifteen, as Reynolds turned in his saddle: Ibid.*, p. 110.

205 *The fate of Alfred Iverson's Brigade:* "Reports of Brig. Gen. Alfred Iverson," *OR* (vol. 27, series 1, part 2), pp. 578–81.

According to one eyewitness, the slaughter of his brigade had a catastrophic effect on Iverson, who "went to pieces and became unfit for further command." Lee virtually dismissed him from the army, transferring him to Georgia, where he commanded state forces. He recouped his reputation later in the war by capturing a Union cavalry unit.

206 *From where he stood, in front of his brigade: High Tide at Gettysburg,* pp. 156–58.

209 *July 2 began early for both men: Oates,* p. 199.

209 *For Chamberlain, the march to the battlefield:* "Report of Col. Joshua L. Chamberlain, Twentieth Maine Infantry," *OR* (vol. 27, series 1, part 1), p. 622.

209 *At just before two P.M.:* "The Struggle for 'Round Top,' " Major General E. M. Law, in *Battles and Leaders of the Civil War* (vol. 3), pp. 319–20; see also *Gettysburg: The Second Day,* Harry W. Pfanz, University of North Carolina Press, Chapel Hill, 1987, p. 161, and *From Manassas to Appomattox,* pp. 364–65.

There is a great deal of disagreement on just when Law's Brigade arrived at Gettysburg. Longstreet and Law say the brigade arrived at just before noon. Oates disagrees, and I believe he is correct. The 15th Alabama did not while away its time until its march behind Seminary Ridge by camping in the fields along the Chambersburg Pike, nor did it stand and wait two hours before receiving orders. Instead, it came to Gettysburg, arriving closer to one P.M., broke ranks for thirty minutes, and then was deployed into line of march. Oates is the authoritative eyewitness: "It was near 4 o'clock [in the morning] when the brigade was put in motion, and after a rapid and fatiguing march, passing the smoking ruins of Thad. Stevens's property, it arrived on the field within sight of Gettysburg at about 1 o'clock P.M. having marched twenty-five miles" (p. 206).

210 *To determine that . . . Lee sent two of his staff officers: High Tide at Gettysburg,* pp. 227–28.

211 *"No, General . . . I want it placed just opposite": Ibid.,* pp. 221–22.

212 *No precise calculations can be made: Oates,* pp. 206–7.

213 *"I am glad to hear you say so": High Tide at Gettysburg,* p. 200. The words were heard and reported by Oliver O. Howard and a number of other officers in attendance.

214 *Which is where Hood found him on the late afternoon:* "The Battle of Gettysburg—Important Communication from an Eye-Witness . . . etc.," Historicus, in *OR* (vol. 27, series 1, part 1), pp. 128–36. "Historicus" is undoubtedly General Daniel Sickles.

214 *Hood was not satisfied: From Manassas to Appomattox,* p. 368.

214 *A rebel battery less than one-quarter mile to his left: Oates,* p. 223.

215 *Slowly, drawn by the fire, the regiment inclined slightly to its right:* "The Confederate Approach to Little Round Top," Gary Kross, *Blue and Gray,* Winter 96, pp. 12–13. Kross is a licensed battlefield guide at Gettysburg. His account

fills in many of the details that Oates left out of his own narrative—giving, for example, the exact location of where Oates's men might have found water for their canteens.

216 *"General Law rode up to me"*: Oates, p. 210.

216 *"I saw Gettysburg"*: Ibid., p. 212.

217 *"I then called his attention"*: Ibid., p. 212.

218 *Chamberlain's regiment was now deployed:* "Through Blood and Fire at Gettysburg," pp. 8–11.

219 *"where heroic men standing bright as golden grain"*: "Through Blood and Fire at Gettysburg," p. 13.

219 *The decision to move up Little Round Top:* Ibid., p. 9.

221 *After the 20th Maine's first volley:* Oates, p. 213.

222 *"It was our time now to deal death"*: "Through Blood and Fire at Gettysburg," pp. 14–15.

222 *Oates's brother John fell:* Oates, p. 226.

223 *"Squads of the enemy"*: "Report of Col. Joshua L. Chamberlain, Twentieth Maine Infantry," *OR* (vol. 27, series 1, part 1), p. 624.

223 *"But we were not a moment too soon"*: Ibid., p. 324.

223 *"The enemy seemed to have gathered"*: Ibid., p. 325.

224 *Down the hill, Oates was also nearing the end:* Oates, p. 215.

225 *All along the line: From Manassas to Appomattox*, p. 372.

225 *"There were never harder fighters"*: Oates, p. 219.

## CHAPTER 10

### God Had Nothing to Do with It

226 *Writing more than a century later: The Civil War: A Narrative* (vol. 2), p. 504.

227 *"The absence of Company A"*: Oates, p. 222.

228 *"laid as on the altar"*: "Through Blood and Fire at Gettysburg," p. 29.

228 *"I do not worship a God who takes sides in battle"*: Oates, p. 247.

229 *Trimble's men came across the wall:* Untitled report of Gen. Winfield Scott Hancock (undated), *OR* (vol. 27, series 1, part 1), pp. 373–74.

230 *Armistead's charge inside the Union lines:* See *High Tide at Gettysburg*, pp. 364–67.

230 *While Pickett reported 232 killed in his command:* Ibid., p. 379.

There are no official returns on the numbers of missing after Pickett's assault. The official records that do exist, *OR* (vol. 27, series 1, part 2), give a minimal figure on the casualties taken in Pickett's Division. They must be underreported. The most accurate figures, by comparison, are from Petigrew's Division—which are detailed: 190 dead of four regiments from North Carolina and 915 wounded, and just from four regiments. After the battle, Pickett wrote his report on the charge and gave it to Lee. Lee returned it to the general, asking him to rewrite it, as he thought it might be bad for morale. The report was never resubmitted, but was lost. After Five Forks, Lee dismissed Pickett from the service, and when he saw him on the road to Appomattox, he is reported to have said: "What is that man still doing with the army?" Pickett was negligent at Five Forks, engaging in a "shad bake" at the same moment that troops led by Joshua Chamberlain were deploying against his lines—and Lee believed that he was fully justified in dismissing him. Nevertheless, it is hard to shake the view that Pickett was a living reminder of Lee's July 3 mistake. The Longstreet and Pickett families became close friends after the war.

231 *"To remain at home in this, the hour of our country's need"*: OR (vol. 27, series 1, part 3), p. 1040.

232 *"I have seen General Lee under various circumstances"*: "Manuscript of William Jordan, 15th Alabama" (unnumbered), Alabama Department of Archives and History, Montgomery, 15th Alabama Regimental Files.

233 *This time both Davis and Seddon agreed*: From Manassas to Appomattox, p. 433.

234 *"At many places, in anticipation of our coming"*: "Manuscript of William Jordan, 15th Alabama."

235 *A martinet, a stickler for regulations*: The Civil War: A Narrative (vol. 2), pp. 171–74.

236 *When five brigades of Hood's Division*: This Terrible Sound, Peter Cozzens, University of Illinois Press, Urbana, 1992, pp. 110–11.

236 *William Oates brought his regiment*: Oates, p. 254.

237 *"The next morning, Saturday, the 19th of September"*: Ibid., p. 255.

238 *"Several were killed and wounded"*: "Manuscript of William Jordan, 15th Alabama."

239 *Longstreet moved down the line of his command*: From Manassas to Appomattox, pp. 445–46.

240 *By eleven A.M., Longstreet could see the federals*: "Report of Lieut. Gen. James Longstreet, CS Army," OR (vol. 30, series 1, part 2), pp. 388–90.

241 *Such massed volleys should have been enough*: From Manassas to Appomattox, pp. 446–47.

241 *The last of these shifts*: "Chickamauga—The Great Battle of the West," in Battles and Leaders of the Civil War (vol. 3), pp. 657–58. See also "The Crisis at Chickamauga," Gates P. Thruston, in Battles and Leaders of the Civil War (vol. 3), p. 662; and "Notes on the Chicamauga Campaign," Emerson Opdycke, in Battles and Leaders of the Civil War (vol. 3), p. 669.

242 *"When we crossed the road it raised a tremendous dust"*: Oates, p. 255.

242 *"The scene now presented was unspeakably grand"*: "Report of Brig. Gen. Bushrod R. Johnson," OR (vol. 30, series 1, part 2), p. 463.

243 *"I discovered that I did not connect"*: Oates, p. 256.

244 *"Don't fire, 15th, until you are ordered!"*: Ibid., p. 257.

244 *"Colonel McSpadden was an honorable man"*: Ibid., pp. 257–58.

244 *Lytle is one of those numerous Americans: This Terrible Sound*, p. 388.

246 *"After we passed the artillery":* "Manuscript of William Jordan, 15th Alabama."

246 *"As we moved through the old field":* Oates, p. 259.

247 *Finally Thomas attempted to head off:* "Report of Maj. Gen. George H. Thomas," *OR* (vol. 30, series 1, part 1), pp. 254–55.

248 *"He was the busiest chap I ever saw":* Oates, p. 262.

249 *"That night . . . I never felt happier":* Ibid., p. 264.

250 *"I waited in breathless silence for them to fire":* Ibid., p. 276.

250 *"I rushed in among the men":* Ibid., pp. 276–77.

251 *Oates was taken to the rear:* Ibid., p. 277.

252 *He was ordered to recuperate:* Ibid., p. 377.


## Chapter 11

### We Know That Some Must Fall

253 *In early August 1863, exhausted by the exertions of army life: In the Hands of Providence*, p. 163.

253 *"It was the most affecting sight I have ever seen": The Twentieth Maine*, p. 157.

254 *"My personal knowledge of this gallant officer's skill":* "James C. Rice to the Hon. William P. Fessenden," September 8, 1863, Maine Historical Society.

255 *On the morning of November 11: In The Hands of Providence*, p. 374.

257 *In mid-March 1864:* Oates, p. 338.

257 *One of the deserters:* Ibid., pp. 335–37. The desertions are duly and bluntly noted in Oates's appendixes to his book, soldier by soldier.

257 *The growing feud:* Ibid., p. 339.

258 *A little after one P.M. on May 5:* "General Lee in the Wilderness Campaign," Lieutenant Colonel Charles S. Venable, in *Battles and Leaders of the Civil War* (vol. 4), p. 241. See also "From the Wilderness to Cold Harbor," Major General E. M. Law, in *Battles and Leaders of the Civil War* (vol. 4), pp. 121–22.

259 *Longstreet began his movement: From Manassas to Appomattox*, p. 559.

259 *"I thought him at that moment":* Oates, p. 344.

260 *Perry called Oates's attack:* "The Wilderness," General W. F. Perry, *Southern Historical Society Papers*, February 1879.

260 *"Colonel, there is a fine chance of a great attack by our right": Recollections of a Confederate Staff Officer*, General G. Moxley Sorrel, Konecky & Konecky (reprint), New York, 1994, p. 241.

262 *"I am happy": From Manassas to Appomattox*, p. 563.

263 *"We must make up our minds":* quoted in *The Civil War: A Narrative* (vol. 3), p. 123.

264 *"About 10 o'clock we heard firing":* Oates, p. 354.

265 *The opening shot of the Battle of Spotsylvania Court House:* "Through

the Wilderness," Brevet Major General Alexander S. Webb, in *Battles and Leaders of the Civil War* (vol. 4), p. 165.

265 *"as brave and true a man"*: In the Hands of Providence, p. 180.

265 *Finally, on May 12, to break the stalemate:* "Through the Wilderness," p. 168.

266 *"Mounting to the crest of the embankment"*: Reminiscences of the Civil War, General John Gordon, quoted in Oates, p. 361.

267 *After Spotsylvania, Chamberlain took command of the Third Brigade:* In the Hands of Providence, p. 181.

269 *"I called out, 'Sergeant, give them double charges' "*: Oates, p. 366.

269 *After the Battle of Cold Harbor:* "Gen. Griffin to Col. J. L. Chamberlain," OR (vol. 40, series 2, part 3), pp. 470–71.

Chamberlain took the transfer without comment, happy to be in charge of a brigade. He was also getting used to the shuffling then occurring in the Army of the Potomac due to mounting combat losses. Others, however, were not so pleased. General Lysander Cutler complained about the loss of his brigade and attempted to have the unit transferred back to his division. Warren maintained the transfer of command, however, because he thought Chamberlain "an officer of the highest reputation."

270 *"old men and boys"*: Oates, p. 368.

271 *"Circumstances lead me to believe"*: "Petersburg and Appomattox," *Lewiston Journal*, September 1–6, 1900, Maine Historical Society.

272 *"Comrades, we have now before us"*: "Patrick DeLacy Manuscript," Manuscripts Division, Library of Congress. DeLacy was a sergeant in the 143rd Pennsylvania Regiment who received the speech from a soldier who wrote it down at the time. DeLacy then passed on the manuscript to Chamberlain. DeLacy wrote to Chamberlain about it in a letter dated January 15, 1904, which can now be found in the Library of Congress.

273 *The ball passed through his body:* In the Hands of Providence, p. 209.

274 *"My darling wife"*: "JLC to Fannie," June 19, 1864, Bowdoin College.

275 *"I haven't a particle of fanaticism"*: "JLC to Sarah Chamberlain" (undated), Bowdoin College.

The contents of this letter make it apparent that it was written near the time of his wounding, but certainly no earlier than the late spring of 1864. Alice Rains Trulock places the date of the letter a little later, no later than the autumn of 1864.

275 *"I went to see General Lee"*: Oates, p. 371.

276 *"hardy mountaineers"*: Ibid., p. 372.

277 *The sudden appearance of the two Alabama regiments:* Ibid., p. 375.

277 *"A moment later a ball struck me"*: Ibid., p. 376.

278 *"I told him that I did not care"*: Ibid., p. 378.

279 *"Doctor Mudd got to me"*: Ibid., p. 381.

280 *Chamberlain returned to the army in November:* In the Hands of Providence, pp. 219–20.

281 *"I do not in the least regret my choice"*: "JLC to Sae Chamberlain" (his sister), March 9, 1865, The Papers of Joshua L. Chamberlain, Bowdoin College, Brunswick, ME.

281 *Chamberlain received his orders on March 28: The Passing of the Armies*, Joshua L. Chamberlain, Morningside Press (reprint), Dayton, OH, 1989, p. 42.

282 *"My dear General, you are gone": Ibid.*, p. 46.

283 *The night of the Union victory: Grant Takes Command*, Bruce Catton, Little, Brown, Boston, 1968, pp. 440–41.

283 *"General Chamberlain, the Fifth Corps is eternally damned": The Passing of the Armies*, p. 72.

As in much of his firsthand account of the various battles south of Petersburg, Chamberlain is writing for the public and not for historians. The result is that it is difficult to follow the precise times of his movements—or even the day on which they occurred. The ambiguities are easily cleared up by reference to "Warren Court of Inquiry," *Official Records of the Union and Confederate Armies* (vol. 3). See also "General Warren at Five Forks, and the Court of Inquiry," eds., in *Battles and Leaders of the Civil War* (vol. 4), pp. 723–24; and "Five Forks and the Pursuit of Lee," Brigadier General Horace Porter, in *Battles and Leaders of the Civil War* (vol. 4), pp. 708–22.

286 *The attack began at four P.M.: The Passing of the Armies*, p. 121.

287 *"Griffin came down from the right": Ibid.*, p. 144.

287 *The next morning he sent a dispatch: OR* (vol. 46, series 1, part 3), p. 1378.

288 *"He was dressed in a suit of new uniform": From Manassas to Appomattox*, pp. 624–25.

289 *William Oates learned of Lee's surrender: Oates*, p. 432.

289 *"We could not look into those brave, bronzed faces": The Passing of the Armies*, pp. 270–71.

CHAPTER 12

## The Passing of the Dead

293 *"Now I see the white flag": The Passing of the Armies*, pp. 239–40.

293 *"I was doubtful of my duty": Ibid.*, p. 241.

294 *"He, too, comes with a single aide": Ibid.*, p. 246.

295 *"As General Lee rode back to his army": From Manassas to Appomattox*, pp. 628–29.

295 *They were "starving": The Passing of the Armies*, p. 247.

295 *"Taking the assignment as I would any other": Ibid.*, p. 255.

296 *"Gordon at the head of the column": Ibid.*, p. 261.

297 *"You're mistaken, sir": Ibid.*, p. 267.

298 *"I never felt better": The Civil War: A Narrative* (vol. 3), p. 977.

299 *"It was no uncommon thing": The Passing of the Armies*, p. 277.

299 *"I must tell you, madam": Ibid.*, p. 280.

301 *"For me, while this division was passing"*: Ibid., p. 343.

302 *He was promoted to a high rank:* "Ellis Spear to Gen. J. L. Hodsdon," March 9, 1866, The Papers of Joshua L. Chamberlain, Bowdoin College, Brunswick, ME.

302 *The total of deaths:* "Notes on the Union and Confederate Armies," eds., in *Battles and Leaders of the Civil War* (vol. 4), pp. 767–78. See also *The Civil War: A Narrative* (vol. 3), pp. 1040–41.

A precise count is impossible, though one was attempted by the Office of the Adjutant General in 1885. A summary of the figures appears in "Notes on the Union and Confederate Armies" and gives a strikingly matter-of-fact narrative of the war's horrific cost to the Union army: "Killed in action, 4142 officers, 62,916 men; died of wounds received in action, 2223 officers, 40,789 men, of which number 99 officers and 1973 men were prisoners of war; died of disease, 2795 officers and 221,791 men, of which 83 officers and 24,783 men were prisoners." The report goes on to state the number of deaths by drownings, executions (267), and "accidents."

The death by disease category is especially striking—four times as many men died from disease as from combat—but the figure is symbolic of warfare at that time. A review of Oates's account of what happened to the men of the 15th Alabama shows that disease carried off far more soldiers than combat. "Disease and sickness incident to camp life killed just three times as many as the enemy's bullets," Oates wrote. This was undoubtedly true in all wars fought in history to that time. World War I is, arguably, the first instance in which combat deaths exceeded deaths caused by disease.

The aggregate total is 360,222 dead in the Union forces alone. The report states: "Northern writers have assumed that the Confederate losses equaled the Union losses; no data exist for a reasonably accurate estimate." A review of the returns by battle for all engaged Confederate forces shows a total similar to that reported for the North by the adjutant general: just over 300,000 men in gray were killed, died from their wounds, or died of disease. The strategy followed by the Union in the war seems to dictate that in terms of sheer numbers, the Union forces suffered more combat casualties—they were the attackers, though they suffered fewer casualties in proportion to the total population of the North.

The figures do not include losses during naval engagements, deaths during or in the course of desertions, and uncounted deaths by sickness. The total casualties directly due to service during the war in both northern and southern armies undoubtedly amount to more than one million men. There is no evidence that women died in combat during the war, but it seems likely. There are at least three known incidents of women serving disguised as men—one was discovered only when beginning childbirth. One served with her husband in the Union army.

The indiscriminate targeting of civilians is a salient, but not unique, feature of twentieth-century warfare—the Thirty Years War in Europe (1618–48) depopulated (by one-third) the inhabitants of Europe—but the targeting of civilians was not a feature of the Civil War. Sherman's March to the Sea in 1865 targeted the war-making capacity of the Deep South, but not its civilians. Wanton murder and rape of the southern population simply did not take place. There is little doubt, however, that the South was plundered. There is no accurate count of civilian casualties directly due to the war, but the number is undoubtedly very low.

303 *Thomas Davee Chamberlain returned to Portland: In the Hands of Providence*, p. 368.

304 *He never emerged: Oates*, p. 709.

305 *"Now that God has smitten slavery unto death": Reconstruction*, Eric Foner, Harper & Row, New York, 1988, p. 28.

306 *At the beginning of the conflict: Oates*, pp. 743–60.

307 *Among them Jesse Carmichael: Ibid.*, p. 637.

308 *John Oates somehow got Merritt out of jail: Ibid.*, p. 695

308 *Alabama was devastated: Civil War and Reconstruction*, pp. 251–53.

310 *On the one side: Reconstruction*, pp. 180–85.

310 *The first attempt at restoring the power of Alabama's government: Civil War and Reconstruction in Alabama*, pp. 343–45.

311 *By the late summer of 1865: Oates*, pp. 704–5.

311 *A second civil war had begun: Civil War and Reconstruction in Alabama*, pp. 137–39.

312 *"Secession must be repudiated"*: "Address of Joshua Chamberlain," August 1865, Maine Historical Society, Augusta.

313 *The August 1865 visit of Ulysses S. Grant: In the Hands of Providence*, p. 330. See also *Grant: A Biography*, William S. McFeely, Norton, New York, 1981, p. 236.

313 *Grant's visit was all Joshua and Fannie could have hoped for:* "Gen'l Grant In Maine," *The Boston Journal* (undated), Pejepscot Historical Society, Brunswick, ME.

315 *Chamberlain gave his wife an expensive gold-and-diamond bracelet:* "Fannie Chamberlain to JLC," March 9, 1866, Chamberlain–Adams Family Correspondence, Radcliffe College. The bracelet was purchased from Tiffany's for $250. According to Alice Rains Trulock, the hourglasses "symbolize the weary hours away from home."

## CHAPTER 13

### *The Bone of Contention*

317 *Rather, Grant came to speak with Oliver O. Howard: Grant: A Biography*, pp. 236–38.

317 *"The presence of black troops": A Documentary History of Reconstruction: Political, Military, Social, Religious, Education, and Industrial, 1865–1906*, Case Western Reserve Press, Cleveland, 1906 (2 vols.), vol. 1, pp. 51–53.

318 *Chamberlain's own views of the freedmen: In the Hands of Providence*, p. 338.

319 *"For slavery alone"*: Oates, p. 498.

320 *"I replied that was quite true"*: Oates, p. 496.

321 *"If slaves will make good soldiers"*: *The Civil War: A Narrative* (vol. 3), pp. 859–60.

The men of the Army of Northern Virginia did not agree with Cobb. According to Shelby Foote, one Alabama regiment petitioned the Confederate government to enlist black soldiers to help them fight. The nub of the question was stated not just by Cobb, but by other former "fire breathers," like Confederate Senator Robert Hunter, who had helped to take the South out of the Union. "If we are right in passing this measure [to enlist slaves], we were wrong in denying the old government the right to interfere with the institution of slavery and to emancipate slaves." His words should serve as a model for those seeking the "cause" of the war—without slavery there would have been no war.

321 *"When the Union armies triumphed"*: Oates, p. 499.

In a number of statements made after the war, in writing, Oates said the best that might have happened—to stave off both war and defeat—would have been for the South to institute a system of gradual emancipation.

322 *Alabama had been under the rule of a military administration*: *Civil War and Reconstruction in Alabama*, pp. 407–9.

323 *These dissenters, a clear majority*: Ibid., pp. 475–78.

324 *"I accept the political and civil equality"*: Ibid., p. 527.

The convention was followed closely by a number of newspapers, which printed its proceedings—the *Selma Times and Messenger* and the *Mobile Nationalist*—and was widely commented on even in the North. Detailed reports of its proceedings appeared in the *New York World* and the *New York Herald*.

325 *To organize opposition to the vote*: Ibid., p. 536.

326 *Just days before the election*: Ibid., pp. 539–40.

326 *When the polls closed*: Ibid., pp. 538–40. See also "Constitution Vote," *Selma Times and Messenger*, March 10, 1868.

327 *"We reiterate the advice hitherto offered"*: "Manifesto," the *Independent Monitor*, Montgomery, April 21, 1868.

328 *The Ku Klux Klan built*: See *The South During Reconstruction*, E. Merton Coulter, Louisiana State University Press, Baton Rouge, 1947, and *Reconstruction*, pp. 425–44.

329 *In Sumter County, west of Montgomery*: *Reconstruction*, p. 426.

Congressional hearings were organized on the KKK, the proceedings of which were then printed by state. They can be found in "KKK Hearings," 46th Congress, 2nd Session, Senate Report 693 (hereafter "KKK Hearings"). The most important cataloguing of KKK crimes in Alabama appears on pages 334–37.

330 *"I have become satisfied"*: "KKK Hearings," p. 404.

331 *"A convention of the white people of Alabama"*: *Civil War and Reconstruction in Alabama*, p. 355.

332 *Chamberlain was feted at almost every turn*: In the Hands of Providence, p. 335.

333 *Chamberlain's war record was enough for him: Ibid.*, p. 337. Chamberlain polled 69,637 votes to his opponent's 41,947.

333 *"Well, Gen, honors have come down on you gloriously":* "Alfred Godfrey to Joshua Chamberlain" (undated, but undoubtedly just days after the inauguration), Maine Historical Society.

334 *She had greeted in sullen silence the news:* "Fannie to JLC," March 8, 1866, Maine Historical Society.

Fannie later testified, and Chamberlain confirmed, that Fannie hated his military and political life equally. She used the word "detested." But in the few letters we have from her, she never stated explicitly why this was so. The letters of hers that do survive are cold and distant.

335 *"I trust it will not be deemed an undue boldness":* "Address of Governor Chamberlain," January 1867, Maine Historical Society, Augusta.

335 *"We are struck with amazement": Ibid.*

336 *By far the most controversial of his acts: In the Hands of Providence*, pp. 338–39. The Harris case is JLC's letters to his mother, in January 1867.

Chamberlain was not a compassionate man when it came to those sentenced to death. In a letter to the warden of the state prison written soon after he became governor, he recommended that all such men be placed "in solitary confinement." He continued, "However the experience of suffering may have affected my personal sympathies, the consideration of the public safety convinces me that this is not the time to soften penalties."

338 *His marriage continued to deteriorate:* "JLC to Fannie Chamberlain," October 29, 1868, The Papers of Joshua L. Chamberlain, Bowdoin College, Brunswick, ME.

Chamberlain's letters to Fannie are viewed by a number of historians as reflective of his "great affection" for her. That is true for some, but not for most. Many of them are imperious—as if he is giving orders to a child. The letter of October 29, 1868, is a case in point: "Come today," he writes her from August, "and *do not* [emphasis in original] forget the flannels and stockings." This tone continued throughout his life and appeared in letters that he wrote her, later, from Florida. On the other hand, Chamberlain often wrote his mother about his own trips, asking her to help "induce" Fannie to accompany him—and to get her away "from that lonely house in Brunswick." This was clearly a troubled marriage, but the fault was on both sides.

338 *"Now last night, after I had gone to bed":* "JLC to Fannie Chamberlain," November 20, 1868, Bowdoin College.

## CHAPTER 14

### *The Same Dark Question*

341 *On one side of the debate: Reconstruction*, pp. 333–45.

342 *The claim was that he had purposely violated: Reconstruction*, p. 333.

342 *"He attempts to govern"*: Ibid., p. 334.

342 *Even Ulysses S. Grant*: Ibid., p. 335.

343 *By early May 1868*: The impeachment records are in the *Congressional Record*, 40th Congress, Second Session, 1868, in the Library of Congress, Washington, D.C.

344 *Joshua Chamberlain supported Fessenden's vote*: "Governors of Maine and Their Times," *Portland Sunday Telegram*, July 9, 1911.

346 *The controversy over Warren's dismissal*: Proceedings, Findings, and Opinion of the Court of Inquiry in the Case of Gouverneur K. Warren (in 3 parts, 2 vols.), Government Printing Office, Washington, D.C., 1883.

347 *Sheridan had then dismissed*: Sheridan: The Life and Wars of General Phil Sheridan, Roy Morris, Jr., Crown, New York, 1992, pp. 290–91.

347 *President Andrew Johnson had reacted*: Ibid., p. 294.

348 *In July 1869*: "Army of the Potomac Reunion" (clipping), The Papers of Joshua Chamberlain, Library of Congress, Washington, D.C.

349 *The party hierarchy*: "Governors of Maine and Their Times," *Portland Sunday Telegram*, July 9, 1911.

350 *The movement had begun in the 1820s*: In the Hands of Providence, p. 341.

352 *He proved to be a formidable opponent*: JLC: A Sketch, p. 21. Smith polled 39,033 votes.

352 *The only incident of note*: In the Hands of Providence, p. 347. See also Soul of the Lion, Willard M. Wallace, Thomas Nelson and Sons, New York, 1960, pp. 222–23.

354 *"As a statesman, he was in advance of his time"*: "President Hyde's Address at the Funeral of Joshua Chamberlain," February 27, 1914, The Papers of Joshua L. Chamberlain, Bowdoin College, Brunswick, ME.

355 *In September 1869, Harriet Beecher Stowe published*: Harriet Beecher Stowe, "The True Story of Lady Byron's Life," *Atlantic Monthly*, September 24, 1869, pp. 295–313.

355 *Stowe visited Lady Byron in 1856*: Harriet Beecher Stowe: A Life, p. 369.

356 *"This question of Woman and her Sphere"*: "What Is and What Is Not the Point in the Woman Question," Harriet Beecher Stowe, *Hearth and Home* 1, August 28, 1869, p. 520.

358 *After rebuilding his law practice in Abbeville*: "Data: Biography of William C. Oates" (written in his own hand), William C. Oates Governor's File, Alabama Department of Archives and History, Montgomery.

359 *"In those dark days of reconstruction"*: "William C. Oates," *Mobile Register* (undated clipping in Governor's file), Alabama Department of Archives and History, Montgomery.

359 *In 1870, Oates was elected to the state legislature*: "Data: Biography of William C. Oates" (written in his own hand), William C. Oates Governor's File, Alabama Department of Archives and History, Montgomery.

360 *Oates served in the state legislature:* "William Calvin Oates" (undated biography), William C. Oates Governor's File, Alabama Department of Archives and History, Montgomery.

360 *He was put forward in both 1870 and 1872:* William Calvin Oates, "William Calvin Oates" (undated biography), William C. Oates Governor's File, Alabama Department of Archives and History, Montgomery.

361 *Oates was brought back:* "Data: Biography of William C. Oates" (written in his own hand), William C. Oates Governor's File, Alabama Department of Archives and History, Montgomery.

361 *The official end of Reconstruction: Reconstruction*, pp. 575–87.

362 *"We must do the best we can for the negroes":* "Address of Joshua Lawrence Chamberlain," Faneuil Hall, Library of Congress, Washington, D.C.

## CHAPTER 15
### *God's Ways Seen by Men*

364 *"I am one of those who do not believe":* "William C. Oates to E. P. Alexander," August 25, 1868, The Papers of Edward Porter Alexander, Georgia Historical Society.

365 *In 1867, disturbed by the mounting violence:* "James Longstreet Letter," *New Orleans Times*, March 18, 1867.

365 *This second letter gained wide circulation:* "James Longstreet Letter," *New York Times*, April 13, 1867.

366 *"It is all important we should exercise such influence":* "James Longstreet Letter," *New Orleans Times*, June 8, 1867. See also "James Longstreet to R. H. Taliaferro," July 4, 1867, quoted in *Lee's Tarnished Lieutenant*, William Garrett Piston, University of Georgia Press, Athens, 1987, p. 106.

The sentiments of the Taliaferro letter quote nearly precisely the letter that appeared in the *New Orleans Times*. Longstreet's sentiments were undoubtedly being formed for quite some time. The Longstreet letter—and his subsequent correspondences—show, in fact, that his sentiments on southern racial questions were not at all outside the mainstream of southern culture at the time; but his strategy for reasserting southern control of the South was.

367 *On January 19, 1872: Lee's Tarnished Lieutenant*, p. 118.

367 *Longstreet's failure "to assault at daylight":* "Personal Recollections of Robert E. Lee," William Nelson Pendleton manuscript, Pendleton Papers, Southern Historical Society Collection, The University of North Carolina.

367 *No one has ever been able to find a record of such an order:* See *Lee and Longstreet at Gettysburg*, pp. 1–35.

Tucker's analysis of the "sunrise attack order" may be the best-written of the tens of thousands of words given over to the Longstreet controversy. See also "The Battle of Gettysburg," Lafayette McLaws, Address to the Confederate Veterans Association, Savannah, Georgia, April 27, 1896.

369 *Early and his followers struck back:* "Causes of the Defeat of Gen'l Lee's

Army at the Battle of Gettysburg," General Jubal A. Early, Southern Historical Society Papers 4, August 1877.

369 *Oates's condemnation of Longstreet:* "Gettysburg—Battle on the Right," William C. Oates, Southern Historical Society Papers 6, October 1878, pp. 172-82.

371 *After 1870, Calvinism collapsed in the South:* See *God and General Longstreet*, Thomas L. Connelly and Barbara L. Bellows, Louisiana State University Press, Baton Rouge, 1982.

371 *Virginian John Daniel was the first to note:* Quoted in "Paper of John Daniel," *Army of Northern Virginia Memorial Volume*, p. 122, John William Jones Papers, Virginia State Library, Richmond, Virginia.

372 *"Man did not conquer her":* "The Land We Love," Fanny Downing, in *The Land We Love*, July 1866.

372 *After finishing his fourth and last term: Soul of the Lion*, pp. 226-27.

373 *"I do not fear these men of science":* "Inaugural Address of Joshua Lawrence Chamberlain," President of Bowdoin College, July 1872, The Papers of Joshua L. Chamberlain, Bowdoin College, Brunswick, ME.

374 *God's plan included woman because:* "The New Education," Joshua Lawrence Chamberlain (manuscript), Bowdoin College Archives, Bowdoin College, Brunswick, ME.

375 *In an attempt to bring the protests: In the Hands of Providence*, p. 346.

375 *The drill rebellion gained widespread attention: Soul of the Lion*, pp. 239-41.

375 *"The same sickly longing":* quoted from a newspaper clipping in *Bowdoin Documentary History*, Bowdoin College Archives, Bowdoin College, May 31, 1874.

377 *Perhaps the most surprising came within a year: JLC: A Sketch*, p. 19.

378 *Other honors had come to Chamberlain:* "Maine, Her Place In History," Address of Joshua Chamberlain at the International Exhibition in Philadelphia, Maine Centennial Commission, Augusta.

378 *That year, Oates ran for Congress:* "Data: Biography of William C. Oates" (written in his own hand), William C. Oates Governor's File, Alabama Department of Archives and History, Montgomery.

379 *relied on "Barbour County Fever": Reconstruction*, pp. 552-53.

380 *"Northern men do not understand the Negro question":* Unpublished manuscript, William C. Oates Governor's File, Alabama Department of Archives and History, Montgomery.

381 *True to his Democratic roots . . . included a repeal of the notorious "cotton tax":* Undated newspaper clipping, William C. Oates Governor's File, Alabama Department of Archives and History, Montgomery.

381 *It was primarily for this reason that Oates married Sarah Toney:* "Married," Mrs. Washington Toney's Scrapbook, Alabama Department of Archives and History, Montgomery. (The notice was undoubtedly copied by Mrs. Toney from the local newspapers.)

382 *was first introduced to her when she lay in her crib: Ibid.* This scrap is apparently a copy of an article which first appeared in the Eufaula newspaper. A similar news clipping apparently appeared in the *Mobile Register*, which, of all of Alabama's newspapers, provides the best information on Oates's career and life. Very, very little is known of Oates's wife.

382 *"The charming bride is the pride of this community"*: "William C. Oates and Miss Toney," undated, *Montgomery Advertiser* (April 1882).

383 *"Her taste for entertaining"*: Ibid.

384 *"He opposed the alien ownership of land"*: Untitled and undated biography, in William C. Oates Governor's File, Alabama Department of Archives and History, Montgomery.

386 *The rise of the Greenback movement: The Greenback and Resumption of Specie Payments, 1862–1879,* John J. Otto, New York, 1882; *The Greenback Era: A Social and Political History of American Finance, 1865–1879,* Irwin Unger, Princeton University Press, Princeton, NJ, 1964. See also *Reconstruction,* pp. 522–25.

387 *In September 1879: JLC: A Sketch* [Supplement], pp. 25–26.

Alice Rains Trulock perceptively notes that the third-person account of Chamberlain's role in the greenback crisis in Maine was undoubtedly written by Chamberlain himself, then inserted in the biography as an afterthought. She entitles it a "Supplement" in her notes on the crisis, while Willard Wallace entitles it "Twelve Days at Augusta."

388 *Maine's most powerful politician: In the Hands of Providence,* p. 357.

388 *He therefore signed an executive order: JLC: A Sketch* [Supplement], p. 31.

389 *"The excitement is now terrific in bitterness"*: "Chamberlain to Judge Appleton," January 12, 1880, Maine Historical Society.

390 *"Men, you wish to kill me, I hear"*:: *JLC: A Sketch* [Supplement], pp. 19–20.

391 *"I consider my trust, under Special Order No. 45"*: Ibid.

391 *He was the "Republican Renegade"*: Ibid.

## CHAPTER 16

### *What Do You Do About Yours?*

393 *Grant's funeral brought together: Grant,* pp. 516–17.

393 *"It was the last of the great scenes"*: "Joshua Lawrence Chamberlain to Fannie Chamberlain," August 8, 1885, Maine State Museum, Augusta.

395 *After hours of testimony and review: OR,* "The Case of Fitz John Porter," (vol. 12, series 1, parts 1 and 2).

395 *"Grant was a strategist"*: *The Passing of the Armies,* pp. 380–81.

396 *Following the lead of others: Soul of the Lion,* p. 277.

396 *"Service was the central fact"*: Ibid., pp. 282–83. See also "Dedication of the Twentieth Maine Monuments at Gettysburg," October 3, 1889, "Speeches

by Joshua L. Chamberlain and Howard L. Prince," Gettysburg National Battlefield Park.

397 *"I am coming to realize"*: "Harold Chamberlain to Fannie Chamberlain" (undated, May 1892), Maine Historical Society.

398 *To meet the growing crisis: Alabama: The History of a Deep South State*, William Warren Rogers, Robert David Ward, Leah Rawls Atkins, and Wayne Flynt, University of Alabama Press, Tuscaloosa, 1994, pp. 277–90.

The Rogers, Ward, Atkins, and Flynt account is the most detailed and comprehensive. However, other reports on the Oates-Kolb competition appear in *From Civil War to Civil Rights: Alabama 1860–1960* (an anthology of the *Alabama Review*), compiled by Sarah Woolfolk Wiggins, University of Alabama Press, Tuscaloosa, 1987; *Retreat from Reconstruction*, William Gillette, Louisiana State University Press, Baton Rouge, 1979; and *Alabama: A Documentary History to 1900*, Lucille Griffith, University of Alabama Press, Tuscaloosa, 1972.

398 *The Ocala convention included: Ibid.*, p. 499.

399 *Alabama's leading populist: Ibid.*, p. 515.

400 *When Kolb announced that he would run for governor: Ibid.*, p. 517.

401 *Kolb responded to this challenge: Ibid.*, p. 520.

402 *Reuben F. Kolb probably won the Alabama governor's election: Ibid.*, pp. 305–9.

403 *Oates returned to Alabama: Ibid.*, p. 509.

404 *"Your valiant one-armed hero": Ibid.*, p. 510.

405 *In one incident during the campaign:* Alabama Secretary of State, Proceeding of the State Assembly and Legislature, 1894, in Alabama Department of Archives and History, Montgomery. See also "The Emancipation of Pure, White, Southern Womanhood," Virginia Foster Durr, *New South*, Winter 1971.

The incident is difficult to trace and prove, but is so notorious that it is still part of the legacy of the Oates governorship in Alabama. Historians at Chickamauga and at the Alabama Department of Archives and History say they "have heard the rumor" of Oates's illegitimate children. Virginia Foster Durr, in her own memoirs, says she heard the rumor from her family during her childhood and that it was generally known that Oates kept a black woman in "a shack" (she is apparently quoting from an Alabama legislator) behind the governor's mansion.

Virginia Foster Durr and her husband—who was a well-known judge—are heroes of Alabama history. Virginia Durr was an outspoken ally of the civil rights movement and her husband was called to account before the House Un-American Activities Committee during its heyday in the 1950s.

When the *Nation* magazine called the Vietnam Antiwar Movement "the only radical movement now going on in the United States" in 1963, she penned an angry letter to the editor: "This reflects the unconscious ignoring or the conscious ignoring on the part of the rest of the country to the really momentous struggle that is going on here—in the South. We are fighting down here for the fundamental tenets of the American form of government and the people who are in the fight are being shot, beat up, disgraced, put in jail, denied all economic aid or the chance to make a living, and the Government of the United States is being defied, riot and revolution are in the air, and the rest of the country stands by and seems to think it is nothing but a Southern oddness as usual."

406 *In the end, the Democrats won the election: Alabama: The History of a Deep South State*, p. 522.

406 *"The inauguration of William C. Oates"*: "Editorial," *People's Advocate*, Columbiana, AL, December 6, 1894.

407 *"This event was one of pronounced distinction"*: Undated, *Montgomery Advertiser* (news clipping) Governor's Vertical File, Alabama Department of Archives and History, Montgomery.

408 *"You would refuse to register"*: *Alabama: The History of a Deep South State*, p. 523.

409 *In addition to his work for the Institute: JLC: A Sketch*, p. 25.

410 *The first ceremonies dedicating the battlefields: Dedication of the Chickamauga and Chattanooga National Military Park*, September 18–20, 1895, compiled by H. V. Boynton, vol. 4, Government Printing Office, Washington, D.C.

411 *"This great gathering and the fraternal feeling"*: Ibid., pp. 181–82.

411 *"It is complimentary to the Confederate veteran"*: Ibid., pp. 181–82.

412 *"He should have been hung"*: Ibid., p. 183. The response from the crowd to Oates's speech is contained in the minutes of the address as given by Oates, undoubtedly by those responsible for providing a transcript of the event. He was interrupted a number of times, though in some cases the nature of the interruption is not detailed.

413 *He vacationed in New Hampshire*: Governor's Vertical File, Alabama Department of Archives and History, Montgomery.

413 *Chamberlain wrote a series of articles*: "JLC Letter," *Bangor News*, March 5, 1898. There were five letters in all. Chamberlain believed that the United States had no choice but to avenge the sinking of the *Maine* in Havana harbor, thinking the incident was "no accident."

413 *"I cannot but think that my day is not yet over"*: "Chamberlain to the Honorable Wm. P. Frye," April 22, 1898, National Archives, Washington, D.C.

413 *On May 28, 1898: Oates*, p. 555.

415 *Oates was given a new brigade: Ibid.*, p. 558.

415 *Oates traveled to Gettysburg: Ibid.*, p. 561.

416 *"Col. Nicholson has sent to me your letter to him"*: "Gen. Joshua L. Chamberlain" (from Wm. Oates), April 4, 1905, Gettysburg National Military Park; also in "The Trulock Collection," Pejepscot Historical Society, Brunswick, ME.

417 *"In [your] letter, I find your impressions place me"*: "[To] General William C. Oates" (from J. L. Chamberlain), May 1, 1905, Gettysburg National Military Park.

418 *"To the memory of Lt. John A. Oates"*: "The Alabamian Attack on Little Round Top," Gary Kross, *Blue and Gray*, Winter 1996, p. 61.

420 *"White men have gotten to cheating each other"*: Alabama Secretary of

State, 1901 Constitutional Convention Proceedings (SG 5546–5550), Alabama Department of Archives and History, Montgomery.

421 *"Your husband and children 'rise up and call you blessed' "*: "Joshua Chamberlain to Fannie Chamberlain," August 12, 1905, Maine Historical Society.

EPILOGUE

*Montgomery and Brunswick*

425 *John Bell Hood, Oates's division commander: Historical Times Illustrated Encyclopedia of the Civil War*, ed. Patricia L. Faust, Harper & Row, New York, 1986, p. 369.

425 *Jubal Early, who convinced Oates to add his voice: Ibid.*, p. 233.

Early's nemesis, James Longstreet, outlived Early by twenty years, living into his eighties before dying at his home in Gainesville, Georgia, on January 2, 1904. By the time of his death, a new generation of historians was reassessing his role in the Civil War.

425 *The colorful and strange Richard Ewell: Ibid.*, p. 248.

425 *Richard Taylor, the head of the Louisiana Tigers: Ibid.*, pp. 743-44.

426 *Oates's favorite commander: Ibid.*, p. 426.

426 *Joseph Bartlett, who vied with Chamberlain: Ibid.*, p. 43.

426 *Charles Griffin, who pushed for Chamberlain's promotion: Ibid.*, p. 326.

426 *Adelbert Ames, the first commander of the 20th Maine: Ibid.*, p. 11.

# Bibliography

### Manuscripts

Alabama Historical Society, Montgomery, Alabama
    The Papers of Governor William C. Oates
Chicago Historical Society, Chicago, Illinois
    James Longstreet Papers
Chickamauga-Chattanooga National Military Park
    William C. Oates File
    Fifteenth Alabama File
Duke University, Durham, North Carolina
    Jubal A. Early Papers
    Daniel Harvey Hill Papers
    Micah Jenkins Papers
    E. M. Law Papers
    Augustus Baldwin Longstreet Papers
    James Longstreet Papers
    James Longstreet Letters
Georgia Historical Society, Savannah, Georgia
    James Longstreet Papers
Gettysburg National Military Park
    William C. Oates Correspondence Scrapbook
    Twentieth Maine Volunteer Infantry File
The Hawthorne-Longfellow Library, Bowdoin College, Brunswick, Maine
    The Papers of Joshua L. Chamberlain
    Bowdoin College Archives
    Oliver O. Howard Papers
Museum of the Confederacy, Richmond, Virginia
    Robert E. Lee Papers
    William Nelson Pendleton Papers
Pejepscot Historical Society
    Joshua L. Chamberlain Collection
    Joshua L. Chamberlain Letterbook

Arthur E. and Eliza Schlesinger Library on the History of Women in America
    Beecher-Stowe Collection
Sterling Memorial Library, Yale University, New Haven, Connecticut
    Beecher Family Papers
University of North Carolina, Chapel Hill, North Carolina
    Southern Historical Collection, *Southern Historical Society Papers*
    E. P. Alexander Papers
    Lafayette McLaws Papers

## ARTICLES AND MONOGRAPHS

Alexander, E. P., "Longstreet at Knoxville," in *Battles and Leaders of the Civil War* (vol. 3), Castle Books, New York, 1956.

Colgrove, Silas, "The Finding of Lee's Lost Order," in *Battles and Leaders of the Civil War* (vol. 2), Castle Books, New York, 1956.

Cox, General Jacob D., "The Battle of Antietam," in *Battles and Leaders of the Civil War* (vol. 2), Castle Books, New York, 1956.

Downing, Fanny, "The Land We Love," *Land We Love* 1 (July 1886): 161–62.

Early, Jubal A., "Leading Confederates on the Battle of Gettysburg: A Review by General Early," *Southern Historical Society Papers* 4 (Dec. 1877): 241–302.

——, "Letter from J. A. Early," *Southern Historical Society Papers* 4 (Aug. 1877): 50–68.

——, "Reply to General Longstreet's Second Paper," *Southern Historical Society Papers* 5 (June 1878): 270–87.

Elam, W. C., "A Scalawag," *Southern Magazine* 8 (April 1871): 456–59.

Evans, Clement, "Genl. Gordon and Genl. Longstreet," *Independent* (Feb. 11, 1904).

Galloway, G. Norton, "Hand-to-Hand Fighting at Spotsylvania," in *Battles and Leaders of the Civil War* (vol. 4), Castle Books, New York, 1956.

Hassler, William W., "The Ghost of General Longstreet," *Georgia Historical Quarterly* 65 (Spring 1981): 22–27.

Henderson, G. F. R., "Review of General Longstreet's Book, 'From Manassas to Appomattox,'" *Southern Historical Society Papers*, n.s., 1 (April 1914): 104–15.

Hennessey, Melinda M., "Reconstruction Politics and the Military: The Eufaula Riot of 1874," *Alabama Historical Quarterly* 38 (Summer 1976): 112–25.

Hill, Daniel H., "Chickamauga—The Great Battle of the West," in *Battles and Leaders of the Civil War* (vol. 3), Castle Books, New York, 1956.

——, "Lee's Attacks North of the Chickahominy," in *Battles and Leaders of the Civil War* (vol. 2), Castle Books, New York, 1956.

Howard, Oliver Otis, "The Eleventh Corps at Chancellorsville," in *Battles and Leaders of the Civil War* (vol. 3), Castle Books, New York, 1956.

Hunt, Henry J., "The First Day at Gettysburg," in *Battles and Leaders of the Civil War* (vol. 3), Castle Books, New York, 1956.

——, "The Second Day at Gettysburg," in *Battles and Leaders of the Civil War* (vol. 3), Castle Books, New York, 1956.

——, "The Third Day at Gettysburg," in *Battles and Leaders of the Civil War* (vol. 3), Castle Books, New York, 1956.

Imboden, John D., "The Confederate Retreat from Gettysburg," in *Battles and Leaders of the Civil War* (vol. 3), Castle Books, New York, 1956.

——, "Stonewall Jackson in the Shenandoah," in *Battles and Leaders of the Civil War* (vol. 2), Castle Books, New York, 1956.

Irwin, Lieutenant-Colonel Richard B., "The Case of Fitz John Porter," in *Battles and Leaders of the Civil War* (vol. 2), Castle Books, New York, 1956.

Johnson, Robert Underwood, and Clarence Clough Buel (eds.), "General Warren at Five Forks and the Court of Inquiry," in *Battles and Leaders of the Civil War* (vol. 4), Castle Books, New York, 1956.

Kershaw, Joseph, "Kershaw's Brigade at Fredericksburg," in *Battles and Leaders of the Civil War* (vol. 3), Castle Books, New York, 1956.

Law, E. M., "From the Wilderness to Cold Harbor," in *Battles and Leaders of the Civil War* (vol. 4), Castle Books, New York, 1956.

——, "On the Confederate Right at Gaines's Mill," in *Battles and Leaders of the Civil War* (vol. 2), Castle Books, New York, 1956.

——, "The Struggle for Round Top," in *Battles and Leaders of the Civil War* (vol. 3), Castle Books, New York, 1956.

Longstreet, James, "The Battle of Fredericksburg," in *Battles and Leaders of the Civil War* (vol. 3), Castle Books, New York, 1956.

——, "General James Longstreet's Account of the Campaign and Battle," *Southern Historical Society Papers* 5 (Jan. 1878): 54–86.

——, "The Invasion of Maryland," in *Battles and Leaders of the Civil War* (vol. 2), Castle Books, New York, 1956.

——, "Lee's Invasion of Pennsylvania," in *Battles and Leaders of the Civil War* (vol. 3), Castle Books, New York, 1956.

——, "Lee's Right Wing at Gettysburg," in *Battles and Leaders of the Civil War* (vol. 3), Castle Books, New York, 1956.

——, "Letter from General Longstreet," *Southern Historical Society Papers* 5 (Jan.–Feb. 1878), 52–53.

——, "Our March Around Pope," in *Battles and Leaders of the Civil War* (vol. 2), Castle Books, New York, 1956.

——, "The Seven Days, Including Frayser's Farm," in *Battles and Leaders of the Civil War* (vol. 2), Castle Books, New York, 1956.

McClellan, George B., "The Peninsular Campaign," in *Battles and Leaders of the Civil War* (vol. 2), Castle Books, New York, 1956.

McLaws, Lafayette, "The Battle of Gettysburg," *Philadelphia Weekly Press* (April 21, 1886).

——, "The Confederate Left at Fredericksburg," in *Battles and Leaders of the Civil War* (vol. 3), Castle Books, New York, 1956.

——, "Gettysburg," *Southern Historical Society Papers* 7 (Jan. 1879): 64–90.

McMahon, Martin T., "Cold Harbor," in *Battles and Leaders of the Civil War* (vol. 4), Castle Books, New York, 1956.

———, "From Gettysburg to the Coming of Grant," in *Battles and Leaders of the Civil War* (vol. 4), Castle Books, New York, 1956.

Melcher, H. S., "The 20th Maine at Little Round Top," in *Battles and Leaders of the Civil War* (vol. 3), Castle Books, New York, 1956.

———, "The 20th Maine at Little Round Top," *Lincoln County News*, Saldoboro, ME, March 13, 1885.

Moore, J. H. "With Jackson at Hamilton's Crossing," in *Battles and Leaders of the Civil War* (vol. 3), Castle Books, New York, 1956.

Oates, William C., "Gettysburg—Battle on the Right," *Southern Historical Society Papers* 6 (Oct. 1878): 172–82.

Pearce, Thomas Nelson, "Longstreet's Responsibility on the Second Day at Gettysburg," *Georgia Historical Quarterly* 10 (March 1926): 26–45.

Pendleton, William Nelson, "Personal Recollections of General Lee," *Southern Magazine* 15 (Dec. 1874): 603–36.

Pope, John, "The Second Battle of Bull Run," in *Battles and Leaders of the Civil War* (vol. 2), Castle Books, New York, 1956.

Porter, Fitz-John, "Hanover Court House and Gaines's Mill," in *Battles and Leaders of the Civil War* (vol. 2), Castle Books, New York, 1956.

Porter, General Horace, "Five Forks and the Pursuit of Lee," in *Battles and Leaders of the Civil War* (vol. 4), Castle Books, New York, 1956.

Richter, William L., "James Longstreet: From Rebel to Scalawag," *Louisiana History* 11 (Summer 1970): 215–30.

Sanger, Donald Bridgman, "Was Longstreet a Scapegoat?" *Infantry Journal* 26 (1936): 39–46.

Smith, J. B., "The Charge of Pickett, Pettigrew, and Trimble," in *Battles and Leaders of the Civil War* (vol. 3), Castle Books, New York, 1956.

Stowe, Harriet Beecher, "An Appeal to the Women of the Free States of America, On the Present Crisis in Our Country," *Independent* 6 (Feb. 23, 1854): 57.

———, "The True Story of Lady Byron's Life," *Atlantic Monthly* 24 (September 1869): 473–81.

Taylor, Walter H., "Lee and Longstreet," *Southern Historical Society Papers* 14 (Jan.–Dec. 1896): 73–79

Thruston, Gates P., "The Crisis at Chickamauga," in *Battles and Leaders of the Civil War* (vol. 3), Castle Books, New York, 1956.

Tucker, Glenn, "Longstreet: Culprit or Scapegoat?" *Civil War Times Illustrated* 1 (April 1962): 5–9.

Walker, Francis A., "Meade at Gettysburg," in *Battles and Leaders of the Civil War* (vol. 3), Castle Books, New York, 1956.

Walker, General John G., "Sharpsburg," in *Battles and Leaders of the Civil War* (vol. 2), Castle Books, New York, 1956.

## BOOKS

Ayers, Edward L., *The Promise of the New South, Life After Reconstruction*, Oxford University Press, New York, 1992.

Bauer, K. Jack, *The Mexican War*, University of Nebraska Press, Lincoln, 1974.

Belz, Herman, *A New Birth of Freedom: The Republican Party and Freedmen's Rights, 1863–1869*, Westport Publishing, Westport, CT, 1976.

Boydston, Jeanne, Mary Kelley, and Anne Margolis, *The Limits of Sisterhood: The Beecher Sisters on Women's Rights and Woman's Sphere*, University of North Carolina Press, Chapel Hill, 1988.

Braude, Ann D., *Radical Spirits: Spiritualism and Women's Rights in Nineteenth-Century America*, Beacon Press, Boston, 1989.

Brown, Kent Masterson, *Cushing of Gettysburg*, University of Kentucky Press, Lexington, 1993.

Caskey, Marie, *Chariot of Fire: Religion and the Beecher Family*, Yale University Press, New Haven, CT, 1978.

Catton, Bruce, *Grant Moves South*, Little, Brown, Boston, 1960.

———, *Grant Takes Command*, Little, Brown, Boston, 1968.

Chamberlain, Joshua Lawrence, *The Passing of the Armies*, Morningside Press (reprint), Dayton, OH, 1989.

Cleaves, Freeman, *Meade of Gettysburg*, Morningside Press (reprint), Dayton, OH, 1980.

Coddington, Edwin B., *The Gettysburg Campaign: A Study in Command*, Morningside Press (reprint), Dayton, OH, 1983.

Connelly, Thomas L., and Barbara L. Bellows, *God and General Longstreet*, Louisiana State University Press, Baton Rouge, 1982.

Coulter, E. Merton, *The South During Reconstruction*, Louisiana State University Press, Baton Rouge, 1947.

Cozzens, Peter, *This Terrible Sound: The Battle of Chickamauga*, University of Illinois Press, Urbana, 1992.

Davis, William C., *Battle at Bull Run*, Louisiana State University Press, Baton Rouge, 1977.

———, *Jefferson Davis: The Man and His Hour*, HarperCollins, New York, 1991.

———, *The Orphan Brigade*, Doubleday, New York, 1980.

De Trobriand, Regis, *Four Years with the Army of the Potomac*, Ticknor, Boston, 1889.

Donald, David Herbert, *Lincoln*, Simon and Schuster, New York, 1995.

Early, Jubal A., *Autobiographical Sketch and Narrative of the War Between the States*, Lippincott, Philadelphia, 1912.

Engert, Roderick M. (ed.), *Maine to the Wilderness: The Civil War Letters of Pvt. William Lamson, 20th Maine Infantry*, Publishers Press, Orange, VA, 1993.

Farwell, Byron, *Stonewall*, Norton, New York, 1992.

Faust, Patricia L. (ed.), *Historical Times Illustrated Encyclopedia of the Civil War*, Harper & Row, New York, 1986.

Fiedler, Leslie A., *Love and Death in the American Novel*, Stein and Day, New York, 1975.

Fleming, Walter L., *Civil War and Reconstruction in Alabama*, Reprint Company, Spartanburg, SC, 1978.

Fogel, Robert William, and Stanley L. Engerman, *Time on the Cross: The Economics of American Negro Slavery*, Little, Brown, Boston, 1974.

Foner, Eric, *Reconstruction*, Harper & Row, New York, 1988.

Foote, Shelby, *The Civil War: A Narrative* (vols. 1–3), Random House, New York, 1986.

Foster, Gaines M., *Ghosts of the Confederacy*, Oxford University Press, New York, 1987.

Freehling, William W., *The Road to Disunion*, Oxford University Press, New York, 1990.

Furgurson, Ernest B., *Chancellorsville 1863,* Knopf, New York, 1992.

Garrison, Wendell Phillips, and Francis Jackson Garrison, *William Lloyd Garrison, 1805–1879: The Story of His Life Told by His Children*, Century, New York, 1889.

Gillette, William, *Retreat from Reconstruction*, Louisiana State University Press, Baton Rouge, 1979.

Golay, Michael, *To Gettysburg and Beyond*, Crown, New York, 1994.

Grant, Ulysses S., *Personal Memoirs of U. S. Grant* (vols. 1 and 2), Library of America, New York, 1990.

Hassler, Warren W., *Crisis at the Crossroads: The First Day at Gettysburg*, University of Alabama Press, Montgomery, 1990.

Hedrick, Joan D., *Harriet Beecher Stowe: A Life*, Oxford University Press, New York, 1994.

Helper, Hinton Rowan, *The Impending Crisis of the South*, Burdick, New York, 1860.

Henderson, G. H. F., *Stonewall Jackson and the American Civil War* (2 vols.), Fawcett, New York, 1962.

Hennessy, John J., *Return to Bull Run: The Campaign and Battle of Second Manassas*, Simon and Schuster, New York, 1993.

Hood, John Bell, *Advance and Retreat: Personal Experiences in the United States and Confederates States Armies*, Burk and M'Fetridge, Philadelphia, 1880.

Jones, J. William, *Christ in the Camp*, Sprinkle Publications (reprint), Harrisonburg, VA, 1986.

Krick, Robert K., *Conquering the Valley*, Morrow, New York, 1996.

LaFantasie, Glenn, "Introduction" to *The War Between the Union and the Confederacy*, in *Eyewitness to the Civil War*, Bantam Books, New York, 1992.

Lerner, Gerda, *The Grimke Sisters from South Carolina*, Houghton Mifflin, Boston, 1967.

Lewis, Lloyd, *Captain Sam Grant*, Little, Brown, Boston, 1950.

Longstreet, James, *From Manassas to Appomattox*, Konecky & Konecky, New York, 1984.

McFeely, William S., *Grant: A Biography*, Norton, New York, 1981.

——, *Yankee Stepfather: General O. O. Howard and the Freedmen*, Yale University Press, New Haven, CT, 1968.

McPherson, James M., *Battle Cry of Freedom*, Oxford University Press, New York, 1988.

——, "Introduction" to *The Passing of the Armies*, in *Eyewitness to the Civil War*, Bantam Books, New York, 1993.

Morris, Roy, Jr., *Sheridan, The Life and Wars of General Phil Sheridan*, Crown, New York, 1992.

Nesbitt, Mark, *Through Blood & Fire*, Stackpole Books, Mechanicsburg, PA, 1996.

Nolan, Alan T., *The Iron Brigade*, Hardscrabble Books, Berrien Springs, MI, 1983.

——, *Lee Considered*, University of North Carolina Press, Chapel Hill, 1991.

Norton, Oliver Willcox, *The Attack and Defense of Little Round Top*, Morningside Press, Dayton, OH, 1983.

Oates, Stephen B., *To Purge This Land with Blood: A Biography of John Brown*, Harper & Row, New York, 1970.

Oates, William C., *The War Between the Union and the Confederacy and Its Lost Opportunities*, Morningside Press (reprint), Dayton, OH, 1985.

Olmsted, Frederick Law, *The Slave States*, Paragon Books, New York, 1959 (originally printed in 1860).

Persico, Joseph E., *My Enemy My Brother*, Collier Books, New York, 1977.

Peterson, Merrill D., *The Great Triumvirate*, Oxford University Press, New York, 1987.

Pfanz, Harry W., *Gettysburg: Culp's Hill & Cemetery Hill*, University of North Carolina Press, Chapel Hill, 1993.

——, *Gettysburg: The Second Day*, University of North Carolina Press, Chapel Hill, 1987.

Piston, William Garrett, *Lee's Tarnished Lieutenant*, University of Georgia Press, Athens, 1987.

Potter, David M. *The Impending Crisis*, Harper & Row, New York, 1976.

Pullen, John J., *The Twentieth Maine*, Harcourt Brace, New York, 1957.

Rable, George C., *Civil Wars: Women and the Crisis of Southern Nationalism*, University of Illinois Press, Urbana, 1991.

Robertson, James I., Jr., *General A. P. Hill*, Random House, New York, 1987.

Rugoff, Milton, *The Beechers: An American Family in the Nineteenth Century*, Harper & Row, New York, 1981.

Sears, Stephen W., *Chancellorsville*, Houghton Mifflin, Boston, 1996.

——, *Landscape Turned Red*, Ticknor & Fields, New York, 1983.

——, *To the Gates of Richmond: The Peninsula Campaign*, Ticknor & Fields, New York, 1992.

Shaver, Lewellyn A., *History of the Sixteenth Alabama Regiment*, Barrett and Brown, Montgomery, AL, 1867.

Sherman, William T., *The Memoirs of General W. T. Sherman*, Library of America, New York, 1990.

Silber, Nina, *The Romance of Reunion*, University of North Carolina Press, Chapel Hill, 1983.

Sommers, Richard J., *Richmond Redeemed: The Siege at Petersburg*, Doubleday, Garden City, NY, 1981.

Sorrel, G. Moxley, *Recollections of a Confederate Staff Officer*, Konecky & Konecky (reprint), New York, 1994.

Stampp, Kenneth, *The Peculiar Institution: Slavery in the Ante-Bellum South*, Knopf, New York, 1956.

Stewart, George R., *Pickett's Charge*, Houghton Mifflin, Boston, 1959.

Stowe, Harriet Beecher, *The Pearl of Orr's Island*, Houghton Mifflin, Boston, 1896 (originally published 1862).

——, *Uncle Tom's Cabin; Or, Life Among the Lowly* (2 vols.), Houghton Mifflin, Boston, 1892 (originally published 1852).

Symonds, Craig L., *Joseph E. Johnston: A Civil War Biography*, Norton, New York, 1992.

Tanner, Robert G., *Stonewall in the Valley*, Doubleday, Garden City, NY, 1976.

Taylor, Richard, *Destruction and Reconstruction: Personal Experiences of the Late War*, Appleton, New York, 1879.

Trudeau, Noah Andre, *Bloody Roads South: The Wilderness to Cold Harbor*, Little, Brown, Boston, 1989.

——, *The Last Citadel*, Little, Brown, Boston, 1991.

Trulock, Alice Rains, *In the Hands of Providence: Joshua Chamberlain and the American Civil War*, University of North Carolina Press, Chapel Hill, 1992.

Tucker, Glenn, *Chickamauga: Bloody Battle in the West*, Morningside Press (reprint), Dayton, OH, 1984.

——, *Hancock the Superb*, Morningside Press (reprint), Dayton, OH, 1980.

——, *High Tide at Gettysburg*, Morningside Press (reprint), Dayton, OH, 1983.

——, *Lee and Longstreet at Gettysburg*, Morningside Press (reprint), Dayton, OH, 1982.

Unger, Irwin, *The Greenback Era: A Social and Political History of American Finance 1865–1879*, Princeton University Press, Princeton, NJ, 1964.

Villard, Oswald Garrison, *John Brown: A Biography Fifty Years After*, Houghton Mifflin, Boston, 1910.

Wallace, Willard M., *Soul of the Lion*, Ron R. Van Sickle Military Books, Gettysburg, PA (reprint), 1988.

War Department, *The War of the Rebellion: A Compilation of the Official Records of the Union and Confederate Armies* (128 vols.), Government Printing Office, Washington, D.C., 1880–1901.

Waugh, John G., *The Class of 1846*, Warner Books, New York, 1994.

Wert, Jeffrey D., *General James Longstreet*, Simon and Schuster, New York, 1993.

Wheeler, Richard, *Sword Over Richmond: An Eyewitness History of McClellan's Peninsula Campaign*, Harper & Row, New York, 1986.

Wiener, Jonathan M., *Social Origins of the New South: Alabama 1860–1885*, Louisiana State University Press, Baton Rouge, 1970.

Wiggins, Sara W., *The Scalawag in Alabama Politics, 1865–1881*, University of Alabama Press, Montgomery, 1977.

Wills, Garry, *Lincoln at Gettysburg*, Simon and Schuster, New York, 1992.

# Index

*Italic* page numbers refer to maps and map text. Chronologically ordered sub-entries are run in; thematic subentries are listed alphabetically.